COLLECTED STUDIES SERIES

# Luther and German Humanism

Professor Lewis W. Spitz

Lewis W. Spitz

# Luther and German Humanism

VARIORUM
1996

This edition copyright © 1996 by Lewis W. Spitz.

Published by VARIORUM
Ashgate Publishing Limited
Gower House, Croft Road,
Aldershot, Hampshire GU11 3HR
Great Britain

Ashgate Publishing Company
Old Post Road,
Brookfield, Vermont 05036
USA

ISBN 0–86078–499–1

**British Library CIP Data**

Spitz, Lewis W.
Luther and German Humanism.
(Variorum Collected Studies Series; CS507).
I. Title.  II. Series.
144. 0943

**US Library of Congress CIP Data**

Spitz, Lewis William, 1922–   .
Luther and German Humanism / Lewis W. Spitz.
p. cm. – (Collected Studies Series; CS507).
Includes index (cloth: alk. paper).
1. Luther, Martin, 1483–1546.  2. Humanism–Germany.
3. Germany–Intellectual life–16th century.  4. Germany–Church
history–16th century.  5. Reformation–Germany.
I. Title.  II. Series: Collected Studies Series; CS507.
BR333. 5. H85S65     1995                          95–23340
284. 1' 092–dc20                                         CIP

The paper used in this publication meets the minimum requirements of the
American National Standard for Information Sciences – Permanance of Paper
for Printed Library Materials, ANSI Z39.48–1984. ∞ ™

Printed by Galliard (Printers) Ltd., Great Yarmouth, Norfolk, Great Britain.

COLLECTED STUDIES SERIES C507

# CONTENTS

# LUTHER, REFORMATION, AND HUMANISM

This volume contains xii + 360 pages

# PREFACE

As the distinguished scholar of Renaissance intellectual history Professor Charles Trinkaus perceived, the Leitmotif or basic theme of much of the author's work and of this volume is the close synergistic relationship of Renaissance humanism and the sixteen century transformation of European culture. For decades scholars have been drawn productively to the questions of the relation of the Renaissance to the Medieval mind and in a larger context to the symbiotic relation of the Reformation to the Renaissance. Within that broad framework scholars have centered their attention on biblical humanism heroically exemplified by Erasmus of Rotterdam, prince of the humanists, who provided the philological tools of classical humanism in the way that they could be applied for a new understanding of the Scriptures. Of Augustinian background, Luther understood the power of the authority of antiquity, as he demonstrated during the Leipzig debate of 1519. He adduced both Scriptural and patristic sources for content and interpretation, and classical rhetoric as a means for the conveyance of basic Christian ideas and teaching.

The entire subject of the relation of the Reformation to higher learning has been newly reassessed, no longer within the narrow confines of the Luther and Erasmus debate on the freedom or the bondage of the will, or even in terms of the young humanists who supported Luther and the older humanists who opposed him. The humanist sodalities carried the Reformation in urban centers and the universities and there were forms of coexistence and mutual support an various levels. The attention of scholars is now centered not merely on Melanchthon, the *praeceptor Germaniae,* but on Luther himself, whose knowledge of the classics was astonishing. For Luther along with his dear lifelong personal friend, neighbor and colleague Melanchthon pressed for and achieved an educational revolution along with their religious reformation which in a matter of decades had separated over half of Europe from the medieval theology, church and hierarchical authoritarian church government and culture. Luther's labors for education on the elementary level for both boys and girls are well known. But his insistent preference for a humanist curriculum on the gymnasium or secondary level and that of the university requires the elaboration provided in the chapters which follow. Beyond dialectic or

Aristotelian logic he promoted Ciceronian rhetoric, history, poetry, classical and biblical languages, Latin drama, and the natural sciences, especially botany and iatro-chemistry or medicine. One of his sons became a doctor. Luther's mature thoughts on the natural world are reflected in his multi-volume *Commentary on Genesis,* his last exegetical scholarly effort on which he worked over the course of ten years. The humanistic curriculum served as the basis for the theological superstructure of Lutheranism and Lutheranism in turn carried the values of Renaissance humanism into the next centuries of orthodoxy, enlightenment, rationalism, idealism, and anthropological realism in the nineteenth and twentieth centuries.

The Lutheran evangelicals were, of course, concerned with the theology of the cross rather than the theology of self-glory, with heaven as man's final home. But this anthropological understanding of man as *homo aeveternus* (St. Thomas Aquinas' term), a creature of this life and of eternity, a time when there will be no time, underlined the importance of a cultural paradise in the here and now. Luther was not a cultural freak-out caught between God and Satan expecting momentary eschatological doom, but a university professor and a family man, confident of God's love for man and looking to the future of mankind on this earth and in this life as well as in the life to come. He along with Melanchthon, Johann Sturm, Calvin, Beza and other education-minded reformers formulated plans and put into effect elementary, secondary and university educational change looking toward a better future for and through the young. The Lutheran province of Silesia serves as a good test case of the relation of humanism and Lutheranism, a reflection of the role of humanism in Luther's mind and writings. It was Melanchthon who equipped the third generation of young humanists to carry on the work of the Reformation, despite the opposition he encountered on theological but not on cultural grounds. The influence of both Luther and Melanchthon carried through to the fourth generation of German humanism exemplified by Joachim Camerarius (1500–1574), a most prolific scholar of philosophy and history, and Johannes Wigand (1523–1587), who had studied with both Luther and Melanchthon, and understood philosophy as a maid-servant to theology, both as a necessary part of the elucidation and understanding of Holy Scriptures, but also for the refutation of heretics. As Ulrich Asendorf has explained, in late sixteenth and seventeenth century German Aristotelianism and humanism shared a "peaceful coexistence in philosophy as well as in the pedagogical curriculum." Under the powerful and pervasive influence of Strasbourg's Johann Sturm and other educators, humanist instruction prevailed in both the gymnasium and lycée in the Germanies and in France. Theology in the Christian tradition remains the core and acculturation in a humanist vein continues, though in an attenuated way, to be the essential cultural carrier in Western Civilization down to the present day.

May I draw attention to some recent publications directly relevant to the subject of this book.

Ulrich Asendorf, "Das kulturelle Paradies: Reformation und Humanismus gingen ursprünglich Hand in Hand," *Lutherische Monatshefte*, 1 (1994), 35–38.

Manfred Fleischer, *The Harvest of Humanism in Central Europe* (Saint Louis: Concordia Publishing House, 1992).

Charles Nauert, *Humanism and the Culture of Renaissance Europe* (Cambridge and New York: Cambridge University Press, 1995).

Erika Rummel, *The Humanist-Scholastic Debate in the Renaissance and Reformation* (Cambridge: Harvard University Press, 1995).

Lewis W. Spitz and Barbara Sher Tinsley, *Johann Sturm on Education: The Reformation and Humanist Learning* (Saint Louis: Concordia Publishing House, 1995).

I wish to thank Mr. John Smedley, editor of the *Variorum* series, for his patience, persistence, and helpfulness in seeing this volume through the press. I am grateful also to Dr. Ronald A. Davies, who prepared substantial parts of the text for publication in new typesetting, and to Mr. John Rawlings and Dr. William Fredlund of the Stanford University Libraries, who have helped to build the holdings in Renaissance and Reformation history into one of the best in the country, and through the reference department researched out bibliographical matters helpful to the author of this volume.

Acknowledgement is gratefully made to the journals and publishers for their kind permission to reprint, and in some cases to update and change the type of the chapters in this volume: Walter de Gruyter, Berlin (I); E.J. Brill (II, VII); University of North Carolina Press (III); University of Texas Press (IV); Longman House, Essex (V); Saint Martin's Press (VI); Susquehanna University Press and Associated

Presses (VIII); University of Pennsylvania Press (IX); Duke University Press (X); Concordia Publishing House (XI).

Stanford University                                                      Lewis W. Spitz
Stanford, California

For

Mathew Schepman Spitz
and  Elizabeth Grace Spitz

with Grandfatherly Love

# PUBLISHER'S NOTE

The articles in this volume, as in all others in the Collected Studies Series, have not been given a new, continuous pagination. In order to avoid confusion, and to facilitate their use where these same studies have been referred to elsewhere, the original pagination has been maintained wherever possible.

Each article has been given a Roman number in order of appearance, as listed in the Contents. The number is repeated on each page and quoted in the index entries.

# I

## THE RENAISSANCE:
## HUMANISM AND HUMANISM RESEARCH·

### I. Definitions and Varieties

Humanism, the most characteristic form of Renaissance intellectual life, developed in Italy about the middle of the fourteenth century and persisted through the Reformation period well into the seventeenth century. The term "humanism" or *umanesimo* was coined by a German pedagogue, F.J. Niethammer, who used it in 1808 to refer to a philosophy of education that favored classical studies in the school curriculum. Karl Hagen in a work published 1841–43 and Georg Voigt, 1859, first used the word *Humanismus* as a historical event and an intellectual phenomenon in association with the Renaissance. The term itself is protean and has been used in varying modalities to describe a number of movements involving an anthropocentric emphasis. In a very general way it was tied up with the rationalistic and humanitarian attitudes cultivated by the Enlightenment. Early in the nineteenth century it was used for the so-called second humanism of Wilhelm von Humboldt and his contemporaries, who made reason and experience the sole touchstones of truth. It has been identified with the libertarian ideas of John Stuart Mill and at the other extreme has been appropriated by Marxian socialists as the communist "progressive humanism." The twentieth century has witnessed the development of the "new" or "third humanism," represented by thinkers such as Bertrand Russell and Corliss Lamont, militantly anthropocentric and not infrequently anti-religious. The term has been associated with the attempt to develop a non-theistic religio-ethical movement. Jean-Paul

---

· This essay first appeared in German as "Humanismus/Humanismusforschung," in *Theologische Realenzyklopädie* (Berlin and New York: Walter de Gruyter, 1977ff.), Band 15 (1986): 639–61. It appears here in English for the first time, translated by the author, with minor additions to its selective bibliography. Readers seeking more extensive bibliography on Renaissance Humanism are directed to Volume Three of Albert Rabil, Jr., ed., *Renaissance Humanism: Foundations, Forms, and Legacy* (Philadelphia, 1988).

Sartre and others have argued for existential philosophy as a humanism. The term has been applied indiscriminately to any and every appreciation of human values and is not infrequently confused with simple humanitarianism. Historically, however, humanism has been most often closely associated with the thought and literary culture of the Renaissance.

## Defining Renaissance Humanism

Renaissance humanism was a complex phenomenon embracing many intellectual emphases. It was not static but underwent change and movement throughout three centuries. Paul Joachimsen offered a clear and positive definition of it as an intellectual movement, primarily literary and philological in nature, which was rooted in the love of and desire for the rebirth of classical antiquity. This rebirth of classical antiquity, which presupposed that it had been truly dead, involved two aspects, that of form which was primarily aesthetic and that of norm which included ethical values with the aesthetic. Humanism was not merely antiquarian, but it represented a certain way of looking at antiquity and of relating it to the present. Antiquity gave the humanists not only new forms of thought, literary expression and action, but also new norms for determining the suitability and rightness of the content of thought, word, and deed. The word humanism was derived from the phrase *studia humanitatis,* the liberal arts, a concept derived largely from Cicero, who believed that the orator or poet was best suited to communicate the *humaniora* or humane studies. A student of the humanities in fifteenth-century parlance was a *humanista*.

The term "humanist" was initially applied to the professional public or private teacher of classical literature. It came into use only in the late-fifteenth and early-sixteenth centuries in Italy. In a second phase the word came to assume a more comprehensive and general meaning and referred to the student of classical learning who was not necessarily also a teacher. Outside Italy the word *humanista* appeared first in Germany, four times, for example, in the Latin text of the *Epistolae Obscurorum Virorum,* 1515. The German word *Humanismus,* however, did not appear until the end of the eighteenth century. The word was used in France by Claude Gruget and Michel Montaigne in the middle of the sixteenth century. The word was adopted into the English language late in the sixteenth century from French and Italian sources.

The five subjects which composed the liberal arts curriculum were grammar, rhetoric, poetry, history, and moral philosophy. While the humanist course of studies was related to that of the medieval cathedral schools it was less preoccupied with dialectic or logic, natural science and metaphysics than was the scholastic curriculum. The Florentine Leonardo Bruni expressed a thought common to nearly all the humanists when he wrote to Niccolò Strozzi that these were the studies best designed to perfect and ornament man.

Technically the humanists were continuing the medieval vocation of the *dictatores,* who taught the skills of letter-writing and proper style in written work and in speech. The twelfth-century renaissance was very much an ecclesiastical affair centered in the cathedral schools at Tours, Chartres, Laon, Orléans, and Canterbury. The study of the liberal arts was the customary way of educating the clerical administrators needed for the growing ecclesiastical hierarchy. In the thirteenth century the teachers of the *ars dictaminis,* the epistolary techniques useful not only for ecclesiastical bureaucrats but also for city secretaries or chancellors, developed rhetoric and classicism. Brunetto Latini, the teacher of Dante, had an impressive knowledge of the Latin classics and of Aristotle's politics. The Renaissance humanists of the fourteenth and fifteenth centuries stood in this tradition, but they went beyond their predecessors in their fervent love of the classics and their cultivation of rhetoric as a guide to and expression of wisdom. They loved to quote Cicero's phrase in *De Oratore:* "For eloquence is nothing else than wisdom speaking copiously." The humanists used other names as well, such as orators, since many held chairs of rhetoric or spoke as advocates of city councils or princely courts, poets, philosophers, and even prophets (*vates,* inspired poet-prophets). As professional rhetoricians and teachers of the classics the humanists vied with the scholastics for the place of their discipline in the universities and even for endowed chairs. Much of what has been described as the warfare of humanists and scholastics had to do with such practical matters rather than with intellectual questions, for the humanists considered the dialectical and theological demonstrations of the scholastics trivial and irrelevant compared with the learning which concerned them, man and his life in society and, in a very broad sense, man's place in history and nature. Humanism was cultivated not merely by the educational professionals but by men of letters, historians, moralists, statesmen, and churchmen, regular as well as secular clergy who opposed the *aurea sapientia* or golden wisdom of the philosophers and writers of classical times to the arid dialectic of the scholastic doctors, especially of the dominant *via moderna,* that is the Occamists or advocates of nominalistic or terminist logic, which was often used for physical and mathematical questions.

Several problems have in recent decades preoccupied students of humanism. The first is that of the origins of humanism, whether it developed in Italy from an indigenous classical tradition, memories of the glory that was Rome, and architectural remains, and what it owed to the French medieval tradition. Dante (1265–1321) knew the Latin classics, though his masterpiece was done in the vernacular. Francesco Petrarch read Cicero in his family circle, but still Petrarch's sonnets owed much to Provençal poetry. The question of the Byzantine influence and Greek revival is related to that of origins. The second problem is that of the economic base of humanism. The romantic notion that the humanists were *Wandervögel,* intellectuals living by their wits and pens, has been discarded, for only Francesco Petrarch, Desiderius Erasmus, and a few others made their way by their writings with the help of patrons, and in the latter case, the printers. Most of the leading Italian humanists were financially well off, either members of wealthy families or through their positions as notaries and chancellors gaining wealth in their own right. Their social function was related to the rise of the bourgeoisie in the city-states, a class from which many leading humanists came. By the beginning of the fifteenth century humanism as a profession had become permanently established in four institutions, in the civil service and emerging diplomatic service of the Italian states; in education with university appointments in poetry, eloquence, and moral philosophy, as tutors and teachers and heads of communal or private schools; in ecclesiastical or monastic centers; in private households and in princely courts. A third problem is that of humanism and religion. On the one hand the humanists are no longer considered pre-reformers, but on the other hand there is a tendency now to play down the pagan element of the humanists, some scholars even going so far as to speak of the "great lay priesthood of the humanists." Some even hold that humanism was essentially orthodox and conservative and that late scholasticism was rationalistic, skeptical and radical. Coluccio Salutati and many early fifteenth-century humanists were concerned with the problem, for he wrote to friends defending culture and the poetry of Vergil, while he was also a pious Christian. The relationship of humanist attitudes toward religion and Christian belief was much more subtle than many nineteenth-century historians imagined. A fourth problem is the question of how the Italian Renaissance differed from the Iro-Celtic, Carolingian, Ottonian, and twelfth-century renaissances. A consensus among scholars seems to be developing that the difference consisted not merely in the deeper knowledge of a larger number of Latin and especially Greek classics, but in the fact that the humanists of the fourteenth and fifteenth centuries experienced a greater sense of distance from antiquity and a break in the living cultural continuity, though not complete alienation from the tradition of the medieval centuries immediately preceding. Finally, there is the question as to the extent to which a new individualism was evident, related to the increasingly bourgeois character of a growing urban commercial society. A middle class lay-dominated society, the argument goes, broke with the ecclesiastical and feudal hierarchies and allowed for greater social mobility and expression of individualism. The attempts to relate Renaissance individualism to that of nominalist particularism in contrast to Thomist realism which saw a man as representative of a group or type, have been largely unproductive. The humanists, of course, with their repristination of ancient forms and subservience to classical authorities and to their own models, had a conformity of their own.

## Italian Humanism of the *Trecento*

Toward the end of the thirteenth century and early in the fourteenth a kind of proto-humanism emerged under the aegis of the legal profession to cultivate literature and classical rhetoric. The centers in the North of Italy were Padua, Verona, and Vicenza, and in Tuscany Arezzo and Florence. Many of these proto-humanists were students of the *ars dictaminis,* notaries, lawyers, or judges. Some among them were active in government such as Lovato dei Lovati (1241–1309), Albertino Mussato (1261–1329) and Geremia da Montagnone (c.1260–1321), all of Padua, Francesco da Barberino (1264–1348), a Florentine jurist, and

Geri d'Arezzo (c.1270–c.1339), an *advocatus communis* in Florence. They all imitated classical authors, writing epistles, poems, moral dialogues, tragedies and histories. In 1321 Giovanni del Virgilio was appointed to lecture on Latin poetry at the University of Bologna. Giovanni Mansionario used corrupted classical texts in his *Historia imperialis* and in his *Adnotatio de duobus Pliniis* he showed that there had been two Plinys. While many proto-humanists connected with the legal profession were laymen, there was a renewed interest in the classics also in some ecclesiastical circles such as the cathedral chapter at Verona and the papal court at Avignon, where Petrarch's father settled in 1312. There Petrarch made many friends and patrons interested in the classics such as Raymond Subirani, Giovanni Cavallini, Nicholas Trevet, a Dominican, and Cardinal Giovanni Colonna. Dionigi da Borgo San Sepolcro, an Augustinian, wrote commentaries on such Latin authors as Valerius Maximus and formed a link with the Angevin court at Naples. He lectured at the University of Paris prior to 1329. The Florentine Roberto de' Bardi, another friend of Petrarch, was a professor in Paris and chancellor of the university from 1336 to 1349.

Francesco Petrarch (1304–1374), the "father of humanism" with his depth, brilliance and energy gave to early Italian literary humanism its basic character. He considered his historical studies of the Romans, *De viris illustribus,* and his *Africa,* a Latin epic poem on Scipio, to be his most important works. He was crowned poet laureate on the Capitoline Hill in Rome in 1341. In his *Epistolae de rebus familiaribus et variae* he addressed letters to the ancient dead, Livy, Vergil, Horace, Cicero, revealing a preoccupation with time and the position of his own age in relation to the past and future. He praised the Roman virtues in the hope that they would help restore virtue "in the face of the miseries of the age." In the *Epistolae seniles,* 14, 1, he commended the injunction found in Roman law "to harm no one, to give to each his own, and to live honestly." In a number of treatises such as *De vita solitaria* and the *Secretum* Petrarch developed his religious thought. In artfully constructed dialogues with St. Augustine he probed the melancholy (*accidia*) in his soul. Some of the ambiguities of his position, caught between classical and Christian values, are evident in his *Ascent of Mount Ventoux* in *Le Familiari.* In *De sui ipsius et multorum ignorantia* he wrote as an apologist for the Christian view of man and the humanists' appreciation of individual worth against certain Neo-

Aristotelians, mistakenly called Averroists, whose natural philosophy he believed to be subversive of those values. He touched upon such issues frequently and once confessed: "If to admire Cicero means to be a Ciceronian, I am a Ciceronian.... However, when we come to think or speak of religion, that is, of supreme truth and true happiness, and of eternal salvation, then I am certainly not a Ciceronian, or a Platonist, but a Christian." He was recognized as the founder of a new cultural age.

Along with Dante, the apex of medieval literary culture, and Petrarch, the father of Renaissance humanism, the third man of the great *Trecento* was Giovanni Boccaccio (1313–1375), a friend of Petrarch. His fame rested primarily on the *Decameron,* a collection of one hundred short stories. Three youths and seven young ladies fled Florence to escape the Great Plague of 1348 and found refuge in a country villa. To pass the time away in their rural retreat they tell ten tales a day. The stories are drawn from the old chivalric romances and *fabliaux,* but Boccaccio plays with the tales, mocks and ridicules. His Italian tales and *novelle* reveal the growth of a secular outlook in the lay middle and upper classes of urban Italy. Boccaccio made some great finds while searching for classical manuscripts, a text of Ausonius, another of Martial, a minor work of Ovid, and an important Tacitus selection. He was the author of a manual of classical geography, a book on famous women, *De claris mulieribus,* and the fortunes of great men, *De casibus virorum illustrium,* mostly Greeks and Romans. His encyclopedic *De genealogia deorum* with its literal, moral, and allegorical interpretations and its undiscriminating dependence on classical and medieval compendia was the most important handbook of mythology until the appearance of L.G. Giraldi's *De deis gentium,* Vincenzo Cartari's *Le imagini degli dei,* and Natale Conti's *Mythologiae.* In book 4 he revives the Prometheus myth in a significant new form, for the "second Prometheus" is the learned man, for it is learning that "makes a natural man civil man, remarkable for morals, knowledge, and virtue, whereby it becomes obvious that nature produces man and learning then forms him anew."

## Dissemination of Humanism

The spread of Petrarchan humanism can be traced through a concatenation of literati throughout Italy. Since Petrarch had spent his last years in the lands of the Carraras, his influence was strong in cities in their domain such as Verona and Padua. Giovanni Conversino da Ravenna (1343–1408) was professor of rhetoric at the University of Padua in 1392 and was twice chancellor of Padua. An enthusiastic Ciceronian and admirer of Petrarch, he inspired students such as Poggio Bracciolini, Francesco Filelfo, Guarino da Verona, and Vittorino da Feltre, who became major figures in Renaissance humanism. Gasparino da Barzizza (1359–1431), professor of rhetoric at Padua and author of a famous text, *Orthographia,* opened a humanist school in Padua in 1408. Filippo Maria Visconti, who read Dante and Petrarch, as well as chivalric romances, invited him to open a Latin school for boys in Milan in 1418. Giovanni Malpaghini da Ravenna (1346–1417), Petrarch's copyist, taught in northern Italy and was appointed professor of rhetoric at the University of Florence around 1395.

In Florence an Augustinian monk, Luigi Marsigli (c.1330–1394), a friend and correspondent of Petrarch, gathered a discussion group at the monastery of Santo Spirito concerned with the classics. A similar group of laymen met at the villa of Antonio degli Alberti. Palla Strozzi (1372–1402), influenced by Petrarch and Conversino, became a patron-practitioner of humanist studies. He gave large sums of money to develop the *studia* or University of Florence. He encouraged the Greek scholar Manuel Chrysoloras (c.1350–1415) to come to Florence to lecture, and founded the first public library in Florence in the Santa Trinità monastery. Later he appointed John Argyropoulos, a Greek refugee from Constantinople, as his tutor in Greek. Niccolò Niccoli (1363–1437), a Florentine merchant, attended Luigi Marsigli's lectures, opened his house to students of the new learning, and became a fine classicist, though he never published because he was too inhibited by the excellence of the ancients.

In the search for ancient manuscripts no one was more successful than Poggio Bracciolini (1380–1459). In Cluny he discovered several orations of Cicero and at St. Gall he found Quintilian's *Institutio oratoris,* which along with Cicero's *De Oratore* became the *sedes doctrinae* for the humanists' rhetorical theory. On another expedition to Einsiedeln, Reichenau, and St. Gall he found copies of Ammianus Marcellinus and Lucretius. In later years he also recovered the text of Vitruvius, nine new comedies of Plautus, the letters of Pliny the Younger, some minor works of Tacitus, as well as *Agricola,* the *Dialogue* and the *Germania.* Poggio's *De varietate fortunae* described Roman ruins with an eye for their aesthetic as well as for their historical value. Francesco Filelfo (1398–1481), Poggio's great rival, studied Latin and rhetoric at Padua and in 1417 was invited to teach philosophy and rhetoric in Venice. His importance rests not in original work but in his constant advocacy of humanism and his role in introducing and translating Greek classics.

## The Greek Revival

In Petrarch's day Sicily and southern Italy, known as *Magna Graeca,* had many Greek settlements. Petrarch's Greek teacher, Barlaam, came from Calabria, but Petrarch made little progress in the language. Boccaccio brought the Greek scholar Leontius Pilatus to teach at Florence in 1360, but he had few auditors. The Greek philologist Simon Atumano lectured in Rome in 1380–1381, but he had only a single student. Preoccupied with the revival of Latin antiquity, the Italians had little time left for Greek. During the closing decades of the fourteenth century, however, the eastern Emperor, threatened by the Ottoman Turks, sought renewed contact with the West. Two imperial expeditions in 1374 and 1399 gained no help for him. But some Greek scholars maintained contact: Manuel Chrysoloras, for example, came to Venice in 1393 and was appointed to lecture on the classics in Florence in 1387. From 1397 to 1399 he traveled with Manuel II Palaeologus through northern Italy, to Paris and London, but nowhere was there any great interest in his lectures outside of Florence. There Leonardo Bruni learned Greek from him so well that he was able to translate Plato, Aristotle, Demosthenes, Plutarch, and St. Basil. In 1438 John VIII Palaeologus came to Italy with a large retinue to beg the Council of Ferrara-Florence for help. On July 6, 1439, the reunion of the eastern and western churches was declared, but still no military aid was forthcoming. Among the Greeks accompanying the emperor was Gemistos Pletho (c.1355–c.1450), a Platonist and legist. He urged

Cosimo de' Medici to establish an academy for Greek letters and Platonic philosophy. John Bessarion (1403–1472), metropolitan of Nicea, a distinguished Platonist, served as the chief negotiator at the council. He remained in the West and in 1439 was elevated to the cardinalate. Like Bessarion, Ambrogio Traversari (1386–1439), the prior of the Camaldese Convent of Santa Maria degli Angeli in Florence, was interested in Greek patristic writings. Moreover, two manuscript collectors, Ciriaco de' Pizzicolli of Ancona (c.1391–1457) and Giovanni Aurispa (1374–1450), gathered texts of Thucydides, Euripides, Sophocles and other classical Greek authors. After the fall of Constantinople in 1453 other Greek scholars fled to the West, among them John Argyropoulos, Demetrius Calcondylas, and John and Constantine Lascaris, adding new momentum to the Greek revival and broadening the dimensions of philosophical discussion.

### Civic Humanism

During the medieval period Cicero was thought of primarily as a moral philosopher. His admiration for Greek culture lent legitimacy to the Greek revival. But Cicero was an active statesman and apologist for the Roman Republic. He inspired the humanists to practice the *vita activa* while cultivating the *vita studiosa*. While the gifts of the orator had been used in the service of the state long before the end of the fourteenth century, during the chancellorships of Coluccio Salutati (1331–1406) and Leonardo Bruni Aretino (c.1370–1444) a new urgency came into play, for Florence was seriously threatened by its enemies and forced to fight for its freedom and survival. With Florence threatened by Milan and then by Naples, its humanist chancellors used their rhetorical ability to strengthen the determination of the citizens to resist the tyrants and defend their republic. Salutati, after serving as a notary in obscure posts, then in Rome, in February, 1374, became a notary in the office of elections in Florence; one year later was chosen as chancellor, and held that office for thirty-one years until his death. He served as foreign minister as well as having a strong influence on domestic matters, such as resistance during the Ciompi Revolt in 1378. Salutati's state papers and official correspondence brought much prestige to Florence so that the Florentine government continued to employ humanists as chancellors thereafter. Milan, Venice, Naples, the papal curia and many smaller seignorial courts followed the example of Florence during the course of the fifteenth century. Humanists not only mastered classical Latin, but understood historically Roman precedents and law and increasingly influenced patrons to support literary and artistic projects. Salutati was not the equal of Petrarch or Boccaccio, but his literary production included *De saeculo et religione, De fato et fortuna, De nobilitate legum et medicinae, De tyranno,* and *De laboris Herculis.* His mind was neither agile nor profound, but he touched on questions debated through the decades which followed.

Given the position of Tuscany at the center of the city-state complex, Florence continued to be threatened throughout the century. King Ladislas of Naples advanced from the south, but he died in 1414 in time to save Florence. Then Filippo Maria Visconti took up Milan's efforts once again to conquer Florence. During much of this critical period Leonardo Bruni served as chancellor, following the example of Salutati, who had advanced his career. Unlike Petrarch, who repeatedly withdrew to the contemplative life, Bruni applied humanist learning to social and political life. His dialogue *Ad Petrum Histrum,* an obvious imitation of Plato, developed his ideas of education, the value of learning and of conversation, the greatness of Cicero, the vast knowledge of Varro, and similar subjects. His *Laudatio urbis Florentinae* praised the freedom of the republic, its security as an inland city, the plan of the city with the Palazzo Vecchio in the center surrounded by four concentric circles. He believed Florence to be more beautiful than ancient Athens or Rome. A student of Livy, Polybius, Julius Caesar and Thucydides, he spent nearly three decades working on his *History of the Florentine People,* with liberty as its master theme. Like the classical historians he also wrote contemporary history for posterity, *Commentary on Things Done in His Own Time.*

Civic humanism was more than an ideology of embattled republicanism, for in a broader sense it was understood as a life of action lived for the common good. Giannozzo Manetti (1396–1459), who spoke the eulogy at Bruni's interment in the church of Santa Croce, was the author of a famous treatise *De dignitate et excellentia hominis.* In answer to a question of King Alfonso of Naples as to what composes the whole duty of man, Manetti replied: "To understand and to act." As a man of contemplation and social action no one excelled that great genius of the Renaissance Leon Battista Alberti (1404–1472), a truly "universal man." As an architect he helped restore the papal palace for Nicholas V, ornamented the Trevi fountain, remodeled the church of San Francesco in Rimini, built the Rucellai palace, and designed the façade of the church of Santa Maria Novella in Florence. His most famous treatises were *De re architectura, Della Pittura, Della famiglia.* "Man," he declared, "is born to be useful to man." Such sentiments are to be found in the writings of other humanists as well, such as Matteo Palmieri (1406–1475), author of *Della vita civile,* Carlo Marsuppini (1398–1453), who succeeded Bruni as Florentine chancellor, and Benedetto Accolti (1415–1466), who became Florentine chancellor after Poggio. In his *Dialogus de praestantia virorum sui aevi* he argued for the superiority of the men in his own times over those of the ancient times.

## Humanism and Education

Renaissance humanists were generally optimistic about the educability of man and had a good opinion of the rationality at least of the upper strata of human society. In the medieval period the liberal arts served merely as a basis for the professional study of theology, law and medicine, but now they were seen to be valuable in their own right in producing leaders of cultivation, character and vision. The humanist educators elevated grammar and rhetoric to new dignity in relation to logic in the narrow sense.

One of the most influential treatises on education was that of Pietro Paolo Vergerio (1370–1444), *De ingenuis moribus,* on the morals befitting a free man, which drew extensively on Plato, Plutarch and Cicero. Vergerio, a student of Conversino and Chrysoloras and a friend of Salutati and Bruni, was a professor of logic and rhetoric in Florence, Padua and Verona. He served as Latin secretary to Innocent VII, Cardinal Zabarella, and Emperor Sigismond. Vergerio believed that the liberal arts taught the secret of true freedom and helped the student develop his full individual potential. He ranked the study of history first in importance because it is helpful to both the scholar and the statesman, followed by moral philosophy and eloquence. Among the great humanist educators who put educational theory into practice the most famous were Vittorino da Feltre (1378–1446) and Guarino da Verona (1370–1460).

### Humanism and History

Humanist educators emphasized the importance of history, especially classical history and the history of their own times. The growing sense of distance from ancient times beginning with Petrarch deepened their sense of history. From Leonardo Bruni's *History of Florence* to Niccolò Machiavelli, who wrote a *History of Florence,* and Francesco Guicciardini (1483–1540), who wrote a *History of Italy in His Own Times,* covering 1492–1534, the humanists learned from classical historians a feeling for coherent organization, literary style, historical criticism, and a view of history that differed from that of the medieval chronicler, the pragmatic purpose of history, that is, moral philosophy teaching by examples.

Flavio Biondo (1389–1463) became the founder of modern archeology. As papal secretary he had ample opportunity to study Roman ruins. His two massive works *Rome Triumphant* and *Rome Restored* utilized his knowledge of topography, monuments and archeological finds to reconstruct Roman political institutions and way of life. His encyclopedic *Italia illustrata* provided a topographical-historical survey of all Italy from ancient times.

The most brilliant critical mind was that of Lorenzo Valla (1407–1457), who demonstrated the effective use of historical criticism. A philologist and rhetorician, he wrote the most influential linguistic treatise of the fourteenth century, *Elegantiae linguae latinae* (1444). With his dialogue *De voluptate ac de vero bono* he unfairly earned the reputation of being an epicurean and an anti-religious sensualist. Always a critical genius, in his treatise *De libero arbitrio* he argued that predestination is not inconsistent with free will and that divine foreknowledge and human free will can be harmonized. He did not think that man has the capacity to bridge the natural and supernatural worlds intellectually or to harmonize reason and revelation. Other of Valla's works dealt with problems that were to loom large in the controversies of the Reformation period. In his *Annotationes* on the New Testament he corrected textual errors in the Vulgate and criticized exegetical interpretations of authorities as imposing as St. Augustine. In *De professione religiosorum* he declared that monastic life does not have a higher religious value than the good life of the layman who is motivated from within. In his *Encomium* on Thomas Aquinas he was subtly critical of him for elevating logic and metaphysics in theology and for poor Latin style, praising patristic writers for contrast. Valla's most sensational work was *De falso credita et ementito Constantini donatione declamatio* in which he challenged the authenticity of the document that allegedly proved that when Constantine moved the imperial capital to the East he had given the Lateran Palace and outlying provinces to Pope Sylvester.

## Humanism and Philosophy

By the middle of the *quattrocento* many of the leading Italian humanists were gone. Bruni, Vergerio, Poggio, Vittorino, Manetti, Valla, and humanism transmorphized into a new phase. This new phase was marked by three major developments: the increasing integration of classical scholarship with literary composition in the vernacular, the spread of printing from the establishment of the first press in Italy in 1465, and a new metaphysical emphasis superseding the relatively uncomplicated moral philosophy of the humanists, an intense preoccupation with Neoplatonic, Neo-Pythagorean, Neo-Aristotelian, Hermetic and Cabalistic philosophies and theodicies.

The integration of humanism with vernacular literary composition is best illustrated by the writings of such literary figures as Angelo Ambrogini (1454–1494), known as Politian, who did commentaries on Greek and Latin texts and was an excellent Latin and vernacular poet, Giovanni Pontano (1426–1503) of Naples, a lyricist, Jacopo Sannazzaro (1456–1530), who wrote the *Arcadia* on the beauty of the pastoral life and *De partu virginis,* a poem on the life of the Virgin in classical meter, and Pietro Bembo (1470–1547), of Venice, a prolix and ornate literary exponent of the Neoplatonic doctrine of love in his *Gli Asolani.* The spread of printing through the work of such learned publishers as Aldus Manutius (1447–1515) of Venice naturally broadened the reading public and the influence of humanism. Information storage in great public libraries marked a related cultural advance.

The most prominent and characteristic form of Renaissance philosophy was Neoplatonism which followed upon the Aristotelianism of Thomist scholastic philosophy in the thirteenth century and more immediately upon a brief upsurge of interest in Aristotelian moral philosophy in Florence. In 1457 John Argyropoulos, an Aristotelian from Constantinople, was appointed to the University of Florence. His student Donato Acciaiuoli (1428–1478) and Alamanno Rinuccini (1419–1499) continued the Aristotelian tradition in Florence. But Neoplatonism was to overshadow Aristotelianism during the second half of the century. The revival of a growing number of Greek patristic writings added momentum to the move toward Platonism.

The three most important philosophers of the Renaissance were Nicholas Cusanus (1401–1464), a German churchman who spent many years in Rome, Marsilio Ficino (1433–1499), and Giovanni Pico della Mirandola (1463–1494), a friend and pupil of Ficino. Cusanus' basic philosophical concern was the search for unity, for the infinite One that individualizes and reveals itself in the multiplicity of finite things. The differences and antitheses of all finite creatures coincide in the infinity of God, who is the *coincidentia oppositorum.*

Ficino presided over Cosimo's "Platonic Academy," and edited texts and wrote works of his own which became the basic texts of Neoplatonic philosophy in the late Renaissance. He edited the *Enneads* of Plotinus, and other works by him, as well as by Proclus, Porphyry, and Dionysius the Areopagite, not yet definitively identified. He translated from Greek to Latin a number of texts from the second and third centuries ascribed to a mythical character named Hermes Trismegistus, typical of the gnosticism of that age. Ficino's own two most significant works were *De religione christiana* and the *Theologia platonica.* As a Christian priest he was clearly using Neoplatonism to bind Renaissance classics-minded intellectuals to the Christian faith.

Pico della Mirandola, a wealthy young nobleman, inspired by Ficino, was concerned with finding the truth that Platonism, Aristotelianism, Hermeticism, Islam, and the Jewish Cabala had in common. In Rome he published nine hundred *Conclusiones,* a summation of all learning, which were to serve as theses for a public disputation. His *Oratio de dignitate hominis,* the rhetorical introduction to the *Conclusiones,* declared that man is not merely the middle link of the great chain of being, but is the object of a special creation with the ability to rise upward toward the angels or to sink downward to the level of the beasts by indulging in sensate appetites.

Despite the predominance of Neoplatonism, Neo-Aristotelianism also found its proponents. Pietro Pomponazzi (1462–1525) of Padua wrote such works as *De immortalitate animae* and *De fato, libero arbitrio, praedestinatione, providentia Dei libri V.* He argued that the human soul, having only one nature, is absolutely mortal, and only in certain respects immortal. Immortality cannot be proved but must be accepted on the authority of the church. In the sixteenth century the Aristotelian tradition was continued by Bernardino Telesio and Francesco Patrizzi. Giordano Bruno (1548–1600) has been called the martyr of the Renaissance, for he was burned at the stake in Rome for heresy. He combined Cusa's Neoplatonism and the Hermetic tradition with the implications of the new astronomy of Copernicus into a philosophy that verged on pantheism. Neoplatonism had a broad influence on literature and art as well as on philosophy.

### German Humanism

During the late fifteenth and the sixteenth centuries there was a two-way traffic of men and ideas between Italy and northern Europe. Italian humanists and artists traveled north as diplomatic emissaries, ecclesiastical legates, secretaries to northern princes and cities, lecturers in universities or business representatives. Northerners went to Italy either as students, primarily in law and medicine, or simply as admirers of the learned Italians, whose wisdom they hoped to absorb.

The new humanist culture came earlier to the Germanies than to other countries of the North. There were many close political ties between the Empire and Italy, and a lively trade prospered between the Italian cities and the German cities along the Danube and Rhine. The old medieval tradition of student wandering brought literally thousands of German students to the Italian universities each year. The "German nations" at the universities of Bologna, Padua and Pavia were large and active. The transition from wandering student to roving humanist was not hard to make. German humanism was characterized by strong cultural nationalism and by the desire for religious enlightenment.

During the second half of the fifteenth century, a few pioneers of the movement made their appearance, wandering poets like Peter Luder (c.1415–1474), schoolmaster humanists such as Johannes Murmellius and Rudolf von Langen, scholastic humanists like Conrad Summenhart and Paul Scriptoris, moralistic critics of society and church like Heinrich Bebel and Jacob Wimpfeling (1450–1528), an Alsatian who warned against the encroachments of the French king and in his *De integritate* attacked simony and concubinage. His friends Sebastian Brant (1457–1521), author of the *Narrenschiff*, and Johann Geiler von Kaisersberg (1445–1510), a powerful preacher, were also earnest moralists. But the most representative figure of the older generation was Rudolf Agricola (1444–1485), known as the "German Petrarch." After a decade in Italy he returned to preside over a circle of young humanists in Heidelberg. More a rhetorician than a philosopher, he preferred Cicero to Aristotle, and in his *De inventione dialectica* (1479) he emphasized discovery over judging in rhetorical theory.

One of Agricola's disciples was Conrad Celtis (1459–1508), the German "Arch-Humanist," whom Emperor Frederick III crowned poet laureate of the Empire in 1487. He wrote love poems such as the *Amores* and *Odes*. After a trip to Italy he called upon the Germans to take up cultural rivalry with Italy. He published the plays of Roswitha, a tenth-century nun, and the epic poem *Ligurinus* in praise of Frederick Barbarossa. Celtis organized the Rhenish and Danubian sodalities, loose associations of local societies of humanists in Linz, Ingolstadt, Augsburg, Heidelberg and other cities and recruited their members as contributors to his *Germania illustrata,* modeled on Biondo's *Italia illustrata,* and did *Norimberga* as an example of a topographical-historical work. In 1497 on the invitation of Emperor Maximilian I he founded the College of Poets and Mathematicians at the University of Vienna, where he ended his days.

While humanists struggled for prestige and positions in the universities, humanism spread to courts and cities. In 1520 it had penetrated not only the imperial Habsburg courts in Linz and Vienna, but that of many territorial princes and the powerful ecclesiastical prince-bishops of Mainz, Trier and Cologne. The prosperous cities of south Germany served as centers for humanist and artistic activity. The lawyer Conrad Peutinger (1464–1547) promoted classical learning and served Augsburg and Maximilian as councilor. The historian Johannes Aventinus (1477–1534) wrote the *Annales* of Bavaria. In Nürnberg the city councilor Willibald Pirckheimer (1470–1528), a friend of Celtis and of Albrecht Dürer, turned his patrician house into a center of humanist discourse.

The celebrated Reuchlin controversy brought the issue of humanism and scholasticism into sharp focus. Johannes Reuchlin (1455–1522), chancellor to the duke of Württemberg and later professor at Ingolstadt and Tübingen, did a Hebrew grammar and vocabulary. In two major works, *De verbo mirifico* and *De arte cabalistica,* he used the Jewish mystical cabala in support of Christianity. Defending some Hebrew books from a vicious obscurantist attack by Johannes Pfefferkorn, Reuchlin was attacked by certain scholastic doctors at Cologne. The young humanists Ulrich von Hutten (1488–1523) and Crotus Rubeanus (c.1480–1545) published in Reuchlin's defense the *Epistolae Obscurorum Virorum,* a biting satire on the "obscurantists" who supported the book-burners. In Gotha the canon Mutianus Rufus (1471–1526) gathered a circle of young humanists from the University of Erfurt to promote humanist learning.

## French Humanism

The Hundred Years War and the duel of France and Burgundy delayed the flowering of neoclassical culture in France. Historians formerly dated the French Renaissance from the invasion of Italy by Charles VIII, but it is now understood that there was a buildup from the Avignonese papacy and provençal contacts with Italy long before the invasion. In the first half of the fifteenth century the chancellor Jean de Montreuil (1354–1418) and the great preacher Nicholas de Clémanges admired Cicero and used rhetoric in their callings.

During the reign of Francis I French literary culture truly flourished. Guillaume Budé (1468–1540) wrote a commentary on the *Pandects* or digest of Justinian's law, published *De asse,* a treatise on coinage, and did *Commentarii linguae graecae,* and a major work *De transitu hellenismi ad christianismum,* 1535, which established his reputation as a leading hellenist.

Lefèvre d'Étaples (1455–1536) applied humanist philological principles to Biblical texts, publishing his *Quintuplex Psalter,* 1509, in which he placed five Latin versions of the Psalms in parallel columns, a *Commentary on the Epistles of St. Paul,* 1512, and a *Commentary on the Four Gospels,* 1522. He had a significant influence on Luther as well as upon French reformers such as Gerard Roussel, Guillaume Farel, and John Calvin. Marguerite d'Angoulême, sister of Francis I, a literary figure in her own right, and Bishop Guillaume Briçonnet, patronized and protected Lefèvre and other humanists at Meaux.

François Rabelais (c.1495–1553) is renowned as the author of the witty and satirical *Gargantua and Pantagruel,* the story of a giant and his son which serves as a vehicle for Rabelais' critique of society. A one-time Franciscan and medical doctor, Rabelais has puzzled commentators who analyze him variously as a skeptical freethinker, a crypto-Protestant, and of late more often as an Erasmian humanist. The greatest literary figure was Michel de Montaigne (1533–1592), famous essayist, moralist, skeptical philosopher and humanist.

## Spanish Humanism

Although Spanish humanism is sometimes associated almost exclusively with that giant of Spanish literature Miguel de Cervantes (1547–1616), author of *Don Quixote,* Spanish culture had much earlier been influenced both by Erasmian humanism and Lutheranism. Cardinal Francisco Ximénez de Cisneros (1436–1517) reformed the church with rigor, founding the University of Alcalá, with one of the colleges trilingual for the study of Latin, Greek and Hebrew. He also directed the publication of the Complutensian Polyglot Bible with the Hebrew, Latin, and Greek texts in parallel columns. The leading humanist was Antonio de Nebrija (1441–1522), an outstanding Latinist and Castilian grammarian. At Salamanca he educated an entire generation of Spanish humanists.

## English Humanism

As humanism began to penetrate English thought during the fifteenth century it was absorbed into traditional scholasticism and was not thought of as a competitive intellectual system. Most English humanists were ecclesiastical civil servants who cultivated classical studies for pleasure. During the century various Italians came to England, Poggio, Polydore Vergil, and five bishops of Worcester. Duke Humphrey of Gloucester, brother of Henry V, employed Italian secretaries and promoted humanistic studies at Oxford. William Grey, bishop of Ely, was a student of Guarino as well as a friend of Poggio and Bessarion. Serious study of the classics began at Oxford with Thomas Linacre (c.1460–1524), William Grocyn (c.1466–1519), and William Latimer (c.1460–1543). Grocyn taught John Colet, Thomas More and Erasmus, the three most important Christian humanists of the first phase of the English Renaissance.

John Colet (c.1467–1519) took his degrees at Cambridge, studied at Oxford, came into contact with Ficino and fell under the spell of Neoplatonism. When in 1496 he returned from Italy, he began his famous lecture series on Paul's Epistle to the Romans. He stressed man's sinfulness and need for God's grace and mercy. He became dean of St. Paul's and founded St. Paul's school, modeled after the humanist schools of Italy. His friend Sir Thomas More (1478–1535), remembered for his political career and execution by Henry VIII for opposing his divorce, was also a distinguished man of letters, though a vicious polemicist, and the author of the *Utopia,* the most famous work by an English humanist.

The prince of the northern humanists was without doubt Desiderius Erasmus (1469–1536), who combined an invincible love of the classics with a high regard for the church fathers. His much over-rated debate with Luther on the question of free will has been taken by some scholars as marking a watershed between humanism and Reformation theology.

## II. Humanism and the Reformation

Luther thought of the Renaissance as a John the Baptist, heralding the coming of the resurgent Gospel. He held that humanism made the Reformation possible, for the knowledge of the languages, the critical handling of the sources, the attack on abuses, the romantic cultural nationalism, the war on obscurantism and scholasticism, the exploitation of the printing press, and an army of young humanists who rallied to the evangelical cause were indispensable for the success of the Reformation. The reformers in return contributed to the continuity, the broadening influence, the increase in classical learning, and the perpetuation of many humanist values and the liberal arts into later centuries.

Certainly there was a broad chasm between evangelical theology and the religious assumptions of the classical world and even of Christian humanism in the areas of anthropology and soteriology, in the sin/grace, law/gospel antinomies. But the reformers viewed higher culture, too, as a sphere of faith's works and were for the most part strong advocates of humanist learning. They reformed the curricula of universities and established new gymnasia to promote both humanist learning and evangelical religion. They broadened the base of learning by insisting upon universal compulsory education for boys and girls, upon the calling of the teacher as a lofty divine vocation, and by insisting upon a humanist curriculum on the arts level in the new Protestant universities, the reformed older universities, and in the gymnasia and lycées.

Luther took the initiative in promoting the *humaniora* at the University of Wittenberg, where from its founding in 1502 humanists such as Martin Pollich of Mellerstadt and Nicolaus Marschalk had been active. Luther's personal love of the classics and preference for humanism over scholasticism was reinforced by his close relation with Philipp Melanchthon (1497–1560), grand-nephew of Reuchlin, and a brilliant young humanist, who became professor of Greek in the arts faculty. He was the author of brilliant confessional and theological writings. As in Italy a strong emphasis was placed on rhetoric, history, poetry, and moral philosophy. One of the great polymaths of the century, Joachim Camerarius (1500–1574) studied at Leipzig, Erfurt, and Wittenberg, taught history and Greek at the Nürnberg gymnasium, helped Melanchthon write the Augsburg Confession in 1530, led the reorganization of Tübingen in 1535 and of Leipzig in 1541, where he spent most of his remaining years doing classical scholarship. Other key Protestant figures in promoting humanist learning were Johannes Sturm (1507–1589), educator and director of the Strasbourg Gymnasium, Johannes Sleidan (1506–1556), historian of the Reformation and reign of Charles V, and Georg Calixtus (1586–1656) of Helmstedt, an irenic theologian with a humanist view of history. The many neo-Latin poets included Eobanus Hessus, Euricius Cordus, Lorentius Corvinus, Ursinus Velius, Georgius Logus, Joachim Vadianus, Nathan Chyträus, and Nikodemus Frischlin. The medieval *Fastnachtspiel* and the humanist drama were developed further during the sixteenth and seventeenth centuries as a dramatic form. The reformers appreciated the great value of drama, combining as it did poetry, rhetoric, moral philosophy, and the possibility of presenting Biblical as well as secular history and parables both as popular theater and as school dramas for the youth.

Humanism made an important cultural contribution in reformed Switzerland as well, where Ulrich Zwingli set the tone. In Geneva John

Calvin, a young French humanist who had himself edited a work of Seneca, was a well-read classicist, and a superb French stylist, founded the Academy, which later became the University of Geneva. On the festive opening Theodore Beza, professor of Greek, delivered an *Address at the Solemn Opening of the Academy in Geneva,* in which he praised the liberal arts and learned disciplines. Calvin's own Latin teacher, Mathurin Cordier, who had followed him into exile from France, lived out his days in Geneva as a model of the evangelical humanist educator. Representative of those Calvinist educators who carried the Genevan ideal to France, Scotland, England, and other areas of Calvinist penetration was Claude Baduel, who taught for many years as a humanist professor and reformer of Nîmes. Calvinist academies were modeled on the humanist pattern.

The Catholic reformers, especially the Jesuits, followed a similar pattern. Their secondary schools emphasized languages, rhetoric, history, and moral philosophy. Catholic universities such as Louvain developed a humanist curriculum. In Catholic as in Protestant areas humanist culture became normative and remained an essential part of the educational systems right through the period of the so-called wars of religion and persisted into the Enlightenment.

### III. Research on Renaissance Humanism

Research on humanism has been intimately connected with the problem of historical periodization. The consciousness of living in a new age was common both to Renaissance humanists with their admiration for the golden age of antiquity and to the reformers with their devotion to the New Testament Scriptures and the purity of the early church in contrast to the darkness of the centuries under the papacy. Late in the seventeenth century a Lutheran historian with classical training, Christoph Keller or Cellarius, gave currency to the term *medium aevum,* reducing the Middle Ages to a secondary historical status compared with ancient and modern times. Pierre Bayle (1647–1706), compiler of the *Historical and Critical Dictionary* (1697), saw the renewal of reason in the Renaissance as being of critical importance and considered the Enlightenment to be the continuation of the Renaissance. The eighteenth-century rationalists such as Voltaire, Condorcet, Gibbon, and Robertson were highly critical of the medieval period or "dark ages." The romanticists such as Johann Herder, Friedrich Schlegel, Wilhelm Wackenroder, or Adam Müller sought to rescue medieval civilization from the long-standing charges of religious and moral decline, clerical tyranny and feudal anarchy. In the context of this enlightenment-romanticist polemic modern research on Renaissance humanism emerged.

The most influential work was that of Jacob Burckhardt, *Die Kultur der Renaissance in Italien: Ein Versuch* (Basel, 1860), who saw the Italian Renaissance as making a distinct break with the Middle Ages and the beginning of modern times. The Renaissance was characteristic of modernity in its amoral political calculations, its interest in the human personality and the world of nature, and in its paganism and immorality. Jules Michelet in his history of France had used the phrase "the rediscovery of the world and of man." The fundamental characteristic of the age, Burckhardt felt, was egocentric individualism in a despotic setting. The political anarchy of the thirteenth century had destroyed the old order and undercut traditional values, creating social insecurity and lack of restraint which made possible the rise of ruthless and unlawful individuals. Humanists with their revival of pagan antiquity articulated, took part in, and reinforced the tendencies of the age, though it was not their cause. Humanism was thus linked with modernity.

This analysis dovetailed nicely with the theme of Georg Voigt, *Die Wiederbelebung des classischen Alterthums, oder das erste Jahrhundert des Humanismus* (Berlin, 1859). Voigt saw humanism with its revival of ancient culture as antagonistic to medieval scholastic modes of thought and expression. The humanists developed a new sense of form, critical method, a new consciousness of the individual self, and modern attitudes toward art, literature and life. Philippe Monier, *Le Quattrocento* (Paris, 1901), very heavily dependent on Voigt, conveyed this view of humanism to France. John Addington Symonds, *Renaissance in Italy,* 7 vols. (London, 1875–1886), disaffected with his own century, idealized the age of the Renaissance as the new birth of liberty, mankind recovering consciousness and the power of self-determination, recognizing the beauty of the outer world, and of the body through art, liberating the reason in science and the conscience in religion, restoring culture to the intelligence, and establishing the principle of political freedom. Ludwig Geiger, *Renaissance und Humanismus in Italien und*

*Deutschland* (Berlin, 1882), developed a Burckhardtian interpretation of German humanism, drawing parallels between Italian and German humanists, describing Agricola, for example, as the German Petrarch.

Although these representatives of the Burckhardtian interpretation did not argue for humanism as a new *Weltanschauung,* this interpretation developed in that direction. If Voigt represented quite conventional *Kulturgeschichte,* Wilhelm Dilthey pioneered a new form of *Geistesgeschichte* in opposition to nineteenth-century scientific positivism. In a famous essay first published in 1891–1892 entitled "Auffassung und Analyse des Menschen im 15. und 16. Jahrhundert," he argued that the unified world view composed of Christian, Greek and Roman elements disintegrated during the Renaissance. The humanists corroded the transcendental worldview and Platonism contributed to the development of pantheistic tendencies leading to the feeling that the ultimate realities in life are to be found within the bounds of human experience and the world of nature. In the twentieth century this view was extended by philosophical historians such as the neo-Kantian Ernst Cassirer, whose *Individuum und Kosmos in der Philosophie der Renaissance* (Leipzig, 1929), focusing on the philosophy of Nicholas Cusanus, argued that the *Weltanschauung* of the age was the sense of mathematically conceived, objective causation in the physical universe accompanied by a new conception of man's ability to create a unified cosmos by virtue of the unity of his own subjective perception of external reality. Giovanni Gentile, in such works as *I problemi della scolastica e il pensiero italiano* (Bari, 1912), *Studi sul Rinascimento* (Florence, 1923), and "La concezione humanistica del mondo," *Nuova antologia,* 277 (1931), 307–317, insisted on the sharp break of humanism with medieval other-worldliness in favor of a new self-consciousness, self-confidence, faith in the dignity of man and in the creative power of the human mind which laid the foundation for the immanent philosophy of scientific idealism. This general view was espoused also by Guido de Ruggiero in part three of his *Storia della filosofia* entitled *Rinascimento, Riforma et Controriforma* (Bari, 1930), and by Giuseppe Saitta, *Il pensiero italiano nell' umanesimo e nel Rinascimento* (Bologna, 1949–1951). Thus the Burckhardtian interpretation of humanism developed into the traditional view of humanism as establishing a clear break with medieval Christian and scholastic thought in favor of individualism, new secular values, and a more modern view of life, which led eventually to liberalism, critical rationalism, this-worldliness, and a modern scientific view of man and nature.

Revision and even outright rejection of the traditional Burckhardtian view took two forms, that of "root-stretching" and that of a reevaluation of humanism on the basis of a closer study of humanist writings. The medievalists believed that the Burckhardtians failed to understand the true nature of medieval culture, for classical learning constituted an important dimension of medieval culture and there were many "renascences" before the Renaissance, the Iro-Celtic, the Carolingian, the Ottonian, and the twelfth-century Renaissance. The art historian Heinrich Thode, for example, in *Franz von Assisi und die Anfänge der Kunst der Renaissance in Italien* (Berlin, 1885), maintained that the characteristic attitudes of Renaissance man were rooted in a complex of medieval religious impulses triggered by Saint Francis a century before Petrarch, the importance of individual experience and closeness to nature. Francis and the Franciscans contributed much to Giotto and Renaissance realism in art. Charles Homer Haskins, *The Renaissance of the Twelfth Century* (Cambridge, MA, 1929) pointed to the achievements in classical studies and the inappropriateness of speaking of a "revival" of antiquity in the Renaissance. The neo-Thomist philosopher Etienne Gilson in *Les idées et les lettres* (Paris, 1932) and other volumes argued that all elements found in Renaissance humanism were to be found already in scholastic philosophy. Heinrich Hermelink, *Die religiösen Reformbestrebungen des deutschen Humanismus* (Tübingen, 1907) accepted Thode's thesis and argued that the Italian Renaissance was derivative from medieval religious sources such as St. Francis, Dante, and the *via antiqua* or Thomism, and found the source for German humanism basically in the North. Similarly, Konrad Burdach, ed., *Vom Mittelalter zur Reformation. Forschungen zur Geschichte der deutschen Bildung,* 6 vols. (Berlin, 1912–1939), and *Deutsche Renaissance. Betrachtung über unsere künftige Bildung* (1916, rev. ed., Berlin, 1920) and other works, believed that the mainspring of Renaissance culture was the renewal of the human soul, which resulted from a new consciousness of religious, personal and national rebirth. The causative consciousness of rebirth arose in Italy during the thirteenth century under the influence of Franciscan mysticism, qualified by classical traditions of national rebirth inherited from ancient Rome, and was carried to the German court of Charles IV in Bohemia by Cola di Rienzo, where the German Renaissance began with writers such as Johann von Neumarkt and Johannes von Saaz, author of the *Ackermann aus Böhmen*. More recently P. Renucci, *L'aventure de l'humanisme européen au moyen âge* (Paris, 1953) has sought to document the extent of classical learning in the medieval period.

Moreover, the revisionists maintain that Renaissance humanism was not anti-Christian or pagan, and some have stressed that it was in line with patristic and medieval humanist thought, in contrast to the untraditional and perhaps even unchristian Aristotelian rationalism of Thomistic scholasticism. Francesco Olgiati, *L'anima dell' umanesimo e del Rinascimento* (Milan, 1924), argued that Renaissance humanism was fundamentally Catholic. Ernst Walser, *Studien zur Weltanschauung der Renaissance* (Basel, 1920), and *Gesammelte Studien zur Geistesgeschichte der Renaissance* (Basel, 1932) described Renaissance humanism as a great flowering of Christian piety. The most extreme statement in favor of the Christian nature of humanism and the rationalistic and virtually unchristian nature of scholasticism was that of Giuseppe Toffanin, *Che cosa fu l'umanesimo* (Florence, 1919), *Storia dell' umanesimo* (Naples, 1933), and *La religione degli umanisti* (Bologna, 1950). For Toffanin humanism stood for Catholic Christianity, a universal, objective, rational order, international politically and in its use of Latin. He saw it as antithetical to Protestantism, unbelief, subjectivism, romanticism, scientific naturalism, and individualism. Douglas Bush, *The Renaissance and English Humanism* (Toronto, 1939), emphasized the medieval continuity of humanism and its Christian character.

A small number of historians such as Johan Nordström, *Moyen âge et Renaissance* (Paris, 1933), have depreciated the importance of Renaissance humanism compared with that of the twelfth century. Moreover, some historians of science have argued that with their literary emphasis and their deference to ancient authorities the humanists inhibited the growth of science, the discipline most essential for the modern world. Some scholars have maintained that the science of the Renaissance developed out of the workshops of the artists and artisans and not in the universities or among the humanists.

The scholarship of recent decades has tended toward greater appreciation of the complexity and pluralistic nature of humanism. The emphasis on social, economic, and institutional history has tended to decrease the importance of humanism along with intellectual and cultural history in general. A closer study of the sources has revealed the diversity of humanism, some aspects notable for their novelty, others solidly traditional. Ludwig von Pastor in the introduction to the first volume of his *Geschichte der Päpste seit dem Ausgang des Mittelalters,* 16 vols. (Freiburg im Breisgau, 1886–1933), stressed the partial continuation of medieval religiosity through the age of humanism. Paul Joachimsen, "Aus der Entwicklung des italienischen Humanismus," *Historische Zeitschrift,* 121 (1920): 189–233, and "Der Humanismus und die Entwicklung des deutschen Geistes," *Deutsche Vierteljahrsschrift für Literaturwissenschaft und Geistesgeschichte,* 8 (1930): 419–480, drew significant distinctions between the various types of humanist thought, moral, aesthetic, political, hedonistic, and critical, demonstrating the successive phases of development in what had commonly been regarded as a unified intellectual movement. Pastor and Joachimsen foreshadowed the major tendencies of the past half century.

The major contemporary figure representing this diversity in the interpretation of humanism has been Paul Oskar Kristeller, authority on Ficino and great master of Italian humanist bibliography and sources. In an impressive array of articles and books, including *Renaissance Thought, the Classic, Scholastic, and Humanist Strains* (New York, 1961), *Eight Philosophers of the Italian Renaissance* (Stanford, 1964), and *Renaissance Thought and its Sources* (New York, 1979), he has stressed the varieties of humanism. He holds that humanism derived from the *studia humanitatis* in the Italian universities and offered an educational alternative to the scholastic curriculum, which emphasized logic, natural philosophy, and metaphysics. As an academic curriculum it was compatible with a wide variety of philosophical positions and religiously it might be Christian, anti-Christian, or non-Christian. Although he acknowledges the continuity of humanist rhetoric with the medieval tradition, he emphasizes the contributions of humanism to modernity thanks to its progress in classical scholarship, textual criticism, historical method, and influence on philosophy, art, and literature. One of several *Festschriften* in Kristeller's honor spells out the implications of his thought for humanism in other lands, Heiko A. Oberman and Thomas A. Brady, Jr., eds., *Itinerarium Italicum. The*

*Profile of the Italian Renaissance in the Mirror of its European Transformations* (Leiden, 1975). Kristeller's interpretation finds corroboration in the many writings of B.L. Ullman gathered together in his *Studies in the Italian Renaissance* (Rome, 1955). Ullman acknowledged the importance of medieval classicism, but he emphasized the Renaissance recovery and acceptance of the classics as literary norm.

Among the major figures in humanist scholarship are Hans Baron, William Bouwsma, Eugenio Garin, Federico Chabod, and Charles Trinkaus. Hans Baron in *The Crisis of the Early Italian Renaissance. Civic Humanism and Republican Liberty in an Age of Classicism and Tyranny* (Princeton, 1955; rev. ed., 1966), developed the concept of civic humanism, arguing that during the decades before and after 1400, when Republican Florence was threatened by the tyrants of Milan and later Naples, the humanists as patriots proclaimed the need for all citizens to participate in public life and defend liberty, drawing inspiration from the freedom of the Roman Republic. William J. Bouwsma, *Venice and the Defense of Republican Liberty. Renaissance Values in the Age of the Counter Reformation* (Berkeley and Los Angeles, 1968), developed an analogous theory with regard to Venetian humanism.

Eugenio Garin, *Umanesimo italiano: filosofia e vita civile nel Rinascimento* (Bari, 1952), saw humanism as a reflection of the new urban civic life and the varied interests and activities of townsmen. He found humanism to be anti-scholastic and pragmatic, stressing the knowledge of most value to private and civic life. Humanism contributed to a more critical mentality, a new sense of history, concern for social improvement, and a new interest in the world of nature, basic elements of modernity. Federico Chabod in his studies of Machiavelli, for example, *Machiavelli and the Renaissance* (tr. David Moore, New York, 1965), like Baron and Garin argued the necessity of combining cultural with political history, held that humanism marked a major shift from medieval to modern attitudes, and noted that the medieval unity of experience was yielding to a dissolution of God, man, and nature into independent aspects of reality. The most comprehensive and impressive recent study of humanism is that of Charles Trinkaus, *"In Our Image and Likeness." Humanity and Divinity in Italian Humanist Thought,* 2 vols. (Chicago, 1970), who argues that the humanists, using their professional skills and following their passionate interests, were better able than theologians or philosophers to integrate the surging secular activities and achievements of a dawning new world into the beliefs and practices of the Christian inheritance. The humanists transformed the Christian layman's understanding of man and human vocation. Erwin Panofsky in many studies explored humanistic themes in the art of the Renaissance and Jean Seznec, *La Survivance des Dieux Antiques* (Nouvelle ed., Paris, 1980), analyzes the changing attitudes in the Renaissance toward classical mythology, as revealed in both literature and art.

In contrast to the earlier attempts such as those of Heinrich Hermelink, Conrad Burdach, Albert Hyma and others to find indigenous roots for the Northern Renaissance in the North, current scholarship tends to stress the importance of Italian origins and influence, though to describe this tendency as neo-Burckhardtian would be an overstatement, since the total nexus is so much more complex than his essay suggested. The older authorities such as Johannes Janssen, *Geschichte des deutschen Volkes* (Freiburg im Breisgau, 1897), Willy Andreas, *Deutschland vor der Reformation. Eine Zeitenwende* (Stuttgart, 1932), Arthur Tilley, *The Dawn of the French Renaissance* (Cambridge, 1918) and *The Literature of the French Renaissance* (Cambridge, 1904), or Lewis Einstein, *The Italian Renaissance in England* (London, 1902) understood septentrional humanism as liberal, secular, and inclined toward modernity. The scholars of recent decades have reacted against the traditional conception of humanism, have emphasized the peculiar aspects of humanism characteristic of the North, and have spelled out the differences from Italian humanism. Franco Simone, *Il Rinascimento francese* (Turin, 1961) gives an account of fifteenth-century French humanism with roots in Avignon and Provence but coming increasingly under Italian influence and developing a new sense of history. Lucien Fèbvre, *Le problème de l'incroyance au XVI^e siècle. La religion de Rabelais* (Paris, 1942) argued for an Erasmian Christian humanist interpretation of Rabelais, although very recently Michael Screech in two studies sees Rabelais as a more complicated figure. The study by the distinguished translator and editor of Montaigne's works, Donald Frame, *Montaigne's Discovery of Man. The Humanization of a Humanist* (New York, 1955) recounts his appreciation of the common man as well as of the man of learning. Quirinus Breen, *John Calvin, a Study in*

*French Humanism* (Chicago, 1931) and Andre Bieler, *The Social Humanism of Calvin* (Richmond, 1964) relate the French reformer to humanism.

In the case of German humanism recent historiography has emphasized particularly two themes, cultural nationalism and the desire for religious enlightenment. Among the significant efforts to explain the Renaissance humanist conception of Germany and its past the best work was that of Paul Joachimsen, *Geschichtsauffassung und Geschichtsschreibung in Deutschland unter dem Einfluss des Humanismus, Beiträge zur Kulturgeschichte des Mittelalters und der Renaissance,* VI (Leipzig and Berlin, 1910). He recognized the importance of the newly discovered medieval sources, the historical writing of the German humanists, and some of the myths about the German past. Various authors have treated aspects of the theme, Friedrich Gotthelf, Erich Schmidt, Hans Tiedemann, Theobald Bieder, Hedwig Riess, Paul Hans Stemmermann, H. Dannenbauer, Ludwig Sponagel, Gerald Strauss, but among the very best monographs is that of Ulrich Paul, *Studien zur Geschichte des deutschen Nationalbewusstseins im Zeitalter des Humanismus und der Reformation, Historische Studien,* 297 (Berlin, 1936), tracing the influence of Aeneas Sylvius, Pseudo-Berosus, and Trithemius' Hunibald through the other humanists in Germany. A recent excellent volume that goes well beyond these older works is Frank L. Borchardt, *German Antiquity in Renaissance Myth* (Baltimore and London, 1971).

From Paul Wernle, *Die Renaissance des Christentums im 16. Jahrhundert* (Tübingen, 1904) to Lewis W. Spitz, *The Religious Renaissance of the German Humanists* (Cambridge, MA, 1963), scholars have emphasized the religious dimension of German humanism as well as the patriotic theme. Wernle saw the Italian dominated Renaissance as highly important for the reformers such as Calvin and Zwingli and held Renaissance and Reformation to be kindred movements. While recognizing the theological differences between Luther's evangelical emphasis and the Christian humanism of the northern humanists, scholars today acknowledge the contribution of humanism to the success of the Reformation and the continuity of humanism, thanks to the positive attitude of the magisterial reformers, through the Reformation period. Representative studies are Maria Grossmann, *Humanism in Wittenberg 1485–1517* (Nieuwkoop, 1975); Martin

Greschat and J.F.G. Goeters, eds., *Reformation und Humanismus* (Witten, 1969); and *XIII<sup>e</sup> Colloque International de Tours. L'Humanisme Allemand (1480–1540)* (Munich and Paris, 1979). There is a trend away from understanding the link between Reformation and humanism so much in terms of the Erasmus-Luther debate on the will, for there is a new appreciation of the fact that humanism was a broad movement not so easily confined to a few issues. The role of Melanchthon, for example, is receiving renewed attention.

The study of English humanism has moved well beyond the old classic of Frederic Seebohm, *The Oxford Reformers: John Colet, Erasmus and Thomas More* (rev. ed., London, 1869). Roberto Weiss, *Humanism in England during the Fifteenth Century* (Oxford, 1941) acknowledged the Italian origins of English humanism, but emphasized its persistently medieval and religious character. C.S. Lewis, *English Literature in the Sixteenth Century* (Oxford, 1954) and George B. Parks, *The English Traveler to Italy: The Middle Ages (to 1525)* (Stanford, 1954) stress the influence of Italian humanism. The intimate connection of English humanism and the Tudor political and social order is underlined by such works as Fritz Caspari, *Humanism and the Social Order in Tudor England* (Chicago, 1954) and Gordon Zeeveld, *Foundations of Tudor Policy* (Cambridge, MA, 1948). Other works such as Lawrence V. Ryan, *Roger Ascham* (Stanford, 1963), demonstrate the continuity of humanism from the "Oxford reformers" through the sixteenth century to the age of Queen Elizabeth and its gradual spread beyond the court to the middle class and gentry.

SELECTED BIBLIOGRAPHY

## I.  *Historical Background*

Barbagallo, Corrado. *L'Età della Rinascenza e della Riforma (1454–1556)*. Turin, 1956.

Cheyney, Edward Potts. *The Dawn of a New Era, 1250–1453*. New York, 1936.

Daniel–Rops, Henri. *L'Église de la Renaissance et de la Réforme*. 2 vols. Paris, 1955.

Gilmore, Myron Piper. *The World of Humanism, 1453–1517*. New York, 1952.

Goetz, Walter, et al. *Das Zeitalter der Gotik und Renaissance, 1250–1500*. Berlin, 1932.

Hassinger, Erich. *Das Werden des neuzeitlichen Europas, 1300–1600*. Brunswick, 1959.

Hauser, Henri, and Augustin Renaudet. *Les débuts de l'âge moderne. La renaissance et la réforme*. Paris, 1929; 3rd ed., 1946.

Hay, Denys. *The Italian Renaissance in Its Historical Background*. Cambridge, 1961; 2nd ed., 1977.

Monfasani, John and Ronald G. Musto, eds. *Renaissance Society and Culture: Essays in Honor of Eugene F. Rice, Jr.* New York, 1991.

Ozment, Steven. *The Age of Reform, 1250–1550: An Intellectual and Religious History of Late Medieval and Reformation Europe*. New Haven, 1980.

Potter, G.R. *The Renaissance, 1493–1520*. (The New Cambridge Modern History) Cambridge, 1957.

Spitz, Lewis W. *The Renaissance and Reformation Movements*. 2 vols. St. Louis, 1980; 2nd ed., 1987.

Spitz, Lewis W. *The Protestant Reformation, 1517–1559*. New York, 1985.

Trimborn, Hermann, et al. *Weltkulturen: Renaissance in Europa*. Vol. 6 in *Propyläen Weltgeschichte: Eine Universalgeschichte*, ed. Golo Mann and August Nitschke, Frankfurt and Berlin, 1964– .

## II.   Modern Humanism

Borinski, Karl. *Die Antike in Poetik und Kunsttheorie vom Ausgang des klassischen Altertums bis auf Goethe und Wilhelm von Humboldt.* 2 vols. Leipzig, 1914–1924.

Coates, Willson H. *The Emergence of Liberal Humanism: An Intellectual History of Western Europe.* New York, 1966.

Guistiniani, Vito R. "*Homo, Humanus* and the Meanings of 'Humanism,'" in *Renaissance Essays II.* William J. Connell, ed. Rochester, NY, 1993, pp. 29–57.

Heidegger, Martin. *Über den Humanismus.* Frankfurt a. M., 1947.

Jaspers, Karl. *Existentialism and Humanism: Three Essays.* Ed. Hanns E. Fischer. Tr. E.B. Ashton. New York, 1952.

Kurtz, Paul W. *In Defense of Secular Humanism.* New York, 1983.

Lamont, Corliss. *The Philosophy of Humanism.* 5th ed. New York, 1965.

Mordstein, Friedrich. *Ist der Marxismus ein Humanismus?* Stuttgart, 1969.

Sartre, Jean-Paul. *L'existentialisme est un humanisme.* Paris, 1946.

## III.   Renaissance Humanism: Italy and Europe

Abbagnano, Nicola. "Italian Renaissance Humanism." *Journal of World History,* 11 (1963): 267–83.

Arbesmann, Rudolph. *Der Augustiner-Eremitenorden und der Beginn der humanistischen Bewegung.* Würzburg, 1965.

Bentley, Jerry H. *Humanists and Holy Writ: New Testament Scholarship in the Renaissance.* Princeton, 1983.

Bezold, Friedrich von. *Das Fortleben der antiken Götter.* Bonn and Leipzig, 1922.

Breen, Quirinus. *Christianity and Humanism: Studies in the History of Ideas.* Grand Rapids, MI, 1967.

Brink, Jean R. and William F. Gentroup, eds. *Renaissance Culture in Context: Theory and Practice.* Aldershot, England, 1993.

Chastel, André, and Robert Klein. *Die Welt des Humanismus, 1480–*

*1530*. Munich, 1963.

Cochrane, Eric W. *Florence in the Forgotten Centuries, 1527–1800.* Chicago, 1973.

Cochrane, Eric, ed. *The Late Italian Renaissance, 1525–1630.* New York, 1970.

D'Amico, John F. *Renaissance Humanism in Papal Rome: Humanists and Churchmen on the Eve of the Reformation.* Baltimore, 1983.

D'Amico, John F. *Roman and German Humanism, 1450–1550.* Aldershot, Hampshire, 1993.

Dresden, Sem. *Humanism in the Renaissance.* New York and Toronto, 1968.

Edwards, Mark U., Jr. *Printing, Propaganda, and Martin Luther.* Berkeley and Los Angeles, 1994.

Fleischer, Manfred. *The Harvest of Humanism in Central Europe: Essays in Honor of Lewis W. Spitz.* St. Louis, 1992.

Fryde, E.B. *Humanism and Renaissance Historiography.* London, 1983.

Garin, Eugenio. *La cultura filosofica del Rinascimento italiano.* Florence, 1961.

Garin, Eugenio. *Il pensiero pedagogico dell' umanesimo.* Florence, 1958.

Geanakoplos, Deno J. *Greek Scholars in Venice: Studies in the Dissemination of Greek Learning from Byzantium to the West.* Cambridge, MA, 1962; republished as *Byzantium and the Renaissance.* New Haven, 1978.

Goodman, Anthony, and Angus McKay, eds. *The Impact of Humanism in Western Europe.* New York, 1990.

Grafton, Anthony, and Lisa Jardine. *From Humanism to the Humanities: Education and the Liberal Arts in Fifteenth- and Sixteenth-Century Europe.* Cambridge, MA, 1986.

Grendler, Paul F. *Critics of the Italian World, 1530–1560: Anton Francesco Doni, Nicolò Franco, and Ortensio Lando.* Madison and Milwaukee, 1969.

Harran, Marilyn J., ed. *Luther and Learning: The Wittenberg University Luther Symposium.* Selinsgrove, PA, 1985.

Hermans, Francis. *Histoire doctrinale de l'humanisme chrétien.* Tournai, 1948.

Holmes, George A. *The Florentine Enlightenment, 1400–1450.* New York, 1969.

Jacob, E.F. "Christian Humanism." In John Hale *et al.,* eds., *Europe in the Late Middle Ages.* London, 1965.

Kristeller, P.O. *The Philosophy of Marsilio Ficino.* New York, 1943.

Lewis, Archibald R., ed. *Aspects of the Renaissance: A Symposium.* London, 1967.

Martines, Lauro. *The Social World of the Florentine Humanists, 1390–1460.* Princeton, 1963.

Müller, Gregor. *Bildung und Erziehung im Humanismus der italienischen Renaissance.* Wiesbaden, 1969.

Rabil, Albert, ed. *Renaissance Humanism: Foundations, Forms, and Legacy.* 3 vols. Philadelphia, 1988.

Rice, Eugene F., Jr. *The Renaissance Idea of Wisdom.* Cambridge, MA, 1958.

Robb, Nesca A. *Neoplatonism of the Italian Renaissance.* London, 1935.

Ruegg, Walter. *Cicero und der Humanismus.* Zurich, 1946.

Trinkaus, Charles. *"In Our Image and Likeness": Humanity and Divinity in Italian Humanist Thought.* 2 vols. Chicago, 1970.

Trinkaus, Charles. *The Scope of Renaissance Humanism.* Ann Arbor, 1983.

Walser, Ernst. *Gesammelte Studien zur Geistesgeschichte der Renaissance.* Basel, 1932.

Watkins, Renée Neu. *Humanism and Liberty: Writings on Freedom from Fifteenth-Century Florence.* Columbia, SC, 1978.

Weiss, Roberto. *The Dawn of Humanism in Italy.* London, 1947.

Weiss, Roberto. *The Spread of Italian Humanism.* London, 1964.

Whitfield, J.H. *Petrarch and the Renaissance.* Oxford, 1943.

Wind, Edgar. *Pagan Mysteries in the Renaissance.* Rev. ed. New York, 1968.

Witt, Ronald G. *Coluccio Salutati and His Public Letters.* Geneva, 1976.

Witt, Ronald G. *Hercules at the Crossroads: The Life, Works, and Thought of Coluccio Salutati.* Durham, NC, 1983.

IV.   Renaissance Humanism:
      Germany and the Low Countries

Brann, Noel. *The Abbot Trithemius (1462–1516): The Renaissance of Monastic Humanism*. Leiden, 1981.

D'Amico, John F. *Theory and Practice in Renaissance Textual Criticism: Beatus Rhenanus between Conjecture and History*. Berkeley and Los Angeles, 1988.

Fleischer, Manfred. *Späthumanismus in Schlesien: Ausgewählte Aufsätze*. Munich, 1984.

Holborn, Hajo. *Ulrich von Hutten and the German Reformation*. New Haven, 1937.

Holzberg, Niklas. *Willibald Pirckheimer: Griechischer Humanismus in Deutschland*. Munich, 1981.

Hyma, Albert. *The Christian Renaissance: A History of the Devotio Moderna*. New York, 1925; Hamden, CT, 1965.

Hyma, Albert. *The Brethren of the Common Life*. Grand Rapids, MI, 1950.

Kittelson, James. *Wolfgang Capito: From Humanist to Reformer*. Leiden, 1975.

Kleehoven, H. Ankwitz von. *Johannes Cuspinian*. Graz, 1969.

Lutz, Heinrich. *Conrad Peutinger: Beiträge zu einer politischen Biographie*. Augsburg, 1958.

Näf, Werner. *Vadian und seine Stadt St. Gallen*. 2 vols. St. Gallen, 1944–1957.

Nauert, Charles G., Jr. *Agrippa and the Crisis of Renaissance Thought*. Urbana, 1965.

Post, R.R. *The Modern Devotion: Confrontation with Reformation and Humanism*. Leiden, 1968.

Spitz, Lewis W. *Conrad Celtis, the German Arch-Humanist*. Cambridge, MA, 1957.

Spitz, Lewis W., ed., *Humanismus und Reformation als kulturelle Kräfte in der deutschen Geschichte. Ein Tagungsbericht.* (Veröffentlichungen der Historischen Kommission zu Berlin, 51)

Berlin and New York, 1981.

Spitz, Lewis W., and Barbara Sher Tinsley. *The Reformation and Humanist Learning: Johann Sturm on Education*. St. Louis, 1995.

Spitz, Lewis W. *The Religious Renaissance of the German Humanists*. Cambridge, Mass., 1963.

Strauss, Gerald. *Historian in an Age of Crisis: The Life and Work of Johannes Aventinus 1477–1534*. Cambridge, MA, 1963.

Strauss, Gerald. *Sixteenth-Century Germany: Its Topography and Topographers*. Madison, WI, 1959.

Verbeke, G. and J. Ijsewijn, eds. *The Late Middle Ages and the Dawn of Humanism Outside Italy*. Louvain and the Hague, 1972.

## V.  Sourcebooks and Literary Histories

### German Humanism

Becker, Reinhard P., ed. *German Humanism and the Reformation*. New York, 1982.

Rupprich, Hans. *Die Frühzeit des Humanismus und der Renaissance in Deutschland*. Leipzig, 1938.

Rupprich, Hans. *Humanismus und Renaissance in den deutschen Städten und Universitäten*. Leipzig, 1935.

Spitz, Lewis W., ed. *The Northern Renaissance*. Englewood Cliffs, NJ, 1972

### French Humanism

Bohatec, Josef. *Budé und Calvin: Studien zur Gedankenwelt des französischen Frühhumanismus*. Graz, 1950.

Busson, H. *Le rationalisme dans la littérature française*. Paris, 1957.

Chamard, Henri. *Les origines de la poésie française de la Renaissance*. Paris, 1932.

Levi, A.H.T., ed. *Humanism in France at the End of the Middle Ages and in the Early Renaissance*. Manchester, 1970.

Mousnier, Roland. *Leçons sur l'humanisme et la Renaissance de la fin du XVe siècle au milieu du XVIe siècle*. 3 vols. in 1. Paris, 1966.

Renaudet, Augustin. *Préréforme et humanisme à Paris pendant les premières guerres d'Italie, 1494–1517.* Paris, 1916; 2nd ed., 1953.

Schmidt, A-M. *La poésie scientifique en France au XVI^e siècle.* Paris, 1938.

Screech, M.A. *L'évangelisme de Rabelais: Aspects de la satire religieuse au XVI^e siècle.* Genf, 1959.

Simone, Franco. *Il Rinascimento francese: Studi e ricerche.* Turin, 1961.

Yates, Frances A. *French Academies of the Sixteenth Century.* London, 1947.

## Spanish Humanism

Bataillon, Marcel. *Érasme et l'Espagne: Recherches sur l'histoire spirituelle du XVI^e siècle.* Paris, 1937.

Cione, Edmondo. *Juan de Valdés: La sua vita e il suo pensiero religioso.* 2nd ed. Naples, 1963.

Green, Otis. *Spain and the Western Tradition.* 4 vols. Madison, WI, 1963–1966.

Nieto, José C. *Juan de Valdés and the Origins of the Spanish and Italian Reformation.* Geneva, 1969.

Starkie, Walter F. *Grand Inquisitor, Being an Account of Cardinal Ximenes de Cisneros and His Times.* London, 1940.

## English Humanism

Borinski, Ludwig. *Englischer Humanismus und deutsche Reformation.* Göttingen, 1969.

Bush, Douglas. *The Renaissance and English Humanism.* Toronto, 1939.

Hale, John R. *England and the Italian Renaissance.* London, 1954.

Hexter, J.H. *More's Utopia: The Biography of an Idea.* Princeton, 1952.

Hunt, Ernest W. *Dean Colet and His Theology.* London, 1956.

Jayne, Sears R. *John Colet and Marsilio Ficino.* Oxford, 1963.

Leube, Hans. *Reformation und Humanismus in England.* Leipzig, 1930.

Marc'Hadour, Germain. *The Bible in the Works of Thomas More, 1.* Nieuwkoop, 1969

Surtz, Edward, S.J. *The Praise of Wisdom.* Chicago, 1957.

40

## VI. Humanism Research

Baron, Hans. "Burckhardt's *Civilization of the Renaissance* a Century after its Publication." *Renaissance News,* 13: (1960): 207–22.

Bouwsma, William. *The Culture of Renaissance Humanism.* Washington, DC, 1973.

Conrady, Karl Otto. "Die Erforschung der neulateinischen Literatur: Probleme und Aufgaben." *Euphorion,* 49 (1955): 413–45.

Dannenfeldt, Karl, ed. *The Renaissance — Basic Interpretations.* Lexington, MA, 1974.

Ferguson, Wallace K. *The Renaissance in Historical Thought: Five Centuries of Interpretation.* Cambridge, MA, 1948.

Helton, Tinsley, ed. *The Renaissance: a Reconsideration of the Theories and Interpretations of the Age.* Madison, WI, 1961.

Jantz, Harold. "German Renaissance Literature." *MLN,* 81 (1966): 398–436.

Kristeller, Paul Oskar. "Renaissanceforschung und Altertums-wissenschaft." *Forschungen und Fortschritte,* 33 (1959): 363–69.

Wuttke, Dieter. *Deutsche Germanistik und Renaissance Forschung.* Bad Homburg, 1968.

# II

## THE COURSE OF GERMAN HUMANISM

### Ode to Apollo

Phoebus, who the sweet-noted lyre constructed,
Leave fair Helicon and depart your Pindus,
And by pleasant song designated, hasten
  To these our borders.

You perceive how joyous the Muses gather,
Sweetly singing under a frozen heaven;
Come yourself, and with your melodious harp-strings,
  Gaze on these wastelands.

So must he, whom sometime a rude or rustic
Parent fostered, barbarous, all unknowing
Latium's splendors, choose you now as his teacher
  At writing verses.

Just as Orpheus sang to the old Pelasgians,
Orpheus, whom swift stags, beasts of savage custom,
Whom the lofty trees of the forest followed,
  Charmed by his plectrum.

Swift and joyous, once you forswore, and gladly,
Greece for Latium, passing the mighty ocean;
There you wished your delectable arts to broadcast,
  Leading the Muses.

Thus it is our prayer you may wish to visit
Our abode, as once those Italian reaches.
May wild tongue take flight, and may all of darkness
  Come to destruction.[1]

---

[1] The *Ode to Apollo,* trans. George C. Schoolfield of Yale University, is from *Conrad Celtis the German Arch-Humanist* by Lewis W. Spitz (Cambridge, MA, 1957), 10, reprinted by permission of the Harvard University Press. For recent studies of German Humanism and the Reformation, see Manfred P. Fleischer, ed.,

2

In these beautiful lines Conrad Celtis, christened by Friedrich von Bezold the "German arch-humanist," called on Apollo to continue his *itinerarium* beyond Italy to the lands across the Alps. In his inaugural address at the University of Ingolstadt he challenged the youth of Germany to enter into cultural rivalry with the Italians. "Take up again, O German men," he called, "that old spirit of yours with which you so many times were a specter and terror to the Romans!"[2] To his friend the jurist, Sixtus Tucher of Nuremberg, Celtis wrote:

> When you read my writings, you will be convinced that I did not send them to you to display my poetic genius..., but you will understand that I spared no trouble to accomplish a certain end. For if these efforts do not match those of the Italians, I wish to stimulate and awaken those men among the Germans who excel in learnedness and genius.... Then the Italians, most effusive in self-praise, will be forced to confess that not only the Roman imperium and arms, but also the splendor of letters has migrated to the Germans.[3]

Apollo did indeed leave the lands of the blue Mediterranean with their sun-bleached white marble classical remains and came to the frozen

---

*The Harvest of Humanism in Central Europe: Essays in Honor of Lewis W. Spitz* (Saint Louis, MO: Concordia Publishing House, 1992; Lewis W. Spitz, "Humanism and the Protestant Reformation," in Albert Rabil, ed., *Renaissance Humanism: Foundations, Forms, and Legacy* (Philadelphia: University of Pennsylvania Press, 1988), III: 380–411; Noel L. Brann, "Humanism in Germany," Albert Rabil, ed., *Renaissance Humanism*, II: 123–155; Otto Herman Pesch, ed., *Humanismus und Reformation—Martin Luther und Erasmus von Rotterdam in den Konflicten ihrer Zeit* (Freiburg: Katholische Akademie; Munich and Zurich: Verlag Schnell & Steiner, 1985).

[2] *Conradus Celtis Protucius Oratio in Gymnasio in Ingolstadt Publice Recitata cum Carminibus ad Orationem Pertinentibus*, ed. Hans Rupprich (Leipzig, 1932), 1–11.

[3] Konrad Celtis to Sixtus Tucher, Ingolstadt, 1491, in *Der Briefwechsel des Konrad Celtis*, ed. Hans Rupprich (Munich, 1934), 28 f., No. 15.

north under the septentrional stars. Especially the young men of the North responded to his melodious harp strings.

The culture of the North, however, could not be a Renaissance in the sense of a rebirth of classical antiquity such as Italy experienced in its springtime following its cultural lag of two centuries behind the great achievements of medieval France, for the Germans were not the Romans and did not have the artistic and architectural monuments, the learned notaries and *dictatores* who kept the memory of antiquity partly alive in even ordinary Italian minds. The culture of the North became rather a bookish culture more than a visual culture. Its characteristic Renaissance expression was that of humanism. Petrus Lotichius Secundus (1528–1560), a German poet, wrote from Italy: "Moreover, I am free of those hindrances which formerly kept me from studies: I am alone and live entirely for myself and my studies."[4] The Germans became students of the Roman and Greek authors and like the Italian *umanisti* they devoted themselves to the *studia humanitatis* because these complete and ornament man. Classical letters served as their measure and ideal.

No problem in intellectual history, Wilhelm Dilthey once observed, is so interesting as that of the changes which Renaissance humanism underwent as it crossed the Alps. The study of German humanism is, in fact, studded with controversial issues, controverted interpretations, unresolved problems, great bodies of literature still unexplored, and gaps in the material available for examination. Werner Näf, the great Swiss biographer of Vadianus, once commented upon the need for scholarly editions of the humanists' writings and new biographies of famous men as well as of men undeservedly obscure.[5] Much work remains to be done. The present study cannot pretend to provide lexicographical completeness in such a limited space. It will have to be highly selective, seeking to point up representative figures without

---

[4] "Careo praeterea iis molestiis, quae prius a studiis me avocabant: solus sum solique mihi et meis studiis rectissime inservio," cited by Karl Otto Conrady, "Die Erforschung der neulateinischen Literatur. Probleme und Aufgaben," *Euphorion. Zeitschrift für Literaturgeschichte*, XLIX (1955), 413.

[5] Werner Näf, "Aus der Forschung zur Geschichte des deutschen Humanismus," *Schweizer Beiträge zur Allgemeinen Geschichte*, II (1944), 214.

4

dealing with even all the important figures or categories. It will, therefore, be highly personal in nature.

## I. Problems Of Origins, Nature, Continuity, And New Directions

*Origins*

History, said Lord Acton, should deal with problems and not with periods. The first and one of the most vexing problems of German humanism is that of its origins. Just as the origins of the Italian Renaissance have been variously explained as to be found in the native Roman soil, in French medieval or Provençal influence or as resulting from the Byzantine or Greek influx, so the origins of German humanism have been sought variously in northern sources such as the Brethren of the Common Life, or the precocious court of Charles IV, or in the Italian influence. The extent to which the roots of German humanism were autochthonous and indigenous to the North or were Italian in source is still a highly controverted issue. R.R. Post in a highly revisionist work on the Brethren of the Common Life argued vociferously against the position of Albert Hyma, Augustin Renaudet and other scholars that the Brethren were heavily into education and from the 14th century on (Groote d. 1384), promoted the study of the "safe classics," and led dozens if not hundreds of German students in the Rhineland and the North to an appreciation of the classics.[6] While

---

[6] R.R. Post, *The Modern Devotion. Confrontation with Reformation and Humanism, Studies in Medieval and Reformation Thought,* III (Leiden, 1968). See the excellent review by Helmar Junghans, in *Luther-Jahrbuch,* XXXVII (1970), 120–127, which says approximately what my own response to Post would have been, had he lived, yielding some but not all on the points of controversy. See also the outstanding article by H. Junghans, "Der Einfluß des Humanismus auf Luthers Entwicklung bis 1518," *Luther-Jahrbuch,* XXXVII (1970), 37–101, touching on these points. For Albert Hyma's interpretation see esp. his *The Christian Renaissance: A History of the "Devotio Moderna"* (Grand Rapids, MI, 1924), and *The Brethren of the Common Life* (Grand Rapids, MI, 1950). See also Kenneth A. Strand, ed., *Essays on the Northern Renaissance* (Ann Arbor, MI, 1968), especially the articles by Julia S. Henkel, "School Organizational Patterns of the Brethren of the Common Life," 35–50, and by Kenneth A. Strand, "The Brethren of the Common Life and Fifteenth-

one might well argue that in his detailed study Post was too literal minded and did not see the forest for the trees, a certain validity to his revisionism remains. Certainly the Italian influence upon the development of enthusiastic classicism was the critical determinant. One can still argue for the receptiveness and readiness of the northern soil, and one can play with the idea of a preestablished harmony between the non-dogmatic, non-speculative, education-minded pious Brethren and the non-dialectical, moral-philosophical, education-minded Italian humanists; but the great importance of the Italian Renaissance for the development of German humanism has become increasingly evident.

The early flowering of Renaissance culture at the Prague court of Emperor Charles IV was once hailed not only as the debut of the Northern Renaissance, but even heralded as the cradle in the North of the Renaissance itself.[7] But only a thin thread stretched by way of Emperor Maximilian's Vienna provides a tenuous tie between that early dawn and the mainstream of German humanist culture in the late fifteenth and early sixteenth centuries. The impact of Italian Renaissance culture upon the chief centers of German humanist culture can be traced more convincingly from the contacts provided by the great church councils in the early fifteenth century, the various Italians who

---

Century Printing: A Brief Survey," 51–64. See the excellent pages on northern piety by Margaret E. Aston, "The Northern Renaissance," in Richard L. DeMolen, ed., *The Meaning of the Renaissance and Reformation* (Boston, 1974), 71–129, 82–90. W. Lourdaux has contributed important studies underlining the significance of the Brethren of the Common Life for northern humanism, emphasizing their work as critical editors of texts, men of letters with a well-developed aesthetic sense, whose reading included the works of the most important Italian humanists as well as of classical authors. See his *Moderne Devotie en Christelÿijk Humanisme* (Louvain, 1967) and his article "Dévotion Moderne et Humanisme Chrétien," in Professor G. Verbeke and Professor J. IJsewijn, eds., *The Late Middle Ages and the Dawn of Humanism Outside Italy,* Proceedings of the International Conference, Louvain, May 11–13, 1970 (Louvain, 1972), 57–77.

7 Konrad Burdach, *Vom Mittelalter zur Reformation* (Halle, 1893); *Deutsche Renaissance: Betrachtung über unsere künftige Bildung* (Berlin, 1920); *Vom Mittelalter zur Reformation, Forschungen zur Geschichte der deutschen Bildung,* 6 vols. (Berlin, 1912–1939). See Wallace K. Ferguson, *The Renaissance in Historical Thought* (Boston, 1948), 306–311.

6

visited Germany, and the constant stream of German students who poured annually into Italy for a year or more of study—law for the most part—at Bologna, Padua, or some other university. The many political and ecclesiastical contacts of Italy and the Empire nourished the growth of humanism in the North during the fifteenth and sixteenth centuries.

The development of German humanism during the course of the fifteenth century ran parallel in many ways to that of French humanism, gaining steadily in strength from the conciliar epoch on down to its involvement with secular courts and the episcopal courts as well (a fact which is now more fully appreciated by scholars), followed later by urban centers and eventually by the universities, which only gradually came to appreciate the value and utility of humanist learning.[8] The role of cultivated noble women in the patronage of the new learning is also now more fully recognized. There is a revisionist point of view also on the conflict of humanism and scholasticism. Formerly historians placed full credence in the claims of the humanists, vociferously seconded by the reformers, that they were the youthful gladiators locked in deadly combat with fierce and deadly opponents, the scholastic doctors who fought for syllogistic logic and dialectical theology against the rhetoric, refined literature and enlightened religion of the humanists.[9] The humanists overdramatized their struggle, which often had more to do with a battle for endowment and professorial billets than with a sharply differentiated kind of learning or with an essentially different world

---

[8] Franco Simone, *The French Renaissance, Medieval Tradition and Italian Influence in Shaping the Renaissance in France* (London, 1969). Of interest in this connection is Kurt Nyholm, "Das höfische Epos im Zeitalter des Humanismus," *Neuphilologische Mitteilungen,* LXVI (1965), 297–313.

[9] Charles Nauert, "The Clash of Humanists and Scholastics: An Approach to Pre-Reformation Controversies," *The Sixteenth Century Journal,* IV (April, 1973), 1–18; Charles Nauert, "Peter of Ravenna and the 'obscure men' of Cologne: A Case of Pre-Reformation Controversy," *Renaissance Studies in Honor of Hans Baron,* eds. Anthony Molho and John Tedeschi (DeKalb, IL., 1971), 609–640. James H. Overfield, "A New Look at the Reuchlin Affair," *Studies in Medieval and Renaissance History,* VIII (1971), 165–207. Overfield has prepared an article for future publication which makes a very telling argument for the revisionist view on "Scholastic Opposition to Humanism in Pre-Reformation Germany."

view. The scholastic doctors were usually mute or fairly inarticulate in their defence against outrageous charges and were in general not given to taking the offensive against the new learning. Rather, in terms of humanist origins and the relation of the two approaches to studies, many mid- and late fifteenth-century intellectuals can best be described as "half humanist" and "half scholastic" in outlook, as indeed much of the older scholarly literature described them. There was more of a blending and gradual transition than a real clash during the fifteenth century. The relation between them should not be understood retrospectively in the light of the Reuchlin controversy, itself often misunderstood, or by taking literally the thrusts of the satirical literature of the sixteenth century.

*Nature*

The great neo-Kantian philosopher and intellectual historian Ernst Cassirer reflected a very old romantic notion about German humanism as essentially folkish in nature, in contrast to that of Italy and France.[10] He saw the three humanisms as representing three basic types which only in their contrast brought out the ideal whole of the epoch. The Italian Renaissance produced a new relation to political reality which provided the basis and the means for a general intellectual change. In molding the state into a work of art there for the first time the modern personality in its wholeness became conscious of its creative energies, though still bound to the old Roman idea of *imperium*. Freed of this last restrictive factor the development of the concept of personality was the distinct achievement of the French Renaissance. Montaigne as the richest and most multifaceted thinker of the epoch was not a statesman, poet, or philosopher, but a person whose essays present himself in his

---

[10] Ernst Cassirer, *Freiheit und Form. Studien zur deutschen Geschichte* (Berlin, 1922), 3–11. If the monumental study of medieval Latin thought and letters by Ernst Robert Curtius, *Europäische Literatur und Lateinisches Mittelalter* (Bern, 1948), can justifiably be criticized for not differentiating sufficiently between the various areas and traditions in depicting the unity and coherence of medieval culture, much Renaissance scholarship can justifiably be criticized for overemphasizing the differences especially among the northern expressions of humanist culture and between Protestant and Catholic humanist learning.

8

completely private form and individuality. In contrast to these tendencies of Italian and French humanism, German humanism, Cassirer explained, even in the renewal of antiquity still remained in close touch with folkish tendencies. Erasmus was praised as the restorer of the true rights of mankind, Hutten blended the humanist ideal with the cause of German freedom, religious enlightenment, and national consciousness. Humanism and the new concept of human culture was set in opposition to scholasticism which had darkened the picture of antiquity and pure Christianity. Cassirer's analysis of German humanism was derived largely from the romantic tradition which was spawned in the early nineteenth century, a strange quirk for the great historian of the Enlightenment. The folkish nature of German humanism persisted almost as a cliché, especially in histories of literature, and crested in sickening waves with the *Blut und Boden* propagandistic writings of the National Socialist period. German humanism was characterized by the people's community spirit rather than by individualism. The extent to which German humanist culture was not merely particularist, local, spontaneous, and popular, but European, cosmopolitan, created or contrived, and specialized is now receiving renewed attention. In contrast to the romantics' assessment, favorable to medieval culture, which viewed the classical emphasis of humanism as an artificial, unnatural, Roman, overintellectual, formalistic, alien intrusion, necessarily absorbed and transformed by the force of folkish impulses, contemporary scholars are coming increasingly to recognize the classical influence, the simplicity, the formal sophistication, the rhetorical skill, and the European character of much literature of the German Renaissance. This new emphasis is being accompanied by a renewed attention to the literary aesthetic quality of German Renaissance letters and a tapering off of the philological linguistic approach.[11]

---

[11] Harold Jantz, "German Renaissance Literature," *Modern Language Notes,* LXXXI (1966), 398–436, esp. 398–401. See Willi Flemming, *Das deutsche Schrifttum von 1500 bis 1700* (Potsdam, n.d.), 9: "So nahm die starke bürgerliche Kultur auch ein gut Stück bäuerlicher Gesundheit und Bodenverbundenheit in sich auf. Urkräfte des Blutes pochten in den Adern dieser Geschlechter und sangen sich im Lied volksmäßig aus, ergriffen die ewigen Erlebnisse des Menschenherzens wie die Sondererlebnisse der Einzelberufe. Ganz aus dem Alltag greift Fastnachtsspiel und

That German humanist literature was a bourgeois phenomenon providing a middle-class interlude between the medieval and the "courtly" values of the seventeenth century is one of the commonplaces of literary scholarship.[12] Its bourgeois character gave to German humanist literature its new direction. Even authors who were not personally of middle-class background adapted to the demands of this tendency. Marxist literary historians gladly embraced this general bourgeois assessment of humanist culture, refining it when being mindful of the orthodox historical timetable by labeling it "early-bourgeois."[13] During this phase in the development of capitalism, literature became the organ of the new collective self-consciousness. It is possible to haggle over the definitions and to niggle over specific instances, but in general the interpretation of the bourgeois character of humanist literature must be refined in two ways. First of all it must be

---

Schwankerzählung, Schnurre und Anekdote die Menschentypen und Geschehnisse. Bürgerliche Tüchtigkeit wird in der Erzählung ernsthaft geschildert und propagiert."

[12] A.J. Krailsheimer, ed., *The Continental Renaissance 1500–1600* (Penguin Books, 1971), 351. See the very commendable recent survey, Barbara Könneker, "Deutsche Literatur im Zeitalter des Humanismus und der Reformation," *Neues Handbuch der Literaturwissenschaft,* ed. Klaus von See, *Renaissance und Barock* (II. Teil), eds. August Buck *et alii* (Frankfurt am Main, 1972), 145–176.

[13] Ingeborg Spriewald, Hildegard Schnabel, Werner Lenk, Heinz Entner, *Grundpositionen der deutschen Literatur im 16. Jahrhundert,* Deutsche Akademie der Wissenschaften zu Berlin, Zentralinstitut für Literaturgeschichte (Berlin and Weimar, 1972), 45: "Die im Schoße der feudalen Gesellschaftsordnung sich vollziehenden ökonomischen Veränderungen der Umschichtungsprozesse im sozialen Gefüge und die damit verbundenen Umbrüche im geistig-ideologischen Bereich führten während der zweiten Hälfte des 15. Jahrhunderts zu einem massiven Anwachsen bürgerlicher Ansprüche gerade auch auf kulturellem Gebiet. Die allmähliche, wenn auch nur zögernd und sehr unterschiedlich sich vollziehende Zersetzung feudalen Denk- und Lebensformen, vor allem aber die einschneidenden Wandlungen im Bereich der sozialen Wirklichkeit und das neue Verhältnis des Menschen zu dieser Wirklichkeit implizierten eine Aufgabenstellung der Literatur, die von den gekennzeichneten Intentionen und Möglichkeiten der hochmittelalterlichen Dichtung qualitativ verschieden war." Strobach, *Geschichte der deutschen Literatur von den Anfängen bis zur Gegenwart,* by a scholarly collective of the DDR, vol. V (Berlin, 1963), Vorbemerkung.

acknowledged that many of the attitudes and virtues characterized as bourgeois had long been inculcated by the church and were appreciated by non-urban segments of society. The new literary expressions were in large measure derived from and blended with those of an earlier day, the play from the *Fastnachtsspiel,* for example. The German prose novel goes back to the inspiration of the nobility, its origins to be sought in the creations of Elisabeth of Nassau-Saarbrücken who translated four French verse novels into German prose novels between 1430 and 1440. Secondly, the so-called chivalric or courtly revival developed in a unique way only in the second half of the seventeenth century and constituted only a part of the literary scene during those decades. To allow a simple identification of humanist culture with bourgeois or urban middle-class values, however, would be to create a pseudomorph or caricature of the reality. Clearly the cities and especially the free imperial cities were important centers of humanist learning.[14] But the humanists themselves came from all segments of society, from peasants such as Celtis to nobles such as Hutten. Moreover, the patrons dwelt in episcopal palaces and courts as well as in patrician houses. The readers and enthusiasts were drawn from all occupations as the universities increasingly served as ladders of social mobility for the intellectually able. And this social mixture in the case of author, patron and audience persisted into the seventeenth century. In the case of the baroque poets, for example, it is the humanistic education and not the vocation which provides the social common bond. In terms of calling, those men of letters had no guild or corporate character, but their social base extended from Protestant ministers, judges, Latin teachers, university professors all the way to princely and city bureaucrats and medical doctors. It reached throughout the world of the half-cultured part-time academics who never graduated from the universities, the merchants, publishers, book dealers, apothecaries, lawyers, sextons, and teachers in the law schools.[15] It is clear that short of a very broad definition of bourgeois,

---

[14] Bernd Moeller, *Imperial Cities and the Reformation. Three Essays* (Philadelphia, 1972), "German Humanists and the Beginnings of the Reformation," 19–38.

[15] Jörg-Ulrich Fechner, *Der Antipetrarkismus Studien zur Liebessatire in Barocker Lyrik* (Heidelberg, 1966), 31.

the term has less applicability and utility than those who bandy it about assume.

Above all, the significance of the classical models for humanist letters must be reemphasized. The humanists, it is true, were Germans who happened to be writing in Latin. But that circumstance was determinative for the course of German literary culture. The introduction of classical forms, modes, and ideas was of critical importance not only for neo-Latin literature, but for the vernacular as well. German letters would have been severely retarded if they had not benefited from the inspiration and above all from the classical standards of the Renaissance.

*Continuity*

One of the great misreadings of German intellectual history is reflected in the average textbook account of German humanist culture in the sixteenth century. Every school child is told that there was an irreconcilable contrast between the Reformation and Renaissance humanism, which wilted away under the hot blasts of religious assertions and controversy. The old and unfortunately still standard picture is one of the feeble beginnings of humanist culture, a brief flowering between 1500 and 1520, and then total submersion with some revivification in the neo-classical during the *Aufklärung*. A completely revised assessment is in order. Sixteenth century German culture continued to be remarkably rich in classical letters and learning, in Greek and Hebrew as well as in Latin, paying tribute to the antique spirit as well as to classical form.[16] The reformers did not devote themselves exclusively to the propagation of their religious faith, but saw the place of the Reformation within the general cultural situation and were genuinely devoted to the cultivation of classical culture. Luther saw human society and higher culture as the "sphere of faith's works." Wittenberg became a center of neo-Latin letters. The Empire

---

16 Harold Jantz, *op. cit.*, 410–411. Jantz draws attention to the second volume of the second edition of Karl Goedeke's bibliography of German literature which records on pages 87–119 a selection of 273 neo-Latin poets of the time which reveals that a great part of the humanistic publication took place in Wittenberg precisely during the most active decades of the Reformation.

was fortunate in enjoying over half a century of relative calm following the Peace of Augsburg, 1555, and the cultivation of letters and learning flourished in a benign climate.[17] The classic Dilthey and Troeltsch debate over the relation of the Renaissance and Reformation finds its local application with respect to German humanism and, when it is thought through in the light of all the knowledge now available regarding sixteenth-century German culture, must definitely be resolved in favor of the continuity of German humanism throughout the sixteenth century.[18]

The question of the termination of the Renaissance is intimately related to that of the continuity of German humanism through the Reformation period. With western Europe in mind, H.R. Trevor-Roper chose the year 1620 for the end of the Renaissance period.[19] A very good argument could be made for 1618 as a convenient date for the *terminus ad quem* of German humanism, for the Thirty Years' War had such a disruptive and depressing effect on German intellectual as well as social life that it serves as a very convenient watershed, not to say bloodshed. There is no utility whatsoever to the great scholar Georg Ellinger's artificial distinction between humanistic and neo-Latin literature, for the generic character of Latin letters remained too much the same.[20] Similarly it is not possible to mark the end of humanistic–

---

[17] See Heinz Liebing, "Die Ausgänge des europäischen Humanismus," *Geist und Geschichte der Reformation* (Berlin, 1966), 357–376; Lewis W. Spitz, "Humanism in the Reformation," in A. Molho and J.A. Tedeschi, eds., *Renaissance Studies in Honor of Hans Baron*, 641–662; Lewis W. Spitz, "Humanism and the Reformation," in Robert M. Kingdon, ed., *Transition and Revolution. Problems and Issues of European Renaissance and Reformation History* (Minneapolis, MN, 1974), 153–188.

[18] Two key writings on the debate are available in translation, Wilhelm Dilthey, "The Interpretation and Analysis of Man in the Fifteenth and Sixteenth Centuries" and Ernst Troeltsch, "Renaissance and Reformation," in Lewis W. Spitz, ed., *The Reformation—Basic Interpretations* (Lexington, MA, 1972), 11–43.

[19] H.R. Trevor-Roper, "Religion, the Reformation and Social Change," *The European Witch-Craze of the Sixteenth and Seventeenth Centuries and Other Essays* (New York, 1968), 2.

[20] Georg Ellinger, "Neulateinische Dichtung Deutschlands im 16. Jahrhundert," Paul Merker and Wolfgang Stammler, eds., *Reallexikon der deutschen*

neo-Latin culture at any such fixed date, for the continuity through mannerism and the baroque is obvious. While one is being arbitrary, then, one may as well be as audacious as Trevor-Roper and set the terminal point for purposes of discussion at 1620.

## New Directions

Even after more than a century of serious scholarly study, the field of German humanism is far from closed out or its intellectual mines exhausted, for much work remains to be done. It will serve a useful purpose to point out limitations of our knowledge and new directions to be taken in order to place the present account of the course of German humanism into perspective.

The full story of the reception of Italian humanism in Germany is yet to be told, particularly the influence of less prominent figures such as the Carmelite general Baptista Mantuanus, beloved by humanists and reformers alike. The splendid survey by Willy Andreas is weak on beginnings, modest in scope, limited to the Reformation period, and insufficiently detailed. But no recent general work has superseded his. Moreover, the comprehensive literary histories are uniformly limited to letters and do not include in their purview the historical, political, philosophical and religious dimensions of humanism as one intellectual and cultural phenomenon.[21] The influence and cross-fertilization

---

*Literaturgeschichte*, II (Berlin, 1926/1928), 469–494; Georg Ellinger, *Italien und der deutsche Humanismus in der Neulateinischen Lyrik,* 3 vols. (Berlin, 1929–1933).

21 Willy Andreas, *Deutschland vor der Reformation. Eine Zeitenwende,* 5th ed. (Stuttgart, 1948). See the brief observations of Jacques Ridé, "Deux grand synthèses sur l'Humanisme," *Études Germaniques,* XX (1965), 546–550, on Willy Andreas and Georg Voigt. The most thorough recent literary history, almost encyclopedic in nature, is that of the late Vienna scholar Hans Rupprich, *Die deutsche Literatur vom späten Mittelalter bis zum Barock,* Erster Teil, *Das ausgehende Mittelalter, Humanismus and Renaissance 1370–1520* (Munich, 1970), vol. IV/1 of Helmut de Boor and Richard Newald, *Geschichte der deutschen Literatur von den Anfängen bis zur Gegenwart.* The two most ambitious recent volumes are posthumous collections of essays, Michael Seidlmayer, *Wege und Wandlungen des Humanismus* (Göttingen, 1965), and Richard Newald, *Probleme and Gestalten des deutschen Humanismus* (Berlin, 1963), neither providing a comprehensive account.

14

between German and French humanism was lively and continuous, not only with Gaguin, Lefèvre, or Budé, but through to mannerism, to Johann Fischart (1546–1590), for example, whose *Gargantua* was related to, though in some ways independent of, Rabelais, and to the Baroque.

The impact of patristic writings and of Christian antiquity upon German humanism calls for a major study, now that more work has been done on the patristic influence in Italian humanism. Far beyond its obvious importance for Erasmus, that impact is of special importance in the area where humanism and reform overlay and interpenetrate through the sixteenth century.[22] The influence of the pre-Socratic philosophers calls for precise assessment. Similarly the continued influence of such medieval cultural figures as Bernard, Jean Gerson, or of the Friends of God, Rhenish mysticism and scholasticism requires further analysis.[23] Increased attention has been paid in recent years to the dark underside of the Italian Renaissance, and similar studies of the irrational and occult aspects of humanist thought in northern Europe would add completeness to our picture and would make the emergence of the witchcraft craze and other startling developments of the later sixteenth and seventeenth centuries seem less astonishing.[24]

---

[22] Paul Oskar Kristeller, "Studies on Renaissance Humanism during the Last Twenty Years," *Studies in the Renaissance,* IX (1962), 20, stated that further study of patristic influence on the Renaissance would be desirable. Charles Stinger, "Humanism and Reform in the Early Quattrocento: The Patristic Scholarship of Ambrogio Traversari (1386–1439)" (Stanford diss., 1971), and others have since responded with monographic studies. This dimension of antique cultural influences was scarcely appreciated by the Burckhardtians such as Ludwig Geiger, *Renaissance und Humanismus in Italien und Deutschland* (Berlin, 1882). Among the few monographs which take the patristic influence into account is Hans Jürgen Schings, *Die patristische und stoische Tradition bei Andreas Gryphius* (Cologne and Graz, 1966).

[23] An example of an admirable philological-literary study relating to mysticism is Hermann Kunisch, "Die mittelalterliche Mystik und die deutsche Sprache: Ein Grundriß," *Literaturwissenschaftliches Jahrbuch der Görres-Gesellschaft,* VI (1965), 37–90.

[24] Two recent studies which probe the underside of the Renaissance are Robert S. Kinsman, *The Darker Vision of the Renaissance Beyond the Fields of Reason* (Berkeley and Los Angeles, 1973), and Wayne Shumaker, *The Occult Sciences in*

Too often those suspect dimensions of the Renaissance world are passed over in what Eugenio Garin has called a conspiracy of silence. A figure such as Agrippa of Nettesheim very naturally has attracted attention and Johannes Trithemius is being favored with new studies, but there are other lesser figures and there is a dimension of this sort in nearly all the representatives of humanist culture in the North.[25]

Another aspect of the revival of classical antiquity in the German Renaissance calling for further research is the new role of Roman law and its contribution to northern humanism. So far the exploration of this subject has been very much a one-man show, the work of that very distinguished scholar Guido Kisch, who has written on Erasmus, Zasius, Reuchlin, Melanchthon and others. Much work remains to be done on the significance of the revival of Roman law, the advance of the *mos gallicus* over the *mos italicus,* the significance of Italian law studies for the young German legists who returned to ecclesiastical and secular courts, to city secretariats and to universities.[26]

---

*the Renaissance. A Study in Intellectual Patterns* (Berkeley and Los Angeles, 1973). See Lewis W. Spitz, "Occultism and Despair of Reason in Renaissance Thought," *Journal of the History of Ideas,* XXVII (1966), 464–469. H.C. Erik Midelfort, *Witch Hunting in Southwestern Germany 1562–1684. The Social and Intellectual Foundations* (Stanford, 1972) reveals the popular depths of belief in witchcraft and offers some startling revisionist explanations.

[25] Charles Nauert, *Agrippa and the Crisis of Renaissance Thought* (Urbana, 1965). On Trithemius see the chapter on "Der Magier" in Klaus Arnold, *Johannes Trithemius (1462–1516). Quellen und Forschungen zur Geschichte des Bistums und Hochstifts Würzburg,* XXIII (Würzburg, 1971), 180–200, reviewed by Ulrich Bubenheimer in the *Zeitschrift der Savigny-Stiftung für Rechtsgeschichte, Germanistische Abteilung,* LXXXIX (1972), 455–459. Arnold recently translated and edited *Johannes Trithemius "De Laude Scriptorum" "Zum Lobe der Schreiber"* (Würzburg, 1973).

[26] Guido Kisch, "Forschungen zur Geschichte des Humanismus in Basel," *Archiv für Kulturgeschichte,* XL/2 (1958), 194–221; *Erasmus und die Jurisprudenz seiner Zeit* (Basel, 1960); *Zasius und Reuchlin* (Constance and Stuttgart, 1961); *Die Anfänge der juristischen Fakultät der Universität Basel, 1459–1529* (Basel, 1962); *Melanchthons Rechts- und Soziallehre* (Berlin, 1967). A recent study of a practicing humanistic jurist worthy of emulation is Hartmut Boockmann, *Laurentius Blumenau, Fürstlicher Rat, Jurist, Humanist* (Göttingen, 1964). R.C. Van Caenegem, "The

In the area of education many problems require explanation before a new general account can be undertaken. Otto Herding, the great scholar of German humanism at Freiburg University, has contributed more than any other specialist to the analysis of German humanist education. He has pointed to the need for distinguishing carefully the various genres of educational treatises. He has himself edited Wimpheling's *Adolescentia* and is doing further work on Socrates, Pseudo-Isocrates, and the early Greek influence on Erasmus and educational theory.[27] The comparison of German humanist with Italian educational treatises must be extended. The comparison of humanist with Reformation educational emphases on the classical curriculum, compulsory universal education, the role of teaching as a divine vocation, and the different concepts of calling of humanists and reformers, needs a major treatment. The impact of humanist-reformation education as represented by Johann Sturm's Strasbourg Academy upon French Calvinist as well as upon English secondary education is crying

---

'Reception' of Roman Law: A Meeting of Northern and Mediterranean Traditions," M.G. Verbeke and J. IJsewijn, eds., *The Late Middle Ages and the Dawn of Humanism Outside Italy*, 195–204, offers a brief sketch in general terms of "reception" through the medieval and Renaissance periods. Thomas Burger, *Jakob Spiegel, Ein humanistischer Jurist des 16. Jahrhunderts* (Augsburg, 1973, a Freiburg i. Br. diss.), recounts the relation of the legist Spiegel, Wimpheling's nephew, to the leading humanists and to the Reformation. See the bibliographical study by Myron P. Gilmore, "The Jurisprudence of Humanism," *Traditio*, XVII (1961), 493–501, and his *Humanists and Jurists. Six Studies in the Renaissance* (Cambridge, MA, 1963).

[27] Otto Herding, "Zur Problematik humanistischer Erziehungsschriften. Textforschung und Menschenbild," *XII^e Congrès International des Sciences Historiques: Rapports. III. Commissions* (Vienna, 1965), 87–94. Otto Herding, *Jakob Wimpfelings Adolescentia* (Munich, 1965); "Der elsässische Humanist Jakob Wimpfeling und seine Erziehungsschrift 'Adolescentia'," *Zeitschrift für Württembergische Landesgeschichte*, XXII (1963), 1–18. See also Herding's *Jakob Wimpfeling/Beatus Rhenanus, Das Leben des Johannes Geiler son Kaysersberg* (Munich, 1970), the review of which edition in the *Renaissance Quarterly*, XXVI/2 (Summer, 1973), 206–208, is a bit capricious and does not fully acknowledge the erudition and insight in evidence in the introduction.

for a major comprehensive study.[28] While there have been several significant recent contributions to the history of humanism in the universities, going well beyond the justly famous studies of the venerable Gustav Bauch, including the monograph on the personal role played by Luther in promoting a humanist arts curriculum, much work remains to be done on the continued interplay of humanism and reform in the universities of both Protestant and Catholic areas of Germany into the seventeenth century.[29] The very number and regional spread of the universities suggests a difference in the nature of university influence than was true in England, for example, with its concentration of university manpower in London, Oxford and Cambridge.

If scholarly interest in German humanist expressions of cultural nationalism has noticeably cooled during the post-war years, the attention directed toward the religious thought of the humanists and the

---

[28] Pierre Mesnard, "La pédagogie de Jean Sturm et son inspiration évangélique (1507–1589)," *XII ͤ Congrès International des Sciences Historiques Rapports*. III. *Commissions* (Vienna, 1965), 95–110. A sample of the influence on the Melanchthon-Sturm approach to education on the French scene is provided by Claude Baduel's reform of the academy at Nîmes. Cf. Theodore W. Casteel, "The College and University of Arts in Nîmes: An Experiment in Humanistic Education in the Age of Reform" (Stanford diss., 1973). Lewis W. Spitz and Barbara Sher Tinsley, *The Reformation and Humanist Learning: Johann Sturm on Education* (Saint Louis, MO: Concordia Publishing House, 1995), 429 pp., provides an analysis of Sturm's life, pedagogical method, bibliographic essay, and a translation from Latin to English of Sturm's major treatises and letters on education. The story of Sturm's Gymnasium and Academy as the cradle of the University of Strasbourg is told in the splendid book, with documents, by Pierre Schang, director of the Chapter of Saint Thomas and Georges Livet, scholarch of the Gymnasium, *Histoire du Gymnase Jean Sturm: Berceau de l'Université de Strasbourg 1538–1988* (Strasbourg: Éditions Oberlin, 1988).

[29] Representative recent studies are Gustav Benrath, "Die Universität der Reformationszeit," *Archiv für Reformationsgeschichte*, LXVII (1966), 32–51, and Gottfried Kliesch, *Der Einfluß der Universität Frankfurt auf die schlesische Bildungsgeschichte, dargestellt an den Breslauer Immatrikulierten von 1506–1648* (Würzburg, 1961).

religious life and practices of the people has markedly increased.[30] There is a very natural bridge from the question of the religious positions of the humanists and the interrelation of humanism and the Reformation. Attention has been increasingly centered upon the influence of humanism on the magisterial and lesser reformers as well as upon the points of variance between humanism and reform. More scholarship also has been devoted to the transmission by the reformers of humanist cultural values to later generations.

At issue in the first instance is the question of the classical learning and humanist sympathies of the reformers, preeminently of Luther himself. Oswald Schmidt's limited and badly outdated work on the subject of Luther's knowledge of the classics needs to be superseded by a new study using the Weimar edition.[31] Secondly, Luther's relation to basic humanist disciplines such as rhetoric needs further detailed examination. Luther once wrote to Eobanus Hessus:

> Plane nihil minus vellum fieri aut committi in iuventute, quam ut poesin et rhetoricen omittant. Mea certe vota sunt, ut quam plurimi sint et poetae et rhetores, quod his studiis videam, sicut nec aliis modis fieri potest, mire aptos fieri

---

[30] For example, Lewis W. Spitz, *The Religious Renaissance of the German Humanists* (Cambridge, MA, 1963).

[31] Oswald G. Schmidt, *Luthers Bekanntschaft mit den alten Klassikern* (Leipzig, 1883). Wilhelm Pauck, "The Historiography of the German Reformation during the Past Twenty Years," *Church History,* IX (1940), 15, stated that the problem of Luther's relation to humanism needs a new and thorough investigation. Many of the older analyses must be rethought, such as Carl Stange, "Luther und der Geist der Renaissance," *Zeitschrift für systematische Theologie,* XVIII (1941), 3–27. For a solid discussion of Luther's appreciation of language, see Peter Meinhold, *Luthers Sprachphilosophie* (Berlin, 1958), esp. chap. 4 ("Die Abgrenzung vom Sprachverständnis des Humanismus"), 28–38, showing how Luther defended the classical and biblical languages against the spiritualists or enthusiasts who believed that knowing the Scriptures in the vernacular sufficed and against the anti-humanists of the old church who held the Church to be the proper interpreter of the Scriptures. Luther held the revival of the languages to be further evidence of God working in history.

homines ad sacra tum capessenda, tum dextre et feliciter tractanda.[32]

Luther's involvement with rhetoric and other humanist modalities was far more extensive and intimate than has generally been recognized. For him also higher culture was a "sphere of faith's works" so that he could gladly and enthusiastically recommend humanist rhetoric and poetry. Luther's contemporaries and his admirers for the next three centuries were fond of calling Luther the "German Cicero." While the power of the Word was conveyed by the Holy Spirit, the power of speech is to be properly cultivated by every *vir doctus,* for man is, as the humanists held, characteristically a *Zoon logikon echon,* a living being having the power of speech. The way in which rhetorical principles affected Luther's hermeneutics in the combination of a christological and tropological interpretation requires further exploration.[33] For Luther, who repeatedly in his *Table Talks* cited the

---

[32] *WA Br,* III, 50, ll. 25–39, No. 596: Luther to Eobanus Hessus, [Wittenberg], 29 March 1523. Peter Sandstrom, *Luther's Sense of Himself as an Interpreter of the Word to the World* (Amherst, MA, 1961), is a clever little *Jugendarbeit* drawing some connections between rhetoric and the *verbum evangelii vocale* or the church as a "mouthhouse." See Reinhard Breymayer, "Bibliographie zum Thema 'Luther und die Rhetorik'," *Linguistica Biblica,* 21/22 (February, 1973), 39–44.

[33] Gerhard Ebeling, *Einführung in theologische Sprachlehre* (Tübingen, 1971), newly translated by R.A. Wilson as *Introduction to a Theological Theory of Language* (London, 1973), is not based upon a thorough awareness of the extensive scholarship in the secular rhetorical tradition, particularly with reference to the immediately relevant humanist culture. See the lengthy critique by Klaus Dockhorn, "Luthers Glaubensbegriff und die Rhetorik. Zu Gerhard Ebelings Buch *Einführung in theologische Sprachlehre,*" *Linguistica Biblica,* 21/22 (February, 1973), 19–39. For a critique of Ebeling's "hermeneutical theology" as being "dated" along with Heidegger's obsolete philosophy, see Rüdiger Lorenz, *Die unvollendete Befreiung vom Nominalismus. Martin Luther and die Grenzen hermeneutischer Theologie bei Gerhard Ebeling* (Gütersloh, 1973). See also Dockhorn's article, "Rhetorik und germanistische Literaturwissenschaft in Deutschland," *Jahrbuch für internationale Germanistik,* III, no. 1, 168–185, esp. 178–179. Dockhorn traces the significance of rhetoric through the centuries down, in fact, to Nietzsche and Sartre. See Klaus Dockhorn, *Macht and Wirkung der Rhetorik,* Respublica Literaria. Studienreihe zur

formula *Dialectica docet, Rhetorica movet,* saw the enthroning of rhetoric once again as the *regina artium* as a necessary prerequisite for a purified and affective theology. Luther's application of rhetorical principles has been demonstrated with respect to both his treatise *On the Liberty of the Christian Man* and his *Sermon on the Necessity of Sending Children to School.*[34] It is becoming increasingly obvious that the great contrast between the reformer Luther and the humanist Melanchthon, a cliché so dear to many writers, is on this operative level of worldly culture and at the plane of maximum contact with theology not really tenable.[35] It is to be hoped that the major work on Luder and rhetoric promised by the distinguished literary scholar Klaus Dockhorn will materialize and that a theologian learned in Luther's exegetical and hermeneutical principles will produce a complementary work taking this perspective fully into account. What is said here of rhetoric could

---

europäischen Bildungstradition vom Humanismus bis zur Romantik 2, eds. Joachim Dyck and Günther List (Bad Homburg, 1968). See the brilliant essay by Wesley Trimpi, "The Quality of Fiction: The Rhetorical Transmission of Literary Theory," *Traditio,* XXX (1974), 1–118, for the contribution of rhetoric to the continuity of literary theory. Wilfried Barner, *Barockrhetorik. Untersuchungen zu ihren geschichtlichen Grundlagen* (Tübingen, 1970), demonstrates the great importance of rhetoric for Baroque literature through the 17th century. Ulrich Nembach, *Predigt des Evangeliums. Luther als Prediger, Pädagoge und Rhetor* (Neukirchen-Vluyn, 1972), has a fascinating chapter on the sermon as oration in which (117–174) he analyzes Luther's sermons in relation to Quintilian's rhetorical principles, finding that Luther adopted Quintilian's *Volksberatungsrede* form and technique as the most appropriate and effective homiletical method.

[34] Birgit Stolt, *Studien zu Luthers Freiheitstraktat mit besonderer Rücksicht auf das Verhältnis der lateinischen und der deutschen Fassung zu einander und die Stilmittel der Rhetorik,* Stockholmer Germanistische Forschungen, 6 (Stockholm, 1969). Birgit Stolt, "Docere, delectare und movere bei Luther. Analysiert anhand der 'Predigt, daß man Kinder zur Schulen halten solle'," *Deutsche Vierteljahrschrift,* XLIV (1970), 433–474

[35] Thus Wilhelm Maurer, *Der junge Melanchthon zwischen Humanismus und Reformation,* I: *Der Humanist;* II: *Der Theologe* (Göttingen, 1967, 1969). So also Adolf Sperl, *Melanchthon zwischen Humanismus und Reformation* (Munich, 1959). For a bibliographical survey, Peter Fraenkel and Martin Greschat, *Zwanzig Jahre Melanchthonstudium. Sechs Literaturberichte (1945–1965)* (Geneva, 1967), 72–77.

easily be repeated with respect to moral philosophy, poetry, history, or virtually any other humanistic discipline.

Thirdly, the final word on Luther's *Auseinandersetzung* with humanism embodied in Erasmus on the central theological issues has not yet been spoken despite the volume of literature devoted to it.[36] Actually, Luther's very radical existential theology clarified the relation of theology to philosophy in a way not possible for the sapiential theology of the Thomists or the prudential moralistic theology of humanism theologians, for it delineated the spheres of the divine and the humanistic so clearly that each could rest more firmly on its own base without confusing overlapping or hazardous overhangs.

The history of literature, poetry and prose, from the fifteenth to the seventeenth centuries has been favored with some excellent comprehensive treatments.[37] However, the argument has been made

---

[36] See Friedrich Schenke, "Luther und der Humanismus," *Luther. Zeitschrift der Luther-Gesellschaft,* XXXIII/2 (1962), 77–85, reexamines the theological issues involved in the Luther-Erasmus exchange and rebuts the absurd assertion of Friedrich Heer, who is all too frequently totally unreliable (*Die dritte Kraft.* [Frankfurt, 1959]), that Luther's theocentrism undercuts the validity of *humanitas.* Harry J. McSorley, C.S.P., *Luther Right or Wrong?* (New York and Minneapolis, 1969), discusses the Luther-Erasmus debate over free will, the issue which Luther called the "hinge" and "jugular." The most recent scholarly work on Luther during the critical years of 1518 to 1521 is the excellent volume of Leif Grane, *Martinus Noster: Luther in the German Reform Movement 1518–1521* (Mainz: Verlag Philipp von Zabern, 1994), *Veröffentlichungen des Instituts für Europäische Geschichte Mainz. Abteilung Religionsgeschichte,* herausgegeben von Rolf Decot, vol. 155. In Part V Grane carefully analyzes the support for Luther by the humanists and the misgivings of some, and in Part VI he spells out with precision and in great detail the growing tension of Luther, the humanists, and the *magistri nostri,* followed by the disintegration of the reform party, 147–187, 189–229. Helmar Junghaus, ed., *Leben und Werk Martin Luthers von 1526 bis 1546: Festgabe zu seinem 500. Geburtstag,* I (Berlin: Evangelische Verlagsanstalt, 1983), undertakes to correct the balance between the mountain of scholarly work on the "Young Luther" and the relatively neglected final two decades of his life.

[37] Wolfgang Stammler, *Von der Mystik zum Barock 1400–1600* (Stuttgart, 1927), remains a standard work. The newer work edited by August Buck, *Renaissance und Barock, I, Neues Handbuch der Literaturwissenschaft,* ed. Klaus von See (Frankfurt

that the canon of approved authors was fixed by the nineteenth-century literary historians under romanticist influence. Other figures deserving to be more fully appreciated should be studied and rescued from neglect: Maternus Steyndorffer, author of the comedy *Ein hubsch Lustig und nutzlich Comödia* (Mainz, 1540); Johann Ditmar, *Von der Heimfahrt und Beylager Des... Herrn Friederich Wilhelms, Hertzogen zu Sachsen, etc.* (Jena, 1583); Philipp Camerarius, son of one Joachim and brother of the other, the author of genial essays the *Operae Horarum Subcisivarum Sive Meditationes Historicae* (1602 ff.), in German the *Historischer Lustgarten;* Ruprecht von Moshaim (1493–1543), Valerius Herberger (1562–1627), Leonhart Thurneysser zum Thurn (1530–1596). The three areas which are most neglected are those of fiction, the essay, and the sermon.[38] The relation of the lyric, music, and hymnody needs further exploration.[39] The continuity of the literary tradition from fifteenth century humanism into the age of the Baroque needs to be reemphasized.[40]

---

am Main, 1972), places German literature into its European setting. Friedrich Gaede, *Humanismus-Barock. Aufklärung. Geschichte der deutschen Literatur vom 16. Jahrhundert* (Bern and Munich, 1971), is strong minded and independent in challenging older authorities (e.g., Ernst Curtius), in considering neo-Latin and the vernacular together, and in distinguishing counter-mainstream literature from the dominant mode. Heinz Otto Burger, *Renaissance, Humanismus, Reformation. Deutsche Literatur im europäischen Kontext* (Bad Homburg, 1969), offers a sprightly survey. The work of Hans Rupprich, *Vom späten Mittelalter bis zum Barock,* cited above is particularly notable for its thoroughness and for its inclusion of Catholic writers and Jesuit authors.

[38] Harold Jantz, *op. cit.,* 420–433.

[39] Hans Joachim Moser, "Renaissancelyrik deutscher Musiker um 1500," *Deutsche Vierteljahrsschrift für Literaturwissenschaft und Geistesgeschichte,* V, (1927), 381–412. This article, which Jantsch, *op. cit.,* 405, calls a "great new beginning," points the way to a reassessment of many lyrics which have long been viewed romantically as folksongs but which in reality are classical in structure, such as Luther's "Jesaia dem Propheten das geschah."

[40] Renata Hildebrandt-Günther, *Antike Rhetorik und deutsche literarische Theorie im 17. Jahrhundert* (Marburg, 1966), stresses the contribution of classical antiquity to literary theory. Richard Alewyn, *Deutsche Barockforschung: Dokumentation einer Epoche* (Cologne, 1965), includes essays which underline the

The whole question of the importance of printing for humanism and the Reformation is begging for a thorough and comprehensive study, for, from the first published book, Gutenberg's Constance Missal, and the Bible, printing became a major force with astonishing rapidity and continued to expand its production through the century. Only Italy rivaled Germany in the number of presses and productivity.[41] The German humanists heralded the invention of printing patriotically as a unique contribution of German culture that rivaled Italian achievements.

Enough has been said to suggest that, far from being a closed chapter for historical research, the course of German humanism is wide open to further study. The account which follows must be viewed then as partial in a two-fold sense. For it is a brief statement from one individual's perspective and it is provisional since many aspects of the total picture remain to be more thoroughly explored.[42] Fortunately a

---

contribution of German humanism to the baroque: Erich Trunz, "Der deutsche Späthumanismus um 1600 als Standeskultur," 147–181, and Wolfgang Kayser, "Der rhetorische Grundzug von Harsdörffers Zeit und die gottesgebundene Haltung," 324–335.

[41] A great many very valuable studies have appeared, notably such articles as Maria Grossmann's "Wittenberger Drucke von 1502 bis 1517," *Das Antiquariat* XVII (1964), 153(1)–156(4), 220(4)–226(10), and "Wittenberg Printing, Early Sixteenth Century," *Sixteenth Century Essays and Studies* (St. Louis, MO, 1970), I, 54–74. Especially notable are Elizabeth L. Eisenstein, "The Advent of Printing and the Problem of the Renaissance," *Past and Present*, no. 45 (Nov., 1969), 27ff., and "The Advent of Printing and the Protestant Revolt: A New Approach to the Disruption of Western Christendom," in Robert M. Kingdon, ed. *Transition and Revolution* (Minneapolis, 1974), 235–270.

[42] See the excellent report on the current state of research by Dieter Wuttke, *Deutsche Germanistik und Renaissance-Forschung. Ein Vortrag zur Forschungslage, Respublica Literaria. Studienreihe zur europäischen Bildungstradition vom Humanismus bis zur Romantik*, eds. Joachim Dyck and Günther List, No. 3 (Bad Homburg, 1968), 1–46. A very useful recent bibliography is Günter Albrecht and Günther Dahlke, eds., *Internationale Bibliographie zur Geschichte der Deutschen Literatur von den Anfängen bis zur Gegenwart* (Berlin, 1969), Teil I: *Von den Anfängen bis 1789.* Karl Otto Conrady, "Die Erforschung der neulateinischen Literatur. Probleme und Aufgaben," *Euphorion. Zeitschrift für Literaturgeschichte* XLIX (1955), 413–445, regrets the lack of new research works on the total complex

solid phalanx of well trained and highly endowed young scholars, German and American for the most part, is prepared to take up the pursuit of knowledge in this fascinating area of research. In the words of Vadianus, "Est enim amor omnium studiorum fomes."

## II. THE EARLY PHASES

Antiquity knows of many encounters between the prophet or the philosopher and the king. The story is told that when King Alfonso of Naples once asked Gianozzo Manetti (1396–1459) what comprised the whole duty of man, he replied, "Intellegere et agere," to understand and to act. Johannes Regiomontanus (Koenigsberger), a representative of the natural scientific interest of the northern Renaissance, in the dedication to King Matthias Corvinus of his *Tabulae ac problemata primi mobilis* (ca. 1465) raised the question as to whether one should take the works of the ancients as one's guide or one's own experience. He answered that one should combine them, for experience alone is not adequate and to follow the ancients alone leads to life with the dead. The course of German humanism moved very rapidly away from the early preoccupation with the ancient dead for the sake of antique culture to an active engagement with real problems in the present. Whether the humanists were involved in religious enlightenment, cultural nationalism, ecclesiastical reformation, educational innovation, or literary production, they were not merely antiquarian but action-oriented and people-directed. The movement itself began with a fitful start, followed by a caesura and a second beginning, but then built up continuously and persisted well into the seventeenth century, and some would argue even into the age of the Enlightenment.

Traditionally the birth of the northern Renaissance has been associated with the Prague chancellery of Johann von Neumarkt, the chancellor of Emperor Charles IV (ruled 1346–1378). Johann von Neumarkt (ca. 1310–1380) was an admirer of Petrarch's Latin style and

---

of neo-Latin literature, for no one since Georg Ellinger has had the courage to undertake the study of the entire *corpus* and nexus of ideas. The questions which Ellinger posed in his article "Grundfragen und Aufgaben der neulateinischen Philologie," *Germanisch-romanische Monatsschrift*, XXI (1933), 1–14, have scarcely been answered.

was inspired by the Roman patriotism of Cola di Rienzo. But aside from his own improved style, his contribution consisted of the transmission of two ancient writings ascribed to St. Augustine rather than of works by pagan authors. In that court milieu Johann von Tepl (ca. 1350–1414) (in the older literature he was known as Johann von Saasz after the city where he served as notary and rector of the Latin school for a good number of years) created the *Ackermann aus Böhmen,* the famous dialogue between a peasant whose wife had just died and death. The peasant challenges the right of death to steal away his wife. Death responds coldly and cynically, asserting his power over all that is in and of the world. The peasant derides death as mere negation whose power is limited for it depends upon the prior existence of life. God as judge concludes by commending both for disputing well and declares that the honor goes to the plaintiff and victory to death. In a letter written the evening before St. Bartholemew's Day, 1401, to an old friend Peter von Tepl, Johann described his dialogue as a rhetorical exercise, that is, it was a humanist piece similar to others that Johann von Neumarkt had made native to Bohemia. His concern with style was reminiscent of the work of the Prague court poet Heinrich von Mügeln some decades earlier. Experts have pointed to the probable influence of some pseudo-Seneca dialogues on the piece. The debate continues as to whether the *Ackermann* is medieval as a juridical, controversial dialogue rather than following the style of an antique Platonic dialogue, but it should be possible to agree that while the subject is as somber as a medieval *Jedermann,* in style it shows clear evidence of classical humanist influence.[43]

---

43 Heinz Otto Burger, *op. cit.,* 49–53. A good text edition is Johannes von Tepl, *Der Ackermann aus Böhmen,* ed. with a glossary and notes by M. O'C. Walshe (London, 1951). See also the article by Walshe, "Der 'Ackermann aus Böhmen', a Structural Interpretation," *Classica et Medievalia,* XV (1954), 130–145. The older classic scholarly treatment was Konrad Burdach, *Der Dichter des 'Ackermann aus Böhmen' and seine Zeit,* III, 2, *Vom Mittelalter zur Reformation* (Berlin, 1926, 1932). Among the more recent treatments of special value are Gerhard Hahm, *Die Einheit des "Ackermann aus Böhmen." Studien zur Komposition* (Munich, 1963); Renée Brand, *Zur Interpretation des "Ackermann aus Böhmen"* (Basel, 1944); Franz Bäuml, *Rhetorical Devices and Structure in the "Ackermann aus Böhmen"* (Berkeley, 1960);

26

If the position of Johann von Tepl between the Medieval and Renaissance was ambiguous, the specific humanistic character of two other early fifteenth-century writers, Heinrich Wittenwiler and Oswald von Wolkenstein, is even more debatable. Wittenwiler's *Der Ring,* written before 1418, was basically a medieval work, half didactic and half a verse narrative, describing a world already in decline. A good portion relates a medieval *Schwank,* a form of Middle High German tale similar to the *fabliaux.* Oswald von Wolkenstein, a Tyroler, was a gifted lyric poet. He led an adventurous life, wandering about the world for some thirteen years preparing for knighthood. But Wittenwiler's work was not widely known, and, despite Wolkenstein's love of the world and of adventure, his life-style was more medieval than modern. These individuals can be considered progenitors of Renaissance humanism with even less plausibility than Johann von Tepl or the Prague court.

There is a real question as to whether the Prague beginnings can with justice be considered the cradle of German humanism because of the virtual lack of direct influence and continuity within the Empire. A link does exist, although an indirect one, for the style of Charles IV's court influenced Emperor Maximilian and the connection with later German humanism may be a genuine, if tenuous, one over the route from Prague through Vienna.

The actual inception of a direct continuous movement is to be found rather in the Italian contacts which were accelerated anew by the church councils of the earlier fifteenth century. The councils of Constance (1414–1418) and Basel (1431–1449) gave the German churchmen an opportunity to see the rhetorically schooled Italians in action. Italian humanists and artists travelled north as ecclesiastical legates, diplomatic emissaries, lecturers on rhetoric and poetry in the universities, secretaries to northern princes and cities, and as business representatives. Poggio and Vergerio travelled in the Empire. Enea Silvio Piccolomini served as secretary at the court of the Habsburgs and wrote a description of Bohemia and of Germany in which he lauded the great cultural progress achieved under the aegis of the Roman church. Some of the stimulation came by way of a reaction to Italian superciliousness. Like Petrarch's letter to Urban V so critical of the

---

Ernst Schwarz, ed., *Der Ackermann aus Böhmen des Johannes von Tepl und seine Zeit* (Darmstadt, 1968).

French, Vespasiano's contemptuous remarks about those *ultramontanes* who lacked spirit, or Boccaccio's reference to the English as "thickheads," Sabellicus in his *Decades* ridiculed the Germans for lacking an early history and Antonio Campanus contrasted the Danube and the Tiber. One effect of Italian condescension, in the reaction also of later humanists such as Celtis who left Italy hurriedly in anger, was to stimulate a cultural rivalry which proved to be productive. There was throughout the fifteenth century a lively two-way traffic between Germany and Italy. Following the medieval student-wandering tradition, literally thousands of German students trekked down to Bologna or Padua to study Roman or canon law and sometimes acquired a taste also for classical Latin literature, although rarely for Renaissance art. On their return, they used their classical knowledge in order to ornament their festive orations and to add tone to their letters and diplomatic papers. Jurists and diplomats found classical literature to be a useful accoutrement professionally and led the way in the acquisition of antique Latin culture.

It is a matter of special interest to note the significant role of women in these early phases of humanism as author and patroness. Countess Elisabeth of Nassau-Saarbrücken may justly be considered the creator of German prose novels. The daughter of Duke Frederick V of Lorraine, she was married in 1412 as a mere girl to Count Philip of Nassau-Saarbrücken. As his widow she governed while her sons were still minors. Between 1430 and 1440 she translated four French verse novels into German prose novels. In the best known of her prose novels, *Hugo Scheppel,* the hero, the illegitimate son of a butcher's daughter, strove to win the French crown. Although the background of the prose novels lay in the world of the nobility, this story differed in its greater naturalness, for its outcome depended upon a series of developments, not upon extraordinary qualities in the "hero" or upon divine intervention. The shift from verse to prose has by a long standing critical convention been viewed as a decline of a medieval form, but it can with equal justice be viewed as a step into Renaissance literature, for Italian authors even earlier and, be it said, more artistically had produced novels of this kind. Noble women of other courts encouraged early humanists in cultivating the new style. Eleanor, wife of Duke Sigismund of the Tyrol (1448–1480) did translations from French and had ties to the humanist-physician Heinrich Steinhöwel. The

28

archduchess Mathilde communicated with Hermann von Sachsenheim, Jakob Pütterich von Reichertshausen, and Niklas von Wyle, pioneers of humanist letters in the fifteenth century.[44] The role of women enlarged during the sixteenth century as patrician families such as the Pirckheimers in Nuremberg educated their daughters.

After the primary contacts between German and Italian humanists in the first half of the fifteenth century, enthusiasm for the classics and for Italian humanist learning continued to mount. Italians continued to travel in the Empire, such as the Florentine Publicius Rufus from 1466 to 1467, who came to Erfurt, Leipzig, Cracow, Basel and other cities. Ecclesiastical rulers such as the Bishop of Augsburg, Peter von Schaumburg, and secular princes such as the Count Palatine Frederick the Victorious and Margrave John the Alchemist in Franconia patronized humanist learning. A new generation of pioneers busied themselves like bees gathering Italian and classical lore, editing and translating, representing a stage of the primary accumulation of cultural material. Among a considerable number deserving of special notice are Niklas von Wyle, Heinrich Steinhöwel, and Albrecht von Eyb. These intermediaries served as cultural transmitters and were indispensable forerunners of the major figures who followed them. They cited the Italian humanists liberally and incorporated whole paragraphs and pages into their writings. Wyle, Eyb, and Peter Luder, for example, used the same passage from Leonardo Bruni in order to describe the content of the liberal arts. Hermann Schedel, the uncle of Hartmann Schedel, author of the Nuremberg Chronicle, in his correspondence copied out whole passages from Petrarch, Poggio and Enea Silvio. Filelfo, Guarino, Poggio, Valla, Gasparino di Barzizza, and many others are excerpted

---

[44] Willi Flemming, *op. cit.*, 21. Since we shall not be returning to the specific theme of women's contributions, attention may be drawn to the book by Roland Bainton, *Women of the Reformation in Germany and Italy* (Minneapolis, 1971), and to his brief introduction to three papers, "The Role of Women in the Reformation," *Archive for Reformation History*, LXIII (1972), 141ff. On Eleanor, the sixth child of King James I of Scotland, who was the wife of Duke Sigmund of the Tyrol, see Morimichi Watanabe, "Humanism in the Tyrol: Aeneas Sylvius, Duke Sigmund, Gregor Heimburg," *The Journal of Medieval and Renaissance Studies* IV (1974), 177–202, here at 186–188.

and cited in addition to the even more popular Petrarch, Enea Silvio, and Bruni.

Niklas von Wyle (ca. 1410–1478), a schoolmaster in Zurich and from 1447 in Esslingen, a small city near Stuttgart, where he served as city-secretary and later as a diplomat in the princely employ, served the cause of cultural transmission through his pupils and by his translations of classical and Italian authors. He "transferred" Latin into German as his life's work, the first of these *Tranzlatzen* being dated 1461. These translations, eighteen in all, done in part on direct commission from his patroness Mathilde, included writings of Petrarch, Poggio, and Aretino, Boccaccio's *Guiscardo and Sigismonda* and Enea Silvio's *Euriolus and Lucretia*. His tenth translation, the letter of Enea Silvio in which he commented on the cultural milieu of Germany, was of special importance for the elevation of the *nobilitas literaria* to the side of the nobility of birth. His aim was to Latinize German and to raise its formal level as a vehicle for literary expression and epistelography. Other translators were active such as Antonius von Pforr, Mathilde's chaplain and a Nuremberger who called himself Arigo and translated a part of the *Decameron*.

The Ulm physician Heinrich Steinhöwel (1412–1482/3) served Count Eberhard in Württemberg, Mathilde's son by her first marriage. He translated Rodericus de Arevato's chronicle of the world, the *Speculum humanae vitae* and some of Boccaccio, notably the *De claris mulieribus,* which he dedicated to Eleanor, wife of Duke Sigismund of the Tyrol. To her he also dedicated a highly successful *Esopus,* done between 1474 and 1480, a collection of ancient fables and *facetiae* of Poggio and Petrus Alfonsi.

The role of lawyers in the introduction of humanist culture was significant. The Franconian Albrecht von Eyb (1420–1475) made an even greater contribution with his *Margarita poetica* (finished 1459, published 1472) in which he offered *florileges* drawn from the works of classical orators and poets.[45] He had studied law at Pavia, Bologna, and

---

[45] The basic work is still Max Herrmann, *Albrecht von Eyb und die Frühzeit des deutschen Humanismus* (Berlin, 1893). Herrmann also edited the *Deutsche Schriften des Albrecht von Eyb* (Berlin, 1890). See also Joseph Hiller, *Albrecht von Eyb, a Medieval Moralist* (Washington, DC, 1939). On the problematics of early humanism

Padua. During the course of his legal studies he was attracted to Roman culture and to humanistic letters. Gregor Heimburg (ca. 1400–1472), for example, was born in the imperial city of Schweinfurt on the Main, attended the University of Padua, served as the representative of the elector of Mainz at the Council of Basel, and though he disclaimed literary merit of his own, he frequently cited Cicero, Juvenal, Terence and even Plato in Latin. Sigismund Gossembrot was similar to Heimburg in his classical interests. But Albrecht von Eyb was more productive in literature. His work was pragmatic and didactic, aimed at improving life, and as a schoolmaster of the people he at times substituted German names and popular phrases for foreign or difficult expressions. To his "Mirror of Morals" he added translations of three Latin comedies, Plautus's *Menaechmi* and *Bacchides* and Ugolino's *Philogenia*.[46] Around 1450 he did a book on marriage on the pattern of Franciscus Barbarus's *De re uxoria* (1415), using several Italian sources and including translations once again. He was less interested in Latinizing German than in transmitting the cultural and moral content of the classical and Italian humanistic writing to the people.[47] In that respect he pointed toward the didactic and pedagogical emphasis of later German humanism.

In assessing the early phases of German humanism it is necessary to come to terms with a giant figure of the century, Nicolaus Cryffs, better known as Cardinal Nicholas Cusanus (1401–1464). The philosopher Leibniz considered Cusanus and Valla to be the two most brilliant men of the Quattrocento. Born in Cues on the Moselle, he studied at Deventer, then went to Padua where he studied law, Greek, Hebrew, mathematics, and astronomy. He lost the only legal contest he ever handled to Gregor Heimburg and is said as a consequence to have moved from the law to theology. He served as a representative of the Archbishop of Trier at the Council of Basel, as a convinced conciliarist, but he became disillusioned with the constant bickerings of the

see Otto Herding, "Probleme des frühen Humanismus in Deutschland," *Archiv für Kulturgeschichte*, XXXVIII (1956), 344–389.

[46] See Karl Conrady, "Zu den deutschen Plautusübertragungen. Ein Überblick von Albrecht von Eyb bis zu J.M.R. Lenz," *Euphorion*, XLVIII (1954), 373–396; Max Herrmann, *Albrecht von Eyb*, 161–173, 356–397.

[47] *Ibid.*, 285–355, including a detailed analysis of his sources.

conciliarists and in 1437 he swung over to the papal side. He became a cardinal in 1448, bishop of Brixen in 1450, and retired to Rome in 1460. He was a true Renaissance man in his broad intellectual interests in philosophy, nature, and the classics, and he even discovered several classical manuscripts. Cusanus became a cultural hero, a symbol of philosophical achievement, influential in Italy as well as in Germany for his "Platonism" and *via negativa* speculation. But his place is rather on the metaphysical side of Renaissance thought and he does not belong to the mainstream of German humanism.[48]

The second half of the fifteenth century saw the founding of a whole new wave of universities by territorial princes and city councils: Freiburg im Breisgau (1457); Basel (1459), very early renowned for the study of Roman law; Ingolstadt (1472); Trier (1473); Mainz (1476); and Tübingen (1477). Then in 1502 Elector Frederick the Wise founded the University of Wittenberg. The universities old and new served as resting places for the wandering humanists who continued the medieval *Studentenwanderung* with a *Professorenwanderung*. Peter Luder, Samuel Karoch, and other Germans followed a similar pattern of wandering from university to university serving as guest lecturers in poetry and rhetoric. Luder (ca. 1415–1474) was born in Kislau in Franconia, studied in Italy, lectured subsequently in Heidelberg, Erfurt, Leipzig and elsewhere before entering the diplomatic service of Sigismund of Austria. Count Palatine Frederick I encouraged the new learning at Heidelberg. In 1456 at Heidelberg Luder, a hard-drinking, aggressive personality, announced that he would "deliver a public lecture on the *studia humanitatis,* that is, the books of the poets, orators, and historians." From 1456 to 1460 he played a very important role in advancing humanist learning at Heidelberg. There is a direct line

---

[48] The key book on Cusanus remains Ernst Cassirer, *Individuum und Kosmos in der Philosophie der Renaissance* (Leipzig, 1927). A. Meister, "Die humanistischen Anfänge des Nikolaus von Cues," *Annalen des historischen Vereins für den Niederrhein,* LXIII (1896), 1–26, on his early contacts with northern humanism. More recent is K.M. Volkmann-Schluck, *Nicolaus Cusanus* (Frankfurt, 1952). A fairly good summary is Henry Bett, *Nicholas of Cusa (1401–1464)* (London, 1932). The attempt to link Cusanus with Biblical humanism in an essential way is not persuasive, Herbert Werner Rüssel, *Gestalt eines christlichen Humanismus* (Amsterdam, 1940), 125ff.

from these early wandering humanists to Conrad Celtis and humanists of the high tide of humanism at the end of the century. One of Luder's most gifted and important students, Stephan Hoest, succeeded him in Heidelberg where he maintained that both scholastic philosophy and the *studia humanitatis* are necessary for the study of theology.[49]

During the second half of the fifteenth century printing presses were established in the commercial cities first of all, but then in university towns. The confluence of humanists and printers in the university environment was a fortuitous circumstance for the spread of German humanism, as we shall observe later.

Besides loose-living poets like Luder there were schoolteacher humanists such as Johannes Murmellius and Rudolf von Langen, scholastics such as Conrad Summenhart and Paul Scriptoris, and moralists such as Heinrich Bebel. The dominant characteristic of humanism during the last two or three decades of the fifteenth century was its practical, didactic, and moralistic nature. A pedagogical purpose directed toward an ethical end led the humanists to draw upon antique moral philosophy as well as upon religious sources. The cultivation of Ciceronian Latin in the city schools, now more under governmental than under monastic or ecclesiastical control, promised a generation of youths better schooled for humanist studies.

No doubt the most influential author of those decades was Sebastian Brant, whose great satire *The Ship of Fools* (1494) had an international impact, for it was translated into Latin by his pupil, the bumptious Jakob Locher, and from the Latin into various European languages. Brant (1458–1521) worked as a lawyer, from 1489 on as a professor in Basel, and from 1501 on as a city secretary in Strasbourg. He composed a collection of *varia carmina* (1498), moral, religious, and political in nature. He translated a collection of sayings from Cato, Facetus,

---

[49] On Luder, see Wilhelm Wattenbach, *Peter Luder, der erste humanistische Lehrer in Heidelberg* (Erfurt, 1869), *Sonderdruck aus Zeitschrift für die Geschichte des Oberrheins, XXII* (1869), 33–127, and Frank Baron, *The Beginnings of German Humanism: The Life and Work of the Wandering Humanist Peter Luder* (diss., University of California, Berkeley, 1966). On Karoch, see W. Wattenbach, "Samuel Karoch von Lichtenberg, ein Heidelberger Humanist," *Zeitschrift für die Geschichte des Oberrheins,* XXVIII (1876), 38–50. On Hoest, see Frank Baron, *Stephan Hoest. Reden und Briefe* (Munich, 1971).

Moretus, and others, and published a volume of perorations, highly didactic in nature. In 1502 Brant published an edition of Baptista Mantuanus's *Opus Calamitatum* with a commentary concluding that *astra inclinant, non necessitant.* His *Narrenschiff* was a classic in a rather long tradition of "ship of fools" literature, in clever verses needling the foibles and follies of all mankind. It has been a commonplace since the romantics to view the *Ship of Fools* as a medieval folkish work, but it was intended as a humanistic work and has a classical rhetorical structure, a blend of the new with the traditional. It was the first independent work of poetry in German so that Ulrich von Hutten later could rightly praise Brant as the new founder of German poetry.[50] Johann Geiler von Kaisersberg (1445–1510), the great moralistic pulpiteer, preached a series of sermons on the *Ship of Fools.*[51]

This satirical and pedagogical tradition persisted at Strasbourg with the work of Matthias Ringmann Philesius (1482–1511), who did translations of Caesar (1507), and of Johann Adolf Müling, the city physician, who did satires on the immorality, ignorance, and lack of culture of the clergy. Peter Schott (1460–1490), who belonged to an aristocratic Strasbourg family, wrote two extant works in humanistic

---

[50] Edwin H. Zeydel, *Sebastian Brant* (New York, 1967), a biography; trans. and ed., *The Ship of Fools by Sebastian Brant translated into Rhyming Couplets with Introduction and Commentary* (New York, 1944). On the theme of fools and folly see Barbara Könneker, *Wesen und Wandlung der Narrenidee im Zeitalter des Humanismus. Brant. Erasmus. Murner* (Wiesbaden, 1966). Two studies by Ulrich Gaier merit special mention, *Studien zu Sebastian Brants "Narrenschiff"* (Tübingen, 1966), and "Sebastian Brant's *Narrenschiff* and the Humanists," *PMLA*, LXXXIII (1968), 266–270. Friedrich Zarncke's edition, *Sebastian Brants Narrenschiff* (Leipzig, 1854) was reprinted at Darmstadt, 1964. Dieter Wuttke, "Sebastian Brants Verhältnis zu Wunderdeutung und Astrologie," in Werner Busch, *et alii, Studien zur deutschen Literatur und Sprache des Mittelalters. Festschrift für Hugo Moser* (Berlin, 1974), 272–286, describes Brant as no Enlightenment figure, but bound by his times in his attitude toward wonders and astrology.

[51] See E. Jane Dempsey Douglass, *Justification in Late Medieval Preaching. A Study of John Geiler of Keisersberg* (Leiden, 1966).

Latin, *De mensuris syllaborum epithoma* and the *Lucubraciunculae,* which was edited by Jakob Wimpheling and published in 1498.[52]

But the most influential of this group was Jakob Wimpheling (1450–1528), a humanist priest, a moralist, educator and German patriot. Wimpheling was born in Schlettstadt, the "pearl of Alsace," attended the Latin school of Ludwig Dringenberg, who had studied at Deventer and emphasized ethical-religious training in the manner of the Brethren of the Common Life. He went as a boy of fourteen to the University of Freiburg where he came under the influence of Geiler von Kaisersberg (1445–1510), sharp critic of vanity and worldly splendor. He studied further at Erfurt and Heidelberg, where he had some contact with the humanist circle of Bishop Johannes von Dalberg. He rose to become dean and rector of the university, then for fourteen years he served as cathedral preacher at Speyer, lived then in Strasbourg to be near Geiler, and retired to Schlettstadt for his closing years. Wimpheling's two major contributions as a humanist were as a playwright and as an organizer of a sodality. He was the author of *Stylpho,* a "prodigal son" play, a theme very popular in later sixteenth-century drama, with an unhappy ending. In Strasbourg he organized the *Sodalitas literaria Argentinensis,* a loose association of friends of the classics. He held Baptista Mantuanus to be the best poet of Italian humanism. The classics for him had only the provisional utility of enabling students the better to understand Christian writings. He wrote two educational works on education, the *Isidoneus,* concerned with Latin grammar and literature, and the *Adolescentia,* an omnibus volume containing materials from Petrarch, Vergerio, Baptista Mantuanus and other Italian humanists from classical and Christian authors, from Augustine to Thomas and Gerson, useful for ethical distinction.[53] In his *De Integritate* he attacked the concubinage and poor morals of the priests. Living on a frontier endangered by the French, he played the German patriot by arguing against Thomas Murner in favor of the German character of Alsace. The *Germania* and the *Epitoma rerum Germanicarum,* in which he and his friend Sebastian

---

[52] Murray A. and Marian L. Cowie, eds., *The Works of Peter Schott (1460–1490),* I, University of North Carolina Studies in the Germanic Languages and Literatures, No. 41 (Chapel Hill, 1963).

[53] The best edition is Otto Herding, *Jakob Wimpfelings Adolescentia* (Munich, 1965).

Murrho described the Rhine and its valley as a German stream, were patriotic and historical pioneering works contributing to the cultural nationalism of German humanism and the Reformation. Peter Schott was the granduncle and Wimpheling the teacher of Jacob Sturm, a leading Protestant councillor in Strasbourg. At Heidelberg Wimpheling's paths crossed those of Rudolf Agricola the so-called "father of German humanism."

Agricola (1444–1485) stands at the border between the early phases of humanism and the high generation of humanists. If he had lived longer than the forty-one years allotted him, he might well have been the acknowledged leader of German humanism at high tide. He had a direct personal influence on the younger men and his major work on rhetoric was republished often during the sixteenth century and was influential from Italy to England. "It was Rudolf Agricola," Erasmus wrote, "who first brought with him from Italy some gleam of a better literature."[54] Agricola wrote a life of Petrarch to honor the "father and restorer of good arts," and many humanists considered the Dutch humanist the Petrarch of the North. He was educated at St. Martin's school in Groningen, Erfurt, and Louvain, and then spent ten years in Pavia and Ferrara. Returning to the North in 1479 he found that he "froze after the sun." After three years in Groningen he accepted the patronage of Elector Philip of the Palatinate and spent the last three years of his life in Heidelberg in close touch with the circle of Bishop Johannes von Dalberg, whom he accompanied on a trip to Rome to congratulate Innocent VIII on his election to the papacy. Agricola was a reticent author and his greatest impact was perhaps through the people such as Conrad Celtis, whom he inspired. His *De Formando Studio* laid out a humanist educational plan along the lines of Vergerio, Bruni or Vittorino's educational philosophy. His Christmas oration of 1484 and his *Exhortatio ad clerum Wormatiensen*[55] leave no doubt as to his deep and orthodox Christian faith.

---

[54] "Letter to Joannus Botzhemius," Erasmus, *Opera,* I (Leiden, 1703), front matter.

[55] Lewis W. Spitz and Anna Benjamin, "Rudolph Agricola's *Exhortatio ad clerum Wormatiensen,*" *Archive for Reformation History,* LIV (1963), 1–15. Johannes Janssen, *Geschichte des deutschen Volkes seit dem Ausgang des Mittelalters,* I, 1. abt., 4, A (Freiburg i. B., 1876), 51, already pointed to Agricola's religiosity, for he

His major work was an introductory manual for teachers in the arts course, *De Inventione Dialectica,* in which he taught the function of logic in marshalling arguments, *ars inveniendi,* useful in rhetoric which by effective style produces conviction and action, *ars iudicandi.* [56] He presents two dozen topics, grounds for proofs, indicates how they are to be used, and demonstrates how rhetoric helps to achieve conviction in the hearer. The work is highly eclectic and draws materials from the entire Greek and Latin rhetorical tradition. It was translated into Italian, summarized in a handbook, republished often, and was particularly influential in England.

In the historical introduction to his *Ausführliche Redekunst,* Johann Christoph Gottsched described Friedrich Riedrer's *Spiegel der waren rhetoric, Usz Marco Tulio Cicerone, und andern getütsche* (Strassburg, 1509) as the first German rhetoric, first published in 1493, combining the medieval *ars dictaminis* teaching with ancient rhetoric. These books of rhetoric and epistelography remained popular throughout the sixteenth century and into the age of the baroque, when Johann Meyfart's *Teutsche Rhetorica* (1634) proved to be very popular. But Agricola's *De Inventione* towered above them all not only because it was in Latin, but because Philipp Melanchthon drew his own highly influential rhetorical teaching from the work and inspiration of Agricola, and he became *the praeceptor Germaniae.* Agricola marked the end of the preparatory stages and the advent of the mature generation of German humanism.

### III. THE HIGH GENERATION

"I congratulate myself often on living in this glorious century in which so many remarkable men have arisen in Germany!" exclaimed

---

was even at one time pointed toward the priesthood, but it is absurd to suggest that anyone would necessarily be dependent upon Janssen for such an obvious fact about Agricola, least of all anyone familiar with the fervor of the *Exhortatio.*

[56] The best assessment of Agricola's place-logic is that of Walter Ong, S.J., *Ramus, Method, and the Decay of Dialogue* (Cambridge, MA, 1958), 92–130. Neal W. Gilbert, *Renaissance Concepts of Method* (New York, 1960), 117 *et passim* places Agricola's rhetoric within the general context of Renaissance discussions of method.

Nikolaus Gerbellius in 1507.[57] The two decades following the turn of the century, 1500–1520, marked a special period in the course of German humanism. The preliminary steps had been taken in many fields of learning. Humanism was ensconced in episcopal and princely courts, in cities, and now in the universities as well. The Reformation was not yet underway. The humanists of this generation were devoted to three purposes, the further cultivation of the classics, the development of national culture and German freedom from foreign domination, and religious enlightenment. Nearly all parts of the Empire from Alsace to Silesia were involved in the movement, but there were four particularly vital centers which served as foci and intersections of the humanist cross currents, Heidelberg, Vienna, Nuremberg and Erfurt.

The key figure in the Heidelberg circle was Bishop Johannes von Dalberg (1455–1503). His connections with Agricola, Wimpheling, Conrad Celtis, Johannes Reuchlin and a host of lesser men such as Dietrich von Pleningen (ca. 1420–1520), counselor to the Elector of the Palatinate and later to the Duke of Bavaria, who devoted himself to Seneca, made Dalberg an important force in the promotion of humanism.

The brightest planet to wander across the Heidelberg scene was Conrad Celtis (1459–1508), whom Friedrich von Bezold dubbed the "German arch-humanist." Celtis was the best lyric poet among the German humanists, and was crowned by Emperor Frederick III as the first German poet laureate upon the citadel at Nuremberg, April 18, 1487. His ambition was to be remembered as the German Horace. "Oh sacred and mighty works of the poets, you alone free all things from fate and lift up mortal ashes to the stars!" he exclaimed.[58] Born in 1459 as the son of a peasant, Celtis ran away to school in Cologne, then moved to Heidelberg, known for its humanist learning, to Rostock, and to Leipzig. In 1487 he made a quick trip to Italy, seeing Venice, Padua, Bologna, Florence, and Rome. Angered at the airs of superiority of the Italians he hurried north to Cracow, Nuremberg, and Ingolstadt, where he taught as a frequently truant professor of rhetoric. At last he

---

[57] The basic book on Gerbellius remains Wilhelm Horning, *Der Humanist Dr. Nikolaus Gerbel, Förderer lutherischer Reformation in Strassburg (1485–1560)* (Strassburg, 1918).

[58] *Quattuor Libri Amorum*, II, 9, lines 153f.

accepted the invitation of Emperor Maximilian to the University of Vienna in 1497, and there he founded the College of Poets and Mathematicians. He lies buried beneath the short tower of St. Stephen's Cathedral. To say that Celtis was the best poet among the German humanists is both to pay him tribute and to define the modest achievements of German humanism in poetry. In his *Amores* he celebrated in four books four of his loves symbolizing the four parts of Germany. In his *Odes* he rose occasionally to lofty levels in writing of love, life, and learning. His *Epigrams* were pungent and pointed. He called the Germans to cultural rivalry with the Italians and stirred up their national spirit. In 1500 he published a student edition of Tacitus's *Germania*. His descriptive book *Nuremberg* was to serve as an example for contributors from all parts of Germany to the *Germania Illustrata,* and his *Germania Generalis* was intended to be a preliminary to the large topo-historical work on the Empire. In his *Inaugural Address* at Ingolstadt he called on the youth of Germany to take up the cultural rivalry with the Italians. Celtis organized Rhenish and Danubian sodalities of friends of humanism and encouraged the organization of many local sodalities to sponsor humanist writings and to carry out with local topo-historical descriptions the complete *Germania Illustrata,* modelled after Flavio Biondo's *Italia Illustrata*. Celtis's role as promoter of humanist culture was perhaps his greatest contribution.[59]

---

[59] For Celtis, see Lewis W. Spitz, *Conrad Celtis the German Arch-Humanist* (Cambridge, MA, 1957). The most exciting development in Celtis studies is the preparation by Dieter Wuttke, Klaus Arnold and others of a new scholarly edition of his works, superseding the various editions in the *Bibliotheca Scriptorum Medii Recentisque Aevorum,* ed. years ago by Ladislaus Juhász. Wuttke has found the manuscript prepared for use by the printer of Celtis's five books of epigrams; Arnold is working on a new edition of the *Norimberga*. See Dieter Wuttke, "Unbekannte Celtis-Epigramme zum Lobe Dürers," *Zeitschrift für Kunstgeschichte,* XXX (1967), 321–325; "Zur griechischen Grammatik des Konrad Celtis," *Silvae. Festschrift für Ernst Zinn zum 60. Geburtstag* (Tübingen, 1970), 289–303. Recent articles include Kurt Adel, "Konrad Celtis und Wien," *Österreich in Geschichte und Literatur,* X (1966), 237–244; Joseph Arno von Bradish, *Von Walther von der Vogelweide bis Anton Wildgans. Aufsätze und Vorträge aus fünf Jahrzehnten* (Vienna, 1965), 33–48: "Der 'Erzhumanist' Celtes und das Wiener 'Dichter-Kollegium'"; 49–62: "Dichterkrönungen im Wien des Humanismus."

It was Maximilian I who invited Celtis to Vienna, the emperor who was the patron and darling of the humanists. Maximilian is habitually referred to in the literature as "der letzte Ritter," as though he were the last in a long line of important and frivolous rulers. Perhaps Johan Huizinga's picture of the decaying Burgundian court has been transferred, via the marriage with Mary, to the Habsburg court. But his talent for self-projection, his flair for the dramatic, his interest in art and letters—even to the point of commissioning Dürer to do the "Arch of Triumph" and of becoming personally involved in the *Heldenbuch,* the poetic allegory *Theuerdank* and the *Weiskunig,* which related his own daring deeds—his love for lavish display, and his respect for men of learning and support of the university, all suggest that he should really be considered the first in a long line of Renaissance rulers in the North whose lifestyle resembled that of the Italian princes, who played their role on a smaller stage. Maximilian made Vienna one of the lively centers of Renaissance culture in the early sixteenth century.[60]

Having followed Celtis down the Danube to Maximilian's Vienna we must return now to the upper Rhineland to take up the story there once again. The most intriguing friend of Celtis in that area was the learned and mysterious friend, Johannes Trithemius (1462–1516), Benedictine Abbot of Sponheim from 1506 on at Würzburg. A contemporary admirer, Arnold Wion, hailed him as the *orbis miraculum ac totius arca sapientiae,* though posterity has remembered him more for his association with the mysterious Dr. Faustus, who visited Sponheim, for

---

[60] The first volume of a projected four-volume biography of Maximilian I has appeared. Hermann Wiesflecker, *Kaiser Maximilian I. Das Reich Österreich und Europa an der Wende zur Neuzeit,* I: *Jugend, burgundisches Erbe und Römisches Königtum bis zur Alleinherrschaft, 1450–1493* (Munich, 1971), emphasizing the political, economic, and social forces within which Maximilian developed. On the Renaissance in Vienna, see Otto Rommel, ed., *Wiener Renaissance* (Vienna and Zurich, 1947); Conradin Bonorand, "Die Bedeutung der Universität Wien für Humanismus und Reformation, insbesondere der Ostschweiz," *Zwingliana,* XII (1965), 162–180; Peter von Baldass, *et al., Renaissance in Österreich* (Vienna, 1966). Harold Jantz, *op. cit.* 411–412, argues that Maximilian was the first of a new Renaissance order represented in Lodovico Ariosto's *Orlando Furioso,* which made use of the *Heldenbuch,* in Torquato Tasso's *Gerusalemme Liberata* (1581), Spenser's *Faerie Queene* (1590–96), and the like.

his pious frauds, and for his friends in the Rhenish sodality. He was a monastic figure, a theological writer, a bibliophile, a historian, a hagiographer, the first theoretician of cryptography, and diligent epistelographer. But he also wrote in a monotonous style, was a dilettante though erudite, was fascinated with witchcraft, black magic, and demonology, and readily fabricated sources for the early history of the Benedictines and carried the Habsburg genealogy back to the Trojans. He wrote of himself in a fragmentary autobiography, *Nepiachus,* "quicquid in mundo scibile est, scire semper cupiebam... Sed non erat in mea facultate satisfacere, ut voluissem, desiderio." Trithemius collected a great library of over two thousand volumes and a hundred Greek books. His *De scriptoribus ecclesiasticis* presented a bibliography of 963 authors. In his *Catalogus illustrium vivorum Germaniae,* written on Wimpheling's urging, he made his contribution to cultural nationalism. Even his fabrications, Hunibald and the Meginfrid, were related to this patriotic impulse.[61]

Humanist historical writings developed gradually during the fifteenth century out of roots in the medieval chronicles. The work of Felix Fabri (ca. 1441–1502) was still very much a part of ecclesiastical culture. Sigismund Meisterlin did an Augsburg chronicle (1456) and some thirty years later a Nuremberg chronicle. He showed historical critical sense, rejecting, for example, the myth of the Trojan origins of the Swabians. Lorenz Blumenau, who died in 1484, as the historian of the Teutonic Knights was influenced by Italian humanism, as was Matthias von Kemnat, the historian of Frederick the Victorious. But the most notable German historical production of the fifteenth century was the rightly renowned *Weltchronik* (1493), which was published in Latin and German by Hartmann Schedel, who was influenced by his uncle Hermann and his teacher Peter Luder in the direction of humanism. It

---

[61] Klaus Arnold, *Johannes Trithemius,* cited in note 25 above, is detailed, thorough, sound, and vastly superior to older biographies such as Oliver Legipont's *Vita* (1754) or Isidor Silbernagl's *Johannes Trithemius* (1868, 1885). It is reviewed by Ulrich Bubenheimer, *Zeitschrift der Savigny-Stiftung für Rechtsgeschichte, Germanistische Abteilung,* LXXXIX (1972), 455–459. Bubenheimer has contributed an interesting bit of new information on Trithemius's use of medieval sources, "Der Aufenthalt Burchards von Worms im Kloster Lobbes als Erfindung des Johannes Trithemius," in the same journal, vol. LXXXIX (1972), 320–337.

became the most famous of the topographical historical works at which the Germans excelled.[62] The Renaissance myths of origins so prevalent in their works and only partially rejected were largely medieval in origin, but the humanist historians organized them and sought coherence. Later the Reformation historians, Carion, Melanchthon, Sebastian Franck, John Sleidan and others, were to make further critical progress but also to give a new theological dimension to their reading of history.[63]

The histories of the sixteenth century show a marked maturation. Johann Turmair or Aventinus (1477–1534) on the encouragement of Duke William IV wrote *The Annals of Bavaria* (1521).[64] In Nuremberg the patrician Willibald Pirckheimer (1470–1528), a friend of Celtis and Albrecht Dürer, presided over humanist intellectual life. When his learned father Johann sent Willibald off to study in Italian universities he gave him this advice:

Audias lectiones in studiis humanitatis.
Item, ubi private leguntur et fit contributio.
Discas carmine facere.

He took the advice and studied both law and the classics in Italy. He could read and write Greek as well as Latin. He composed a history of

---

[62] Gerald Strauss, *Sixteenth-Century Germany: Its Topography and Topographers* (Madison, WI, 1959). On humanist historiography the old classics are still of great value. Paul Joachimsen, *Die humanistische Geschichtsschreibung in Deutschland,* I: *Die Anfänge. Sigismund Meisterlin* (Bonn, 1895); and his *Geschichtsauffassung und Geschichtsschreibung in Deutschland unter dem Einfluß des Humanismus* (Leipzig and Berlin, 1910).

[63] See the outstanding volume by Frank L. Borchardt, *German Antiquity in Renaissance Myth* (Baltimore, 1971); and his articles, "The Topos of Critical Rejection in the Renaissance," *Modern Language Notes,* LXXXI (1966), 476–488; "Etymology in Tradition and in the Northern Renaissance," *Journal of the History of Ideas,* XXIX (1968), 415–429. For a review of Borchardt's book, see *Speculum,* XLVIII (1973), 733–736.

[64] Gerald Strauss, *Historian in an Age of Crisis: The Life and Work of Johannes Aventinus, 1477–1534* (Cambridge, MA, 1963).

42

the Swabian-Swiss war in which he had participated, in the humanist and classical tradition of doing contemporary history.[65]

The collection of historical sources and artifacts became a passion, as it had with Italians such as Cyriaco de' Pizzicolli of Ancona or Giovanni Aurispa. In Augsburg the city secretary Conrad Peutinger (1465–1547), who became a counselor of Maximilian I, was a highly influential legist and humanist. While a law student in Italy he became a devotee of classical learning. He collected art work, ancient coins, and classical manuscripts. Celtis presented to him the famous *Tabula Peutingeriana*, a military map of the Roman Empire.[66] A full discussion of humanist historiography would have to include the names of Albert Krantz, Nauclerus and Irenicus, and others. Historical writing, moving away from the medieval universal or world chronicle, became a vehicle for the expression of German cultural interest, inspired in part by the republication of Tacitus's *Germania*, altered then by the Reformation's reemphasis on the importance of ecclesiastical history.

This generation of mature humanism experienced the impact of Italian Neoplatonism. Just as Italian humanism went through its various literary and civic phases culminating in (or retreating to?) the Platonic revival in the second half of the *quattrocento*, so German humanism moved from a classical literary phase into a cultural nationalist and religious enlightenment phase, which included a substantial

---

[65] Willehad Paul Eckert and Christoph von Imhoff, *Willibald Pirckheimer Dürers Freund im Spiegel seines Lebens, seiner Werke und seiner Umwelt* (Cologne, 1971), 138–172: "Schweizerkrieg." Johann's counsel is to be found in *Willibald Pirckheimers Briefwechsel*, Emil Reicke, ed., I (Munich, 1940), 29. See Hans Rupprich, "Pirckheimers Elegie auf den Tod Dürers," *Anzeiger der Phil.-hist. Klasse der österreichischen Akademie der Wissenschaften* (1956), no. 9, 136–150. The best succinct portrayal of Pirckheimer's intellectual and personal essence is that of Hans Rupprich, "Willibald Pirckheimer. Beiträge zu einer Wesenserfassung," *Schweizer Beiträge zur Allgemeinen Geschichte*, XV (1957), 64–110. See the charming commemorative volume of sources and essays, *Willibald Pirkheimer 1470/1970 Dokumente Studien Perspektiven Anläßlich den 500. Geburtsjahres herausgegeben von Willibald-Pirkheimer-Kuratorium* (Nuremberg, 1970).

[66] Heinrich Lutz, *Conrad Peutinger. Beiträge zu einer politischen Biographie* (Augsburg, 1958).

Neoplatonic component.⁶⁷ Giles of Viterbo, general of the Augustinian order, knew Marsilio Ficino in Florence and very probably saw Martin Luther on his 1510–1511 trip to Rome. He believed that the triumph of Platonic theology marked the return to a golden age. He was familiar with Pico's interpretations of the Cabala and corresponded with Johannes Reuchlin about the Cabala. His opening oration at the Fifth Lateran Council called for reform—men must be changed by religion, not religion by men. In his own person Giles linked together the worlds of Italian and northern humanism, of Renaissance and Reformation.⁶⁸ He is representative of many major Italian figures with close contacts with the Germans. The most popular of the Italian humanists among the Germans, judging impressionistically from the frequency of citation, were Valla, Ficino, Pico, and Baptista Mantuanus.

Ficino was respectful of the northerners and maintained personal contacts with various northern men of letters. He welcomed many to Florence, who came to see him or stopped on the way to Rome. In March, 1482, he welcomed a delegation of Duke Eberhard of Württemberg which included Johannes Reuchlin, Gabriel Biel, Ludwig Vergenhans, and Matthias Preninger, a canon lawyer. Ficino corresponded with Reuchlin, Vergenhans, and Preninger. Many young Germans interested in Greek learning came to Ficino for inspiration. Georg Herivart of Augsburg in later years cherished the memory of his visit with him in Florence. At Basel Paulus Niavus, the "German Filelfo," expounded on Ficino's writings. Konrad Pellikan was inspired by Ficino and Pico, whose interest in Hebrew led Pellikan to do the first guide to Hebrew studies in the North, *De modo legendi et intelligendi Hebraeum* (1501), before Reuchlin's *Rudimenta hebraica*. Froben and Auerbach published various works of Ficino. Among the northern humanists with a keen interest in Ficino's philosophy were Nicolaus Gerbel and Nicolaus Ellenbogen, a Benedictine prior who published an anthology from Plato, Peutinger, Celtis, Pirckheimer, Albrecht Dürer,

---

⁶⁷ Lewis W. Spitz, "The *Theologia Platonica* in the Religious Thought of the German Humanists," *Middle Ages—Reformation Volkskumde. Festschrift for John G. Kunstmann* (Chapel Hill, 1959), 118–133.

⁶⁸ John W. O'Malley, S.J., *Giles of Viterbo on Church and Reform, Studies in Medieval and Reformation Thought,* V (Leiden, 1968), 5, 8, 139.

44

Mutianus Rufus, Beatus Rhenanus, Trithemius, Agrippa of Nettesheim and many other figures of the Reformation generation, notably Zwingli.

Pico's influence among the Germans was almost as powerful as that of Ficino. His theses on the Cabala and his stress on the importance of Hebrew letters were of critical importance for Christian Hebraism throughout the century, especially for Johannes Reuchlin. Moreover, Pico's philosophical goal of doing a grand synthesis of Plato and Aristotle appealed to the harmonizers such as Philipp Melanchthon, who once wrote, "Let us love both Plato and Aristotle." His defence of scholastic philosophy also found a sympathetic response in the North. His nephew Giovanni Francesco Pico spent years of exile in the Empire and became an intimate friend of German humanists and reformers. The knowledge of Hebrew was given added impetus by the Protestant emphasis on the importance of the biblical languages. By the end of the sixteenth century a knowledge of all three languages, Latin, Greek, and Hebrew, the triple linguistic tiara, was a very common achievement in the learned world. The importance of the Cabala, itself heavy with Neoplatonic philosophy, can best be seen in the thought of Johannes Reuchlin.

Johannes Reuchlin (1455–1522) studied at various northern universities. He read Cusanus and learned to know Ficino and Pico, as we have seen, on two trips to Italy. He served as chancellor to the duke of Württemberg for many years and his last years taught at Ingolstadt and Tübingen universities. Reuchlin believed that the most ancient wisdom was to be found in the Hebrew Cabala. Hebrew was more ancient than Greek, Moses centuries earlier than the Greek philosophers. He believed that Moses and the prophets had transmitted divine truths orally through the seventy wise men in a continuous tradition until they were embodied in the Jewish Cabala. "Marsilius produced Plato for Italy. Lefèvre d'Etaples restored Aristotle to France. I shall complete the number and… show to the Germans Pythagoras reborn through me!" he exclaimed. He believed the Cabalistic number-mysticism was related to the Pythagorean belief in the mysterious power and quality of numbers. In his works *De Verbo Mirifico* and the *De Arte Cabalistica* he sought to demonstrate that Cabalism and

Pythagoreanism harmonized with Christian revelation and that Cabalistic messianism supported the Christian doctrine of the incarnation.[69]

It is ironic that this Christian apologist who in his later years even stood firmly against the Reformation should have become the target of a ferocious assault by obscurantists. In 1506 a converted Jew named Pfefferkorn wrote A *Mirror for Jews* on the dangers of Hebrew books and argued for their confiscation. The Dominicans of the University of Cologne backed his demand. In 1509 Emperor Maximilian issued a decree ordering the Jews to turn in their books. Reuchlin ventured the opinion that Hebrew books should not be destroyed and thereby attracted to himself the lightning of Pfefferkorn who assaulted him with an outrageous pamphlet *The Hand Mirror*. Reuchlin detested controversy but replied in his own defense with *The Eye Mirror* and published a volume of testimonials in his behalf, *Letters of Famous Men*. The affair smoldered on and finally in 1520 the pope condemned Reuchlin's *The Eye Mirror*. Reuchlin's comment on Luther when the Reformation exploded was "God be praised that now the monks have found someone else who will give them more to do than I."[70]

---

[69] For a fuller account, see Spitz, *The Religious Renaissance of the German Humanists*, 61–80: "Pythagoras reborn." For a fine appreciation, see the commemorative volume, *Reden und Ansprachen im Reuchlinjahr 1955* (Pforzheim, 1956); and *Johannes Reuchlin 1455–1522. Festgabe seiner Vaterstadt Pforzheim* (Pforzheim, n.d.). The scholarly world awaits the new eleven-volume edition of Reuchlin's *Sämtliche Werke*, edited by Hermann Greive, *et al.*, to be published by De Gruyter, Berlin, beginning with vol. 5 in 1975.

[70] James H. Overfield, *Humanism and Scholasticism in Late Medieval Germany* (Princeton University Press, 1984), chapter 8, studies it against the background of the classical humanism-scholasticism conflict, arguing that the scholastics were not so actively opposed to humanism as the humanists and reformers alleged. Werner L. Gundersheimer, "Erasmus, Humanism and the Christian Cabala," *Journal of the Warburg and Courtauld Institutes,* XXVI (1963), 38–52, comments on the irony that Erasmus viewed the Cabala, i.e., Jewish anti-scholasticism, as more dangerous to Christendom than Scotism. That is to say, while Erasmus did not deny that cabalism had a well-established claim for scholarly attention, within the *letter* of humanism, he nonetheless felt that it was altogether antithetical to the *spirit* of his approach to learning. Clearly a mere scholastic vs. humanist antithesis is too simple a formula to catch all the counter-currents in the situation.

46

The Reuchlin controversy galvanized into action Ulrich von Hutten, Crotus Rubeanus, and a phalanx of young humanists ready for the fray. Two strains came together in their polemic in behalf of Reuchlin, the critical and partially skeptical wit of Lucian and the spirit of cultural nationalism. As a knight Hutten belonged to a class that was rapidly losing its social utility and this loss of purpose played a role in Hutten's acerbic psychological set. Born in the fortress of Steckelberg, he was sent at the age of eleven to the monastery at Fulda. But at seventeen he fled, studied at Cologne, Erfurt, and Frankfurt an der Oder, where he took his A.B., then wandered on to Leipzig, Greifswald, and Rostock. He devoted his life to poetics and polemics, excoriating the exploitation of the Germans by the Roman church, criticizing abuses, and stirring up the young to rival the Italians. The Reuchlin controversy was made to order for his polemical talents and in the *Letters of Obscure Men* he and Crotus Rubeanus published a devastating satire on the "obscurantists" of Cologne, addressing to them fake letters designed to mock their ignorance.[71] In 1517 he published an edition of Valla's *On the Donation of Constantine,* which proved so shocking to Luther. In his last years Hutten threw himself into the Reformation controversy with all the strength remaining. In a letter to Pope Leo X in December, 1520, he concluded with the biblical phrase: "Let us break their chains asunder and cast their yoke from us." He was too ill to play an active role in the Knights' Revolt of 1522 and died in August, 1523; he lies buried on the island of Ufenau where his grave was rediscovered only a few years ago. Both Hutten and Crotus Rubeanus had close ties to Mutianus Rufus, the canon of Gotha, who presided over the Erfurt school of humanists.

---

[71] Thomas W. Best, *The Humanist Ulrich von Hutten. A Reappraisal of His Humor* (Chapel Hill, 1969); and Alga Gewerstock, *Lukian und Hutten. Zur Geschichte des Dialogs im 16. Jahrhundert* (Berlin, 1924, 1967). Walther Brecht explored the problem of authorship, *Die Verfasser der Epistolae Obscurorum Virorum* (Strassburg, 1904). Cf. Robert Herndon Fife, "Ulrich von Hutten as a Literary Problem," *Germanic Review*, XXIII (1948), 18–29. The best biography remains Hajo Holborn, *Ulrich von Hutten and the German Reformation* (New Haven, 1937), which superseded David Friedrich Strauss, *Ulrich von Hutten* (Leipzig, 1914; originally, 1871).

Erfurt was the first university in central and northern Germany to introduce humanist studies into its curriculum, and it was at Erfurt that the first books in that region containing Greek type were printed.[72] The university played a pivotal role in the development of humanism in the entire North and Northeast and was of critical importance for the Reformation because of Luther's study at Erfurt and the many close ties to Wittenberg. Hutten's co-author Crotus Rubeanus studied there and served as rector in 1520–1521. He and a university delegation of forty or more people met Luther at the city gates on the way to his ordeal at the Diet of Worms. He declared Luther to be the "judge of evil to see whose features is like a divine appearance." Eobanus Hessus, the young Erfurt poet, who became the leading poet among the evangelicals called out: "Rejoice, exalted Erfurt, crown thyself... for behold, he comes who will free you from disgrace."

The literary arbiter and key personality among the Erfurt humanists was the highly intellectual canon at nearby Gotha, Conrad Mutianus Rufus (1471–1526). From 1503 on Mutian was the leader of the humanists in Erfurt. Georg Spalatin was perhaps the first of his disciples, followed by Petreius Aperbacchus and Eobanus Hessus. From 1505–1506 an ever growing number of Erfurt students came to Mutian in Gotha for instruction and comradery, for he was now a canon at St. Mary's. Over the door of his house he had the words *Beata tranquillitas,* an epicurean haven, for as he wrote, "Tranquillitas dat vires ingenio." He was such a perfectionist and so tentative in his speculations that he wrote one book, a manuscript on rhetoric which Melanchthon declined to publish in later years because of its neglect of Greek rhetorical sources. His influence was rather, like that of Agricola, through the impact of his own person on his many pupils. Over six hundred letters survive from the years 1502 to 1525, despite his repeated admonition to Urban, a young Cistercian monk in the monastery of Georgenthal and his confidant, to tear up or burn letters compromising for their radical

---

[72] Gustav Bauch, *Die Universität Erfurt im Zeitalter des Frühhumanismus* (Breslau, 1904) corrected the excessive enthusiasm and claims of F.W. Kampschulte's *Die Universität Erfurt in ihren Verhältnissen zu dem Humanismus und der Reformation,* 2 vols. (Trier, 1858). Erich Kleineidam, "Die Universität Erfurt in den Jahren 1501–1505," *Reformata Reformanda. Festgabe für Hubert Jedin,* 2 vols. (Münster, 1965), I, 142–195.

religious ideas. His influence in terms of caustic wit and acerbic commentary on abuses in the church was very pronounced on Hutten and Crotus Rubeanus, although scholars have long known that he did not himself personally contribute to the *Epistolae obscurorum virorum*.[73]

This remarkable man was born as Konrad Muth (Mutian) in Homberg, Hesse, the son of a prosperous patrician and a mother of noble family, which may have contributed to his aristocratic and elitist attitude toward the masses. As a red-headed boy (Rufus) he studied under Alexander Hegius at Deventer at the same time as Erasmus. At Erfurt he heard Celtis lecture on rhetoric and poetry, shortly after Celtis left Heidelberg in 1486 after the death of Agricola. Mutian spent seven years in Italy, 1495–1502, where he was completely won over by the Neoplatonism of Ficino and the eclectic thought of Pico. He was intrigued by late classical learning including religious mysteries and occult lore, devoting himself to the *studia humanitatis* for enjoyment not for professional advantage; "frui, non uti," as he put it. Though he became *doctor decretorum* in Ferrara, he was to choose a quiet life living on a small prebend as a canon rather than the pressures of the active life or the university. He brought from Italy a genuine enthusiasm for classical antiquity, which he apostrophized as a "virgo nubilis et formosa," a strong skeptical streak, and a bent for religious and philosophical speculation, for he considered himself to be a "priest both of Christ and of philosophy." His *religio docta* was universalistic, for he believed that there was *una religio in varietate rituum*. Like Ficino he compared the life of Christ with that of Apollonius of Tyana, for he had available Philostratus in the Aldine edition of 1504. In his private letters to Urban he denied that Christ was crucified in the flesh and held a "docetist" view of Christ as righteousness, love, and spirit rather than God truly incarnate. In some of his more extreme passages in which he confided arcane truths to Urban he described nature as a goddess in pantheistic phrases reminiscent of Celtis's nature enthusiasm. In August, 1505, he wrote to Urban, "Est unus Deus et una Dea... Sed haec cave ennuncies!" It is "our goddess the earth" who is "omnipares mater, augusta regia, diva, sanctissima." The many names for God and divine men, Jupiter, Sol, Apollo, Moses, Christ, Luna, Ceres, Proserpina, Tellus,

---

[73] Walter Brecht, *Die Verfasser der Epistulae Obscurorum Virorum* (Strassburg, 1904), 4ff.; A. Bömer, ed., *Epistolae obscurorum virorum,* I (Heidelberg, 1924).

Maria, are not only *nomina* of the nature-God, but also her *numina*. The sun is the "verus totius mundi animus." He is glad to be alive just as a man, wordly styles and titles aside. These excursions into natural religion (non-revelatory, non-Biblical, not exclusively Christian) were as radical as German humanism became. The ideas were clearly derivative from Florentine currents and their Neoplatonic and late classical antique sources. There is no reason to believe on the basis of his hints of dark secrets and admonitions to discretion that he had access to an arcane philosophy beyond these derivative notions from known sources. Nor did he develop these radical ideas into a systematic or coherent unified philosophy or natural theology. He seemed to be too uncertain or insecure to organize such thoughts into a coherent system, and they remained almost more poetic expressions than a philosophy, though he wished to be a philosopher rather than a poet. As a complex human being he held disparate ideas to be true on different levels. He was psychologically so bound by the received tradition and his clerical calling that he repeatedly took recourse to Christian piety, and did not merely return to Catholic orthodoxy in his old age. He preferred St. Paul's epistles to the gospels, but his "Platonic" exegesis was a far cry from the Paulinism of that Augustinian professor at Wittenberg, who studied at Erfurt after Mutian's departure.[74]

One of the pioneers of humanist learning at Erfurt and at Wittenberg was Nicolaus Marschalk (1470–1525), who studied at Louvain and Heidelberg, and matriculated at Erfurt, where he studied with Mutian, taking an A.B. in 1492 and an M.A. in 1496.[75] He published a

---

[74] See the scintillating pages of Heinz Otto Burger, *op. cit.*, 362–366, Willy Andreas, *op. cit.*, 518–520, Aufklärische Religionsphilosophie des Mutianus Rufus; Fritz Halbauer, *Mutianus Rufus und seine geistesgeschichtliche Stellung, Beiträge zur Kulturgeschichte des Mittelalters und der Renaissance*, 38 (1929); F.W. Krapp, *Der Erfurter Mutiankreis and seine Auswirkungen* (diss., Cologne, 1954); Lewis W. Spitz, *The Religious Renaissance of the German Humanists*, 130–154.

[75] Edgar C. Reinke and Gottfried G. Krodel, eds., *Nicolai Marscali Thurii Oratio habita albiori academia in Alemania iam nuperrima ad promotionem primorum baccalauriorum numero quattuor et viginti anno domin mcccciii* (St. Louis, 1967), 3–26 (introduction), 27–55 (text and translation). See also Gustav Bauch, "Wolfgang Schenk und Nikolaus Marschalk," *Zentralblatt für Bibliothekswesen*, XII (1895), 354–409.

comparative study of Greek and Latin, *Orthographia*, a *Grammatica exegetica,* and a *Laus musarum,* printed on his own press. In the winter of 1502 he accepted Elector Frederick's call to the new University of Wittenberg, and there in 1504 he became *utriusque iuris doctor,* teaching in the liberal arts faculty while he studied law. On January 18, 1503, he delivered the commencement address for Wittenberg's inaugural session in which he praised classical studies for the foundation which they provide for the development of sound moral character. Marschalk moved on from Wittenberg, but his humanist influence lasted on. His pupil, Johannes Lang at Erfurt, gave Luther his earliest classical training. At Wittenberg between 1512 and 1517 Luther's interest in Latin, Greek, Hebrew, and the natural sciences as necessary subjects of study for well-educated clergy grew to the point that he led the way in the humanistic reform of the university. In 1510 Otto Beckmann delivered an oration at Wittenberg *In laudem philosophiae ac humaniorum literarum* and became a strong advocate of humanistic studies. It was to this Beckmann that Melanchthon dedicated his own inaugural address in 1518, *De corrigendis adolescentiae studiis.* So closely was the development of humanism at Erfurt and at Wittenberg interwoven.

One giant figure looms above the heads of all the German humanists of this high Renaissance generation, Desiderius Erasmus of Rotterdam, whose brilliant intellect dominated much of the intellectual life in the Empire from 1500 to 1520 and who lived in Basel and Freiburg for fourteen years. The Netherlands were still nominally part of the Empire, and Erasmus like Agricola and Hegius spoke of *Germania nostra* and spoke of "us" and "our people" with reference to the low Germans in general. He was important for the major humanist figures and reformers alike, be it Wimpheling, Pirckheimer, Reuchlin, Hutten, Mutian, Zwingli, or Melanchthon.[76] For no one, however, did Erasmus play a more

---

[76] The discussion of Erasmus must be reserved to the section on Dutch humanism, but a few particularly relevant and recent titles may be cited here: J. Beumer, "Erasmus von Rotterdam und sein Verhältnis zu dem deutschen Humanismus mit besonderer Rücksicht auf die Konfessionellen Gegensätze," *Scrinium Erasmianum,* I, ed. J. Coppers (Leiden, 1969), 165–201; E.W. Kohls, "Erasmus und die werdende evangelische Bewegung des 16. Jahrhunderts," *ibid,* 203–219; Augustin Renaudet, *Érasme et l'Italie* (Geneva, 1954); Gerhard Ritter,

important role than for Luther, for thanks to Erasmus he was able to make clear exactly where the line was to be drawn between the *philosophia Christi* and the *theologia crucis et passionis.*

## IV. HUMANISM DURING THE REFORMATION ERA

Luther considered the Renaissance revival of learning a happy development preceding the coming of the Reformation just as John the Baptist once heralded the coming of Christ. Humanism made the Reformation possible, for the knowledge of the languages, the critical handling of sources, the attack on abuses, the national feeling, the war on scholasticism, and an army of young humanists who rallied to the evangelical cause were indispensable preconditions for the success of the Reformation. The Reformation in turn contributed to the continuity, the broadening of influence, the increase in classical learning, and the perpetuation of many humanist values into later centuries. A broad chasm did indeed separate evangelical theology from the religious assumptions of the classical world and from Christian humanism in the area of soteriology, in the sin/grace, law/gospel antinomies. But the reformers viewed worldly culture also as a "sphere of faith's works" and were for the most part strong advocates of humanist learning, specifically in the universities and in the newly founded secondary schools. They broadened the base of learning by insisting upon a humanist curriculum on the arts level, on compulsory universal education for boys and girls, and upon the calling of the teacher as a lofty divine vocation.

---

*Erasmus and der Deutsche Humanistenkreis am Oberrhein* (Freiburg i. B., 1937); James D. Tracy, "Erasmus Becomes a German," *Renaissance Quarterly,* XXI, (1968), 281–288; James D. Tracy, *Erasmus. The Growth of a Mind* (Geneva, 1972); Roland H. Bainton, *Erasmus of Christendom* (New York, 1969); Brian Gerrish, ed., *Reformers in Profile* (Philadelphia, 1967), 60–85; Richard L. DeMolen, *Erasmus of Rotterdam. A Quincentennial Symposium* (New York, 1971); John C. Olin, *et alii,* eds., *Luther, Erasmus and the Reformation. A Catholic-Protestant Reappraisal* (New York, 1969); Georges Chantraine, S.J., *"Mystère" et "Philosophie du Christ" selon Érasme* (Namur and Gembloux, 1971).

Italian humanism also played a role in Wittenberg indirectly and directly.[77] Elector Frederick the Wise was determined to ornament his "Sparta" not only with new buildings such as the Castle and Castle church in Wittenberg or with the artistic work of Dürer, Cranach, and Vischer, but by building up the university in his capital city and by bringing teachers of the *humaniora*. He preferred peace to war, construction to destruction, learned humanist culture to barbarity. There were two literary sodalities in Wittenberg, the *Sodalitas Polychiana*, so named for Martin Pollich of Mellerstadt who was to became the first rector of the university, and the *Sodalitas Leucopolitana*, named for the town. To these sodalities belonged Matthäus Lupinus, Cuspinian's teacher, Bohuslas von` Hassenstein, the Bohemian humanist, and Heinrich von Bünau, who was also a member of the Rhenish Sodality and a friend of Johannes von Dalberg, Trithemius, and Celtis.[78] The University of Wittenberg was the first German university founded without church permission. Emperor Maximilian in the founding letter gave the University the right to teach *scientiae, bonae artes* and *studia liberalia* as well as *theologia*. Mellerstadt came to Wittenberg from Leipzig and as rector in the early years favored humanism, though he later moved more deeply into Thomism. Johannes von Staupitz, the first dean of the theological faculty was not a humanist, but he was an open, reflective person who favored the renewal of the church.[79] Mellerstadt brought Hermann Buschius along from Leipzig, as the first

---

[77] Maria Grossmann, "Humanismus in Wittenberg, 1486–1517," *Luther Jahrbuch*, 39 (1972), 11–30. Maria Grossmann, "Wittenberger Drucke von 1502 bis 1517," *Das Antiquariat*, XVII (1964), 153–157; XIX (1966), 220–226. E.G. Schwiebert, *Luther and his Times* (St. Louis, 1950), 268–274 (the pre-Lutheran Faculty), 275–302 (Triumph of Biblical Humanism in the University of Wittenberg). The old history of Walter Friedensburg, *Geschichte der Universität Wittenberg* (Halle, 1917) remains standard. The East German commemorative volume *450 Jahre Martin Luther—Universität Halle-Wittenberg*, I: *1502–1816* (Halle, 1952), contains useful essays and underlines the initiative and important role of Luther in support of humanistic studies at Wittenberg.

[78] M. Grossmann, "Humanismus in Wittenberg," 17.

[79] David Steinmetz, *Misericordia Dei. The Theology of Johannes von Staupitz in its Late Medieval Setting* (Leiden, 1968), reveals Staupitz in the Augustinian tradition of viewing man as the instrument of God.

professor of humanistic subjects. He had studied with Hegius at Deventer and with Rudolf Agricola and Rudolf von Langen in Heidelberg and spent several years in Italy. He is best known for his *Vallum humanitatis,* or defence wall for the *studia humanitatis* (1518). Marschalk was especially important for his emphasis on Greek language and literature, a tradition carried on by Trebelius, Andreas Carlstadt, Johannes Lang, who taught Luther, and Melanchthon.

But once again the Italian influence made itself felt, for three of the jurists who were strong advocates of humanism were inspired by Italian humanism. Peter of Ravenna and his son Vicentius were enthusiastic humanists. Johann von Kitzscher had been a member of the humanist circle of Cardinal Ascanio Sforza in Rome and was a friend of Filippo Beroaldo the elder. Christopher Scheurl, who came in 1507, was born in Nuremberg, studied in Heidelberg, and studied law and humanities in Bologna, spending nine years in Italy. He was elected rector three weeks after his arrival and on May 1 published a university catalog, *Rotulus doctorum Wittenberge profitentium,* in the manner of the Italian universities, which listed thirteen members of the arts faculty. In 1508 the *poeta laureatus* was made a member of the arts faculty. After he moved to Nuremberg Scheurl kept in close touch with Wittenberg as a friend of humanism and the Reformation.[80] Another key figure for the success of humanism in Wittenberg was Georg Spalatin, who had studied with Marschalk, Henning Goede, and Jodocus Trutvetter in Erfurt. Spalatin had come to Wittenberg in 1502 with Marschalk, left and returned to Wittenberg again in 1508 as a tutor to Johann Friedrich, the elector's nephew. The humanists clustered about him and he became a key liaison for Luther with the Elector.[81]

Initially the theological faculty at Wittenberg taught the *via antiqua,* Thomism and Scotism, but Elector Frederick brought the nominalist Jodocus Trutvetter from Erfurt in 1507 to broaden the approach and his student, Martin Luther, came soon after, though only for a year. When Luther returned to stay in 1511, humanism was well established in Wittenberg and the way prepared for his Biblical humanism, a return to

---

[80] Maria Grossmann, "Humanismus in Wittenberg," 19–22; on the great importance of the library which Frederick assembled, 26–28.

[81] See the exemplary biography by Irmgard Hösz, *Georg Spalatin, 1484–1545. Ein Leben in der Zeit des Humanismus und der Reformation* (Weimar, 1956).

the sources. The triumph over scholastic theology came, however, not with the victory of classical letters over scholastic philosophy, but through the return to the Scriptures led by the reforming circle of "Augustinians." Luther not only maintained a positive attitude toward classical culture, but, partially under the influence of Melanchthon, invested what time and energy remained for him during his later years to humanist studies, notably history, for he felt he had been deprived of these good things in his early years. He showed the initiative and played an important role in the major university reform of 1518 and encouraged Melanchthon, the *praeceptor Germaniae*, in his humanist and educational efforts.[82] Luther's confrontation with Erasmus over the theological issue of freedom of the human will to keep the law perfectly and to accept Christ as Savior of its own power did not prevent him from recommending to students Erasmus's humanist writings and did not lead him to discourage Melanchthon's continued correspondence with the prince of humanists. Luther could distinguish much more clearly than most Reformation scholars in our day between a right relationship with God of everlasting importance and the supreme benefits of culture for the very limited time allotted to man in the here and now.

The young Melanchthon, grand-nephew of Reuchlin, was a brilliant young humanist. At Tübingen in 1517 young Melanchthon had laid down a program for humanist studies in an oration *De artibus liberalibus*. Elector Frederick chose Melanchthon for the professorship of Greek in the arts faculty, a position he retained the rest of his life despite Luther's importuning him to take a chair in theology. Luther had wanted little Peter Mosellanus, but the wise elector fortunately prevailed. Melanchthon's inaugural address in 1518, *De corrigendis adolescentiae studiis*, developed the power of rhetoric and the function

---

[82] Scholarship on the question of Luther's relation to humanism has moved well beyond the flat denial that Luther's early development was totally independent of the influence of humanism, Hans von Schubert, "Reformation und Humanismus," *Luther-Jahrbuch*, VIII (1926), 1–26. Perhaps the very best study is that of Helmar Junghans, "Der Einfluß des Humanismus auf Luthers Entwicklung bis 1518," *Luther-Jahrbuch*, XXXVII (1970), 37–101. See also Lewis W. Spitz, *The Religious Renaissance*, 237–293, and the bibliographical notes, 345–354.

of dialectic in the service of rhetoric, the value of history and of moral philosophy.[83]

It is true that Melanchthon was drawn by Luther's magnetic personality and powerful message to evangelical theology, distracted from the humanist program of 1518 to the authorship of the *Loci communes rerum theologicorum* of 1521. Now for Melanchthon the law of God shows the sinner his lost condition and is no longer a mere stimulus to virtue. Now philosophy is of no use as a preparation for theology or its handmaiden. Now antiquity is no longer the norm, but the Scriptures alone are the source of divine revelation.[84] His evangelical anthropology now coincides with Luther's view that the will is an *arbitrium servum* in matters of sin and grace. Nevertheless, the very form of the *Loci* is derived from the rhetorical topics and Erasmus heaped elaborate praise upon him for his effort, even though he considered the *Loci* to be competition for his own *Ratio seu methodus*. Melanchthon learned to differentiate the spheres of the human and divine in Luther's way, even though in later years he tended to blur the line and to fuzz up the picture. Many of his humanist writings and

---

[83] The most convenient collection of Melanchthon's humanist writings is Robert Stupperich, ed., *Melanchthons Werke in Auswahl,* III: *Humanistische Schriften,* ed. Richard Nürnberger (Gütersloh, 1961), 29–42. Selections in English translation from the *De corrigendis* and the *In laudem novae scholae* (1526) are included in Lewis W. Spitz, "Humanism and the Reformation," in Robert Kingdon, ed., *Transition and Revolution* (Minneapolis, MN, 1974), 153–188, 167–175. Cf. Carl S. Meyer, "Melanchthon as Educator and Humanist," *Concordia Theological Monthly,* XXXI (1960), 533–540. On the humanistic and theological development of young Melanchthon, see especially Wilhelm Maurer, *Der junge Melanchthon zwischen Humanismus und Reformation,* I: *Der Humanist;* II: *Der Theologe* (Göttingen, 1969); Adolf Sperl, *Melanchthon zwischen Humanismus und Reformation* (Munich, 1959); Ernst Bizer, *Theologie der Verheißung. Studien zur theologischen Entwicklung des jungen Melanchthon (1519–1524)* (Neukirchen-Vluyn, 1964). A noteworthy thesis showing the mediating role of the humanistic reformer is by Judith Law Williams, "Philipp Melanchthon as an Ecclesiastical Conciliator, 1530–through 1541" (diss., University of North Carolina, 1973).

[84] Ekkehard Mühlenberg, "Humanistisches Bildungsprogramm und reformatorische Lehre beim jungen Melanchthon," *Zeitschrift für Theologie und Kirche,* LXV (1968), 431–444.

orations came after the *Loci* of 1521. In 1557, as a sixty-year-old professor, he ghost-wrote an oration for a beginner, Bartholomäus Kalkreuter, in praise of Erasmus.

Melanchthon was only the most prominent figure in a multitude of Reformation intellectuals who cultivated the classics and adopted humanistic literary forms.[85] Peter Mosellanus at Leipzig delivered a forceful *Oration Concerning the Knowledge of Various Languages Which Must Be Esteemed.* He proved to be an inspiration for Andreas Althamer, who became the leading reformer of Brandenburg-Anspach. Leipzig turned Lutheran after the death of Duke George and a school of "evangelical humanists" developed, several of whom, such as J. Lonicerus and Arnold Burenius, had studied with Mosellanus.

One of the greatest polymaths of the century, Joachim Camerarius (1500–1574) studied at Leipzig, Erfurt, and Wittenberg, taught history and Greek for several years at the Nuremberg gymnasium, helped Melanchthon write the Augsburg Confession in 1530, led in the reorganization of the University of Tübingen in 1535, and that of Leipzig in 1541, where he spent most of his remaining years with classical scholarship. He wrote more than one hundred and fifty works and translated into Latin many Greek authors, such as Homer, Sophocles, Lucian, and Demosthenes. His interest in history was especially keen, and he delivered many orations praising classical learning, for he believed that when combined with evangelical faith, humanist learning made possible the fullest development of man's humanity. Joachim's son with the same name carried on the tradition in Saxony. His other son Philipp was a talented essayist whose *Operae Horarum Subcisivarum Sive Meditationes Historicae* (1602 ff.) or *Historischer Lustgarten* was translated into French and into English as *The Walking Librarie* or *The Living Librarie.* A grandson, Ludwig, helped to negotiate the Peace of Westphalia.

---

[85] For a fuller account which serves, however, merely as an introduction to the continuity of humanism through the Reformation era, see Lewis W. Spitz, "Humanism in the Reformation," A. Molho and J.A. Tedeschi, eds., *Renaissance Studies in Honor of Hans Baron*, 641–662. For a translation of Johann Sturm's *De amissa dicendi ratione libri duo*, see Lewis W. Spitz and Barbara Sher Tinsley, *Johann Sturm on Education* (Saint Louis: Concordia Publishing House, 1995), 119–132.

Given Luther's emphasis upon the *verbum evangelii vocale* and the response of the believer's *fides ex auditu,* the instrumental importance of rhetoric gained a new dimension of significance during the Reformation era, despite the comeback staged by Aristotelian dialectic, thanks again in part to Melanchthon. From Melanchthon's *De Rhetorica libri Tres* (1519) and his *Encomion eloquentiae* (1523) on rhetoric was firmly entrenched in the Protestant cultural tradition. Camerarius did a very successful *Elementa rhetoricae* (Basel, 1541 and later editions). Johann Sturm did a *De amissa dicendi ratione libri duo* (Lyons, 1542) and other rhetorical works.

In history, too, the continuity from the fifteenth century through to the seventeenth is very remarkable. Peter Luder in his Heidelberg address had praised rhetoric and poetry but gave first place to history. From Fabri, Meisterlin, Blumenau, Schedel, Celtis, Wimpheling, Nauclerus, and Pirckheimer an unbroken succession of authors adopted the humanist pragmatic approach to history, though the Reformation historians took even greater pains to perceive the footsteps of God in history. Luther read more history during his later years and even prepared a chronology of universal history for his own use. He wrote prefaces for the historical worlds and editions of Galeatius Capella, Lazarus Spengler, Georg Spalatin, Robert Barnes and others. Melanchthon wrote his *Chronicon* based on Carion's and the famous prefaces to Caspar Hedio's and Johannes Cuspinian's histories. Sebastian Franck's German chronicle (1538) was "intended to point out the true kernel and main themes of our history," but not from a highly patriotic or nationalistic point of view. He merely wished to make up for the previous neglect of German history and to fill in the picture. Jacob Sturm in Strasbourg was one of the patrons of Johann Sleidan (1506–1556), who wrote the *Commentarii de statu religionis et rei publicae Germanorum Carolo V. Caesare* on which he labored until just before his death and which enjoyed a tremendous popularity. He saw the German nation at its height under Charles V with a mission to the world. The learned Jesuit Heinrich Schütz in 1761 did a critical commentary on all the works which were dependent on Sleidan or related to his great history.[86] Flacius Illyricus gave to Protestant

---

[86] Werner Kögl, *Studien zur Reichsgeschichtsschreibung deutscher Humanisten* (diss., Vienna, 1972), 16–18, n. 37. See also Gerald Strauss, "The Course of German

historiography a polemical cast with his *Catalogue of the Witnesses of Truth* (1556) and the *Magdeburg Centuries* (1559ff.).[87] The historiographical line leads directly to the "Centurions" of the seventeenth century and the pragmatic secular and church historians of the eighteenth century, to Veit Ludwig von Seckendorff and to Johann Lorenz Mosheim.

The focus placed upon the history of the early church and of the Councils at the Leipzig debate in 1519 underlined the importance of patristic studies and early church history.[88] Luther did a preface for Georg Major's *Vitae Patrum* (Wittenberg, 1544). Melanchthon wrote a "little patrology" in which he advised the reader as to how Augustine, Ambrose, Origen and other teachers ought to be read.[89] The *Catalogus Testimoniorum* of the church fathers figured prominently in the confessional and apologetic writings of the time, continuing a tradition of serious scholarly interest in patristic literature begun by Ambrogio Traversari and the Italian humanists.[90] Georg Calixt (1586–1656) at Helmstedt serves as an instructive example of how a humanist view of history combined with an Aristotelian philosophy in a moderate orthodoxy could develop a theologian of an ironic and ecumenical disposition during the seventeenth century.[91]

"Education is a divine gift to be seized upon by all," exclaimed Luther. The reformers followed the humanists as strong advocates of

---

History: The Lutheran Interpretation," A. Molho and J.A. Tedeschi, eds., *Renaissance Studies in Honor of Hans Baron,* 663–686.

[87] Heinz Scheible, *Die Anfänge der reformatorischen Geschichtsschreibung. Melanchthon, Sleidan, Flacius and die Magdeburger Zenturien* (Gütersloh, 1966), offers the texts of key prefaces.

[88] Donald J. Ziegler, ed., *Great Debates of the Reformation* (New York, 1969), 3–34.

[89] CR, XX. 703ff.

[90] The knowledge and use of patristic writings in the 16th century is a subject begging for a major study. A model for such a study is Peter Fraenkel, *Testimonia Patrum. The Function of the Patristic Argument in the Theology of Philip Melanchthon* (Geneva, 1961).

[91] Hermann Schüssler, *Georg Calixt. Theologie und Kirchenpolitik. Eine Studie zur Ökumenizität des Luthertums* (Wiesbaden, 1961), 35–39: "Humanistische Geschichtsbetrachtung."

education. Their primary motivation was clearly the religious need of literacy for the reading of the Scriptures. But that was not by any means the sole motivation. The phrase that recurs constantly is for the good of the church and of the commonwealth. In his famous treatise *Of the Upbringing and Education of Youth in Good Manners and Christian Discipline,* Zwingli carried on the humanist pedagogical tradition emphasizing along with religion the importance of virtue and honor. Luther's *Address to the Municipalities, Sermon on Keeping Children in School,* and other educational writings stressed the needs of the child, church, and society. The role of Melanchthon, Bugenhagen and other reformers in encouraging the founding of secondary schools, in reforming the system in Denmark, and in promoting a humanist liberal arts curriculum on the secondary and university levels was of crucial importance to the prospering of humanist learning down to the colleges of liberal arts and the university divisions of humanities and sciences of the present day. Johann Sturm's famous school in Strasbourg served as an inspiration and model for Claude Baduel, reformer of the academy in Nîmes, for Roger Ascham, the English educator, and for many others. In his *Vallum humanitatis* (1518) Hermann Buschius urged the thorough study of the classics in the schools. This emphasis was international and interconfessional, for the Catholic schools, preeminently those of the Jesuits as well as for Protestant schools. The Catholic Conrad Heresbach was typical rather than exceptional when at Freiburg he delivered an oration in praise of Greek letters.[92]

In poetry, drama, and prose the continuity with the early and mature phases of humanism is very impressive. The sixteenth century was remarkably rich in its emulation of classical Latin, Greek, and even Hebrew poetry. Salutati had declared poets to be "much more friends and open witnesses of the truth than the philosophers," a point on which the Germans were in tune with the Italians. A look at Karl

---

[92] The literature on the Reformation and education is enormous, although a truly thorough and well documented history is yet to be written. Of interest for the elementary level are the articles by Gerald Strauss, "Reformation and Pedagogy: Educational Thought and Practice in the Lutheran Reformation," 272–293, and Lewis W. Spitz, "Further Lines of Inquiry for the Study of 'Reformation and Pedagogy'," 294–306, in Charles Trinkaus and Heiko A. Oberman, eds., *The Pursuit of Holiness in Late Medieval and Renaissance Religion* (Leiden, 1974).

60

Goedeke's bibliography of German literature reveals that of the selected 273 neo-Latin poets of the time a very large number of their humanist works were published in Wittenberg during the most active years of the Reformation.[93] This poetry had a strong moral and didactic emphasis, stressed the immortal fame of the poet, revitalized the religious component of life, and expressed a deep longing for a knowledge of the nature of things. But the unabashed eroticism of a Celtis is rarely found, although there is a deep strain of individualism and personalism, despite the adherence to classical forms. Some poets such as Eobanus Hessus (d. 1540) and Euricius Cordus (d. 1538) belonged to the old humanist circle but entered the new poetic guild. Laurentius Corvinus (d. 1527), Ursinus Velius (d. 1539), Georgius Logus (d. 1553), and Joachim Vadianus (d. 1551), the reformer of St. Gallen, carried over into the Reformation their humanist cultural concerns. Like Eobanus and Cordus, Jacobus Micyllus (d. 1558) and Joachim Camerarius (d. 1574) had belonged to Mutian's circle but were younger and clearly belonged to the new generation of Reformation humanist poets. The Wittenberg school of neo-Latin poetry included Georg Sibutus, Thiloninus Philhymnus, Andreas Crappen, Wolfgang Cyclopius, Johannes Eisenmann, and the Italian poet Richard Sbrulius. From the late 1520s on Melanchthon became the leader of a lively group of poets which included his son-in-law Georg Sabinus (d. 1560) and Johannes Stigel (d. 1562). A brash young poet Simon Lemnius (d. 1550), who roused Luther's anger by mocking older professors, produced a sensual *Amores* as well as harmless eclogues. Other members were Melchior Volz or Acontius (d. 1569), Johannes Gigos (d. 1581) and Georg Amilius (d. 1569). In Melanchthon's last years yet another generation of young humanists came forward, Friedrich Widebram (d. 1585), and the most talented of the group, Johannes Major (d. 1600). The greatest and most original of Germany's neo-Latin poets was Petrus Lotichius Secundus (1528–1560),whose four books of elegies, two books of carmina, and six eclogues were of the highest order, the elegies revealing a sensitive inner life. These poets experimented with various forms, lyrics, epics, eclogues, landscape descriptions (hodoeporicon), satires, and epigrams. The tie-in with hymns and religious song is worth noting. Two Swabian poets in the second half of the sixteenth century who were exceptional

---

[93] Harold Jantz, *op. cit.*, 410.

in depicting their personal inner life and experiences were Nathan Chyträus (1543–1598) and Nikodemus Frischlin (1547–1590). At the end of the sixteenth and early seventeenth century a group of poets known as the "Anakreontiker" which included Georg Rollenhagen, Julius Mynsinger the younger, and Jakob Fabricius copied Italian models, doing landscape poetry, shepherd poetry, and allegorical heroides.

At the beginning of neo-Latin poetry in Germany some of the less impressive Italian poets served as the models, Filippo Beroaldo the elder, Tifernas, Fausto Andrelini, half French, Octavius Cleophilus and above all Baptista Mantuanus. But gradually the influence of the better Italian poets made itself felt during the course of the century, Pontano, Poliziano, Sannazaro, Fracastoro, Bembo, and above all Flaminius. Religious fervor and deep personal feeling found expression in poetry that was good, if not the greatest. Many poets of the seventeenth century did both German and neo-Latin poetry, such as Martin Opitz (d. 1639), Johann Heermann, Fleming, Gryphius, Lauremberg and others. The Jesuit Jakob Bidermann carried on the neo-Latin tradition as did other Catholic poets. It is not possible to complete the roster or to develop the subject further, but enough has been said to document the importance of the Italian influence, to show the continuity between the early phases of German humanism and the Reformation century, and to suggest that literary life became a more powerful movement under the aegis of the Reformation than it had been before.[94] The romantics of the

---

[94] A major work on neo-Latin poetry during the second half of the 16th century into the baroque period needs to be done. Georg Ellinger provided the sketch drawn on extensively here, "Neulateinische Dichtung Deutschlands im 16. Jahrhundert," Paul Merker and Wolfgang Stammler, eds., *Reallexikon der deutschen Literaturgeschichte*, II (Berlin, 1926/28), 469–494. His premature death prevented him from doing a complete work on the subject begun with his *Geschichte der neulateinischen Literatur Deutschlands im sechzehnten Jahrhundert*, 3 vols. (Berlin and Leipzig, 1929), on Germany and the Netherlands. Dr. C. Reedijk, *The Poems of Desiderius Erasmus* (Leiden, 1956), 19–24, provides a brief survey of German humanist poets. Gerald Gillespie, "Notes on the Evolution of German Renaissance Lyricism," *Modern Language Notes*, LXXXI (1966), 437–462, quite correctly argues (p. 437) that "because our sensitivity for rhythm and diction is historically conditioned, it is only a seeming paradox that, after Luther, 'really' native German verse sounds strange to us. The nature of German poetry was fundamentally altered

nineteenth century may have appreciated more deeply Hans Sachs and
the indigenous German tradition so indebted to the *Meistergesang* and
the medieval *Volksbuch* tradition, but it is hard to see how German
letters of its golden age could have reached the splendor of Weimar
without the input of Italian Renaissance classicism and the development
of the Baroque.[95]

A similar double track between humanist drama and the folkish
*Fastnachtsspiel* with its medieval roots ran parallel through the sixteenth
century. The *Fastnachtsspiel* developed further during the fifteenth and
sixteenth centuries as a dramatic form, originating from among the
burghers as had the *Meistergesang* and running side by side with the
religious dramas, where again there is a marked continuity through the
Reformation era. It was cultivated by Hans Rosenplüt and Hans Folz in
Nuremberg, and flourished especially in the Tyrol and at Lübeck. It
developed from a primitive form of individual, unrelated speeches to
dialogue.[96] While humanist drama no doubt owed something to the
medieval tradition, the critical event was the discovery and widespread
popularity of Terence. The first school edition of Terence was
published in Strasbourg in 1470. But the widespread use of Terence and
of Plautus began in the 1490s. The actual start of humanist drama in

---

by the end of the sixteenth century through the influence of Romance and ancient
classical models."

[95] See Fritz Strich, "Hans Sachs und die Renaissance," Festschrift für Hans R.
Hahnloser, E.J. Beer, ed. (Basel, 1961), 361–372; Barbara Könneker, *Hans Sachs*
(Stuttgart, 1971); Eugen Geiger, *Der Meistergesang des Hans Sachs* (Bern, 1956);
Archer Taylor, *The Literary History of Meistergesang* (New York, 1937).

[96] The important edition of Adelbert von Keller, *Fastnachtspiele aus dem 15.
Jahrhundert*, 4 vols. (Stuttgart, 1853–1858) has been reprinted in three volumes,
Darmstadt, 1965. See also Eckehard Catholy, *Das Fastnachtsspiel des späten
Mittelalters. Gestalt and Funktion* (Tübingen, 1961); M.J. Rudwin, "The Origin of
German Carnival Comedy," *Journal of English and Germanic Philology*, 18 (1919)
402–454; Werner Lenk, *Das Nürnberger Fastnachtsspiel des 15. Jahrhunderts. Ein
Beitrag zur Theorie und zur Interpretation des Fastnachtsspiels als Dichtung* (Berlin,
1966). Pamphilus Gengenbach in Basel in the years 1515 and 1516 adapted the
*Fastnachtsspiel* to religious and moral ends. See Derek Van Abbé, "Development of
Dramatic Form in Pamphilus Gengenbach," *Modern Language Review*, XLV (1950),
46–62.

Germany began with the presentation of original pedagogical dramatizations, with actual dramatizations of Terence's dramas done later. Credit for the first original drama goes to Wimpheling who wrote his *Stylpho* in 1480. Jakob Locher's *Historia de rege Franciae* was performed in one of the gardens of Freiburg University. He was a pupil of Celtis and of Sebastian Brant and developed his interest in theater during his studies in Italy in the 1490s, where he perhaps saw Verardi's *Historia Baetica* performed. German students at Italian universities did classical comedies. Locher also did the *Judicium Paridis,* in which he introduced the device of having a character on stage describe the approach of another off stage until his arrival. Johannes Reuchlin had his students perform his *Henno* in Dalberg's house on January 31, 1497, for the Heidelberg sodality. Reuchlin had previously written one comedy, the *Sergius,* mocking Holzinger, the chancellor of Duke Eberhard the younger, but Dalberg had advised against its performance. Celtis credited Reuchlin with being the founder of humanist comedy.[97]

In his *Ingolstadt Oration* Celtis praised the value of ancient drama and urged the German youth to initiate those public performances in which they "exhorted the spectators to virtue, piety, moderation, courage, and the patient endurance of all hardships." In Vienna during the winter semester of 1502/1503, Celtis directed the performance of the *Eunuchus* of Terence and the *Aulularia* of Plautus, the same two plays which his Cracow student Laurentius Corvinus, now at St. Elizabeth School in Breslau, had his students perform. The drama was a natural metier for Celtis, for it contained all the elements at which he excelled:

---

[97] For German humanist drama see Wolfgang F. Michael, *Frühformen der deutschen Bühne* (Berlin, 1963), 67–86; *Das deutsche Drama des Mittelalters* (Berlin, 1971), which discusses in three chapters "Geistliches Drama," "Das weltliche Volksdrama," and "Das Humanistendrama," centering on the years 1440–1520, critically reviewed by Dieter Wuttke in the *Archiv für Reformationsgeschichte, Literaturbericht,* I (1972), 80, no. 293. See also Derek Van Abbé, *Drama in Renaissance Germany and Switzerland* (London and New York, 1961); Henning Brinkmann, "Anfänge des modernen Dramas in Deutschland. Versuch über die Beziehungen zwischen Drama und Bürgertum im 16. Jahrhundert," *Studien zur Geschichte der deutschen Sprache und Literatur,* II (Düsseldorf, 1966), 232–288; Leicester Bradner, "The Latin Drama of the Renaissance (1346–1640)," *Studies in the Renaissance,* IV (1957), 31–70.

64

display, festivity, and comradery. Some members of the Danubian Sodality presented on March 1, 1501, Celtis's first drama, the *Ludus Dianae* in Linz at the court of Maximilian and his Italian bride, Bianca Maria Sforza. It was done in the Italian style with a free use of classical forms and figures as in the festival plays, using rhetorical declamation and pantomime. In the *Rhapsodia* performed in Vienna he celebrated a minor victory of Maximilian against some Bohemian mercenaries during the Bavarian War of Succession in 1504.[98]

The reformers saw the great value of drama, combining as it did poetry, rhetoric, moral philosophy and the possibility of presenting Biblical as well as secular history both as popular theater and as school dramas for the youth. In the traditional *Fastnachtsspiel* some playwrights attacked abuses and developed Biblical themes. The Swiss Niklaus Manuel wrote a play on the "Ablaszkrämer" and also on "Vom Papst und seiner Priesterschaft". Burkard Waldi's "Parabell vam vorlorn Szohn" (1527) held up the pharisaism of the monks for criticism in the person of the prodigal son's older, self-righteous brother. In the 1530s in the Lutheran schools and parishes a widespread use of dramas developed with the prodigal son, Abraham, Tobias, Jacob, Susanna and the Elders, Esther and similar themes often repeated.[99] Like the evangelical hymns, these German dramas constituted a genuinely creative contribution of the Reformation. Two Dutchmen, Wilhelm Graphäus and Macropedius, first shaped Biblical materials into the classical model, thus uniting the formal interests of the humanists and the religious interests of the reformers. The school dramas appeared in the 1530s in Saxony and in Switzerland, done by Paul Rebhun, Heinrich Bullinger, Valten Voith, Hans Ackermann, Sixtus Birck and others.[100]

---

[98] Alfred Schütz, *Die Dramen des Konrad Celtis* (diss., Vienna, 1948). Lewis W. Spitz, *Conrad Celtis the German Arch-Humanist*, 72–82, 129–130, the playwright.

[99] Barbara Könneker, "Deutsche Literatur," 164–173. See Richard Froning, ed., *Das Drama der Reformationszeit* (Stuttgart, 1894; reprinted, Darmstadt, 1964). The old classic work is Hugo Holstein, *Die Reformation im Spiegelbilde der dramatischen Literatur* (Halle, 1886). On the Susanna theme, Robert Pilger, "Die Dramatisierungen der Susanna im 16. Jahrhundert," *Zeitschrift für deutsche Philologie,* IX (1880), 129–217.

[100] Hermann Palm, *Paul Rebhuns Dramen* (Stuttgart, 1859) was reprinted in Darmstadt, 1969.

Jacob Ruf and Bartholomäus Krüger depicted world history as a battle of God and Satan, like Luther and the pope. Thomas Naogeorgus in his *Pammachius* (1538) presented the history of the "devil's church" from the Donation of Constantine to the present, with Luther pushing it to destruction, but with the fourth act breaking off with the admonition that the audience must complete the destruction of that church which was not yet complete. Hans Sachs alone did over a hundred comedies and tragedies, but mostly on non-Biblical themes, using about all the material available in his day from the Bible to Homer, the Roman historians, or Boccaccio.[101] In Alsace Jörg Wickram wrote farces, although his prose novels were better known. The tradition persisted in lively form into the second half of the sixteenth century and into the seventeenth with the dramas of Nikodemus Frischlin (1549–1590), Johann Fischart (1546–1590), Georg Rollenhagen (1542–1609), author of the *Battle of Frogs and Mice (Froschmeuseler)*, and others.[102] Luther had urged the performance of the plays of Terence in the schools and once reprimanded a Silesian schoolmaster for bowdlerizing his plays. As the century wore on the influence of Greek drama became increasingly powerful, especially in Strasbourg, which had the first permanent German theater. The history of sixteenth century drama closes with the work of Jacob Ayrer (1543–1605). This Nuremberg playwright wrote over a hundred tragedies, *Fastnachtsspiele,* and other works. He was very eclectic and drew on the materials of contemporary English plays as well as upon German humanist dramas and such authors as Hans Sachs, Frischlin, Wickram and others. A direct line runs from German humanist and Reformation drama to the great dramatist of the seventeenth century Andreas Gryphius (1616–1664), a Silesian who travelled in Italy as well as in the Netherlands and France, and wrote remarkable tragedies and comedies.[103]

From Saxony and Switzerland the school drama spread to other evangelical areas and was adopted in due course by Catholic authors

---

[101] Barbara Könneker, "Deutsche Literatur," 165–167. Edmund Goetze, ed. *Sämtliche Fastnachtsspiele,* 7 vols. (Halle, 1880–1887).

[102] Eli Sobel, "Georg Rollenhagen, Sixteenth-Century Playwright, Pedagogue, and Publicist," *PMLA*, LXX (1955), 762–780.

[103] Willi Flemming, *Andreas Gryphius. Eine Monographie* (Stuttgart, 1965), 194ff. on the influence of Italian comedy on Gryphius.

such as the Swiss Hans Salat (1498–1561) and Wolfgang Schmetzl (ca. 1500–ca. 1560), who were fond of applying the prodigal son theme to Protestantism. Georgius Macropedius (1486–1558) from the Netherlands was also a Catholic. His play *Asotus* (1537) was on the prodigal son theme and his *Hecastus* (1539) was influenced by the morality play style of the *Jedermann*. He was influenced by Plautus. The Jesuits drew upon classical and humanistic sources for their famous school dramas, drawing strength from the medieval tradition of church plays. Jesuit dramas were very rhetorical and the Jesuits regarded tragedies as representing a higher form of dramatic art than comedies. They contributed in turn to the achievements of the age of the baroque.[104]

It is not possible to develop here even an outline of prose literature during the course of the sixteenth and seventeenth centuries. Two general observations, however, are called for. One is that no artificial distinction should be made between neo-Latin and German prose literature during this period, for the borrowing of themes and techniques was extensive and many of the same authors wrote in both languages. Secondly, not only the positive and constructive, pragmatic and moralistic literature owed much to Renaissance letters, but also the satirical, negative, and critical literature, the grotesque, the "verkehrte Welt," was derived in part from the humanist literature of satire and folly.[105]

The humanist interest in the natural sciences was continued and reinforced during the Reformation era by both Protestants and Catholics. Luther and the Wittenberg reformers showed a lively interest in natural philosophy. The combination of the propagation of the faith with an interest in geography, alchemy, botany, zoology and the

---

[104] Of the many studies of Jesuit drama especially to be recommended are W. Flemming, *Geschichte des Jesuitentheaters in den Ländern deutscher Zunge* (Berlin, 1923); J. Müller, *Das Jesuitendrama in den Ländern deutscher Zunge vom Anfang (1555) bis zum Hochbarock (1665),* 2 vols. (Augsburg, 1930); N. Scheid, "Das lateinische Jesuitendrama im deutschen Sprachgebiet," *Lit. wiss. Jahrbuch,* V (1930), 1–96. The most significant Jesuit dramatists were Jakob Gretser (*Udo*), Jakob Pontanus (martyr and Biblical drama), Jakob Bidermann (Cenodoxus, 1609), the Vienna court dramatist Nikolaus Avancinus (*Pietas victrix*).

[105] See Friedrich Gaede's brilliant pages, *Humanismus. Barock. Aufklärung,* part 3, 79–114, "Verkehrte Welt, Realistische Literatur im 16. und 17. Jahrhundert."

practice of medicine, which was often considered a part of pastoral care, was common. The *Schola Wittenbergensis* figures in the histories of medicine as a prominent school of medicine, and Luther and Melanchthon were listed as honorary members. The *uomo universale* of sixteenth-century Lutheranism was *historicus, philosophus,* and *medicus* as well as *theologus.*[106] Melanchthon's son-in-law, Kaspar Peucer (1525–1602), served as the elector's physician as well as cultivating an interest in mathematics, astronomy, and theology. The achievements of Paracelsus in iatrochemistry were celebrated in the decades which followed and the tradition cultivated. A host of interesting sixteenth-century physicians and scientists await their biographers. Leonhard Rauwolf (b. 1535/40, died 1596), the Augsburg physician, studied at the University of Wittenberg, travelled widely in the Levant, and made remarkable contributions to botany. Many physicians and botanists studied at Wittenberg such as Valerius Cordus (1515–1544), Carolus Clusius, and Caspar Ratzenberg. The full story of the German Reformation and science is yet to be written.[107]

Just as eighteenth-century scholarship has become increasingly conscious of the dark underside of the Enlightenment and the loss of faith in reason especially during the second half of the century, so Renaissance scholarship has become increasingly aware of the "darker vision of the Renaissance," the non-rational, irrational, and suprarational

---

[106] I owe this observation to Professor Manfred Fleischer of the University of California, Davis, who is currently at work on a study of the interrelationship between humanism and the Reformation in Silesia. See his article, "The Institutionalization of Humanism in Protestant Silesia," *Archiv für Reformationsgeschichte,* LXVI (1975). See also Fleischer's thorough chapter on "Humanism and Reformation in Silesia: Imprints of Italy—Celtis, Erasmus, Luther and Melanchthon," 27–109, in Manfred Fleischer, ed., *The Harvest of Humanism in Central Europe: Essays in Honor of Lewis W. Spitz* (Saint Louis: Concordia Publishing House, 1992).

[107] Karl H. Dannenfeldt, *Leonhard Rauwolf, Sixteenth-Century Physician, Botanist and Traveler* (Cambridge, MA, 1968), 13–14. John Dillenberger, *Protestant Thought and Natural Science* (New York, 1960), explores the reception of Copernicanism over the subsequent century, but a detailed history of science and Protestantism remains to be written, one free of the polemics surrounding the debate about 1640, Puritanism and science, and other Weberian or Marxian hypotheses.

events of the period 1300 to 1650 A.D. Not only was there a popular undercurrent of credulity, belief in the occult powers, resort to astrology, fear of demonic powers and witchcraft, but there was a strong component of these non-rational forces in the minds of many intellectuals and representatives of the social upper classes, humanists, reformers, princes, kings, and popes. This reassessment has been done most systematically for the Italian Renaissance, but some recent studies have pointed to new dimensions and new facets of the northern Renaissance and Reformation.[108] Early German humanism was already associated with the dark Faustian tradition.[109] Agrippa of Nettesheim (1486–1535), a skeptic and fideist, has been associated with a more general movement which was producing "a sense of debility, cultural decline, and decadence."[110] How thin the cultural veneer of humanist enlightenment actually was in the very area where it had prospered relatively early can be seen from the upsurge of witch hunting in Southwestern Germany, where in a period of 120 years there were more than 480 trials and 3,200 people executed for witchcraft. Ironically it was the fact that the upper classes, judges, and other establishment figures, were implicated as victims that led to the abating of the craze, though the opposition especially of evangelical preachers defending the sovereignty of God did help.[111]

A fusion of certain elements of Renaissance culture, Reformation theology, and the mystical and alchemical tradition occurred in the mind of Jacob Böhme (1575–1624), a not-so-simple shoemaker of Görlitz. The quintessence of his theosophy and natural philosophy was contained in his book *Aurora, oder Morgenrothe im Aufgang,* which had an enormous influence in Silesia, other parts of Germany, the

---

[108] Natalie Zemon Davis, *Society and Culture in Early Modern France* (Stanford, 1975). See also footnote 24.

[109] Dieter Harmening, "Faust und die Renaissance-Magie. Zum ältesten Faustzeugnis. (Johannes Trithemius an Johannes Virdung, 1507)," *Archiv für Kulturgeschichte,* LV (1973), 56–79.

[110] Charles G. Nauert, Jr., *Agrippa and the Crisis of Renaissance Thought,* 333.

[111] An epochal book which has proved to be very stimulating for scholars in the field of intellectual and religious history is Keith Thomas, *Religion and the Decline of Magic. Studies in Popular Beliefs in Sixteenth and Seventeenth Century England* (London, 1971). Cf. Midelfort, cited in footnote 24 above.

Lowlands, and even in France and England down to the nineteenth century. His fellow countryman, Abraham von Franckenberg (1593–1652), helped to spread his ideas. Angelus Silesius (1624–1677), a Breslau physician, drawing inspiration from Johannes Tauler, the fourteenth-century mystic, and from Böhme, turned Catholic and produced two volumes of poetry, the *Heilige Seelen-Lust* (1657) and *Geistreiche Sinn- und Schlussreime* (1657), known in its second edition as *Der cherubinische Wandersmann* (1674).[112]

The pattern of cultural development diverged in art and music from the unity in evidence in German humanism under the presence of the Reformation. The visual arts after Albrecht Dürer clearly suffered.[113] But the tradition of music from Luther, who so warmly admired Ludwig Senfl and the Flemish composers, built up to the great hymnody of Paul Gerhardt (1607–1676) and the musical triumphs of Johann Sebastian Bach. The lifespan of Renaissance lyrics was long indeed and the romantic enthusiasm for the *Volkslied* and *Gesellschaftslied* as the major source of music must be radically revised.

Conrad Celtis boasted of the German inventor of printing, whom he could not name. Luther considered the printing press to be the last and greatest gift of God to man whereby the gospel would be disseminated to the ends of the earth. Printing not only served the cause of learning as its instruments for multiplying pages, but in important ways it changed the nature of the enterprise, of the way in which people

---

[112] On Böhme, see Arlene A. Miller (Guinsburg), "The Theologies of Luther and Boehme in the Light of Their *Genesis* Commentaries," *The Harvard Theological Review*, LXIII (1970), 261–303; "Jacob Boehme from Orthodoxy to Enlightenment" (diss., Stanford, 1971), 720 pages. Erich Beyreuther, author of *Der geschichtliche Auftrag des Pietismus in der Gegenwart* (Stuttgart, 1963), has a very impressive knowledge of Böhme's impact upon thought in Pietism.

[113] Carl G. Christensen, "The Reformation and the Decline of German Art," *Central European History*, VI (1973), 207–232; Hans Rupprich, "Dürers Stellung zu den agnoëtischen und kunstfeindlichen Strömungen seiner Zeit," *Bayerische Akademie der Wissenschaften. Philosophisch-Historische Klasse Sitzungsberichte*, Jahrgang 1959, Heft 1, 3–31. A model of how artistic and literary cultural research should be pursued is Dieter Wuttke's article, "Methodisch-Kritisches zu Forschungen über Peter Vischer d. Ä. und seine Söhne," *Archiv für Kulturgeschichte*, XLIX (1967), 208–261.

thought and expressed themselves, and became a blender through which humanist and reformation thought fused as well as interacted. The sixteenth century was notable for the tremendous growth of private and public libraries, collections such as those of Frederick the Wise, that is, used by officials, professors, and the ruler himself. They invariably contained many humanist and classical as well as medieval and reformed theological writings.

Trithemius, like a very minuscle group of Italian humanists, set himself against the future. In his *De laude scriptorium Manuelium* he argued that parchment will last five times as long as paper (although paper cost only fifteen percent as much), that publishers are profit oriented and therefore many important books will not be printed and so lost (Trithemius a prophet!), and that printed books are less beautiful. But the days of the manuscript were numbered as the volume of printed books became virtually numberless. By 1520 all the major Latin authors had been published. Valla's *De Elegantiis Linguae Latinae* (1444) went through sixty editions between 1471 and 1536. Within two generations after the supreme invention there were presses in 250 towns, first of all in the commercial cities and then in the university towns. The leading German publishing centers during the early decades of the Reformation were Nuremberg, Wittenberg, Strasbourg, Augsburg, Magdeburg, Frankfurt, Basel and Zurich. Anton Koberger in Nuremberg kept twenty-four presses going and employed over a hundred workers. Just as in Italy, where printers and whole dynasties of publishers such as the Aldines were learned humanists, so also many of the German printers were learned men in their own right and advocates of humanism and reform. Pamphilus Gengenbach (d. 1524), for example, a printer and Meistersinger of Nuremberg, living later in Basel, adapted the *Fastnachtsspiel* to moral and religious ends.[114] He also published tracts of Eberlin von Günzburg, the most prolific and effective pamphleteer of the Reformation. Hans Lufft, one of Luther's favorite printers, became mayor of Wittenberg. A very large number of printers became evangelical preachers, possibly moved by the tracts they published and freed by the frequent bankruptcies of printing firms. If printing served humanism and reform, the humanists and reformers

---

[114] Derek Van Abbé, "Development of Dramatic Form in Pamphilus Gengenbach," *Modern Language Review*, XLV (1950), 46–62.

served publishing in turn. There was a steadily ascending curve in the volume of publications, but controversies triggered great upsurges in the number of books and pamphlets published. Like the Savonarola incident in Florence, the Reuchlin affair in Germany, the Carlstadt skirmish with the Thomists, the events of the Reformation opened the floodgates. The number of books published in Germany increased by ten times between the posting of the Ninety-Five Theses and the year 1524, which marked the high tide in the printing of religious and social treatises. On February 14, 1519, the humanist publisher Johannes Froben in Basel wrote to Luther:

> We sent six hundred copies of your collected works which I published to France and Spain. They are sold in Paris, read and appreciated at the Sorbonne. The book dealer Clavus of Pavia took a sizable number to Italy to sell them everywhere in the cities. I have sent copies also to England and Brabant and have only ten copies left in the storeroom. I have never had such good luck with a book. The more accomplished a man is, the more he thinks of you.[115]

The statistics tell an exciting tale of the proliferation and power of the press. Estimates vary, but a reasonable conjecture is that 40,000 titles were published in Europe during the fifteenth century. If the average edition numbered 250 volumes, and it may well have been closer to 300, there must have been a total of ten to twelve million incunabala published, many traditional medieval titles, but many also humanist and classical texts. By the year 1517 another ten million volumes were published, but by 1550 under the pressure of the Reformation 150,000 more titles had been published for a total of sixty million volumes.[116] Some 25,000 works were printed in Germany before

---

[115] Froben to Luther, February 14, 1519, in *D. Martin Luthers Werke: Briefwechsel*, I (Weimar, 1930), 332.

[116] See Richard C. Coles, "The Dynamics of Printing in the Sixteenth Century," *The Social History of the Reformation*, Lawrence W. Buck and Jonathan Zophy, eds. (Columbus, Ohio, 1972), 93–105; Elizabeth L. Eisenstein, "The Advent of Printing and the Protestant Revolt: A New Approach to the Disruption of Christendom," Robert M. Kingdon, ed., *Transition and Revolution* (Minneapolis, MN, 1974), 235–

1500, not including broadsides and leaflets, but once the Reformation was underway the annual number rose to five hundred and then to a thousand. In Wittenberg alone over six hundred different works were published between the years 1518 and 1523, whereas in the British Isles the total for these years was less than three hundred.[117] Classical learning and religious thought no longer contributed exclusively to what Vico was to call "the conceit of the learned," but became the property of an ever broader range of the literate population. The French humanist Louis Le Roy rightly declared later in the sixteenth century:

> Besides the restoration of learning, now almost complete, the invention of many fine new things ... has been reserved to this age. Among these, printing deserves to be put first.... The invention has greatly aided the advancement of all disciplines. For it seems miraculously to have been discovered in order to bring back to life more easily literature which seemed dead.[118]

Luther, like Erasmus, was quick to see the power of the press, but he held that the message was still more powerful than the medium. In 1522 he wrote: "I have only put God's Word in motion through preaching and writing. The Word has done everything and carried everything before it."

## V. CONCLUSION

In the first of his Martin Classical Lectures delivered at Oberlin College two decades ago, Paul Oskar Kristeller observed that "the Renaissance is a very complex period and it encompassed, just as do the Middle Ages or any other period, a good many chronological, regional, and

---

270, has a useful bibliography, 268–270; Rudolf Hirsch, *Printing, Selling and Reading, 1450–1550* (Wiesbaden, 1967).

[117] Harold Jantz, *op. cit.,* 418.

[118] Louis Le Roy, *De la vicissitude ou Varieté des Choses en L'Univers* (Paris 1575), tr. J.B. Ross, *The Portable Renaissance Reader* (New York, 1965), 98.

social differences."[119] Our review of the *Itinerarium studii renascentium litterarum* to the North underscores the truth of Professor Kristeller's statement. German humanism was related by strong bonds of consanguinity to Italian humanism, and yet its historical development followed an independent course.

Italian humanism has been traditionally considered the fountainhead of all Renaissance humanism. The full development of humanism in the other European countries has usually been attributed to the late fifteenth or to the sixteenth century at the very point when the movement in Italy itself had supposedly reached the end of the line.[120] Our review of the course of German humanism leads to the conclusion that whatever claims can be made for the indigenous or medieval roots of northern humanism, the influence of Italian humanism was the critical determinant during the early and the mature phases of German humanism in stimulating interest in classical culture as form and norm and in defining the cultural significance of the classical revival for the Germans. The tendency in some of the more recent scholarship to stress the native roots and the independent development of northern humanism, especially of Germany and the Low Countries and of France and England as well, must be very much attenuated. The distinctive Renaissance thrust, the classical revival, received its impetus from Italy in the fifteenth century, whatever the carry-over from earlier medieval renaissances in the North and the contribution of the Brethren of Common Life or the *via antiqua* may have been. Moreover, the influence of Italian humanism in the German speaking lands, as in the case of France, has been traced back to the early fifteenth century and even to the fourteenth, so that many of the "pre-humanists" in the North can be claimed as "humanists" with almost as much justice as the newly appreciated pre-Petrarchan forerunners of humanism in Italy.[121]

---

[119] Paul Oskar Kristeller, *Renaissance Thought. The Classic, Scholastic, and Humanist Strains* (New York, 1961), 4.

[120] Paul Oskar Kristeller, "Studies on Renaissance Humanism during the Last Twenty Years," *Studies in the Renaissance*, IX (1962), 8–9.

[121] *Ibid.*, 9. The claims made for the *via antiqua* as the cradle of humanism have long since been abandoned as argued by Heinrich Hermelink, *Die religiösen Reformbestrebungen des deutschen Humanismus* (Tübingen, 1907).

Just as the vitality of the Italian Renaissance and the creativity of Italian humanism especially in Florence and Venice is said to have lasted far beyond the *sacco di Roma* (1527), so German humanism, too, remained a powerful cultural force in alliance with the Reformation.[122] Partially subsumed under the religious drive of the Reformation, it received through the approbations of and amalgamation with the Reformation a broader, deeper, and long lasting impact through the sixteenth and seventeenth centuries. The study of the course of German humanism from the early fifteenth century to the seventeenth century demonstrates the tremendous continuity of that intellectual movement. The commonplace notion of a sharp break between Renaissance and Reformation so far as humanism in intellectual and cultural terms is concerned has proved to be a *fable convenue* which must be relegated to the historians' shelves of outmoded curiosities along with the idea of the Middle Ages as the dark ages or the Enlightenment as an antihistorical period.[123]

The Holy Roman Empire experienced over half a century of uneasy calm following the Peace of Augsburg in 1555, which gave to the German areas a distinct advantage over Italy, weighed down by Spanish control, and over France, torn for decades by religious wars and massacres. Neo-Latin publications, Greek and Hebrew studies, like natural science and education, made notable progress in Germany during the course of the sixteenth century. As early as the twelfth

---

[122] Eric Cochrane, *Florence in the Forgotten Centuries 1527–1800. A History of Florence and the Florentines in the Age of the Grand Dukes* (Chicago, 1973), maintains that the Florentines retained their creativity long after they had lost their position as the cultural leaders of Europe, although some reviewers of his work insist upon the great qualitative difference between the epigoni and the greats of the *Quattrocento*. William J. Bouwsma, *Venice and the Defense of Republican Liberty. Renaissance Values in the Age of the Counter Reformation* (Berkeley and Los Angeles, 1968), follows the development of Venetian republican consciousness from the relatively backward and inarticulate early Venetian Renaissance to the rich and sophisticated thought of late sixteenth and early seventeenth-century writers such as Gasparo Contarini, Paolo Paruta, Enrico Davila, and Paolo Sarpi.

[123] Heinz Liebing, "Perspektivische Verzeichnungen. Über die Haltbarkeit der *fable convenue* in der Kirchengeschichte," *Zeitschrift für Kirchengeschichte*, III (1968), 289–307.

century the *carmina burana* expressed nostalgia for the good old days when *Florebat olim studium.* It was only natural for men later in the sixteenth century to look back on the early decades of Renaissance humanism and the heroic days of the Reformation as the good old days. In actual fact, the literary and linguistic achievements of the later sixteenth century are very noteworthy and in some ways marked the maturation of cultural efforts begun in an amateurish way early in the century.

There was perhaps a loss of verve and fire as the century moved on. Humanism became more a matter of classical study than of spontaneous expression or style of life. But this change must not be exaggerated and it was in some measure compensated for by the much broader spread of humanist learning as the century advanced thanks to the educational program which combined Renaissance humanist and reform goals. Cicero's intellectual definition of life, *docto homini et erudito vivere est cogitare,* gained the approval of a growing number of people drawn from all classes of society. This spread of humanism was less a result of a chance trickle-down process than it was the product of an educational system designed toward that end. Even the persistence of dialectic and the resurgence of Aristotle could not repress the humanist learned tradition of rhetoric, poetry, moral philosophy, history, Platonism, and natural philosophy. One is struck by the concatenation of influences from person to person, teacher to student, mind to mind. The spread of humanism to a reasonably broad segment of the German population began with the attendance of German youth at the Italian universities, increased as the German universities served as ladders of social mobility, and broadened as the reformers, Protestants and Jesuits alike, developed the gymnasium ideal of secondary education.

Renaissance humanism was an international phenomenon, and our survey has pointed to the many ties binding German to Italian, Dutch, French, and even English humanism. Many questions remain unanswered, and a library of books is yet to be written on unexplored aspects of this subject. One of the most intriguing questions begging for an answer is why, with the growing number of erudite and cultivated men, German humanism failed during the second half of the sixteenth century to produce any real genius comparable to those who made

Elizabethan England a golden age from Spenser to Shakespeare.[124] Looking ahead from the year 1555 one might have expected Germany to take over the cultural leadership from Italy, with France and England following after, but just the reverse order actually occurred. Two centuries later, when German literature seemed doomed to tertiary status as imitative and unoriginal, it bloomed into the garden of Weimar genius just as French and English letters wilted away. Perhaps the centrifugal force of political particularism, the shift of economic activity to the Atlantic seaboard, the passing of the agonizing decades of religious struggle and the stalemate acknowledged and legalized by the Peace of Augsburg, the insistence on orthodoxies, or other considerations may be adduced as contributing factors. But the human spirit must not fare too well in this world, for creative genius responds to suffering and conflict and grows dull with overmuch prosperity. The German humanists such as Reuchlin were fond of quoting the line from Horace, *Exegi monumentum aere perennis.*[125] Compared with the golden age of the Italian Renaissance it was indeed a monument of bronze. But it also had a lasting quality, though it gave way in the end to the iron age of an industrial society.

---

[124] Harold Jantz, *op. cit.,* 435
[125] Horace, *Carmina,* III, 30.

# III

## THE *THEOLOGIA PLATONICA* IN THE RELIGIOUS THOUGHT OF THE GERMAN HUMANISTS

In the entire range of problems associated with Renaissance humanism there is none so controversial and difficult to penetrate as that of the precise nature of the religious thought and sentiments of the period. The range of scholarly opinion is wide indeed, from Burckhardt's own reference to "religious indifference" to Toffanin's ordination of a "great lay-priesthood of the humanists." Thanks to the work of the revisionists, scholarship has moved far from the judgment of Milman in his *History of Latin Christianity:* "Between the close of this age [scholasticism], but before the birth of modern philosophy, was to come the Platonizing, half Paganizing, school of Marsilius Ficinus: the age to end in direct rebellion, in the Italian philosophers, against Christianity itself."[1] Ficino's efforts to develop a constructive theology, synthetic in character, attempting to conciliate divergent philosophies in a "great peace" is at last understood in something near its true terms. The conciliatory formula in his commentary on the *Timaeus* can now be correctly appreciated in the light of Ficino's high regard for Thomas: "The peripatetics have positive reasons, the Platonists superior reasons."[2] The new evaluation of the Florentine's *religio docta* has implications also for northern humanism which have not as yet been fully assessed.

The changes which Renaissance ideas underwent as they crossed the Alps offer an instructive object lesson in intellectual history. Now that the theories of the autochthonous origin and development of northern humanism have been laid to rest, there remains the task of studying more closely the nature of the Italian influence in a cultural milieu which lacked most of the antique-aesthetic elements everywhere present in the Latin homeland. The task of evaluating the cultural amalgam resulting frcm the combination of northern and southern influences presents a real challenge. The present study is intended to be a contribution toward the solution of one facet of the larger problem, namely, the effect of the *Theologia Platonica* on a select number of representative German humanists, who were really German men of letters who happened to write in Latin.[3] It will be a kind of intellectual spectral analysis revealing the

Platonic coloration of northern humanists resulting from the dispersion of the pure white light of Florentine philosophy upon entering the northern atmosphere.

Egidio da Viterbo, who was named a cardinal in the fateful year 1517, believed that the triumph of the Platonic theology marked the return to a golden age. This faith in the validity and power of the *philosophia pia* was characteristic of the verve of the Italian Platonists. The influence of the Florentine Academy in Germany was in part a direct result of conscious zeal for the propagation of the faith, as well as of their earnest, subjective, contagious enthusiasm. The most popular Italian humanists among their German counterparts, in fact, were Valla, Ficino, Pico, and Baptista Mantuanus, possibly in that order. One reason for the sympathetic hearing accorded Ficino was his high regard for the ultramontanes, in contrast to the pose of superiority adopted by Poggio, Antonio Campano, or Aeneas Silvius.

Ficino maintained many personal contacts with German men of letters. In Florence he played host to a good many of the German savants on their *Italienische Reise,* a tradition of medieval standing. In March, 1482, for example, he welcomed the learned retinue of Duke Eberhard of Wuerttemberg including Ludwig Vergenhans, Matthias Preninger, Gabriel Biel, and Johannes Reuchlin. Ficino carried on an extensive correspondence particularly with Preninger, a noted canon lawyer, and also wrote to Vergenhans and Reuchlin.[4] Though he informed the minor German humanist Martin Uranius in 1492, who had asked him for a list of his students, that properly speaking he had no students, only Socratic *confabulatores* and younger auditors, the Germans recommended to him many young men aspiring to Greek learning *et dona ferentes*.[5] In Basel Paulus Niavus, the "German Filelfo," expounded on Ficino's writings. Konrad Pellican, the pioneer Hebraist, was inspired both by Ficino's and Pico's writings. Both Froben and Amerbach published various works of Ficino. In Augsburg Georg Herivart always cherished the memory of his visit with Ficino in Florence and commemorated the day he learned to know him. The list of Germans who knew Ficino and Pico, read their works, or were influenced at least indirectly by them might be extended to great length to include such lesser humanists as Nicolaus Gerbellius or Nicolaus Ellenbogen, the Benedictine prior who assembled an anthology of passages from Plato, and more illustrious figures as Konrad Peutinger, Mutianus Rufus, Conrad Celtis, Willibald Pirckheimer, Albrecht Dürer, Beatus Rhenanus, Trithemius, Agrippa of Nettesheim, and many leading reformers such as Zwingli as well.

It would be pretentious indeed to undertake to discuss in brief compass the impact of all phases of the *Theologia Platonica* on the entire humanist movement. Prudence would dictate a more modest course. To that end it will be necessary first to epitomize the key ideas of the Platonic theology and then to examine the role these ideas played in the thought of a few representative German humanists. The *sedes doctrinae* are, of course, Ficino's *Theologia Platonica, De religione christiana,* and in a more literary philosophical garb, the *Commentarium in convivium platonis de amore.*[6] Pico's popularity in the North was perhaps due to the appeal of that theme in his writings to which he intended to give full expression in the *De concordia Platonis et Aristotelis,* a hope never realized. For Pico's humanist-scholastic synthesis was sure to find a sympathetic response wherever the *viae,* especially realism, still showed some vitality. His famous letter to Ermolao Barbaro, June 5, 1485, defending scholastic philosophy, would have found many sympathetic recipients in the North.

Ficino, an ordained priest, considered himself a fisher of men like Peter, using the Platonic philosophy to catch especially the intellectuals. The apologetic goal determined to a large degree the structure of his theosophy. He was interested in exploiting the Platonic and Neoplatonic philosophies in the interest of a constructive theology. In one passage he has Plato say to Plotinus, "This is my beloved son in whom I am well pleased." But Ficino read Plotinus, whose *Enneads* and other works he knew well, as translator and editor, to a degree through the eyes of Dionysius the Areopagite, as had the long medieval tradition before him. The result was not a lifeless repristination of the thought of Pletho, Dionysius, Plotinus, or Plato, but Ficino's own system tuned to the needs of his time. Certain features of his thought are particularly characteristic and readily identifiable.

The *religio docta* presupposed an epistemology of poesy and faith. Divine poetry provides a veil for the true religion. Formally Ficino's theory of knowledge was premised on Plato's dictrine of innate ideas. In the religious area Ficino tended to the rhapsodic and mystical. True poesy is theology encompassing more than can be included in a precise intellectual formula. "I certainly prefer to believe by divine inspiration," wrote Ficino, "than to know in human fashion."[7] It is interesting to discover that the term *sola fide* was a favorite expression of Ficino's, though with it he meant essentially merely a tool for the apprehension of trans-empirical reality, and not Luther's faith that moves mountains. True religion is identified closely with wisdom and is not coterminous with Judaeo-Christian revelation. Truth is revealed in many forms and wisdom has been transmitted through a long tradition from the ancient philosophers. All the elements of this *prisca gentilium theologia* are to be found in Plato and the Platonic tradition. The border between revealed truth and inspired wisdom was quite indistinct in the *philosophia pia*. It might even appear from the arguments that the Christian faith found authority in its wisdom rather than the reverse. There is, then, clearly a tendency discernible toward a syncretistic universalism.[8]

Basic to the cosmology and anthropology of the Florentine Platonists was their conception of the hierarchy of being. The basic concept is that of God as the ultimate unity of all things. Plotinus, building on Philo, described the "One" as the absolute and uncontradicted original essence, prior to any specific beings which imply pluralities. The relationship of the "One" embracing in itself numberless numbers to the lesser creatures is to be understood in terms of the great chain of being. There is a stepladder of bodies, qualities, soul and heavenly intelligences to the eternal "One" which marks the way of ascent to God. Man's position in the universe is a guarantee of his dignity and moral worth. Yes, God's immanence in man should lead man to trust his own divinity. The goal of life is to enjoy God *(Deo frui)* and to make this possible for men, Christ became the intermediary (the *Tò metaxú* concept) between God and man. Christ is the archetype of the perfect man serving as example. At the same time he demonstrates God's love for man, freeing the soul for the ascent to God. Here church and sacrament, priests and saints, above all Mary, play their part in the highly spiritualized understanding of dogma and ecclesiology. Some day man will enjoy God's presence without mediation.

Certain prominent threads run through the entire texture of Florentine Platonism. The light metaphysic is exploited for literal and symbolic representation. Involved in this problem besides questions of general ontology is the notion of astral influence and Saturnine melancholy. The theory of love directing man's preferences in terms of good and evil, beautiful or displeasing, for the problem of aesthetics runs parallel to that of ethics in his thought, is intimately related to his epistemology, since it is harmony with an innate idea in man and its correspondence in quality to that unity which binds the world together, turning chaos into cosmos, which determines man's judgment. The Platonic assumption of a substantive soul involving the issue posed by the Averroists and Alexandrists of the nature of immortality is a major concern of the Florentines. These are basic themes of Ficino and his *conphilosophi* which should reappear in the assumptions of the German humanists who came under their influence.

It is common knowledge that Neoplatonism had been a major ingredient of the medieval intellectual tradition. It was important in the thought of the Dominican mystics as well as being frozen in formalized scholastic structures. The temptation for the "revisionists", therefore, is to write off the evidence of Neoplatonic influence on the thought also of the German humanists as merely a carry-over of medieval Neoplatonism. On the surface this seems plausible enough and a measure of continuity can in the course of things be assumed, particularly among those humanists who came from the Rhenish areas where mysticism was common or had been trained in the *via antiqua*. To isolate the distinctive influence of the Florentine *Theologia Platonica* requires a close examination of the particulars, therefore, since merely asserting arguments *a priori* must in the nature of the case be unrewarding. Wessel Gansfort illustrates neatly how a man who moved naturally within the traditions of medieval Platonism can not possibly be associated with the Florentine variety. A comparison of his Platonism with that of the humanists under Florentine influence reveals the differences between a late medieval reformer type and more distinctively "Renaissance" personalities.[9]

Significantly, many outstanding members of the older generation of humanists, nearer in point of time and intellectual background to the main line medieval tradition, are practically devoid of Platonic or Neoplatonic philosophy. A case in point is the "father of German humanism", Rudolf Agricola, the first man of major stature after such poet-rhetoricians as Peter Luder, Albrecht van Eyb, the old-time scholastic Konrad Sum-

123

menhart, or the half-literary jurist Gregor Heimburg. Agricola, like Petrarch, opposed scholasticism because its abstractions covered over the real heart of Christianity. Agricola set strict limitations to speculative knowledge and ascribed new value to example over precept as depicted by historian, poet, and rhetorician, echoing the tenets of his teacher, Battista Guarino. He is a prime example of how the basically non-speculative, practical, and moralistic aspect of the *Devotio Moderna* coincided with the corresponding emphases of his pious Italian teachers. The familiar Neoplatonic themes, medieval or Florentine, are not to be found in his thought. He illustrates what German humanism might have remained if it had not been for the impact of the Villa Careggi.[10]

That even a knowledge and a certain enthusiasm for the Florentine Platonists might leave a humanist's thought not greatly altered is evident from the case of Wilibald Pirckheimer. He typifies the patrician-humanist with deep roots in the imperial city of Nuremberg and a distinguished family with three generations of Italian travel and education. In his twentieth year he went to Italy where he spent almost seven years, mostly at Padua and Pavia, and absorbed a variety of intellectual influences which he never succeeded in integrating into a unified philosophy.[11] At Padua in addition to contact with Scotism and nominalism, he learned to know Averroistic Aristotelianism. The philosophy of Platonism was represented by Giovanni di Rosellis and Gabriel Zerbus. Like the Florentines, they were interested in harmonizing Platonic and Aristotelian teaching in support of Christianity. Pirckheimer once described Ficino as "a man who was most meritorious because of his work on Plato and one worthy of eternal memory."[12] Moreover, his personal feeling toward Pico developed out of his friendship with Pico's nephew, Francesco. Pirckheimer's major literary efforts went into translations of Greek into Latin and both into German. For moral and metaphysical edification he translated the pseudo-dialogues *Axiochum* and *Clitiphon,* in the manner of Ficino, he observed. He also did the *De Justo, Eryxias, Num virtus doceri possit, Demodocus, Sisyphus,* and *Definitiones,* as well as a translation of Proclus' *Sphaera.* He gave preference in his translating to Plato and Plutarch, who, he asserted, had not wandered far from the path of truth, but also did many of the church fathers, church history, and education. The true theologian, Pirckheimer declared in the letter to

Lorenz Behaim preceding his edition of Lucian's *Piscator seu Reviviscentes*, must have studied the divine philosophy of Plato, to whom the palm must go. In 1511 at Maximilian's request Pirckheimer translated the *Hieroglyphica* of Horapollon which had intrigued Ficino and which Pico had exploited for his theosophical speculation. Pirckheimer associated them with the Christian moral teaching of the basic virtues. The wind-up is there, but one looks in vain for the follow-through, a distinctively Neoplatonic or at least mystical pitch in his religious philosophy. The fact is that Pirckheimer was much more conservative in his religious thought than he has generally been portrayed and much less imaginative in exploiting Platonism in the interest of Christianity than might be expected. For the grand superstructure of the *Theologia Platonica* one looks in vain in the works of Wilibald Pirckheimer, who complained all his life about how official public duties prevented his full devotion to thought and letters.

The three leading humanists who best illustrate the positive and varied effect of Florentine Platonism on religious thought are Mutian, Celtis, and Reuchlin. Mutian, the prince of the Erfurt humanists, ranked with Luther, Erasmus, and Reuchlin in the opinion of Crotus Rubeanus and the younger humanists. Educated in Deventer, Erfurt, and Italy in the essentials of the *devotio moderna*, the intricacies of the *via moderna*, and the wisdom of the *philosophia platonica*, he absorbed in one mind the impress of three major intellectual systems. In addition to contact with the medieval Neoplatonic constructs through his encounter, for example, with Johann Wesel, strongly under the influence of Wesel Gansfort, he was deeply impressed by the Florentine Platonists during his long stay in the home of the Renaissance.[13] Mutian's ambition was to transcend literary humanism to the level of philosophy. While Agricola, as a philologist-rhetorician, had a predilection for Cicero, Petrarch, and Quintilian, Mutian preferred Plato, the *philosophus sanctus*.[14] His ideas everywhere reveal the philosophical marks of Florentine Neoplatonism. Very different in personality traits from the tentative, reflective Mutian was that gregarious propagandizer of humanism in the North, Conrad Celtis, the German arch-humanist.[15] He best illustrates the potential contribution of poetic culture for the Renaissance of Christendom. He learned to know Ficino personally in Florence, where at the time Ficino was working on his *De vita triplici*, that "diatetic of the Saturnine man." There Celtis met at first hand a philosophy closely attuned to his poetic spirit. He was himself only a dilettante in philosophy, as a glance at the disparate list of titles which he edited makes plain. But the poetic theosophy of Neoplatonism appealed very strongly to his aesthetic nature.[16] Reuchlin's Neoplatonism came through various channels. Melanchthon in an oration in honor of Reuchlin recalled that he had at first used the Greek works collected by Nicolas Cusanus in Basel.[17] On his first visit to Florence he had met Ficino (1482), on his second, Pico (1490), and was deeply impressed by both. Ficino had urged Hebrew as a most important source and element of wisdom. But from Pico Reuchlin acquired his interest in Cabalism, for in his *Conclusiones* and *Apologia* Pico had advanced the idea that the Cabala provided sure support for Christian dogma and the divinity of Christ. In his *Heptaplus* Pico pointed to the parallel between Pythagorean theosophy and Cabalism. Reuchlin, sharing Ficino's notion that Greek philosophy was derived from the wisdom of Moses and the Hebrews, believed that Pythagoreanism had developed out of oriental philosophy in great antiquity. On such a premise he could easily conclude that Pythagoreanism corresponded to the tradition of the Jewish Cabalists. He determined to exploit the Cabala in the interest of Christian apologetics. But the medieval Cabala was itself steeped in Neoplatonic lore and indeed shared its basic structure. In his early period and in his first philosophical work, *De verbo mirifico* (1494), before he had mastered Cabalism, Reuchlin's Platonic amalgam was basically medieval and Florentine. In his major work, *De arte cabalistica* (1517), his Platonism was structured more extensively on the pattern of Cabalism. For Reuchlin was conscious of the special role he was to play in intellectual history, when he wrote: "Marsilio [Ficino] brought forth Plato for Italy; Lefévre d'Etaples restored Aristotle to France; and I shall complete the number, for I, Capnion, shall show to the Germans Pythagoras reborn through me."[18]

The shift in Florentine thought from a literal exegesis and the *nuda veritas* of the dogmatic traditions to an epistemology of poesy and faith and a consistent "spiritualization" of the theological heritage was reflected also in the poetic-symbolic approach to religious concepts of Mutian, Celtis, and Reuchlin. Mutian's wisdom ideal tended toward the spiritualization of the Hebraic-Christian inheritance. He once suggested, for example, that the spiritual nativity of Christ took place before all ages so that Christ as the true wisdom of God was with the Jews, the Greeks, the Italians, and even the Germans, though they celebrated their religions with different rituals and had various priesthoods.[19] Mutian was as critical of the formal sacramentalism as of the sacerdotalism of the late medieval period. He protested strongly against mere outward ceremonies and the dependence upon sacramental efficaciousness *ex opere operato*. The tone of his criticisms of fasts, rote prayers, veneration of relics, benefice seeking, abuse of the office of the keys as a power instrument and control device, and similar strictures against the church is similar to that of many late medieval critics and rebels but in some cases seems to have been inspired not so much by moral indignation as by a philosophical consideration that viewed the spiritual meaning as the essence and the outward act as a thing of tertiary importance. Mutian found the essence of the Eucharist not in corporeal transubstantiation but in love. Like Ficino, who may have first used the phrase "Platonic love", Mutian urged the universal validity of the law of love and grew rhapsodic over the theme of love as the eternal law and the basic reality in this "great and most beautiful and best arranged world." He protested the externalization and vulgarization of spiritual meaning and emphasized subjective personal responsibility against the objectivization of religion within the institutionalized framework.[20] Celtis, too, when not in a skeptical mood, urged the spiritualization of the sacramental system and of formalized ecclesiastical dogma.. He struck near the heart of the medieval sacramental-sacerdotal system with his jibes at the gross interpretations of transubstantiation. Some of his demurers against the externalization and formalization of dogma seem to suggest that he did not feel bound by the inner dogma of the church, though in reality he held the spiritual essence of the faith to ·the end.[21] Similarly Reuchlin, though he was himself a poor poet and was least in his element when rhapsodizing on light, love, and beauty, much preferred the poetic approach to theology of the Platonists to the syllogistic aridity of those scholastics uninspired by Platonism. His epistemology was precisely the Neoplatonic formula with its familiar theory of innate ideas and process of illumination.[22] Only knowledge reinforced by faith is certain knowledge.[23] Like Ficino, he frequently used the phrase *sola fide* in an epistemological sense. His was preeminently a *philosophia supernaturalis* in which faith was both a tool for knowledge and the elixir of eternal life.

The tendency toward a syncretistic universalism in the *philosophia pia* is in evidence also in the thought of Mutian, Celtis, and Reuchlin. Mutian's wisdom ideal combined with his spiritualization of the Hebraic-Christian inheritance and stress on moral influence over the vicarious atonement implied a universalistic element reducing the uniqueness of Christianity. Mutian discovered the basic moral imperative in various traditions. He wrote: "Moses, Plato, Christ taught it. This is present in our hearts."[24] He believed that although Christ had most fully revealed natural moral law, it was partially set forth by Draco, Solon, Lycurgus, Moses, Plato, Pythagoras, the decemvirs and similar law givers.[25] He concluded that the higher religions viewed morality rather than ceremony as the essence of true religion. He cited from the Alcoran the saying: "Who prays to the eternal God and lives virtuously, he may be a Jew, Christian, or a Saracen, he receives the grace of God and salvation." "Therefore," he asserted, "he is religious, right living, pious, who has a pure heart. All else is smoke."[26] Mutian derived a substantial measure of his universalism from his strong sense of God's immanence and the activity of the Spirit inspiring men to wisdom and virtue. Ficino had based the historical claim to validity upon the Alexandrine myth that theological truths before Christ were derived from the Hebrew revelation. It is refleected as well in Pico's idea of the unity of truth which presupposed a syncretism of philosophical and religious truths. Celtis, too, learned from the *theologia prisca* that the philosophers and poets of old had achieved a proper harmony of nature and grace. Like Mutian, he regularly substituted classic names and phrases for Christian. In his *Carmen saeculare* he addressed God as an abscondite Being and in various odes revealed a surprising development toward universal theism.[27] Celtis' projected work, the *Parnassus biceps,* harmonizing the views of poets and theologians was reminiscent of the apologetic motif of the Florentines. As in Ficino's case, Reuchlin derived a tendency toward religious universalism from the exploitation of a wide variety of non-Christian sources of wisdom, in line with Pico's suggestion in the *Heptaplus* that the cabalists and Pythagoreans shared a common fund of wisdom.

The characteristic marks of the theology proper of Mutian,

Celtis, and Reuchlin indicate affiliation with Florentine thought rather than mere analogy. Mutian's conception of God as a dynamic Spirit, a *deus vivus*, in and with all life and being, followed Ficino's reformulation of theological ontology of Aristotelian scholasticism.[28] Similarly Mutian's image of Christ as the intermediary was a reflection of Ficino's. Christ's true significance lay in his spiritual qualities, for he descended from heaven as righteousness, peace, and joy. Mutian privately went so far as to approximate the ancient Docetic heresy in his abnegation of the human nature of Christ and the veneration of his earthly relics.[29] The poet Celtis was as mercurial theologically as he was temperamentally. On one level he stood securely on the formal dogmatic definitions. He died in the arms of the church and was laid to rest with due honors. In his poetry, however, he often reflected his immediate source of inspiration, Apuleius, Macrobius, Lucretius, Ovid, or Boccaccio. In one passage fate like a blind goddess strides across the earth. In another, man's fate rests securely in God's hands. Doubtless these wild vacillations reflected also his personal perplexity over questions of God's nature, his concern for the universe, or a deistic withdrawal.[30] But the predominant conception of God and his relationship to man and nature corresponded in idea and tone to the views of Florentine Neoplationism. There is the emphasis upon God's immanence, the enlivening of every part of the universe by the omnipresent Spirit, the binding power of Love, the Neoplatonic Eros, as the cosmic principle uniting God the Creator to the creature, the love to which the philosophers ascribed creative power. These expressions all leave the impression of superficiality, of being mere poetic effusions, but they also show in pale reflection the religious mystique and theological notions of the aesthetic Florentines. Reuchlin was far superior as a religious philosopher. His two major works reveal his constructive theology as basically the familiar Neoplatonic system. In the first he was concerned with demonstrating the centrality of Christ as the divine intermediary, exploiting writers from St. John to Ficino. The conception of Christ (the cabalists' Messiah) as the mediator (tò metaxú) between the abscondite God and man is central for Reuchlin. As in Ficino, Christ's revelatory role is more prominent than his redemptive action. He is the Word who illumines men and opens the last gate of understanding.[31] In the second work the Neoplatonic structure stands completed with a true cabalistic facade.

A strong affinity to Neoplatonic anthropology is evident in the place which Mutian, Celtis, and Reuchlin assigned to man as an intermediary being in the universe, bound by the sensate, but drawn towards God and the celestial ideals. In all three man appears as the mirror of the macrocosm, a divine reflection of God himself, a little world, a little god.[32] Man's moral potential and his immortal destiny are his chief claims to glory and preeminence. The goal of man as the microcosm at the midpoint in the universe is to ascend upward to the One, Reuchlin pronounced, using the precise Neoplatonic terminology.[33] Like Ficino, he developed every available argument against Aristotle (Averroes) to prove the immortality of the soul.

Like Ficino, who viewed the world of nature with mystical sentimentality as a living organism, Mutian, Celtis, and Reuchlin hailed the earth as holy, beautiful in form, and reflecting brilliance and soul like the sun. Ficino's cosmology, the macro-microcosm, the bonds of sympathy of the upper and lower worlds, the light metaphysic reappear in them. Like Pico. both Celtis and Reuchlin were intrigued by Pythagorean number mysticism. Reuchlin discovered in the Cabala (Opus de Bereshith) an elaborate cosmic theory which corresponded in basic outline to that of the Neoplatonists.[34] In the first decades of the sixteenth century representative German natural philosophers were highly receptive to the mystical teachings of Pico. Paracelsus, for example, had a strong feeling for the unity of the cosmic order penetrated by the immanent God.

Literary and civic humanism from Petrarch on had evidenced a trend against over-intellectualized and formalized religion. Many Platonic elements in the medieval heritage and many facets of preceding humanist thought pointed toward and contributed to the building up of the mystical metaphysical synthesis of the Florentine Academy. The erudite and poetic spirituality of the Neoplatonic philosophy clearly responded to the religious aspirations of many men in the fifteenth century. This approach, with its frequent recourse to allegory and myth was well designed to capture the imagination and allegiance also of some *literati* in the humanist tradition in the North. Cosimo d'Medici reportedly said to the father of Ficino: "Your business is to care for our bodies, but your son has been sent by Heaven to cure our souls." The philosophical concerns of these northerners, like those of their Italian cultural heros, were essentially theological.

Establishing lines of influence is, of course, one of the more difficult problems in intellectual history. In this case, however, there are controls which establish a high probability for definite conclusions. It is clear that the literary humanists of the older generation like Agricola, who had a long Italian experience, even with a first-hand exposure to medieval influences and with access to such philosophers as Cusanus, did not move in the direction of a *Theologia Platonica*. A careful biographical examination, moreover, reveals that humanists like Mutian, Celtis, and Reuchlin showed no serious inclination toward Platonic theology prior to their first contacts with the Florentines in their persons and writings. Finally, their contemporaries like the great Erasmus, who had direct contact with the medieval piety and thought of the *devotio moderna* and the *via antiqua*, but only indirectly and at a maturer age with the world of Neoplatonic speculation, did not show the same understanding of or enthusiasm for the *Theologia Platonica*. Erasmus' primary contact with the Florentine Academy had had been through Colet and Oxford, where his theological interests received a new orientation. The author of the *Enchiridion* knew Pico's works, but basically retained only his ideas about the dignity of man, detaching them from the metaphysical system in which they were imbedded. Even these faded away into the peculiar amalgam of his own *philosophia Christi*. Valla was his true inspiration.[35]

In Mutian, Celtis, and Reuchlin the presence of the *Theologia Platonica* in varying degrees is unmistakable. There is the greater inwardness and individualism, the spiritualization of the sacramental system, the emphasis on wisdom *(sapientia)* and the attendant universalism, as well as the distinctive Neoplatonic nexus of ideas and characteristic terminology in the areas of theology, anthropology, and cosmology. These northerners, who were selfconsciously the *conphilosophi* of the Florentines, failed to produce a closed system of philosophy which could be reproduced as such at any time in a later age. In fact, the lack of such a system is exactly one of the major differences between Renaissance thought in general and the closed quality of scholastic philosophy.

The philosophical conceptions of the German humanists

were not merely repetitions of a received tradition, but were expressions of a living intellectual response to challenging novel ideas. Agricola was typical of the literary humanists with a long Italian experience, but under no Neoplatonic influence of the Florentine type. Pirckheimer scarcely appropriate Florentine ideas into an integrated philosophy, remaining very much intellectually what he was socially, a conservative patrician. To assert that in view of the Christian apologetic aim of the Florentines the Italian Neoplatonic influence was basically Christian in nature and fused harmoniously with northern piety would yield a pat revisionist solution and the case would be closed. But even the present small sampling suggests that in the case of Mutian and Celtis the heady ideas and broader horizons of the Florentine philosophy served to upset their religious equilibrium and proved to be more disturbing than reassuring. Reuchlin alone had the mental stamina not only to take the Florentines' measure but to go beyond them into a new area of thought toward which they had, to be sure, pointed. There can in any event be no talk of sterile formalism or of northerners as mere epigoni. Ficino was said to have appeared after his death to his student Michael Mercatus to bring him news of the other world. "O Michael, O Michael, vera, vera sunt illa!" he intoned. If only he could add an authoritative affirmation also to this present analysis!

## NOTES

1. Henry Hart Milman, *History of Latin Christianity*, VIII (New York, 1871), 287. Credit is due above all to Paul Oskar Kristeller for his careful technical analysis of Ficino's thought, *The Philosophy of Marsilio Ficino* (New York, 1943), and for his various studies seeking to put Florentine Platonism in its proper place in relationship to its philosophic antecedents and to literary and civic humanism, "Florentine Platonism and Its Relations with Humanism and Scholasticism," *Church History*, VIII (1939), 201ff.; "Humanism and Scholasticism in Renaissance Thought," *Byzantion*, XVII (1945), 346ff.; "Diacetto and Florentine Platonism in the Sixteenth Century," *Miscellanea Giovanni Mercati*, IV (1946), and other articles. A sprightly essay defining Pico's dependence upon scholasticism is Avery Dulles, *Princeps Concordiae: Pico della Mirandola and the Scholastic Tradition* (Cambridge, Mass., 1941), revealing a positive correlation drawn already by Leon Dorez and Louis Thuasne, *Pic de la Mirandole en France* (Paris, 1897). Dr. John Kunstmann contributed to my initial interest in German humanism with a lecture which he delivered on Niklas von Wyle at the University of Chicago many years ago.

2. *Opera*, II, 1438, cited in André Chastel, *Marsile Ficin et l'Art* (Geneva, 1954), 15. The most recent study of this general problem is Michael Seidlmayer, "Religiö-ethische Probleme des Italienischen Humanismus," *Germanisch-Romanische Monatsschrift*, N.F. VIII (1958),

105-126. I am grateful to Dr. Hans Baron for drawing this article to my attention. For detailed bibliography on this whole question, cf. Carlo Angelieri, *Il Problema Religioso de Rinascimento*. *Storia della critica e bibliografia* (Florence, 1952), especially 178ff.

3. Hans Baron, "Zur Frage des Ursprungs des deutschen Humanismus und seiner religiösen Reformbestrebungen," *Historische Zeitschrift*, CXXXII (1925), 446, called for a study which would isolate a number of cultural types and thereby clarify more concretely the nature of northern humanism, a program still not realized.

4. Henri Johan Hak, *Marsilio Ficino* (Amsterdam, 1934), 143-153, gives details on the many personal contacts of Ficino with the Germans.

5. A. Chastel, *op. cit.*, 24.

6. Sears Jayne, *Marsilio Ficino's Commentary on Plato's Symposium*, *University of Missouri Studies*, XIX, no. 1 (Columbia, 1944), 24, argues that the *Commentary* was intended to epitomize Ficino's whole philosophy. Eugenio Garin, *Der italienische Humanismus* (Bern, 1947), 105ff., contains an excellent statement of some of Ficino's basic tenets, though he makes no effort at completeness.

7. *Epistolae, liber* V, fol. 783: "Ego certe malo divine credere, quam humane scire." For a high idealist interpretation of the *religio docta*, cf. Guiseppe Saitta, *Il Pensiero Italiano nell' Umanesimo e nel Rinascimento*, I (Bologna, 1949), 509ff., "La Filosofia di Marsilio Ficino," especially 514ff.

8. Ivan Pusino, "Ficinos und Picos religiös-philosophische Anschauungen," *Zeitschrift für Kirchengeschichte*, XLIV, N.F. VII (1925), 504ff., stresses the universalist element in Florentine Neoplatonism. Cf. *Marsilii Ficini Florentini, insignis Philosophi Platonici, Medici atque Theologi clarissimi, Opera*, etc. (Basel, n.d.), 98: "Unity, truth, goodness are the same, and beyond these there is nothing" (*Theologia Platonica*, 79ff.).

9. Gerhard Ritter, "Romantische und revolutionär Elemente in der deutschen Theologie am Vorabend der Reformation," *Deutsche Vierteljahrschrift für Literaturwissenschaft und Geistesgeschichte*, V (1927), 342-380, especially 373.

10. Cf. J. Lindeboom, *Het bijbelsch Humanisme in Nederland* (Leiden, 1913), 58ff., observes that Agricola never belonged to Ficino's circle. The association of Agricola with the promotion of Neoplatonism is a common error in the general literature, as, for example, L. Häusser, *Geschichte der Rheinischen Pfalz* (Heidelberg, 1845), I, 437: ". . . . auch bei Agricola wird die neuerblühte antike Philosophie, jener florentinische Platonismus . . . hineingezogen." A complete biography of Agricola is that of H. E. J. M. van der Velden, *Rodolphus Agricola (Roelof Huusman) een nederlandsch Humanist der vijftiende Eeuw* (Leiden, 1911). Melanchthon already reported Agricola's constant preoccupation with Aristotle, *Corpus Reformatorum*, XI, col. 443.

11. Hans Rupprich, "Willibald Pirckheimer. Beiträge zu einer Wesenserfassung," *Schweizer Beiträge zur Allgemeinen Geschichte*, XV (1957), 64-110, gives a precise detailed account of Pirckheimer's travels, studies, and literary activities. He concludes that Pirckheimer was basically far more conservative than has been traditionally held. Yet C. J. Burckhardt "Willibald Pirckheimer," *Neue Schweizer Rundschau*, N.F. IV (1936/37), 577ff., depicts Pirckheimer as a bird of paradise in the conservative Nuremberg upper bourgeoisie. The completion of the definitive edition of Pirckheimer's correspondence is a boon to Pirckheimer scholarship, *Willibald Pirckheimers Briefwechsel*, I (Munich, 1940), A. Reimann and Emil Reicke, eds., II (Munich, 1956), Siegfried Reicke and Wilhelm Volkert, eds. For his works we are still dependent upon the old Melchior Goldast, ed. *Bilibaldi Pirckheimeri Opera* (Frankfort, 1610).

12. Letter to Bernhard Adelmann, Sept. 1; 1521, Goldast, ed., *Opera*, 234. Cf. Exkurs III: Pirckheimer und Marsilius Ficinus. Einflüsse auf Dürers Melancholie. Zu P'S Aufenthalt in Rom, E. Reicke, ed., *Pirck-*

133

*heimers Briefwechsel*, I, 10f. On May 29, 1517, Adelmann wrote to Pirckheimer: "That your father ascribed great significance to Marsilius you know perhaps best of all." Pirckheimer had from his father Ficino's Plato translation and the manuscript translation of *Pymander*, Hermes Trismegistus' work on the power and wisdom of God. Cf. *Pirckheimers Briefwechsel*, I, ep. 1, p. 1: "Opus Marsilii Ficini affinibus dedi, qui id se transmissuros dixerunt. Theologiam Marsilii seu Platonis non reperio." A Vienna manuscript which Pirckheimer wrote himself in Italy contains a letter from Ficino in 1472 and his *Commentarium in conviviam Platonis de Amore*, Nationalbibliothek Handschriftensammlung, *Bibl. Pal. Vind.*, Codex 12466.

13. Cf. Carl Krause, *Der Briefwechsel des Mutianus Rufus* (Kassel, 1885), ep. 85, p. 93; ep. 137, p. 175; ep. 392, p. 460; ep. 548, p. 616; ep. 557, p. 626; ep. 311, p. 385. "At quoniam sine sacris et Christo philosopharis, stulto stultior esse et ab academia Platonicisque meis aberrare videris neque nostrae Musae Congruis."

14. *Ibid.*, ep. 233, p. 289.

15. For an account of Celtis, cf. my biography, *Conrad Celtis the German Arch-Humanist* (Cambridge, Mass., 1957), especially pp. 106ff.

16. Celtis criticized the scholastics sharply for not knowing the divine books of Plato, *Amores* III, 10, lines 49ff.; and urged his students to the study of Plato, the Stoics, and Pythagoras. Hans Rupprich, *Der Briefwechsel des Konrad Celtis* (Munich, 1934), ep. 11, pp. 20ff., a student thanks Celtis for extending to him his "deep understanding of Plato."

17. *Corpus Reformatorum*, XI, col. 1002.

18. *De arte cabalistica* in *Opera omnia Ioannis Pici Mirandvlae* (Basel, 1557), 734.

19. Carl Krause, *op. cit.*, ep. 26, p. 32.

20. On the interpretation of the Eucharist, cf. *ibid.*, ep. 85, p. 93. See also, *ibid.*, ep. 596, p. 636; ep. 73, p. 79.

21. Cf., for example, Celtis, *Epigramme* IV, 17; *Ode* III, 15, lines 29ff.; *Ep.* IV, 23; *Amores* III, 9, lines 47ff.

22. Reuchlin, *De arte cabalistica* 739, 740, 747, 765, 782.

23. Reuchlin cites Plotinus, Porphyry, and Iamblichus on the power of God, *ibid.*, 891. On faith, cf. *De verbo mirifico* (Tübingen, 1514) fol. cviv.

24. Carl Krause, *op. cit.*, ep. 52, p. 57.

25. *Ibid.*, ep. 69, p. 75.

26. *Ibid.*, ep. 268, pp. 330f. On veneration for churchyards, cf. *ibid.*, ep. 488, p. 552.

27. Cf. *Ode* I, 16; *Ode* I, 19.

28. Carl Krause, *op. cit.*, ep. 233, p. 291; ep. 10, p. 11, etc.

29. *Ibid.*, ep. 85, pp. 93f.; ep. 27, p. 35.

30. *Amores* IV, 4, lines 89ff.; *Ode* I, 15, lines 137ff.

31. *De verbo mirifico*, fol. hvᵛ; *De arte cabalistica*, 842.

32. Carl Krause, *op. cit.*, ep. 85, p. 94; Celtis, *Briefwechsel*, ep. 275, pp. 494ff., lines 121ff.; ep. 101, pp. 165ff., line 22; *De verbo mirifico*, fol. dv: . . . homo migret in deum et deus habitet in homine; fol. biiii, Est deus in nobis, a phrase taken from Ovid; *De arte cabalistica*, pp. 738f., 740, 773, 820.

33. *De arte cabalistica*, 874.

34. On cosmology, cf. *Marsilii Ficini . . . Opera*, 1082; Carl Krause, *op. cit.*, ep. 25, p. 28; ep. 488, pp. 551ff.; ep. 75, p. 80; Celtis, *Amores* I, 11, lines 49ff.; *Amores* IV, 14, lines 29f.; *Ode* I, 29. In his *De vita coelitus comparanda*, Ficino urged people to remain in the free heaven, in high and pleasant places, so that the stars' rays might work on them without interference.

35. Cf. Augustin Renaudet, *Érasme et L'Italie* (Geneva, 1954), 7, and the superb studies by the same author, *Érasme, sa pensée religieuse et son action, d'après sa correspondance (1518-1521)* (Paris, 1926); *Études érasmiennes (1521-1529)* (Paris, 1939). Louis Bouyer, *Autour D'Érasme* (Paris, 1955) has more recently argued for Erasmus' consistent orthodoxy.

# IV

## The Third Generation
## of German Renaissance Humanists

AFTER A FULL CENTURY of scholarly research, we are much better informed about the relationship of the Renaissance to the Middle Ages, much better informed than we are about its relationship to the period which followed. Similarly, we have learned a good deal more about the relationship of that cultural movement which we call humanism to its medieval sources of origin, to its scholastic predecessors, to its Byzantine inheritance, to its classical fountainhead than we have about its relationship to that movement which followed it, the Reformation. This paper is concerned with one facet of this relationship. Within the framework of the great debate on the medieval or the modern nature of the Reformation, exemplified best by Ernst Troeltsch and Wilhelm Dilthey, progress can be made only in terms of specifics, through an examination of the precise circumstances within which the Reformation developed. The juxtaposition of humanism and the Reformation, of humanists and reformers, may provide more concrete evidences than the general assertions with which the arguments on both sides of the question are usually promoted. The present problem was posed for historians by Luther himself, a man not insignificant in the events of his day, who, perceiving quite early that the Gospel made very little headway among the older men, wondered why. The Reformation was revolutionary, cutting deeper than had humanism, and breaking more decisively with the past. A young man's movement, it was in large part the work of the third generation of humanists in the north.

The Christian humanism of the north reflected the pattern of development familiar from the Italian Renaissance. A literary-philological phase was in many areas followed by a Platonic metaphysical phase. To a greater extent than has heretofore been realized humanism also invaded the courts and chancelleries of the secular and ecclesiastical princes as well as the councils of the city-states in the Empire and played a formative role through Roman law and classical letters. In the case of each of the major countries of the north it is possible to distinguish three generations of humanists: a pioneering generation, exhausting much of its energy in the acquisition of new classical learning and confronting some of the normative issues raised by the classical world view; a second generation, marking the highest achievement of renowned humanists; and a third and younger generation setting out upon a course of action to change that society which their elders merely criticized.

Thus in England the pioneers in classical studies such as Grocyn and Linacre were followed by the high generation of Oxford reformers, More, Colet, and Erasmus. These, in turn, were superseded by the young activists such as Starkey and Morison, who became the founders and expeditors of Tudor policy in statecraft, or Tyndale, Roger Ascham, and others, who became leaders in the religious and educational reform movement. In France the early pioneers such as Fichet, Standonck, and Gaguin were followed by the high generation of French humanism such as Budé and Lefèvre d'Etaples. Then came the young humanists, such men as Jean Calvin, who were no longer satisfied with criticism, but, following upon the impetus of conversion in many cases, were bent upon changing the world. The special vocation which this generation felt can be detected in Guillaume Farel's account of his dramatic interview with the aged Lefèvre. "That pious old man, Jacques Faber, whom you know," wrote Farel, "having taken my hand there forty years ago, said to me: 'It is necessary for the world to be changed and you will see it'."[1]

In German humanism such pioneers as Rudolph Agricola were followed by such great names as Mutian, Reuchlin, Celtis, Pirckheimer, Wimpheling, Erasmus, and Peutinger. The younger humanists of the third generation were impatient for change and became the men who, with Luther, made the Reformation. Bernd Moeller at Heidelberg University asserts with epigrammatic force: Without the humanists there would have been no Reformation.[2] With the singular exception of Luther himself, the leaders of the Reformation in the German cultural

[1] Comité Farel, *Guillaume Farel, 1489–1565* (Neuchâtel and Paris, 1930), pp. 103–104, taken from Johann H. Hottinger, *Historia ecclesiastica Novi Testamenti* (Tiguri, 1665). Though not a learned humanist, to be sure, Farel nevertheless reflects the aggressive spirit of the younger generation.

[2] Bernd Moeller, "Die deutschen Humanisten und die Anfänge der Reformation," *Zeitschrift für Kirchengeschichte*, LXX (1959), 47–61.

area moved from humanism into the Reformation. Major figures such as Zwingli, Melanchthon, Oecolampadius, Bucer, or Vadian come immediately to mind.[3] Scholarship has come increasingly to appreciate the importance of humanist learning also in the case of the radical reformers: Anabaptist leaders such as Balthasar Hubmaier, or the evangelical rationalists, or spiritualists such as Servetus or Sebastian Franck.[4] But the historian must not stay with the major figures, leaping from peak to peak, for, like the alpinist, he must traverse also the valleys and lesser plateaus or foothills between the heights. A host of less well-known men were Christian humanists in their formative years and became local leaders of the evangelical movement. Hubmaier once commented that almost all the learned were Lutherans.[5] "Young men," observed Francis Bacon in his *Of Youth and Age*, "are fitter to invent than to judge; fitter for execution than for counsel; and fitter for new projects than for settled business."

A list of lesser men who fall into this category might prove to be at least statistically reassuring. Johann Forster, a favorite pupil of Reuchlin, worked with Luther as a Hebraist in translating the Scriptures and was later a close friend of Melanchthon. Kaspar Peucer, mathematician and astronomer, was a son-in-law of Melanchthon and the electoral physician. Paul Eber as a philologue, historian, and natural scientist became a student and friend of Melanchthon. Friedrich Taubmann

---

[3] Werner Näf, *Vadian und seine Stadt St. Gallen* (2 vols.; St. Gallen, 1944–1957), is a model study of a humanist turned reformer. Of special importance for the present problem is the section on Vadian's breakthrough to Reformation doctrine (II, 151–180).

[4] Robert Kreider ("Anabaptism and Humanism: An Inquiry into the Relationship of Humanism to the Evangelical Anabaptists," *Mennonite Quarterly Review*, XXVI [1952], 123–141) illustrates the surprising connections between humanism and the radical reformation being established by current scholarship. Kreider is clear about the essential difference, however, stressing that the humanist "was a scholar, the Anabaptist was a disciple." Other representative recent studies are Thor Hall, "Possibilities of Erasmian Influence on Denck and Hubmaier in their Views of the Freedom of the Will," *Mennonite Quarterly Review*, XXXV (1961), 149–170; Guy F. Hershberger, ed., *The Recovery of the Anabaptist Vision* (Scottsdale, Illinois, 1957); John H. Yoder, "Balthasar Hubmaier and the Beginnings of Swiss Anabaptism," *Mennonite Quarterly Review*, XXXIII (1959); Heinold Fast, "The Dependence of the First Anabaptists on Luther, Erasmus, and Zwingli," *Mennonite Quarterly Review*, XXX (1956), 104–119; Robert Friedmann, "Recent Interpretations of Anabaptism," *Church History*, XXIV (1955), 132–151; Paul Peachy, "Social Background and Social Philosophy of the Swiss Anabaptists, 1525–1540," *Mennonite Quarterly Review*, XXVIII (1954), 102–127. See especially the comprehensive work of George H. Williams, *The Radical Reformation* (Philadelphia, 1962).

[5] Torsten Bergsten, *Balthasar Hubmaier* (Kassel, 1961), p. 100.

became professor of poetry at Wittenberg. The list might be extended almost indefinitely to include Aesticampianus, teacher of Hutten, who ended his days in Wittenberg; Franz Fritz (Irenicus); Johann Brenz; Theobald Dillichanus; Heinrich von Eppendorf; Bartholomaeus Bernhardi; Hieronymus Schurff; Johann Rivius, educational reformer in Saxony; Michael Neander, rector of Ilfeld and textbook writer; or Johannes Zwick, the reformer of Constance; and many others.[6]

During the decade of 1510 to 1520 a change is discernible in the atmosphere of the humanist microcosm. No longer satisfied with enjoying intellectually the stimulation of the classics, the humanists seek ways of applying their philosophy to life. The sharp criticism of abuse with its long ancestry back into the late medieval period is coupled now with a determined effort to effect the changes necessary to realize their ethical ideals. The *libido sciendi* is transformed into a wish to shape and form life. The interest in medicine becomes an insatiable desire to control nature. The scholarly pursuit of legal studies is transformed into a new preoccupation with jurisprudence and with entry into the political life of the Empire. In the humanist sodalities the humanist scholars and the political administrators, secretaries and bishops alike, reinforced their common interest in change. In some men, such as Conrad Peutinger, the *vita studiosa* and *vita activa* blended harmoniously. Konstanze Peutinger, in a charming letter addressed to her father, who was representing the city of Augsburg at the Diet of Worms, writes that he should hurry back, for his books are longing for his return. In religious life the criticism of abuses and the desire for religious enlightenment merged into a universal readiness for reform and an eagerness to get on with it.

Luther once commented that his Ninety-Five Theses had been carried within fourteen days throughout the length and breadth of Germany. The humanists were the chief agents for their distribution. Thus Christoph Scheurl in Nuremberg sent them to Peutinger in Augsburg, and they were quickly reprinted in Leipzig, Basel, and possibly Nuremberg. In 1520 Luther was the most read author in Germany, and Ulrich von Hutten the second most. There were strikingly few pamphlets and tracts or popular preachers active in those first years. Humanist support was comprehensive and universal. Without it Luther would not

---

[6] Many of these lesser figures await their biographers. An exemplary illustration of the kind of monographs needed as a basis for sound generalization is Bernd Moeller, *Johannes Zwick und die Reformation in Konstanz* (Gütersloh, 1961), especially pp. 41–54.

have succeeded. Almost all of the humanists of the older generation gave him a friendly word and at least provisional approval. And the younger humanists pledged him their loyalty and enthusiastic support. On May 1, 1518, Bucer wrote about the Heidelberg disputation to Beatus Rhenanus: "He [Luther] agrees with Erasmus in everything, except on one point he seems to excell him, for what he [Erasmus] merely insinuates, he [Luther] teaches openly and freely." Even some theologians such as Fabri and Cochlaeus, who were soon to become his fierce enemies, at first were kindly disposed to Luther. Eck himself reacted in a not un-friendly fashion, however fleetingly. To Crotus, Luther was like a god come to bring justice. His virtue and erudition were everywhere praised. Bernhard Adelmann in Augsburg identified *doctus* and *Lutherus*. "I see the whole world reviving!" exclaimed Beatus Rhenanus. The canon at Constance, Johann von Botzheim, an Erasmian, praised Luther as "the man who, after all the other disciplines have been renewed, is now renewing theology itself."[7]

Specifically, the humanists approved of Luther's uncompromising assault on scholasticism and his return to the pristine sources of Christianity, the Scriptures. Mosellanus in his description of the Leipzig debate wrote, "Ille [Lutherus] Philosophiam Aristotelicam . . . ex theologorum theatro explodit!" Melanchthon described the debate as a battle of primitive Christianity with Aristotle. Only a few, such as the keen-minded Oecolampadius, perceived that Luther's objection to scholasticism was less to its barbarous dialectic than to its *theologia gloriae* and that his drive *ad fontes* was less a preoccupation with antiquity than a thirst for the content, for the gospel itself. The general humanist reaction to Luther's acts proved to be productive misunderstanding and without just this kind of *felix culpa* history would not move forward! But from 1520 on, the Reformation derailed humanism. The humanists had been attracted more by Luther's constructive educational and devotional writings than by his polemical treatises. His *On the Babylonian Captivity of the Church* seems to have opened the eyes of many of the humanists to the real thrust of his reform. Precisely this treatise which offended some of the older humanists inspired some of the younger to join Luther's movement. Many of the mature humanists now discovered that in their heart of hearts they were Catholic and had to stay with the old church. Others, like Mutian, were shocked at the revolutionary *lapidatores* and shrank away from the boisterous reformers. Many of the younger humanists became evangelicals. Almost all of the

---

[7] Moeller, "Deutsche Humanisten," p. 51.

110

evangelicals were young, although not all of the young became evangelicals.

I blush to suggest that what the social scientists refer to as a "generations problem" is apparent here. Sigmund Freud candidly conceded that the poets had anticipated many of his seminal insights. Social scientists must likewise confess that the *literati* first pointed up the conflict of the generations. The theme is time-honored and even biblical, suggested in the mocking of the sons of Noah and given classic form in the story of David and Absalom. Literary historians from Herodotus to Voltaire have been aware of the generation factor. In the second book of his *Histories* Herodotus observed that for the Egyptians three hundred generations in the male line represented ten thousand years, for three generations made up a hundred years. Voltaire conjured with the notion of generation in his *Siècle de Louis XIV*. In modern letters this theme is the main burden of Turgenev's *Fathers and Sons*, Dostoevski's *The Possessed*, or Thomas Wolfe's *You Can't Go Home Again*, and is prominent in Simone de Beauvoir's *Mémoires d'une Jeune Fille Rangée*, not to mention the unmentionable, John Osborne's *Luther*. Social scientists have undertaken to define, structure, and systematize this factor and make it useful to historians.

The most masterful description of the problem of generations is clearly that of Karl Mannheim, who has described the two approaches as "positivist" and "romantic-historical."[8] The different ways in which the two schools approach the problem reflect the contrast in their basically antagonistic attitudes toward reality. The methodological ideal of the positivists naturally is that of reducing all problems, including the generations problem, to quantitative terms, attempting to establish a quantitative formulation of factors which ultimately determine the forms of human existence and the movement of human history. The second approach may be characterized as qualitative, shying away from the clear daylight of mathematics, introverting the whole problem. The intellectual ancestry of the positivist approach can be traced back to David Hume and Auguste Comte. Hume translated the principle of political continuity into terms of the biological continuity of generations. Comte, whose six-volume *Cours de philosophie*, which appeared between 1830 and 1842, linking sociology closely to biology, thought that man's span

---

[8] Karl Mannheim's essay, "The Problem of Generations," is the most useful single summary of the generations factor as seen by social scientists (*Essays on the Sociology of Knowledge* [New York, 1952], pp. 176–320, specifically, pp. 276–282).

of life and the average generation period of thirty years were necessary correlatives of the human organism. The discussion of the length of a generation continues today, with some theorists such as Ortega y Gasset setting the limits dogmatically at fifteen years, others arguing that a generation diminishes rapidly in length as the tempo of social change accelerates.[9]

A man whose importance for historical thought in the twentieth century is enormous and whose influence upon historical methodology has increased tremendously in recent years, Wilhelm Dilthey, in his essays on the *Geisteswissenschaften* gave to the generations problem a peculiarly Germanic romantic-historical turn. He shifted away from the positivistic quantitative approach to an interiorized qualitative method. Possibly taking his cue from St. Augustine—and no Reformation research paper, as Santayana once remarked of sermons, is complete without at least one reference to St. Augustine—Dilthey saw the phenomenon of generations as the problem of the existence of an interior time that cannot be measured but only experienced in purely qualitative terms. Dilthey was concerned with the generations problem primarily because the adoption of the generation as a temporal unit in the history of intellectual development makes it possible to replace purely external chronological units with a concept of measuring qualitatively from within (*eine von innen abmessende Vorstellung*). Dilthey held that the use of generations as interiorized units makes it possible to appraise intellectual movements by an intuitive process of re-enactment.

A second proposition which Dilthey advanced in connection with the generations problem is that the co-existence of a generation in many individuals is of more than mere chronological significance. Not only is the succession of one generation after another important, but the fact that the same dominant influences deriving from the prevailing political, social, religious, and intellectual circumstances are experienced by contemporary individuals, both in their early formative and in their later years, is of great significance to the interior, qualitative measurement of intellectual or cultural evolution or devolution, as the case may be. Individuals are contemporaries and constitute a single generation precisely because they are subject to common influences. Wilhelm Pinder referred to this phenomenon as the "noncontemporaneity of the con-

[9] José Ortega y Gasset, *El Torno a Galileo* (Vol. V of *Obras Completas* [Madrid, 1947]), Leccíon III, "Idea de la generacíon"; Leccíon IV, "El Metodo de las generaciones en historia"; Leccíon V, "De Nuevo, la idea de generación," pp. 29–67, specifically, p. 50.

temporaneous." The generation is thus conceived of as a collective of mentality which tends to become the basis for social groups. From the point of view of intellectual history, contemporaneity, then, means not merely something chronological, but a state of being subjected to similar influences and a state of collectively escaping other influences. This formulation of the concept shifts the discussion, while complicating it, from a level on which it ran the risk of degenerating into a kind of Pythagorean number mysticism to the sphere of interior time which can be appreciated and at least partially comprehended by intuitive understanding.[10] A survey of the extensive literature in the field reveals that a commonly accepted formula for a quantitative/qualitative correlation or even a uniform approach to the problem does not exist today among social scientists (such as Eisenstadt, Mentré, Pinder, Rintala, Berger, or Heberle). Nevertheless, as genial eclectic Renaissance dilettantes we shall make bold to apply some of the social-scientific techniques in a most humanely humanistic fashion.[11]

The quantitative or statistical analysis of the positivists when applied like a census-taking to the men around Luther yields interesting if not deeply satisfying results. In that fateful year 1517 Luther was thirty-four years old, a man who was moving out of his youth toward maturity. It is intriguing to discover that nearly all of Luther's followers at Wittenberg and abroad were younger than Luther, most of them thirty years old or younger, and that nearly all of Luther's opponents (except Eck) were older than Luther, most of them fifty years old, or older.

At the calculated risk of trying the reader's patience, we shall now quantify. The younger Wittenberg faculty members were among the earliest of Luther's followers. Amsdorf was born on December 3, 1483,

---

[10] Mannheim, "Problem of Generations," *Essays,* pp. 280–282. Wilhelm Dilthey, "Über das Studium der Geschichte der Wissenschaften vom Menschen, der Gesellschaft und dem Staat" (1875), *Gesammelte Schriften* (2nd ed.; Stuttgart, 1957), V, 31–73. On Dilthey's contribution to contemporary intellectual movements, see the excellent chapter, "Dilthey and His Influence," in Kurt Müller-Vollmer, *Towards a Phenomenological Theory of Literature: A Study of Wilhelm Dilthey's Poetik* (The Hague, 1963), pp. 1–32.

[11] A few representative titles from the impressive volume of literature on the generations problem are Samuel N. Eisenstadt, *From Generation to Generation: Age Groups and Social Structure* (Glencoe, Illinois, 1956); Marvin Rintala, *Three Generations: The Extreme Right Wing in Finnish Politics* (Bloomington, Indiana, 1962); François Mentré, *Les générations sociales* (Paris, 1920); Wilhelm Pinder, *Das Problem der Generation in der Kunstgeschichte Europas* (2nd ed.; Berlin, 1928); Bennett Berger, "How Long is a Generation?" *British Journal of Sociology,* XI (1960), 10–23; Rudolf Heberle, *Social Movements* (New York, 1957), pp. 118–127.

less than a month after Luther (November 10, 1483). Bartholomäus Bernhardi von Feldkirch was born in 1489. Melanchthon was born in 1497; August Schurff in 1495; Heinrich Stockmann in 1495; Stephan Wild in 1495; Tilemann Plettner in 1490; Paul Knod in 1490; Johannes Eisermann in 1490. Outside of the University and even beyond Wittenberg, Luther's first adherents were younger, with the exception of Link and Lang, who were approximately the same age as Luther and had shared common experiences with him. Bugenhagen was born in 1485; Stiefel in 1486; Jakob Propst in 1486; Heinrich von Zütphen in 1488; Mykonius in 1488; Bucer in 1491; Billican in 1491; Justus Jonas in 1493; Pfeffinger in 1493; Agricola in 1494; Schnepf in 1495; Brenz in 1499; Cruciger in 1504. Oecolampadius was just a few months older than Luther, and Kasper Güttel, Eberlin von Günzburg, and Aesticampianus were the chief exceptions in the long list of Luther's supporters.

Conversely, the older men at Wittenberg and elsewhere for the most part turned against Luther. Staupitz, as is well known, could not stay with him. At the University, Henning Goede, seventy, the first ordinarius in canon law, could not grasp Luther's theology. Peter Burchard in medicine split with Luther on questions of university discipline and returned to his home university at Ingolstadt, in 1523, signing the University's condemnation of Luther. Johannes Dölsch, a canon at All Saints, was only slowly convinced and then later broke with Luther on the question of the Mass. Christian Bayer, second professor for the Pandects, opposed Luther for minimizing the importance of canon law, and Luther often complained of Bayer's legalism. Three older canons at the famous Castle Church, Beskau, Elner, and Volmar, put up a stiff resistance and only when the students broke in Beskau's windows did he see the light. They resisted until 1524. Otto Beckmann continued to read Masses until he was released in 1523. Sebastian Küchemeister remained a convinced Scotist and finally in 1522 left the heretical city for Ducal Saxony. Johann Rochals was fifteen years older than Luther and remained his opponent. Ulrich Dinstedt, born before 1460, undertook no changes in his parish at Eisfeld. The dean of the Castle Church, born sometime before 1450, was a stubborn opponent of Luther. In 1518 Johann Böschenstein was appointed to the chair of Hebrew. He was forty-six years old, or twenty-five years older than Melanchthon. When he did not work out he was replaced after an interval by Arrogallus, who was thirty and who lived until 1543.

Luther's opponents in the larger arena were also older men. Cochlaeus was born in 1479; Berthold von Chiemsee in 1465; Wimpina around

114

1460. Emser was six years older; Dungersheim was eighteen years older; the famous Hochstraten of Cologne was twenty-three years older; and Erasmus, the "flitting Dutchman," as E. Gordon Rupp has dubbed him, was, of course, forty-eight or nearly fifty in 1517. The same age differential exists between Luther and his opponents at Louvain and Paris. Nothing can be gained by multiplying instances.[12]

At this point one might be tempted to conclude that we have arrived at the perfectly obvious. Social scientists, after all, are quite often the apostles of the obvious. It is a clearcut case of the conservative nature of the old and the liberal propensities of the young. In that case we would have advanced very little beyond Pope's lines in his *Essay on Criticism*:

> We think our fathers fools, so wise we grow;
> Our wiser sons, no doubt, will think us so.

Socialization and progressivism tend to decelerate with age, we are told. Such a conclusion would indeed be prosaic to the point of being banal. The reader would justifiably be tempted to quote the lines of Oliver Wendell Holmes' *Apostrophe to a Katydid*: "Thou sayest an undisputed thing in such a solemn way." But complications remain. The generations problem cannot be merely the time-honored or dishonored father-son conflict at work, for in that case the young humanists might have revolted against their humanist mentors. In our own day we see young shallow conservative quietists or noisy conservative activists reacting against their genial bewildered liberal professors. Moreover, not all of the young humanists turned reformer. Not all of the young whom we have surveyed above were humanists. Romantic-historical techniques must be adduced to describe and analyze the qualitative differences of those for whom quantification provides no key. Psychoanalysis will not help, for we do not have the information needed for this approach to a whole generation.[13] As Roland Bainton once expressed the problem, there are

[12] The sociologist of religion and Anglicist Herbert Schöffler (*Die Reformation* [Frankfurt, 1936], pp. 33–40) cites as important factors, and provides much data on, the age differentials of Luther's supporters and opponents, the recent founding of Wittenberg University, and the four zones of the Christianization of Central Europe: the area still within the old Roman limes, the area converted between the seventh and ninth centuries, that between the ninth and tenth, and the last converted between the tenth and twelfth centuries. Protestantism scored its most complete success in the reverse order of their conversion. This interesting essay has been republished in *Wirkungen der Reformation: Religionssoziologische Folgerungen für England und Deutschland* (Frankfurt, 1960), pp. 105–188. His thesis runs into difficulties in view of the Counter-Reformation successes in Eastern Europe.

[13] There is much to be learned from such efforts, for all their limitations so

grave difficulties to psychoanalyzing the dead.[14] More can be gained by a cultural analysis of their "common" humanist experience in order to improve our understanding of why the young humanist reformers reacted as they did, and by an examination of the nonhumanist young reformers in order to underline the "noncontemporaneity of the contemporaneous" or the polyphonous cultural pattern of the epoch, each voice sounding out the *verbum evangelii vocale* in its own way and at its own time.

The young humanists who joined the Reformation did indeed have common experiences which qualify them for collective generational identification. These intellectual coevals played the "sonata appassionata" of their lives upon fundamentally the same keyboard of environment. They were witnesses of the same events, they read the same books, they were all university men. They had all encountered classical culture, posing alternatives to traditional values. They showed an openness to new ideas, they observed the same deficiencies in society, they concurred in the chorus of criticism against abuse. They reacted negatively to scholastic philosophy, many of the younger escaping the study of scholastic theology altogether. They were deeply concerned with the search for religious enlightenment. They were captivated by the evangelical appeal, either from Luther, or, in surprisingly many cases, from the Scriptures themselves. Between 1518 and 1523 most of them changed their callings, many from law, for the preaching office. A certain dynamic in humanism and a set of attitudes with latent implications simply required time and an interiorized appropriation to begin operating in a collective way. For the Germanies, that time began in the 1510's and 1520's with the third generation of humanists.

This pattern is evident in the life of Justus Jonas (1493–1555), who was typical in almost every respect. Precisely because he is less well known, he may be of special interest here.[15] Jonas enrolled at the Univer-

---

obvious to trained historians, at a psychoanalytical approach, as Erik Erikson, *Young Man Luther* (New York, 1958), or even Norman Brown, *Life Against Death* (Middletown, Connecticut, 1959). Thus Erikson's application of the identity crisis to Luther's case or Brown's pointing up the prominence of the Thanatos motif in late medieval culture are definitely useful contributions, even though their work as a whole may not measure up to the demands of sound technical history.

[14] Roland Bainton, "Interpretations of the Reformation," *The American Historical Review*, LXVI (October, 1960), 81.

[15] See the excellent biography by Martin Lehmann, *Justus Jonas Loyal Reformer* (Minneapolis, 1963). Cf. W. Delius, *Lehre und Leben: Justus Jonas 1493–1555* (Gütersloh, 1952).

sity of Erfurt when only thirteen years old. He first studied law, then
theology. At Erfurt he was a friend of Johannes Lang, a man of humanistic interests and a friend of Luther. Jonas became an enthusiastic follower of Erasmus and other leading humanists. He made a pilgrimage
to Basel in order to visit the most famous scholar of the day and returned
to Erfurt with such prestige for his Erasmian friendship that he was
elected rector. This was in 1519, the year in which Luther wrote a post-
script to Lang which reads: "P.S. Especially remember me to our Jonas,
and tell him that I like him" (April 13, 1519). Jonas was drawn to
Luther and accompanied him to the Diet at Worms for his ordeal. On
April 17, 1521, the day of Luther's first appearance before the Diet,
Hutten wrote to Jonas: "And so you have followed the preacher of the
Gospel to be in his garden! O piety worthy of love! Truly, Justus, I
loved you before, but on this account I love you a hundred times more."
On May 10, 1521, Erasmus wrote from Louvain:

There has been a persistent rumor here, dear Jonas, that you were with Martin
Luther at Worms; nor do I doubt that your piety has done what I would have
done had I been present, to assuage the tragedy with moderate counsels, so
that it would not in the future burst forth with greater damage to the world.

But Jonas went all the way with the evangelicals. Some time later
Luther wrote: "Dr. Jonas has all the virtues which a preacher should
have, but he clears his throat too often." The circuit was completed.

The pattern is similar among most of the other Wittenbergers in the
inner circle, Georg Spalatin, Caspar Cruciger, Johannes Bugenhagen,
and Philip Melanchthon. They changed the frontier city in the sandbox
of the Empire into a "little Athens on the Elbe." Spalatin (1484–1545)
had belonged to the most outspokenly critical circle of humanists at Erfurt under the leadership of the intellectual canon of Gotha, Mutianus
Rufus. Mutian once posed for Spalatin the question loaded with universalist implications: "If Christ is the way, the truth, and the life, how
then were people saved before the birth of Christ."[16] At no point in
Spalatin's development, however, did he ever deviate from basically
Christian presuppositions. Since he had never studied theology on the
university level, he was never encumbered with a load of scholastic
learning. Even Hutten had freed himself only gradually from scholastic
dialectic acquired on the arts level, but Spalatin approached Biblical
studies unencumbered, thanks to his early and sustained humanist in-

[16] Irmgard Höss, *Georg Spalatin 1484–1545: Ein Leben in der Zeit des Humanismus und der Reformation* (Weimar, 1956), p. 31.

terest. He followed Erasmus' counsel to approach the Scriptures directly and with benefit of guidance from patristic literature. Luther's exegesis of the Scriptures captivated him and he became a devoted follower of the reformer. Luther's forces were divided between the radicals pressing for a strong confessional stand and the Melanchthonian moderates favoring accommodation and a search for common ground. It is typical that Spalatin, the young humanist turned reformer, belonged to the moderates both at Augsburg in 1530 and thereafter.[17]

The youngest and most precocious of the Wittenberg circle of Luther's associates was Caspar Cruciger (1504–1548), the most regular professor of theology at the University, which was crippled by the frequent absences of its key professors. Cruciger was twenty years younger than Luther and seven years younger than Melanchthon. Instructed as a child by the humanists Georg Helt and Caspar Borner, he enrolled at the University of Leipzig at the age of nine. As a teen-ager he was present at the famous Leipzig debate between Eck and Luther. Though in the opinion of the majority of those present Eck carried the day, Luther convinced young Cruciger, who followed him to Wittenberg in order to study theology. At twenty he was appointed rector of the City School in Magdeburg, but four years later returned to Wittenberg for life. Cruciger was quiet and unassuming, a mediating spirit. In 1529 he accompanied Luther to Marburg. After Zwingli's death he and Melanchthon persuaded the Swiss to come to Saxony for discussions in May, 1536. The Wittenberg Concord was the result. Luther, who had called Cruciger his Elisha "who will teach theology after my death," sent him with Melanchthon to the Colloquies at Worms and Regensburg in 1540 and 1541, the last attempt before Trent to reunite the church. During the period of the Smalkald War, Cruciger as rector stayed in Wittenberg and saved the University. Together with Melanchthon he drew up, shortly before his death, the Leipzig Interim, a compromise document, held by the orthodox to be a compromising document.[18]

A third figure among Luther's intimate friends illustrating the pattern emerging from the bewildering number of humanist reformers is Dr. Pomeranus. On September 20, 1522, Luther directed Spalatin to do

[17] *Ibid.*, pp. 423, 345.
[18] Walter G. Tillmanns *The World and Men around Luther* (Minneapolis, 1959), pp. 94–98. On the role of the humanists in the attempts at effecting the reunion of the church, see Robert Stupperich, *Der Humanismus und die Wiedervereinigung der Konfessionen* (Leipzig, 1936), pp. 133 ff. (*SVRG*, No. 160). Of interest in this context is the modest study by Werner Kaegi, *Humanistische Kontinuität in Konfessionellen Zeitalter* (Basel, 1954).

118

some academic wirepulling: "It remains for you to accept the task of securing from the Elector for John Bugenhagen one of those stipends that have heretofore been thrown away on the sophists. For next to Philip [Melanchthon] he is the best professor of theology in the world."[19] Bugenhagen (1484–1558) was the son of a city councilor in Wollin. He studied at the University of Greifswald and became a teacher at Treptow in 1503. He is an instance of the subtle influence of humanism upon a not very subtle personality. A practical, not particularly creative, type, he is perhaps representative of a large body of clergy who helped effect the reformation on the parish level. Although the sources are not adequate for the study of his early intellectual development, every indication is that his theology was colored by Erasmian humanism. Even before 1517 he was interested in the reform of the church on that level. He wished to combine classical learning with a practical Erasmian piety. The humanist Murmellius recommended to Bugenhagen readings in such modern theologians as Pico, Lefèvre, Bouillus, Reuchlin, and Erasmus.[20] His history of *Pomerania* was in many ways a typical humanist production. But in 1520 upon reading Luther's *On the Babylonian Captivity* he wrote to Luther declaring for the Reformation. The next year he moved to Wittenberg, where he became a professor and preacher. But for the remainder of his life, whenever he was not immediately under Luther's influence, he habitually reverted to a moralistic emphasis not unlike Erasmus' *philosophia Christi*. He seemed to be almost blissfully oblivious to the radical Copernican (Son-centered) revolution Luther had launched in theology.

The story of Melanchthon is so common that, to turn a phrase from Chaucer, every wit that hath discretion knows all or part of it.[21] He remains the true archetype of the young humanist turned reformer. A student of his, Johann Agricola, tagged with the nickname "Magister

[19] Preserved Smith and Charles M. Jacobs, eds., *Luther's Correspondence* (2 vols.; Philadelphia, 1913), II, 141, cited in Tillmanns, *The World and Men around Luther*, p. 90.

[20] Otto Vogt,ed., *Dr. Johannes Bugenhagens Briefwechsel* (Stettin, 1888), pp. 309–310. See Hans Eger, "Bugenhagens Weg zu Luther," *Monatsblätter der Gesellschaft für pommersche Geschichte und Altertumskunde*, XLIV (1935), 123–133. See Otto Clemen, "Bugenhagen als Mensch," *Monatsblätter der Gesellschaft für pommersche Geschichte und Altertumskunde*, XLIV (1935), 112, for such piecemeal information as exists on Bugenhagen's early learning.

[21] See Adolf Sperl, *Melanchthon zwischen Humanismus und Reformation* (Munich, 1959). Of special interest is Heinrich Bornkamm's essay, "Humanismus und Reformation in Menschenbild Melanchthons," *Das Jahrhundert der Reformation* (Göttingen, 1961), pp. 69–88.

Eisleben," was his pale shadow. Agricola (1492– or 1494–1566) studied the arts at Leipzig, escaped any training in scholastic theology, and came to Wittenberg, where he was overwhelmed by the personality of Luther. He studied philology with Melanchthon and theology with Luther. He was embroiled in the antinomian controversy, eventually helped to frame the Leipzig Interim with Melanchthon, and outlived his major opponents.[22] Of the two dozen leaders at the time of the Diet of Augsburg in 1530 all except Luther and Nicholas von Amsdorf (1483–1565) had come to the Reformation from humanism. Very possibly the lack of a humanist experience led Amsdorf in later years to exaggerate the effects of original sin upon man in the loss of the image of God and to caricature Luther's theology, holding to such extreme statements as that good works are harmful. He held to his positions with an inflexibility which can most charitably be described as singlemindedness. He sided with Flacius Illyricus against Melanchthon.[23]

In the other centers of Protestantism the humanist-reformers also assume the leadership. Strassburg had Martin Bucer, Wolfgang Capito, Nicholas Gerbelius, Caspar Hedio, and Jakob Sturm.[24] It was Sturm who wrote to his humanist uncle, Jakob Wimpheling, "If I am a heretic you have made me one!" The Swiss reformers in this pattern included Zwingli, Oecolampadius, Pellicanus, Vadian, Myconius, and preeminently, Calvin. Where the dynamic of humanism was still in process the Reformation took especially creative forms. The leadership of the Reformation was in the hands of the young men with a humanist experience.

Many of the young men who turned reformer did not enjoy a humanist education or even a vicarious experience of humanism. Hajo Holborn has pointed to the fact that at least during the first phase of the Reformation period nearly all of the reformers were recruited from the ranks of disaffected priests and monks.[25] The roster of students at the University of Wittenberg indicates a major flow of such men who came

[22] Joachim Rogge, *Johann Agricolas Lutherverständis* (Berlin, 1960), pp. 253–256.

[23] The recent monograph by Peter Brunner, *Nikolaus von Amsdorf als Bischof von Naumburg* (Gütersloh, 1961), brings interesting new material on Amsdorf as an ecclesiastical figure.

[24] See Heinrich Bornkamm, *Martin Bucers Bedeutung für die europäische Reformationsgeschichte* (Gütersloh, 1952), p. 9.

[25] Hajo Holborn, "The Social Basis of the German Reformation," *Church History*, V (1936), 330–339, specifically 338–339. A typical example of a Dominican turned reformer is Jacob Strauss at Eisenach. He did not really appreciate Luther's central stress on *sola fide* and was a moralist. See Joachim Rogge, *Der*

120

to Wittenberg for education or re-education. Their encounter with humanism was through the Biblical humanist curriculum adopted in 1518. It followed rather than preceded their turn to the evangelical faith. These men did not provide the intellectual or organizational leadership of the movement, but, representing great numerical strength, they responded loyally to the confessional stand of Protestantism and became the bulwark of orthodox conservatism in subsequent decades.

The young humanists who either remained loyal to the Catholic confession or reverted to it shortly, such as George Witzel, born in 1501, are difficult to categorize, and complicate the problem of generations a great deal. Very preliminary studies indicate in some cases a thorough and unreserved commitment to an Erasmian *philosophia Christi* theology which outlasted any evangelical experience.[26] The importance of the humanist ingredient in both confessions during subsequent religious history is a story which carries us well beyond our theme and even more hopelessly beyond our space limitation. You will bestow upon me Spalatin's nickname, "Loquax," for that prolix humanist chancellor wrote over eight hundred letters to Luther alone.

Perhaps the factor of the generation in the historical context of humanism and the Reformation will find its place side by side with such generalized concepts as the growth of bourgeois optimism and self-confidence, the birth of the lay spirit, the rising tide of religious expectations, or the well-worn notion of a new individualism.[27] At that time it was at most only one of many factors at play in the great historical drama. Moreover, only at certain widely separated junctures in history has the generation element been an important contributing cause to

---

*Beitrag des Predigers Jakob Strauss zur frühen Reformationsgeschichte* (Berlin, 1957). Strauss lived from 1480 to 1527.

[26] See John Patrick Dolan, *The Influence of Erasmus, Witzel and Cassander in the Church Ordinances and Reform Proposals of the United Duchies of Cleve during the Middle Decades of the 16th Century* (Münster, 1959); Albrecht B. Ritschl, "Georg Witzels Abkehr vom Luthertum," *Zeitschrift für Kirchengeschichte,* II (1887–1888), 386–417, which I have been unable to consult.

[27] The concept of generations may have at least some minimal value for improving our understanding and conceptualization of the various factors involved in the Reformation, the most drastic spiritual revolution ever experienced by a single people in so short a time, according to Leopold von Ranke. In contributing to a better insight into the casual nexus, the stock in trade of historians, it may help historians beyond the naive description level of Karl Eder, *Deutsche Geisteswende* (Salzburg, 1937), or even beyond Willi Andreas' brilliantly written *Deutschland von der Reformation* (5th ed.; Stuttgart, 1948), a grand narrative, but somewhat lacking in third-dimensional analysis.

historical events. It is not possible to generalize the generation factor into a universally applicable formula.[28] The modest assertion of this paper is simply that the generation factor played a significant though minor part in the genesis and development of the Lutheran Reformation. We must, of course, beware of scientizing and bedeviling the world of history with impersonal abstractions and invisible powers or mysterious entelechies. If the idea of generation, understood in a qualitative even more than in a quantitative sense, as one of the mutually interdependent variables in the etiological syndrome of Reformation history is to be of value, it must be given substance from the realities of history itself. This is the difficult task of the historian. Humanists engaged upon such an undertaking can find solace in Plato's words:

*Chalepa ta Chala*
The good is always difficult!

[28] Henri Peyre, *Les Genérations Littéraires* (Paris, 1948), discusses the difficulties of other divisions in literary history, the antiquity and history of the generations concept, and applies generational grouping to each of the major national literatures. The value of the concept, he argues, is not mysterious, but heuristic and practical. Careful reading and reflection upon the numerous exceptions, however, suggest that this bold attempt is only a qualified success.

# V

# Humanism in Germany

## I

In his sparkling and splendid book *The Italian Renaissance in its Historical Background*, Denys Hay wrote:

> To start with, I accept as a fact that there was a Renaissance in the period (to beg a few questions at any rate for the time being) between about 1350 and about 1700. I accept that this Renaissance occurred first in Italy in the fourteenth and fifteenth centuries and that it later affected to a greater or lesser degree the rest of Europe. I say this, because to my mind the evidence is overwhelming.[1]

It seems also to me, after four decades of reading, research, and writing, the 'three R's' of the historian, that the evidence is quite convincing. The impact of the Italian Renaissance upon both the Renaissance and the Reformation in Germany is clear and indisputable. This essay is designed in part as a *mea culpa* (even St Augustine wrote *Retractiones*) and in part to underline the fact that Denys Hay was right and that other unrepentant and intellectually limited scholarly journalists have often been wrong, but can still be rehabilitated. The Reformation, for example, was not a 'miscarriage' of late scholasticism, but it was a rebirth in the same sense as was the Renaissance. The German Renaissance and German humanism, very much dependent upon Italian

---

1. D. Hay, *The Italian Renaissance in its Historical Background*. (Cambridge, 1961), p. 1.

humanism and the great Italian awakening, naturally fused with cultural elements already present in the North.

As to the origins of the northern Renaissance, an earlier theory proposed an indigenous northern phenomenon blossoming under Emperor Charles IV in Prague, founder in 1348 of the university of Prague. His chancellor, Johannes von Neumarkt, authorized a new book of forms for epistolary and chancery documents which was said to have introduced a 'new style' into German and Latin public documents. The notary Johann von Tepl, author of the *Ackermann aus Böhmen*, a discussion between Death and a simple ploughman about the regrettable demise of his wife, is said to have been influenced by Petrarch, but the cultural passages with their references to Plato, Seneca, and Boethius basically reflect medieval sources. This formal type of 'humanism' was transmitted by Albert of Austria, the son-in-law of Sigismund, the last of the Luxembourg rulers. Scholars such as Conrad Burdach and Karl Brandi decades ago argued that the influence of Cola di Rienzo in Prague, who had declared himself a tribune of a new Roman Republic, and barely escaped with his life, was of humanistic inspirational significance in the Holy Roman Empire. Occasionally what great scholars dig up, they should promptly immediately rebury!

Moreover, the 'northern indigenous theory' urged that because of the revival of the scholastic *via antiqua* in the Germanies around the middle of the fifteenth century, a climate favourable to a classical revival was created.[2] Further, it was argued that in one way or another nearly all of the septentrional humanists were birthed or directed by the Brethren of the Common Life, founded by Gerard Groote, who died in 1384. In the year of our Lord 1988 we are treated to academic sessions in celebration of the six hundredth anniversary of the *Devotio Moderna*, a pale reflection of those in 1983 dedicated to the memory of Luther and Marx (Luther's birth and Marx's death!), following those for Goethe! A bit more research should be devoted to the continued influence and the reasons for the eventual decline and end of the Brethren in the late sixteenth century, despite the fact that the reformer Martin Luther was consistently a defender and protector of the Brethren. Luther argued that they, like all nuns in a convent, should be left in peace to live out their lives in service and tranquillity so long

---

2. Of recent articles, two are the most commendable: N. L. Brann, 'Humanism in Germany,' in A. Rabil, Jr, ed., *Renaissance Humanism: Foundations, Forms, and Legacy*, II: *Humanism Beyond Italy* (Philadelphia, 1988), pp. 123–55; E. Meuthen, 'Charakter und Tendenzen des deutschen Humanismus', in H. Angermeier and R. Seyboth, eds., *Säkulare Aspekte der Reformationszeit* (Munich and Vienna, 1983) pp. 216–66.

as they acknowledged Jesus Christ as their all-sufficient Saviour.[3] The Brethren, whether they taught schools, supported students in schools and at the universities, or published many works of piety, were a major influence in the development of German humanism, which was the foremost expression of the German Renaissance. Of course, there were Albrecht Dürer, Hans Holbein, Lucas Cranach and Catholic Renaissance artists, *creatores* of the baroque which blossomed out in the later beauty that all adore in Würzburg, Munich, and in many lesser localities, centres of baroque and then rococo art. But Professor Miriam Chrisman is correct in referring to the 'academic humanism' of the later sixteenth century, a point to be taken up in this essay. Hans Holbein moved to England, Martin Bucer moved from Strasbourg to England, western Atlantic trade and industry moved to Holland and England, and Germany lost out in these cultural and material things, but not in all. There was a shift to the west in Europe, God's playground, and there is no doubt that Central Europe, Italy, and Germany paid a heavy price for the dislocation.

Some of those who have urged a northern origin of the Renaissance have skated on ice thinner than that of the Dutch canals, arguing that northern humanism and then the Reformation were bred in the festering ferment of German mysticism. This mysticism placed man directly in the presence of the ineffable God and reflected an overwhelming inward religious experience. People as intelligent as Hegel have written about the 'basic inwardness' of the German people. This form of mysticism strove for perfection through an infusion of divine grace which would lead to a life modelled on that of Christ.[4] The three leading German mystics of the fifteenth century were Johann Wesel, Puper von Goch, and Wessel Gansfort, who is purported to have had a determinative influence on Luther, a doubtful proposition. Via the French humanist Lefèvre d'Étaples, who edited the works of Nicholas Cusanus (d. 1464), that Dionysian Neoplatonic philosopher and mystic did influence Luther at a critical juncture in his exegetical work on the

---

3. See the detailed account of the Brethren by R. R. Post, *The Modern Devotion. Confrontation with Reformation and Humanism, Studies in Medieval and Reformation Thought*, III (Leiden, 1968), in which he attacked Renaudet, Hyma and Spitz for their assessment of the Brethren's activities and influence. For some of what could be said in response, see the excellent review of the book by Helmar Junghans, *Luther-Jahrbuch*, 37 (1970), pp. 120–27.

4. For a representative recent book on mysticism, humanism and the Reformation, see Steven E. Ozment, *Mysticism and Dissent: Religious Ideology and Social Protest in the Sixteenth Century* (New Haven, 1973).

Psalms and the Epistles of St Paul.[5] The powerful influence of the Italian Renaissance ideas and style in the arts and letters necessarily fused with northern intellectual streams and formed a unique amalgam.

The main transmitters for this transfusion of Renaissance culture were the monasteries, the ecclesiastical and the secular courts, the urban centres, and in due course the universities.

That monasteries were important centres for the new learning is so surprising that scholars all too often have not taken the fact into account, despite the evidence. Late medieval monasticism has, of course, had a bad press with modern secular scholars, who to a regrettable degree are ignorant of patristic and medieval history. Despite the contributions of the monastic establishments, from the days of Flavius Cassiodorus (*c.* 485–583), who developed the Scriptorium, of the Benedictines down to the Schottenkloster in contemporary Vienna, and the contributions of the Dominicans and Franciscans to the medieval universities, scholars of the Renaissance have neglected the importance of monks, friars, and other religious to the culture of the Renaissance. Paul Oskar Kristeller is an outstanding exception, for he has published brilliant pieces on this very subject. Thus in the fifteenth century the Cistercian cloister of Adwert, outside Gröningen, was a lively intellectual centre, where Alexander Hegius, famous as an educator at Deventer, Rudolf Agricola, the 'father of German humanism' and a 'second Petrarch', and Johann Wessel, who spent much time in Greece and Italy, came for study and visits with the learned abbot, Henry of Rees. Similarly the Benedictine cloister of Sponheim in south-west Germany became under Abbot Johannes Trithemius (1462–1516) a centre of humanist learning and a hospice for the legendary Dr Faustus.[6] An intense admirer of Petrarch, Trithemius befriended German humanists whom he knew from his Heidelberg days, such as Rudolf Agricola, Jacob Wimpfeling, Johannes von Dalberg, and Conrad Celtis, who has been dubbed the 'German Arch-humanist'. He was the first German poet laureate of the Empire, crowned by Emperor Frederick III on the hill outside the castle in Nuremberg in 1487. He was

---

5. The excellent work of P. M. Watts, *Nicholaus Cusanus: A Fifteenth Century Vision of Man* (Leiden, 1982) carries the understanding of this difficult thinker well beyond the older authorities. The great work on Italian humanist thought is that of C. Trinkaus, *In Our Image and Likeness: Humanity and Divinity in Italian Humanist Thought*, 2 vols. (Chicago, 1970), with supplementary essays in his *The Scope of Renaissance Humanism* (Ann Arbor, MI., 1983).

6. N. L. Brann, *The Abbot Trithemius (1462–1516): The Renaissance of Monastic Humanism* (Leiden, 1981), an admirable work.

the founder of the Rhenish and Danubian sodalities, loose associations of humanists, largely in the imperial cities.[7]

A second avenue by which Italian humanist influence reached the 'septentrionals' was via the imperial, princely and ecclesiastical courts. One must start at the top, the court of the Holy Roman Emperors, Frederick III and Maximilian I (1493–1519), in Vienna and three other locales for the distribution of justice. Frederick III was fairly lethargic, but Maximilian was, by way of contrast, fairly manic. He was said to have wrestled with bears, climbed mountains, married twice with vigour, and patronized many Renaissance humanists and artists. He through ghost writers, some allege, composed two epic narratives entirely related to his own life, the *Teuerdank* and the *Weiskünig*. But, as is the case with most rulers and aristocrats, their major contribution to culture is through patronage. Maximilian established a chair for poetry and rhetoric at the University of Vienna, recrowned Conrad Celtis, who founded the 'College of Poets and Mathematicians' next to the old university, and commissioned art by Dürer and others. Celtis urged other princes to equal his generosity, writing to Magnus of Anhalt, for example, to support the good arts, and, in an act filled with historical portent, dedicating his edition of the plays of Roswitha, nun of Gandersheim to Frederick the Wise of Saxony and praising him for bringing poets, artists, teachers of Roman law, and scientists, to his court as well as to his new university of Wittenberg, founded in 1502.

Much has been made of the 'urban reformation,' because for two decades the Lutheran Reformation made progress in the cities, and only then, with sufficient university-trained evangelical preachers, could it expand to the countryside under the aegis of the territorial rulers, the 'princely' reformation. Something more should be said about the 'urban Renaissance'. Nuremberg and Augsburg may serve as case studies of German cities in which humanistic studies were introduced and encouraged by an elite mercantile aristocracy. In Nuremberg the Pirckheimers had a tradition of sending their sons to Italy for legal and humanistic education and of educating their daughters in letters and religion. Their handsome bourgeois house, only yards away from the beautiful fountain in the market-place, served as a hospice for both humanists such as Celtis as well as reformers like Luther. Celtis wrote a topographical-historical description entitled the *Norimberga*, which

---

7. While there are materials available in English on Conrad Celtis, such as L. Forster, *Conrad Celtis 1459–1508: Selections edited with transition and commentary* (Cambridge, 1948), and L. W. Spitz, *Conrad Celtis: The German Arch-Humanist* (Cambridge, MA, 1957), the essential work over the past three decades has been done by Professor Dieter Wuttke of Bamberg University, who has devoted his life to the study of Celtis and has actually succeeded in finding some new and previously unknown odes of the bard.

was to serve as a model for all the humanists who were to contribute to a *Germania illustrata*, modelled on Flavio Biondo's *Italia illustrata*. In Augsburg the Fuggers and other wealthy merchants commissioned works of literature, art and architecture. In many other cities, particularly in the south and west, a partially Italian-educated judiciary and citizenship patronized classical scholars and neo-Latin poets and rhetoricians.

A fourth avenue by which eventually the Italian Renaissance literary, though not artistic, culture reached Germany was the recalcitrant universities.[8] The German universities in which the humanistic discipline made substantial progress in the late fifteenth and sixteenth centuries were, roughly in this order, Vienna, Heidelberg, Basel, Erfurt, Wittenberg, Leipzig, Tübingen, and also Ingolstadt (later to become the university of Munich).[9] The traditional account of a fierce battle in the universities between the scholastics of either the *via antiqua* (Thomists) or the *via moderna* (Occamists) against the humanists has been largely discredited, for many professors were half-scholastic and half-humanistic. Moreover, the great controversy often had more to do with chairs and stipends than with intellectual issues. The humanist lecturers stressed the importance of grammar and rhetoric over logic or dialectic, the essential device of scholastic philosophy. While logic can lead to inevitable conclusions within a given dialectical system, the humanists believed that rhetoric is a superior instrument to be used on behalf of truth, for it leads beyond intellectual conviction to move the will to action (*virtù*: that is, intelligent will in action), a higher form of truth. Poetry stirs emotions and history is philosophy teaching by examples. Moral philosophy is to be preferred to metaphysics, though not divorced from it, for it strengthens the fibre of public as well as of individual life.

There is an interesting generational theory regarding the development of northern humanism that seems to be particularly applicable to German humanism. From a biological-genealogical perspective, it has been argued, mankind's history seems to be a steady and continuous flow of a near infinite number of individual lives upon which no collective periodization can be imposed. But, in contrast, the history of the social production of mankind characteristically moves in stages, in distinctive periods of time. The conceptual model of historical generations leads to the meeting point of these two very different

---

8. See the commendable chapter 'Humanism at the Universities, 1500–1515: The Prelude to Reform,' in J. H. Overfield, *Humanism and Scholasticism in Late Medieval Germany* (Princeton, 1984), pp. 208–46.

9. On Ingolstadt, an interesting insight into conservative reform is offered in the little monograph by E. Iserloh, *Johannes Eck (1486–1543): Scholastiker Humanist Kontroverstheologe* (Aschendorff/Münster, 1981), pp. 14–20, including paragraphs on Eck as humanist.

V

phenomena. Included in 'social production' must surely be cultural productivity, for men are not merely animals, and once again the humanists have preceded the social scientists with a generational theory.[10] In German humanism pioneers such as Rudolf Agricola, first generation, were followed by the high-tide of German humanism, Mutianus Rufus, Johannes Reuchlin, Conrad Celtis, Willibald Pirckheimer, Jacob Wimpfeling, Desiderius Erasmus, Conrad Peutinger, and many others. If the first generation exhausted its energies acquiring classical learning and absorbing what the Italian humanists could teach them, the second generation of humanists did truly creative intellectual and artistic work in their own right. But the third generation of young humanists was impatient. These young men wished to use their learning to change the world for the better. As Bernd Moeller expressed this thought with epigrammatic force: 'Without the humanists there would have been no Reformation.'[11] Luther led the tortuous way in his own life away from late scholasticism to a biblical faith, but did so by totally rejecting scholastic philosophy (whatever carry-overs remained in his theologizing), and using the tools and much of the substance of Renaissance humanism in the cause of the gospel. His supporting cast, Melanchthon, Bucer, Vadian, Zwingli, Oecolampadius, and John Calvin, had a much easier time of it once Luther had made the great evangelical breakthrough. Some few Anabaptists and evangelical humanists also derived much from the tools and religio-intellectual orientation of humanism, including religious leaders such as Balthasar Hubmaier, Michael Servetus, or Sebastian Franck.[12] Hubmaier once commented that nearly all the learned were Lutherans. In his essay *Of Youth and Age* Francis Bacon observed: 'Young men are fitter to invent than to judge; fitter for execution than for counsel; and fitter for new projects than for settled business.' The progamme of the German humanists may be succinctly characterized as being devoted to a form of cultural nationalism and to a vague and ill-defined kind of religious enlightenment.

Luther once commented that to his astonishment his *Ninety-five Theses* had within fourteen days been carried throughout the length and

---

10. H. Jaeger, 'Generations in History: Reflections on a Controversial Concept,' *History and Theory*, 24 (1985), 273–92. Also, L. W. Spitz, 'The Third Generation of German Renaissance Humanists,' in A. R. Lewis, ed., *Aspects of the Renaissance: A Symposium* (Austin and London, 1967), the symposium at which I first met Denys Hay in person.

11. B. Moeller, *Imperial Cities and the Reformation: Three Essays* (Philadelphia, 1972), recently republished by Labyrinth Press; S. Ozment, *The Reformation in the Cities: The Appeal of Protestantism to Sixteenth-Century Germany and Switzerland* (New Haven, 1975).

12. See P. Hayden-Roy, *The Inner Word and the Outer World: A Biography of Sebastian Franck* (Diss., Stanford, 1988).

breadth of Germany. The young German humanists were the chief agents for their distribution, working out of the urban centres where printing presses were established, well before university presses, in Nuremberg, Augsburg, Leipzig, Basel, Constance, Wittenberg, and cities in which humanist sodalities existed, most loosely related to the Rhenish or Danubian sodalities. In 1520 Luther was the most widely published and read author in Germany, and his suspect backer, Ulrich von Hutten, the second most. Indeed, without the support of the humanists in these urban centres Luther's evangelical revival would, humanly speaking, not have succeeded.

The humanists approved of Luther's uncompromising assault on scholastic philosophy, for, he held, the doctors had accommodated theology to the semi-Pelagian practices of a corrupted Church and left the Scriptural existential understanding of the law–gospel, sin–grace, death–life antinomies for a compromised sapiential metaphysical theology of works, a *theologia gloriae* rather than the *theologia crucis et passionis* This radical assault on the theological establishment excited the young humanists, but, of course, aroused the predictable response from the establishment in Cologne, Louvain, Paris, and Rome! The humanists approved of his drive *ad fontes*, back to the Scriptures, but they did not really grasp the depth of his theology. Had they read *On the Babylonian Captivity of the Church* (1520) with more than Erasmian eyes, they would have understood that they were in turbulent waters much over their heads. That treatise, in fact, did frighten some of the older humanists, who began to turn away, a real watershed. From 1520 on the Reformation began to derail humanism in the Erasmian mould. Or did it? Perhaps the Reformation movement saved German humanism from preciosity, irrelevancy, even foppery. It carried the movement on its broad shoulders forward into the seventeenth century, to a point where the *Aufklärung* (German Enlightenment) was able through the Leibniz (Lutheran), Kant (Lutheran), Hamann (Lutheran), and Herder (Lutheran) connection to take an amalgam into the modern world.

Perhaps after all this it would be fitting to include here in brief scope an account of the course of German humanism. In the year 1507 Nicholas Gerbellius, a young humanist, burbled: 'I congratulate myself often on living in this glorious century in which so many remarkable men have arisen in Germany.' The new culture had come to the Germanies earlier than to the other countries of the North thanks to the medieval political ties between Italy and the Holy Roman Empire, the lively trade between Italian and German cities, the cultural ties established by student migration to the universities of Pavia, Padua, and, above all, Bologna, many for legal education. The transition from the medieval 'Wandervogel' and the migrant student, to the rootless

# V

poet (Celtis) and the literary humanist (Erasmus), who declared himself to be a citizen of the world, was easy and natural.

The migratory birds of German humanism, like the medieval troubadours, spread the classical word. Of course, scholars have done root-stretching back to the Councils of Constance and Basel in the first half of the fifteenth century, and have pointed to the influence of Italian churchmen and diplomats such as Aeneas Silvius Piccolomini (later Pius II) in the North. Aeneas had written a flattering picture of Bohemia and of Germany which had flowered under the aegis of the Roman Catholic Church. But during the second half of the fifteenth century the Germans themselves began to trumpet the cause of classical letters and the new Renaissance culture. A poet such as Peter Luder (c. 1415–74) went to Rome as a cleric, travelled about Italy, and joined the German students in Padua. (Centuries later Dr Johnson once commented that anyone who has not been to Italy is always conscious of an inferiority!) In the year 1444 the elector of the Palatinate made him a lecturer for classical languages and literature at Heidelberg University, where he launched an aggressive campaign for classical rhetoric and poetry. More pedagogical types such as Rudolf von Langen, Johannes Murmellius, scholastic humanists such as Conrad Summenhart and Paul Scriptoris, and moralists such as Heinrich Bebel, author of heavy *facetiae*, and Jacob Wimpfeling, cathedral preacher at Speyer and an Alsatian German patriot, carried the cause of moral philosophy and classical letters forward. Friends of Wimpfeling (1450–1528) included Sebastian Brant (1457–1521), author of *The Ship of Fools*, and Johann Geiler von Kaisersberg (1445–1510), the renowned reforming penitential pulpiteer.

The most prominent pioneer of this older generation was Rudolf Agricola (1444–85). Erasmus wrote of him: 'It was Rudolf Agricola who first brought with him from Italy some gleam of a better literature.' 'He could have been the first in Italy,' Erasmus opined, 'had he not preferred Germany.' In Heidelberg, supported by Bishop Johannes von Dalberg and the Palatinate Elector, Agricola inspired an entire circle of young humanists. 'I have the brightest hope,' Agricola proclaimed,

> that we one day shall wrest from haughty Italy the reputation for classical expression which it has nearly monopolized, so to speak, and lay claim to it ourselves, and free ourselves from the reproach of ignorance and being called unlearned and inarticulate barbarians; and that our Germany will be so cultured and literate that Latium will not know Latin any better.[13]

---

13. *Rudolphi Agricolae Phrisii De inventione dialectica libri omnes et integri & recogniti, etc. per Alardum Aemstelradamum* (Cologne, 1539), II, p. 178.

The high tide of German humanism rose during the first two decades of the sixteenth century. The best lyric poet was clearly Conrad Celtis (1459–1508), the son of a peasant, who studied at Cologne, Heidelberg, Rostock and Leipzig. Upon his crowning as the first poet-laureate of the Empire, he proclaimed: 'O sacred and mighty work of the poets, you alone free all things from fate and lift up mortal ashes to the stars!' In his *Amores* he celebrated his four loves, each symbolizing one of the four extremities of Germany. In his *Odes*, done in the manner of Horace, he wrote of love, life, and learning. From Horace and Cicero he learned that poetry has a passionate and rousing power. He referred to himself as a *vates*, not merely a *poeta*, for he was a prophet and a sage. He quickly journeyed through Italy, visiting Venice, Padua, Bologna, Florence, Rome, but disliked the 'superior' posturing of the Italians. His travels took him to Cracow, Ingolstadt, and finally to Vienna, where he died of syphilis at the age of forty-nine and still lies buried in the short tower of St Stephen's cathedral, his gravestone bearing the caption VIVO, 'I live,' as indeed he does. He lived on also then as a hero of the younger humanists.

Other humanists of this generation made remarkable contributions to learning. Although Mutianus Rufus published little, his house in Gotha, where he was a canon, with his library which he called his *beata tranquillitas*, was a hospice for many young humanists at the nearby university of Erfurt. In Augsburg prosperous patricians supported local artistic and literary men. There Conrad Peutinger (1465–1547) became a prominent legist and humanist, the owner of the tremendous *Tabula Peutingeriana*, a military map of the Roman Empire, which Celtis had found and given to him. In Ingolstadt, Johann Turmair, (Aventinus: 1477–1534) served as tutor to the scions of the duke of Bavaria. Duke Wilhelm IV urged him to write *The Annals of Bavaria*, finished in 1521.[14] Willibald Pirckheimer in Nuremberg wrote in Greek as well as in Latin, and though a busy merchant-banker and city counsellor, wrote poetry and a history of the Swabian-Swiss war. Among his friends he counted Celtis, Dürer, and for a time Luther, who was a guest in his house. His sister Charitas, abbess of a local convent, was so learned that Erasmus compared her to the daughters of Sir Thomas More.

Two events of those two decades involving humanist impact merit special attention. The first of these was the Reuchlin controversy about Hebrew books and the second was the role of that most militant humanist, the knight Ulrich von Hutten. Johannes Reuchlin (1455–1522) served most of his adult life as the chancellor to the duke

---

14. The best work on Aventinus is that of G. Strauss, *Historian in an Age of Crisis: The Life and Work of Johannes Aventinus 1477–1534* (Cambridge, MA, 1963).

of Württemberg. While educated in German universities, on two trips to Italy Reuchlin visited the Platonic Academy, and the Villa Corregi, and was captivated by Marsiglio Ficino's Neoplatonism. He was also intrigued by Pico della Mirandola's discovery of the Hebrew *Kabbalah* and his assertion expressed in the 900 *Conclusiones* that light came from the East (*ex oriente lux*) long before the time of the Greeks. From Pico he learned that the thought of the Cabalists corresponded to the philosophy of the Pythagoreans. 'Marsiglio (Ficino) produced Plato for Italy,' he proclaimed, 'Lefèvre d'Etaples restored Aristotle to France. I shall complete the number and . . . show to the Germans Pythagoras reborn through me.'[15] He wrote a manual of Hebrew grammar, the *Rudimenta hebraica*, and two important works using the Jewish *Kabbalah* apologetically as a support for the Christian faith: *De Verbo Mirafico* and the *De Arte Cabalistica*.[16] He became the target of a vicious obscurantist attack and was defended by the humanists and given encouragement by none other than Martin Luther.[17] Reuchlin later expressed gratitude that Luther had now attracted the hostility of the monks, taking the heat off him! Reuchlin ended his days as a professor at Ingolstadt and Tübingen, a dedicated foe of the Reformation. But his grand-nephew Philipp Melanchthon became Luther's colleague and first lieutenant in Wittenberg, the second most important Protestant reformer until the emergence of John Calvin.

Ulrich von Hutten, a knight, was a fighter! When Luther was summoned to appear before the Emperor Charles V and the Diet in Worms, Hutten called to him: 'Long live liberty!'[18] Born in the fortress of Steckelberg on the border of Franconia and Hesse, he was sent at the age of eleven to the ancient monastery of Fulda to lead the life of

---

15. Reuchlin, *On the Cabalistic Art*, dedication to Pope Leo X, in *Renaissance Philosophy*, II: *The Transalpine Thinkers*, ed. H. Shapiro and A. B. Fallico (New York, 1969), p. 28, cited in Brann. 'Humanism in Germany,' p. 155, n. 74.

16. The latest quite felicitous translation of this very difficult book is that of M. and S. Goodman, *Johann Reuchlin: On the Art of the Kabbalah – De Arte Cabalistica* (New York, 1983).

17. The Warburg and Courtauld Institutes seem possibly under the benignant influence of Frances Yates to have turned into a coven. See the interpretation of Reuchlin by C. Zika, 'Reuchlin's *De Verbo Mirifico* and the Magic Debate of the Late Fifteenth Century,' *Journal of the Warburg and Courtauld Institutes*, 39 (1976), pp. 104–38. This reading of Reuchlin is out of character with his basic religious, legal, and philosophical character as revealed in his many other writings and letters. Noel Brann is mistaken to settle for some safe 'middle ground,' 'Humanism in Germany,' p. 146–7.

18. The most recent and very excellent book on Ulrich von Hutten is that of E. Bernstein, *Ulrich von Hutten mit Selbstzeugnissen und Bilddokumenten* (Reinbeck bei Hamburg, 1988). Bernstein is also the author of a valuable monograph, *Die Literatur des deutschen Frühhumanismus* (Stuttgart, 1978). See Helmar Junghans, 'Der nationale Humanismus bei Ulrich von Hutten und Martin Luther,' *Ebernburg-Hefte*, 22. Folge, (1988), *Blätter für Pfälzische Kirchengeschichte und Ic religiöse Volkskunde* (Vol. 55, 1988), pp. 147–70.

a religious. At seventeen he fled from the monastery just a few weeks before Luther entered one in Erfurt. He studied at six different German universities and during the course of his peregrinations he became a fervent anti-scholastic and a humanist given to poetics and polemics. 'Behold, posterity,' he penned, 'the songs of the poet Hutten, whom you are rightly able to call your own!' He aimed to free the Fatherland of ignorance, of the shackles of Rome, and to elevate culture above that of Italy. This angry young man poured out many polemical tracts, like unloading a barrel of grapeshot, all the more devastating for being fired at close range. In one of his dialogues he wrote: 'Even if it cannot be achieved, there is merit in having tried!' He attacked the papacy, following Valla he exposed the False Donation of Constantine, he assaulted the trade in indulgences, and he rallied behind Luther, who, however, kept a safe distance from this firebrand ready to use the sword. Hutten died in 1523 of syphilis and lies buried on the island of Ufenau near Zurich, where he had gone to seek refuge, but was turned away. Many of the younger humanists, such as Beatus Rhenanus, were of a milder more Erasmian disposition. John Sleidan proved to be the best historian of the earlier sixteenth century.[19]

It would outrun the limits of a mere essay to discuss lesser humanists in detail, but the impact of these phalanxes of the hoplites and of the light-armed soldiers, wielding feather pens, upon German literary, artistic, and religious culture would be difficult to overestimate. After this brief survey of the course of German humanism, it is necessary to turn to a problem of much greater complexity, the impact of humanism upon the Lutheran Reformation.

## II

Friedrich Nietzsche was not entirely mistaken when he depicted Luther as a 'vengeful, unlucky priest who brought to shame the one cleverly refined beautiful brilliant possibility – Caesar Borgia as pope.' (*Der Anti-Christ*, aph. 61) Not literally, of course, since Caesar Borgia, duke of Valentinois and Romagna and son of Pope Alexander V perished in 1507 under very difficult circumstances, ten years before Luther published his *Ninety-five Theses*. Contemporary Catholic schol-

---

19. On Beatus Rhenanus, see the superlative book by the late J. F. D'Amico, *Theory and Practice in Renaissance Textual Criticism: Beatus Rhenanus between Manuscript and Conjecture* (Berkeley and Los Angeles, 1988). See also the excellent brief characterization of John Sleidan as a historian in A. G. Dickens and J. Tonkin, *The Reformation in Historical Thought* (Cambridge, MA, 1985), pp. 10–19. See Ingeborg Berlin Vogelstein, *Johann Sleidan's Commentaries: Vantage Point of a Second-Generation Lutheran* (Lanham, MD: University Press of America, 1986). Ms. Vogelstein is currently doing an annotated reduced version of the *Commentaries*.

arship grants the point, and the pioneer of ecumenical Catholic Reformation historical scholarship, Joseph Lortz, declared that some day Luther would be declared a saint. (He would, of course, not acccept, not believing in sainthood, but in a community of forgiven sinners.) For, Lortz reasoned, he gave a decadent Church the shock treatment needed to bring it out of the Italian family – princely concerns back to the true spiritual vocation of the Church.

Nietzsche's idea does point up the fact that one historiographical tradition from the time of Jakob Burkhardt's *The Civilization of the Renaissance in Italy* (1860) to the present has seen Renaissance and Reformation, humanism and Protestantism, as having been antithetical. A second interpretation has been to view them as twin sources of modernity.[20] 'We are at the dawn of a new era!' Luther exclaimed. Erasmus' *alter ego* Beatus Rhenanus responded to the Reformation by declaring: 'I see the whole world reviving!' In the nineteenth century the historian James Froude referred to the Reformation as 'the hinge on which all modern history turns.' By the fateful year 1517, when Luther nailed his theses to the side doors of the Castle Church in Wittenberg, used as a matter of course as a bulletin board since larger university lectures were given in the nave of the church, humanism was well established at Wittenberg University. It was also a cultural force in many universities, though not in some, as events were to reveal. Humanism had also made its impress upon Luther's mind and spirit.

The Lutheran and 'magisterial' Reformation, the Catholic Reformation and to a more limited extent the radical sectarian Reformation owed much to Renaissance humanism and to the classical revival for many reasons. First of all, the humanist emphasis on the importance of classical languages and scholarship, the drive *ad fontes*, was basic to the reformers' return to the Scriptures and to the ancient fathers. Secondly the stress of the humanists upon the importance of education was essential to the whole Reformation programme for change. Thirdly, the shift of the humanists away from dialectic to grammar and rhetoric, the other two major divisions of the *trivium*, and the attendant increased appreciation of history and poetry, marked a major intellectual shift, a culturally paratactic event. Obviously the Protestant emphasis on preaching, the spoken word of the gospel (Luther: *Verbum evangelii vocale*), owed much to the rhetorical emphasis of the humanists. Poetry was related to the rhetorical appreciation of *affectus*, feeling, along with music, a major force touching emotion and thereby the will.

---

20. For an English translation of the archetypical expressions of the Reformation as progenitor of modernity or the Reformation as essentially medieval, as articulated by Wilhelm Dilthey and Ernst Troeltsch, see L. W. Spitz, ed., *The Reformation: Basic Interpretations* (Lexington, MA, 1972), pp. 11–43.

The reformers became increasingly fascinated with history both sacred and secular. The Scriptures came to be viewed as an account of the existential religious experiences of individual believers as well as the history of salvation (*Heilsgeschichte*) of the Old and the New Israel. Sacred history provided case studies of the way in which God deals with man. Secular history provided pragmatic moral lessons, but also retrospectively describes the *locutia*, the words that God has spoken and acted out in history, as he has done and continues to do in nature.

The evangelical Reformation diverged radically from the religious assumptions of the Renaissance classical world, of the Renaissance Catholic world, and of the Christian humanist world of the North. In both anthropology (sin as the root condition of man) and soteriology (Christology, not merely Christocentrism), Luther and the German reformers moved along what proved to be more history-making lines. For Luther Christ was not merely an *exemplum*, a model to be imitated, but an *exemplar*, an example of the way in which God deals with man, as Luther wrote to Reuchlin in his time of troubles, grinding him down into the dust of death, but then, praise God, raising him up again to life eternal! This shift in emphasis from man's contribution to his own salvation towards dependence upon the divine initiative, grace as a benignity, a gift with which the Giver, the God of love and forgiveness, is always present, did indeed mark a dramatic theological and historical change. It also marked a cultural change that Aristotle would have described as a 'transformation from one dimension to another' (*Metabasis eis allo genos*).

'Nevertheless' (*dennoch*) was the word that Luther substituted for Thomas Aquinas' smooth 'therefore' (*ergo*), existential for sapiential. The magisterial reformers provided for the continuity of humanist culture and learning down to the turbulent seventeenth century, a century of crisis, with remnants of their views on culture remaining into the late twentieth century. The reformers were themselves savants. Luther used many more classical references without citation in his famous exchange with Erasmus than did the 'prince of humanists' with his great display of learning. The reformers extended the influence of classical and humanist learning to a much broader spectrum of the European and, in due course, of the American population. They provided for the continuance of the humanist disciplines through their advocacy of universal compulsory education for boys and girls, through their establishment of many classical gymnasia and through humanist curricular changes both on the arts level of the universities as well as through a new approach to theological education. There developed, for example, a greater stress on exegesis based on the biblical language texts, a new approach to homiletics based on humanist rhetorical principles, and a renewed interest in Church history, poetry, drama, and music. The first professor of history was Eobanus Hessus, the most outstanding Protestant poet, appointed at Philipp of Hesse's new university of Marburg in 1524.

St Augustine in his best-known treatise on education reminded the students that to accept what the teacher says uncritically is mistaken, to reject it out of hand is wrong, but to test whatever the teacher tells one, to see in how far it is true, is the right way for the student. Similarly Plutarch wrote that the auditor should not only criticize a lecture, but should be able to improve upon it, as Plato did upon the Greek orator Lysias (who did endlessly boring orations on vineyard property rights). Auditors should not be like the Lacedaemonians, for when they heard that Philip of Macedon had razed Olynthus to the ground they commented: 'Yes, but to create a city as good is beyond the man's power.' Nearly all Protestant reformers were critical of the schooling they had received both on the elementary and on the university level. What could they do by way of improving the educational system?

Luther pounded away on the subject for years! He not only manoeuvred and pioneered curricular changes at the university of Wittenberg along humanist lines, but he effected decisive changes throughout the educational maze. To say system or organization would be saying too much for those times. At the university level he believed that students who came up from the arts faculty with a dialectical mindset were difficult to deal with in the theological school. Those who had taken the revised humanist curriculum with languages, classics, rhetoric, and the like were better prepared for biblical study, and made better evangelical ministers. In his treatise *To the Councilmen of all Cities in Germany that They Establish and Maintain Christian Schools*, he wrote: 'If it is necessary, dear sirs, to expend annually such great sums for firearms, for roads, bridges, dams, and countless similar things, in order that a city may enjoy temporal peace and prosperity, why should not at least as much be devoted to the poor needy youth?'[21] This treatise has been described as a great song of praise for the study of languages. In many of his writings, such as his *Sermon on the Estate of Marriage* (1519) and his *Sermon on Keeping Children in School* (1530), he argued that the civil authorities have the right to compel parents to send their children to school. Luther may well have been the first person in the history of the world to advocate universal compulsory education for boys and girls, for a substantial number of grades. If boys have the ability and nature had not denied them 'sense and wit', they should be urged and financially supported by the State through the university

---

21. Luther, 'To the Councilmen of all Cities in Germany that They Establish and Maintain Christian Schools,' *Luther's Works*, 45, *The Christian in Society*, vol. 2, ed. W. I. Brandt (Philadelphia, 1962), pp. 369–70.

level, so that they could become fully educated to serve Church, State, and Society. In that *Address to the Councilmen* of the Municipalities he wrote: 'The prosperity of a country depends not on the abundance of its revenue, nor on the strength of its fortifications, nor on the beauty of its public building but it consists in the number of cultivated citizens, in its men of education, enlightenment, and character.'[22] Students would eventually serve Church, State, and thereby Society.

If Luther provided the initial thrust, like the first stage of a rocket launching, his learned colleague, Philipp Melanchthon, grandnephew of Reuchlin, known as the *praeceptor germaniae*, provided instruction in method and organization. Certainly the educator who most fully satisfied Melanchthon's ideal was Johann Sturm of Strasbourg, who directed the gymnasium, helped found and organize a good many others, and wrote elaborate treatises on education which gave curricular specifics along the general evangelical humanist philosophy of education. As a friend and correspondent of Roger Ascham, who even named one of his children after Sturm, he influenced advanced education in England, for Ascham was a renowned educator and tutor to Queen Elizabeth I.

German Lutheran education was notable, then, especially for three special emphases. First, it broadened the popular educational base, moving away from the elitism and upper-class orientation of Italian humanism and towards compulsory universal basic education. Second, the curriculum for the secondary schools and at the arts level of the university was to be the humanistic classical curriculum demanding a knowledge of Latin, Greek, and Hebrew, classical literature, grammar, and rhetoric, while not neglecting dialectic, moral philosophy, poetry, history, mathematics and sciences. Third, there was a new emphasis upon teaching as a divine vocation and on the dignity of the teacher, for, Luther asserted, teaching next to preaching is the most useful service a man of God can render to his fellow human beings.

Many aspects of the impact of humanism in Germany remain to be discussed and much research remains to be done, but it is possible here at least to indicate the problematics of the subject. The entire question of the revival of Christian antiquity, along with classical antiquity and patristic study in the sixteenth century, needs to be explored further.[23]

---

22. *Luther's Works*, 45, pp. 355–6.

23. For many years Paul Oskar Kristeller has been advocating rigorous studies of the influence of the patristic writers on humanism and Reformation. A bibliographical guide suggestive for further research to be done is S. Ozment, ed., *Reformation Europe: A Guide to Research* (St Louis, MO.: Center for Reformation Research, 1982). An example of the type of specialized studies needed is Scott H. Hendrix, "Validating the Reformation: The Use of the Church Fathers by Urbanus Rhegius," in Walter Brand Müller, Herbert Immenkötter, and Erwin Iserloh, eds., *Ecclesia Militans: Studien zur Konzilien-und-Reformationsgeschichte*, TT, Paderborn, (1988), 281–305.

V

The problem of change and continuity is perennial for historians and, when the discussion grows tedious, one thinks of Lord Acton's comment: 'Better one great man of history than a dozen immaculate historians.' The continuity of humanism through the Reformation era and the changes that it underwent as it took on a more academic character and became allied with religious and sectarian interests are worth more intense scrutiny. Certainly a great scholar and savant like Joachim Camerarius (1500–74) was not cut of the same cloth as a frivolous and promiscuous poet like Conrad Celtis. Still, the so-called neo-scholastic dogmaticians such as Chemnitz, Calov, or Quenstedt had a knowledge of both classical and Christian antiquity and of the ancient languages, the triple linguistic tiara, far beyond the reach and imagination of the 'high generation' of German humanists as well as of the Italian humanists. Thanks to the magisterial reformers, who not only placed their *imprimatur* upon humanism, but viewed the cultivation of higher culture as a *negotium cum deo*, a business or work carried on with God's blessing and help, humanism made a broader, deeper, and longer-lasting impact upon European and Western culture than might have been the case, had it been confined to the aristocratic elite of the princes and the wealthy. In the final analysis there has been no cultural movement that has enjoyed such a long continuity in its lasting impact, even with its waning intensity.[24] A comparative study of the impact of German humanism with that of other lands would be highly desirable. This could go on, and what used to be known as the 'gentle reader' may by now fear that it will! In the course of time the golden age of German humanism, and the silver age that followed, in the end yielded to the iron age of a technical and industrial society, though

24. On the continuity of humanism in German culture, see H. Liebing, 'Perspektivische Verzeichnungen. Uber die Haltbarkeit der *fable convenue* in der Kirchengeschichte,' *Zeitschrift für Kirchengeschichte*, 3 (1968), pp. 289–307; H. Jantz, 'German Renaissance Literature,' *Modern Language Notes*, 81 (1966), pp. 398–463; and L. W. Spitz, ed., *Humanismus und Reformation als kulturelle Kräfte in der deutschen Geschichte* (Berlin and New York, 1981).

25. This essay has deliberately kept documentation to a minimum and has limited references to more recent works. For more complete documentation, the black-snow of the scholars, and more replete bibliography, the reader may consult a number of my articles on various aspects of the subject dealt with in this *zusammenfassende Darstellung*. For example: 'The Course of German Humanism,' in H. A. Oberman, ed., *Itinerarium Italicum: The Profile of the Italian Renaissance in the Mirror of its European Transformations* (Leiden, 1975), pp. 371–436; 'Humanism and the Protestant Reformation,' in A. Rabil, ed., *Renaissance Humanism: Foundations, Forms, and Legacy*, 3 (Philadelphia 1988), pp. 380–411; 'Humanismus/Humanismusforschung,' *Theologische Realencyclopedie*, 15 (1987), pp. 639–61; 'Luther and German Humanism,' in M. J. Harran, ed., *Luther and Learning. The Wittenberg University Symposium* (Selinsgrove, PA, 1985), pp. 69–94, and the like.

remnants and sherds remain even today. But for that brief moment in geological and historical time humanism was a brilliant inspiration in Camelot.[25]

Yes, Denys Hay was quite correct in his assessment of the impact of Italian Renaissance humanism and the classical revival, perhaps especially in the case of Germany. Rudolf Agricola expressed this thought in this way:

> We are indebted to Petrarch for the intellectual culture of our century. All ages owe him a debt of gratitude – antiquity for having rescued its treasure from oblivion, and modern times for having with his own strength founded and revived culture, which he has left as a precious legacy to future ages![26]

---

26. *Vita Petrarchae illustrata per eruditissimum virum Rudolphum Agricolam Phrisium ad Antonium Scrofinium Papiensem. Anno salutis 1477 (1473) Papiae*; L. Bertalot, 'Rudolf Agricolas Lobrede auf Petrarcha,' *La Bibliofilia*, 30 (1928), pp. 382–404.

# VI

# LUTHER AS SCHOLAR
# AND THINKER

 Emerson spoke of
scholars as "the eyes and the heart of the world." Luther was a
university professor for over thirty-three years and, in addition to
teaching, sent out books, as he put it, "into all the world." He was
not a scholar in today's sense of the term. He was not forced to excel
in a technical way for scholarship's own sake. But he was a great
scholar in his mastery of the latest and best techniques, in his
genuine respect for what was sound in the scholarly inheritance,
in his willingness to follow through to the necessary end the trend
of his thought, in his creativity and imaginative mental thrusts, and
in the vigor and precision with which he expressed his ideas. He
lived his whole life in a world of learned tomes as well as polemical
tracts. "We continue to be disciples," he wrote in his *Commentary
on Psalm 101*, "of those speechless masters which we call books."

Luther described himself to Erasmus as a *rusticus* compared with
the eloquent prince of humanists. We rarely do anything out of
wisdom and precaution, he once confessed, but always out of ignorance. His was not the ignorance of insufficient knowledge or
perplexity as to how to act; rather it was a willingness to think
and to do even without knowing the final result of thought or action, for these he left up to God. He was capable of the most sophisticated theological discourse and able to draw the finest of scholarly

distinctions. Luther did not just assume a position: He took a stand. And the stands which Luther took as a scholar were equally as important, though less dramatic, as his historic stand at the Diet of Worms. His scholarly work led him to ideas which have had a tremendous impact upon modern culture.

"Learning, wisdom, and writers must rule the world," Luther observed in his *Tabletalk (Tischreden)*. "If God out of His wrath would take away from the world all the learned men, what else would the people who are left be except cattle? And law, yes, even the Word itself, are nothing without lawyers and preachers whose service God uses, as of people He cannot get along without. Where there are no people wise through the Word and laws, there bears, lions, goats and dogs possess the government of the world, and govern the household. . . ." Not only was Luther not apologetic for being an intellectual, he believed the vocation to scholarship to be a high calling, and bluntly declared that the work of the scholar was more difficult than that of a knight in armor. Some people, he reflected, believe that to be concerned merely with the word as a writer or teacher, a preacher or jurist, is a comfortable occupation compared with riding in armor and enduring heat, frost, dust, or thirst. "It is true," he wrote in his *Sermon on Keeping Children in School* in 1530, "that it would be hard for me to ride in armor. But, on the other hand, I should like to see the rider who could sit for a whole day and look in a book, even if he did not have to be concerned, write, or think. Ask a chancellor, preacher, or rhetorician what work writing and speaking is; ask a schoolteacher what labor teaching and educating youths is. The quill is light, that is true . . . but in this work the most noble parts of the human body are active and do the most work, the best member (the head), the most noble member (the tongue), and the loftiest labor (speech). In other labors it is the fist, foot, back, or some similar member which works alone, and one may at the same time sing joyously or joke freely. Three fingers do it (they say of writing), but the entire body and soul are involved in the work." (WA 30 II, 573, 574.)[1] Luther went on to relate a story about the German emperor Maximilian, who replied to critics who had complained because he used so many scribes as ambassadors, with "I can make more knights but I cannot make more doctors."

[1] Martin Luther, *Werke*. Kritische Gesammtausgabe (Weimar, 1883 ff), commonly referred to as Weimarer Ausgabe, hence the abbreviation WA; in this case Vol. 30, pt. II, pp. 573, 574.

84

As a student Luther advanced from the middle of the class to the highest academic preferments. When he took his A.B. degree in 1502 he was merely thirtieth in a class of fifty-two. When he took his M.A. on January 7, 1505, he was second in a class of seventeen. And when he received his doctorate in 1512, he was first as well as last in a class of one. The books which he owned reveal what an avid student he was, for he annotated and underlined shamelessly. He did this even in volumes he borrowed from the library of the Elector of Saxony. He memorized countless passages from the Scriptures, the writings of the early church fathers, called patristics, and the classics, and had sufficient confidence in his powers of recall to quote freely (though not always accurately) without checking. He was persistent in mastering a subject. At the Black Bear Inn on the way from the Wartburg Castle to Wittenberg, he showed some Swiss students his Hebrew text and commented: "I read it every day for practice."

Throughout his life Luther worked with a strong sense of purpose because he viewed his work as a divine vocation, like all other useful labor. "If God does not command you to do a work, who are you, fool, that you dare to undertake it on your own?" he asked in 1531. "A certain divine calling belongs to a good work." The calling to the doctoral and preaching offices gave him courage and comfort not only against his foes but against the enemies within, the sense of inadequacy, ennui, fatigue, and futility which regularly beset even the most dedicated scholars.

Luther, a man of many books, is not associated in the minds of men with a single work of his own the way Machiavelli's name is wedded to *The Prince,* More's to *Utopia,* Castiglione's to *The Courtier,* or Copernicus' to *On the Revolutions of the Heavenly Spheres.* His name is linked rather with a translation, his monumental work on the German Bible. It is there that his great genius for languages unfolds. In this linguistic masterpiece the scholar who knew his Latin, was a master of Greek, and very competent in Hebrew, became the creator of a new high German language for his people. In his treatise on translating, the *Sendbrief vom Dolmetschen,* 1530, he set in two statements the limits within which the translator must move:

"One must not ask the letters in the Latin language how one should speak German."

"Nevertheless, I did not on the other hand let the letters go their own free way." (WA 30 II, 637, 640.)

His creative yet faithful translation of the Scriptures was a splendid demonstration of his own principles. In the *Sendbrief* he recounted how he and his "Sanhedrin" of Hebrew scholars searched for days and weeks for exactly the right vocable:

It often happened to us that we searched and asked for a single individual word for fourteen days, three or four weeks and still at times did not find it. On Job we, that is Master Philipp [Melanchthon], Aurogallus and I, worked in such a way that sometimes we could scarcely finish three lines in four days. (WA II, 636.)

Luther combined faithfulness to the text with a desire to make the prophets and evangelists speak German. He related how he listened to the "man in the street," to women in the market and children at play to get the words of the people with just the right nuance and richness for his vernacular translation.

In addition to his feeling for language Luther possessed a mastery of the sources and a knowledge of traditional authorities that revealed not only a brilliant mind but an indefatigable scholar. Even in his reformatory tracts, such as his three great treatises of 1520, he presented an astounding array of source material. In his *Address to the Christian Nobility,* for example, he drew on the Scriptures, church history, secular and constitutional history, canon law, and the humanists, as well as on his own experience. In his controversy with Erasmus on the freedom or servitude of the will he surprisingly used more classical references than did his humanist opponent. His allusions were indirect and entered the stream of the argument naturally. His treatise was longer than that of Erasmus, be it said, but the fact remains that his classical knowledge was at any rate impressive, and it increased during his last years when under the influence of Philipp Melanchthon, a brilliant Greek scholar as well as a reformer, Luther employed his leisure to cultivate it further.

Luther's scholarly control of the sources is most evident in his work as an exegete, that is, as an expositor of the Bible. He characteristically deprecated his own powers as an exegete and stressed that if the expositor does his work properly he will not thrust himself into the picture but will let the meaning of the passage come through clearly under its own power. A typical expression in his treatment of Psalm 17, 13–14:

There is little to be gained from our translation, and even less from Jerome. . . . I must therefore at this point call upon the very worst teacher, namely myself, and I shall therefore invent a story without prejudice or indiscreetness. If anyone knows of something better, let him help me out, but if he knows of nothing better, let him judge me fairly. (Cited by E. Mülhaupt, *D. Martin Luther's Psalmen-Auslegung*, I [Göttingen, 1959], 228.)

Luther was able to handle the text creatively and with a marked independence from the authorities because he had a point of view and a principle of interpretation more clearly delineated than, and distinctly different from most of theirs.

Perhaps the most striking fact about Luther's exegesis is the vastness of the enterprise, for the largest part of his *opera* is devoted to the exposition of the Scriptures. A second surprising aspect of his work is that the bulk of his scholarly commentaries is devoted to the Old Testament rather than the New. He lectured by preference on the Old Testament and would, at a modern university, have held the chair of Old Testament studies. In contrast, Luther preached by preference on the New Testament. He habitually chose his sermon texts from the gospel or epistle lesson for the day. When he did preach on the Old Testament he drew an overwhelming number of his sermon texts from those books which he believed to offer the richest evangelical treasures, above all Genesis and the Psalms. He was less given to singling out specific Messianic or evangelical passages as points of departure than to handling the whole history of God's way with mankind, through the dialectic of command and promise, law and gospel.

Luther commented on a total of fourteen books of the Bible, if one may group as one the minor prophets, that is, the prophets whose books were smaller in bulk than those of Isaiah, Jeremiah, and Ezekiel. Of the Old Testament books he lectured on Genesis (1535–45), Deuteronomy, the Psalms (three times), Ecclesiastes, the Song of Solomon, Isaiah, and the minor prophets. Of the New Testament books he lectured on the epistles, preeminently on Romans, on Galatians (1519 and 1531), I Timothy, Titus, Philemon, I John, and Hebrews. The evangelists as conveyers of the Word, however, seemed to inspire Luther to proclaim the *Kerygma* rather than to analyze the text. To this idealistic explanation must be added the fact that external circumstances frequently dictated Luther's choice of subject for the lectures. Other professors in the theological faculty did lecture on the four gospels. Melanchthon lectured five different times on the Epistle to the Romans, a preoccupation with St. Paul that is strongly reflected in his best known theological work, the *Loci Communes*. Perhaps it was Luther's great respect for Melanchthon's mastery of Greek and his deferring to Melanchthon's theological acumen which led him to yield the key book in his own development to his young colleague.

Luther's own exegetical procedures underwent a very marked development. From his first lectures on the Psalms, the *Dictata*, through his lectures on the Epistle to the Hebrews (1517/18) he followed the time-honored method of writing short notes explaining linguistic, textual, or limited problems of interpretation in marginal or interlinear glosses, which he called *collects*. He wrote out longer, more comprehensive explanations of the text as *scholia* or corollaries. In this he was following the established medieval practice. But he gradually emancipated himself from this traditional structure and, as his confidence increased, he produced a running commentary on the texts in his later works. His growing certainty as to his understanding of the theological substance of the Pauline epistles becomes very evident by a comparison of his early and later treatment of specific texts and themes, in the Psalms or in Galatians, on which he did commentaries separated in time by more than a decade.

Luther saw that the primacy of the Scriptures as the *norma normans*, the criterion which determines right teaching, demanded the priority of Biblical studies over all other theological disciplines and over subjects such as dialectic or Aristotelian philosophy. He therefore pressed for these principles as well as for the precedence of the fathers over later authorities. He regularly contrasted (unfavorably) the subleties of the scholastic theologians with the sounder theology of the early church fathers. Early in 1517 he expressed satisfaction that "our theology and St. Augustine are making propitious progress and rule at our university thanks to God's working." On May 9, 1518, he wrote to his old professor in scholastic theology at Erfurt, Jodokus Trutfetter:

I am absolutely persuaded that it is impossible to reform the church unless from the very ground up the canons, decretals, scholastic theology, philosophy, logic, as they are now pursued, are rooted out and other subjects taught. And I go so far in this conviction that I daily ask the Lord to let things so transpire that a fully purified study of the Bible and of the holy fathers will be restored. (WA Briefwechsel, I, 170, no. 74.)

This double emphasis upon the Scriptures as norm and the fathers as early and more reliable witnesses to correct interpretation found characteristic expression in his own exegetical work. A few examples chosen from commentaries on Old and New Testament books will illustrate his use of authorities.

The true scholar does not skip. It is quite impressive to select a passage in Luther's commentaries, almost at random, and discover the care with which he has consulted the authorities and researched each word and phrase. Consider a brief passage from his second *Psalms Commentary*, 1519, relating to the meaning of that mysterious word "Selah" (Ps. 3, 2, *et passim*). Luther cites the Septuagint, the early writers Cassiodorus, Augustine, and Jerome, Aquila of Pontus (second century translator of the Old Testament into Greek), and the Renaissance humanists Lefèvre d'Étaples and Johannes Reuchlin.

In the *Commentary on the Epistle to the Hebrews*, 1517–18, then still considered to be the work of St. Paul, Luther used an equally impressive array of authorities. The church father John Chrysostom (d. 407) was especially important because of his influential homilies on Hebrews. Luther also cited Dionysius the Areopagite (fifth century), the western fathers Ambrose and Augustine, Pseudo Ambrose and the Jewish historian, Josephus. Among Renaissance humanists he used Erasmus as his prime authority on Greek. He cited Lefèvre d'Étaples' *Commentaries on St. Paul's Epistles* (1512 and 1515). Johannes Reuchlin was his authority for questions involving Hebrew philology. The late medieval theologian Jean Gerson figured prominently, and he cited as well the traditional medieval exegetical predecessors. Above all, his interpretations rested not on authorities, but upon his own linguistic and theological analysis.

Luther knew the authorities, was willing to consult and compare them, but was essentially independent of them. When he differed from them, he usually did so in a calm, academic manner, although occasionally scorn or sharp disagreement over some absurdity or distortion prompted a cutting comment. Typical of this is his response to the fathers and to Lefèvre in his corollary on Romans 5:14, "Even over them that had not sinned after the likeness of Adam's transgressions":

Blessed Augustine interprets this in the same work as follows: over them that had not yet sinned from their own will in the same way as he did. Also blessed Ambrose understands it in this way. . . .

Faber Stapulensis [Lefèvre d'Étaples], however, understands the matter differently and he reconciles the contradiction between the phrases "in that all had sinned" and "over them that had not sinned" in a different way. But I doubt whether he does it well; indeed, I fear he does not. He says that the phrase "after the likeness" must be referred to the word "reigned", and I am willing to grant this on account of John Chrysostom, who in expounding this passage says: "How did [death] reign? After the likeness of the transgression of Adam," etc. (WA 56, 316, 317.)

Never does one find in Luther a blind or subservient compliance with authorities ancient or modern. But this independence is not marred by disrespect for them or by an unwillingness to be guided by their wisdom where their views seem to him to be exegetically sound.

The deepest theme in history, observed Goethe, has been posed by the conflict of faith and unfaith. Luther's lifework as an exegete was necessarily tied very closely to his total religious and theological method. In his exegetical analysis Luther was not interested in merely establishing critically the historical or literal meaning of the text. Rather, as a *homo religiosus,* he struggled to grasp the theological or spiritual meaning of the message. A recurring phrase is *Das ist theologische Grammatik.* In the *Commentary on Romans 8: 24-25:* "For we are saved by hope. But hope that is seen is not hope . . .," Luther observes: "Grammatically, this way of speaking may be figurative, yet, theologically understood, it expresses a most intense feeling in a most direct and telling way. For it is ever so that when the hope that rises from the longing for a beloved object is delayed, love is made all the greater." For Luther the Scriptures were inspired by the Holy Spirit in order to convey a spiritual message, therefore their basic meaning, the literal meaning, had to be spiritual-prophetic. The essential hermeneutical or interpretative principle is to properly distinguish between law and gospel, threat and promise. The touchstone of correct evangelical exegesis is whether the interpretation of a passage magnifies the promise of God and its fulfillment in Christ. The way in which Luther drove past the philological questions to get to the theological heart of the text, never wishing to confuse the scaffolding with the structure itself, is clearly illustrated in his discourse on faith in his last work, the *Commentary on Genesis:*

I shall not dispute about the Hebrew word *haschab* whether you translate it with *reputare* or *cognitare,* since both words deal with the same idea. For when the divine Majesty considers me righteous, forgiven of my sins, and set free from eternal death, by faith I thankfully lay hold of these thoughts of God concerning me. Thus I am just, not from my works, but out of faith, by means of which I apprehend God's thoughts.

For God's thought is infallible truth. So when I grasp it, not with uncertainty or doubt, but with steadfast heart, then I am justified.

Faith is a steadfast and certain thought about God or trust in Him, that He is gracious through Christ, and that for Christ's sake, He thinks about us thoughts of peace, not thoughts of affliction or wrath. (WA 42, 563, 564.)

Luther's interpretation of the Old Testament turned upon this very fulcrum of faith. Faith is essential to seeing beyond mere profane history in the Old Testament to spiritual history, the history of God's people and the plan of salvation. His interpretation of the Old Testament was not historical in the sense of a modern critical historical science, but in the sense of divine or spiritual history seen through the believing eyes of faith. Faith makes sacred history. And sacred history is as different from the profane history of the gentiles as heaven and earth, light and shadow, life and death.

He praised the Psalms as a miniature Bible, containing in the most beautiful and compact form, like a little *enchiridion* or handbook, the totality of Scriptures and a picture of the whole Christian church done in living color and form, a mirror of Christendom. There is a double sense to the Scriptures, that which is understood by one's own intellect and that to which the Holy Spirit gives understanding. For that reason it is necessary for the exegete to be a Christian, if he is to be able to perceive the spiritual meaning of the text. The *parole* of the dogmaticians on the relationship of the Old and New Testament is based upon this view of Luther: *Novum Testamentum in vetere latet, Vetus Testamentum in novere patet* — the New Testament lies concealed in the Old, the Old Testament lies revealed in the New. Christ as the Word is the key to the Scriptures. All exegetical rules are subject to one overriding hermeneutical principle, namely that the true prophetic spiritual meaning of the Scriptures can be understood only in terms of Christ. The logic of Luther's exegesis is the logic of his christology. In interpreting the Old Testament the exegete finds a christological meaning not only in the overtly Messianic prophetic passages or in those in which the hidden meaning is certified as Messianic by New Testament references, but Luther is quite convinced that the spiritual meaning of the totality of Scriptures is to be understood in relation to Christ. The Scriptures should be expounded in such a way that man appears to be nothing and Christ everything.

Who would understand the Scriptures must understand Christ. Christ himself laid down the great commission to study the Old Testament in John 5: 39: "Search the Scriptures; for in them ye think ye have eternal life: and they are they which testify of me." In the early patristic period St. Ignatius coined the phrase: *Ubi Christus, ibi ecclesia catholica.* —Where Christ is, there is the universal church. This spirit pervades Luther's understanding of the Scriptures. In the history of Christ everything is said that can be said concerning the history of the church, of the individual, and of the world. It can be argued that for Luther the traditional fourfold interpretation constituted a vague anticipation of this christocentric hermeneutics. Thus the historical-literal sense refers to Christ, the allegorical sense to the church, the tropological sense to the individual, and the anagogical sense to the end of the world and the eschaton. All wisdom and knowledge are hidden in Christ and the exegete's task is to lay out what the Scriptures have to tell man about Christ. The historical-literal sense is thus identified with the spiritual or christological sense of the Scriptures. The spiritual sense is no longer associated with the allegorical meaning in contrast to the literal or to the historico-critical meaning. Luther's exegesis was thus independent of the medieval tradition and is quite at variance with contemporary critical methods of Biblical scholarship. Given, however, his understanding of the Word, his achievement as an exegete is a major monument to spirited, brilliant, and industrious scholarship. His skill as well as his integrity and conviction shine through on every page wrested from the text written in ancient languages.

As a scholar and intellectual Luther had the highest regard for human reason, ranking man's *ratio* as the loftiest of all created things. Luther's position in the long and honorable tradition of Christian rationalism has been questioned, challenged, and often misunderstood not only by his critics and foes, but also by his friends. Scholars such as Hartmann Grisar, S.J., or A. Lunn, author of *The Revolt Against Reason,* or such popular and influential writers as Will Durant, badly distort Luther's fideism into a form of anti-rationalism, if not anti-intellectualism. Another scholar, Hiram Hayden, in his massive volume *The Counter-Renaissance* groups Luther with Machiavelli, Montaigne, and Agrippa of

Nettesheim as taking part in an intellectual pendular swing against the values of the Renaissance, a movement characterized by anti-rationalism, anti-natural law, anti-ordered cosmos views. But even some acknowledged Luther scholars who were sympathetic to his beliefs have done his position less than justice. Otto Ritschel spoke of his *sacrificium intellectus* in giving God all honor. Karl Heim referred to a "basic irrational intellectualism". The great Luther scholar Karl Holl assumed that whenever Luther spoke of reason he meant simply "Christian reason" and had no operative concept of natural reason. Luther is often described as having a concept of instrumental reason, which serves as an agent in determining the meaning of the message to be accepted, but not of magisterial reason, which is the judge and arbiter of what is to be accepted. This analysis simplifies Luther's position far too much.

Faith for Luther is not credulity, an epistemological short circuit of rationalism, but *fiducia,* a loving trust in God the creator and redeemer of rational man. Like the medieval theologians, St. Bernard, Thomas Aquinas, and other stalwarts in the tradition of Christian rationalism, Luther drew a horizontal line which distinguished the areas in which reason and faith are operative, and he drew it between the realms of nature and of grace. In the realm of nature, in worldly matters and in the area of human culture natural reason reigns supreme. Luther as an Augustinian knew and approved of St. Augustine's high regard for reason, arguing for its lofty position on the grounds that in judging all things reason demonstrates its superiority to them. Perhaps the most succinct statement of Luther's position on the high place of reason in the total scheme of things is expressed in the theses which he prepared for the *Disputation Concerning Man* (1536):

1. Philosophy or human wisdom defines man as an animal having reason, sensation, and body.
2. It is not necessary at this time to debate whether man is properly or improperly called an animal.
3. But this must be known, that this definition describes man only as a mortal and in relation to this life.
4. And it is certainly true that reason is the most important and the highest in rank among all things and, in comparison with other things of this life, the best and something divine.
5. It is the inventor and mentor of all the arts, medicines, laws, and of whatever wisdom, power, virtue, and glory men possess in this life.

6. By virtue of this fact it ought to be named the essential difference by which man is distinguished from the animals and other things.
7. Holy Scripture also makes it lord over the earth, birds, fish, and cattle, saying, "Have dominion."
8. That is, that it is a sun and a kind of god appointed to administer these things in this life.
9. Nor did God after the fall of Adam take away this majesty of reason, but rather confirmed it.
10. In spite of the fact that it is of such majesty, it does not know itself *a priori,* but only *a posteriori.*
11. Therefore, if philosophy or reason itself is compared with theology, it will appear that we know almost nothing about man.[2]

Luther used the term reason in three different ways and much of the misunderstanding about his place in intellectual history derives from a failure to distinguish his various uses. He distinguished natural, regenerate, and arrogant reason. Natural reason is the most splendid achievement of God's creation, the crowning glory of the world of nature. Even after the fall of man it remained supreme. Regenerate reason is the reason of the man who has come to faith in God. The outlook of such a man, who sees life as an exercise of faith active in love, is qualitatively different. Regenerate reason is freed for fully creative expression by the positive outlook on life engendered in it, for faith is a *vita cordis,* the life of his heart. Finally, arrogant reason is the harlot reason of unregenerate man who refuses to accept God's revelation and His terms of salvation. It insists, on the one hand, upon offering its own righteousness for salvation or, on the other hand, asserts that since faith saves, good works are no longer necessary. Luther regularly uses the term reason as a synecdoche for the whole man in different spiritual conditions, natural man, regenerate man, reprobate man.

When Luther made his dramatic appeal at Worms to the Scriptures, clear reason, and conscience, the clear reason or *ratio evidens* to which he referred was the reason of a man informed by the Word of God. Luther answered the emperor in these words:

Since then your serene majesty and your lordships seek a simple answer, I will give it in this manner, neither horned nor toothed: Unless I am con-

---

[2] WA 39 I, 175–180. Cited here from *Luther's Works,* American edition, XXXIV, ed. L. Spitz (Philadelphia, 1960), 137.

94

vinced by the testimony of the Scriptures or by clear reason (for I do not trust either in the pope or in councils alone, since it is well known that they have often erred and contradicted themselves), I am bound by the Scriptures I have quoted and my conscience is captive to the Word of God. I cannot and I will not retract anything, since it is neither safe nor right to go against conscience.

I cannot do otherwise, here I stand, may God help me. Amen.[3]

His appeal in this case was to the reason of regenerate man. He is not asserting the right of the autonomous individual to defy the teaching of tradition or the church on the basis of natural reason, but he is affirming the duty of regenerate man, informed by the Spirit, to let himself be directed, indeed bound, by the Word. Natural reason is perfectly capable of working very effectively even on sacred texts in order to establish the literal, historico-critical, philologically sound meaning. Luther was grateful for the aid of Jewish scholars in the translation of the Hebrew text. Regenerate reason is open to the guidance of the Holy Spirit in perceiving the religious meaning of a text. The role of reason in Luther's scholarly work is of central importance. His concern for higher culture as a legitimate sphere of faith's works, and his own achievements as a scholar produced historically a powerful impact upon western culture.

BIBLIOGRAPHICAL NOTE: For Luther's early development see H. Boehmer, *Martin Luther: Road to Reformation,* tr. J. W. Doberstein and T. G. Tappert (New York, 1957); and E. G. Rupp, *Luther's Progress to the Diet of Worms* (New York, 1964). For the complete life the place to start is with R. H. Bainton, *Here I Stand: A Life of Martin Luther* (Nashville, 1950). On Luther as translator see H. Bluhm, *Martin Luther, Creative Translator* (St. Louis, 1965); and on the problem of reason: B. Lohse, *Ratio und Fides* (Göttingen, 1958), and B. Gerrish, *Grace and Reason* (Oxford, 1962).

---

[3] Cited by B. Lohse in *Mitteilungen der Luthergesellschaft* (1958), 124–134.

# VII

## HEADWATERS OF THE REFORMATION

*Studia Humanitatis, Luther Senior, et Initia Reformationis*


Around the year 40 B.C. Sallust said of historical writing : *In primis arduum videtur res gestas scribere* ! In addition to the usual difficulties confronting the student of what Schopenhauer described as "the infinite subject matter of history," the Reformation as the first great historical movement in the post-Gutenberg era provides mountains of printed material. Luther's own works are noted not only for their vast extensiveness, but for their circumstantial nature. Robert of Melun in the twelfth century wrote of the church fathers, *Sacri patres quod non appugnabantur non defendebant* ! Luther's writings, too, were frequently polemical, apologetic, or occasional. Moreover, his thought was paradoxical and he at times took a malicious joy in giving the "contradictionists" occasions for exercizing their misguided ingenuity. But the extent and difficulty of his writings, given the fact that he was a man of outsized mentality, make his work an ever fresh source of insight and inspiration.

Dr. Oberman's paper illustrates again the possibility of gaining new perspectives even on a subject so much examined as the *initia Lutheri et reformationis*. Three major intellectual currents, nominalism, humanism, and Augustinianism, can be identified and delineated quite clearly as tributaries to the Reformation movement. Their importance for Luther personally constitutes a more difficult and delicate problem. Luther's development can best be understood in terms of nominalism and humanism domesticated and put into the service of a new Augustinian theology which conditioned him. For that reason a reexamination of the *via Gregorii* as an important element in Luther's theological conditioning is called for. Our new knowledge about Pierre d'Ailly's extensive dependence upon Gregory of Rimini (d. 1358) suggests that another look at the importance of the *via Gregorii* in the 15th and 16th centuries and especially for Erfurt and Wittenberg is mandatory. Relating the intellectual forces contributing to the Reformation and those operative in Luther sheds light upon the beginnings of both. To acknowledge that Luther's *Werdegang* occurred in a specific intellectual context by no means minimizes his emergence as a creative thinker and original mind, a man who reshaped his inheritance and then reformed the church. Dr. Oberman allows for the "X" in the equation, as E. Gordon Rupp put it in his beautiful opening address to the Third International Congress for Luther Research, "the point at which great men cease to be explained by heredity and environment, and the thought world of their contemporaries."

Dr. Oberman is a man who, like Dr. Johnson, was born to grapple with libraries, and the notes reveal that he has done so. I find his methodology and conception of history most congenial to my own personal predilection. He replaces the natural science paradigm so commonly adopted by historians with homonistic conceptions with a humanistic approach. Historians sometimes substitute "factors" for "causes", thus as Professor Jack Hexter has observed, progressing sideways. The imagery of tributaries, emergence, creativity, impetus, event, movement, the provision for the paratactic element in history and the acknowledgement of the irrationality by which a *felix culpa* can move history ahead all make for a descientized and sound humanistic history. Moreover, he treats the gossamer web of intellectual history with caution and sensitivity. The intellectual history approach has its distinct limitations, of course, for it does not encompass the socio-psychological elements operative in the individual nor the social, psychological, economic, and political forces at work in the broader movement. For some historians, for example, Gabriel Biel's role as superior of the "Clerics of the Common Life" at Butzbach and the part he played in the founding of the University of Tübingen, as well as his progressive views on political economy, are as essential to understanding the man's place in history as is analyzing his exposition of the Canon of the Mass or distinguishing a Scotist from an Occamist influence in the last three books of his commentary on the Sentences. For some, an understanding of the political and legal aspect of Luther's "cause" or "case" is as essential as the theological argument itself.[1] Nevertheless, within carefully defined limits intellectual history as applied here to the problem of *initia Lutheri—initia reformationis* is perfectly legitimate.

## I. COGNITIO INITIORUM DUPLEX AND THE LUTHER SEPTICEPS

The account offered of Luther's development to 1521 is authentic,

---

[1] See Wilhelm Borth, *Die Luthersache (Causa Lutheri) 1517-1524 : Die Anfänge der Reformation als Frage von Politik und Recht* (Lübeck, 1970).

letter perfect in utilizing the latest discoveries of new materials and interpretations.[1] Especially fascinating is the insight that Luther was a member of a reform team including Karlstadt and Amsdorf at the university, and at first not even the most prominent member. The importance of the year 1518 and of the Heidelberg disputation before the Augustinian order, "to which he owed far more than to any other single influence," so often lost in the valley between the years 1517 (95 Theses) and 1519 (Leipzig Debate), is properly assessed.[2] Moreover, the difference between Luther's teaching on justification by faith and the reception accorded his proclamation by Bucer, Karlstadt, Müntzer, or Calvin is neatly drawn. Particularly acute is his observation that after Heidelberg Bucer informed Beatus Rhenanus that for Luther man is justified through the *lex spiritus*.[3] However, a cautionary word is in order at the

---

[1] For example, Kenneth Hagen, "An Addition to the Letters of John Lang : Introduction and Translation," *Archive for Reformation History*, LX (1969), 27-32, and Oswald Bayer and Martin Brecht, "Unbekannte Texte des frühen Luther aus dem Besitz des Wittenberger Studenten Johannes Geiling," *Zeitschrift für Kirchengeschichte*, LXXXII (1971), 229-58.

[2] Oswald Bayer, *Promissio : Geschichte der reformatorischen Wende in Luthers Theologie* (Göttingen, 1971) stresses the importance of the years 1518 to 1520 from the theses *Pro Veritate* on for the development of Luther's theology, understood in the light of the *Promissio* concept. Père Daniel Olivier will soon publish a detailed study of the Heidelberg Theses of 1518.

[3] Bucer described the impression Luther made on the reform-minded humanists in April 1518, when he defended his theses before the Augustinian congregation in Heidelberg, saying that Luther agreed with Erasmus in everything except that he excelled him in one thing, namely that he taught openly and freely what Erasmus merely hinted at. See Helmar Junghans, ed., *Die Reformation in Augenzeugenberichten* (Düsseldorf, 1967), pp. 214-15; Humanismus, pp. 214-38. An excellent analysis of Bucer's interpretation of Luther's justification by grace alone in terms of the *Lex spiritus* is to be found in Karl Koch, *Studium Pietatis* (Neukirchen, 1962), pp. 10-15. W.P. Stephens, however, holds that Koch overemphasizes Bucer's humanism, *The Holy Spirit in the Theology of Martin Bucer* (Cambridge, 1970), p. 11, n. 3. On the identification of the *lex Christi* and *lex regni* in both Karlstadt and Müntzer, see E. Gordon Rupp, *Patterns of Reformation* (Philadelphia, 1969), pp. 49-353, where he perceptively tags the former as "puritan." Martin Brecht, *Die frühe Theologie des Johannes Brenz* (Tübingen, 1966), p. 31, observes that Brenz, like his friends Bucer and Oecolampadius, was under the influence of Augustinian spiritualism and that this distinguished him from Luther, who very soon founded the church exclusively on the Word. Luther was fond of referring to Zwingli and Oecolampadius as Daedalus and Icarus, perhaps with their lofty spiritualizing tendencies in mind. Joachim Rogge, "Die Initia Zwingli und Luthers': Eine Einführung in die Probleme," *Luther Jahrbuch*, XXX( 1963), 107-33, contrasts Luther's broad theological base in the exegetical work of the years 1513-1519 and relative indifference to the external form of the church

point where a clear contrast is drawn between Luther's emphasis upon faith effected by the *verbum dei* and that of Zwingli, Bucer and Calvin upon faith as effected by the *operatio spiritus sancti* (pointing up the *extra-Calvinisticum*), for Luther consistently held to the catechetical truth that "the Holy Ghost calls me by the gospel, enlightens me with his gifts, sanctifies and keeps me in the one true faith." Although the Word produces faith, for Luther, too, the Holy Spirit is the operative agent in inducing faith in the Word. His statements on this point are very numerous such as those following from *The Bondage of the Will*: "Unless the Spirit revealed them [the principle articles of our faith], no man's heart would know anything about the matter"; again, "For no man on earth, unless imbued with the Holy Ghost, ever in his heart knows of, or believes in, or longs for, eternal salvation, even if he harps upon it by tongue and pen." [1] The assessment that Occamism was not important for the *initia reformationis* seems to be well-founded. The importance of humanism, on the other hand, for the beginnings and transmission of the Reformation are rightly stressed in the light of recent research.[2]

The structure of the argument is deceptively simple : *Duplex est cognitio initiorum—Lutheri et Reformationis*. The dual beginnings are related to three tributaries, nominalism, humanism, and Augustinianism, the first two domesticated in the third. The image evoked is that of a three-headed Luther rather than Cochlaeus' *Luther septiceps* in Brosamer's well-known woodcut. The seven heads might well be : 1. nominalism, 2. humanism, 3. Augustinianism, 4. mysticism, 5. apocalypticism, 6. *Historia sacra*, and 7. social conditions and actual ecclesiastical practices and teachings, all attached to the psychosomatic finitude known to us as Dr. Luther. When Luther saw the woodcut he was very

---

with Zwingli's strong humanist background, relatively narrow theological base, and immediate concern with the external form of the church and its relations to the state. The recent volume by Robert C. Walton, *Zwingli's Theocracy* (Toronto, 1967), illustrates the Swiss reformer's ethics which can be regarded as one of the hallmarks of city and social reform. His view of society and its aim, Walton concludes, represented a particular version of the theocratic ideal which dominated political thought in the 16th century.

[1] J.I. Packer and O.R. Johnston, eds., *Martin Luther on the Bondage of the Will* (London, 1957), pp. 139-40.

[2] Herbert Schöffler, *Wirkungen der Reformation* (Frankfurt a. M., 1960), pp. 126-32: Die jugendlichste Fakultät, *et passim*; Bernd Moeller, "Die deutschen Humanisten und die Anfänge der Reformation," *Zeitschrift für Kirchengeschichte*, LXX (1959), 46-61; Lewis W. Spitz, "The Third Generation of German Renaissance Humanists," *Aspects of the Renaissance*, Archibald Lewis, ed. (Austin, Texas, 1967), pp. 105-21.

amused and observed that "Kochleffel" had trouble getting all seven heads on one neck. Three is simpler, and this supplementary lecture will indulge in further reductionism by concentrating upon the importance of one of the three, humanism, for the Reformation movement. It will examine the role of the religious in Renaissance humanism, particularly the Augustinians with an eye to their importance for the *initia Lutheri et Reformationis* and the attitude of *Luther Senior* from 1530 to 1546 toward the *studia humanitatis* as it affected the course of the Reformation.

Humanism is to be defined less in the confining terms of Paul Oskar Kristeller, who relates it closely to the profession of rhetoricians and city-secretaries in the medieval *ars dictamini* tradition, than in the broader sense employed by Hanna Gray in her brilliant articles on rhetoric, Lorenzo Valla and other topics of Italian humanism, or by Paul Joachimsen, who many years ago described humanism as an intellectual movement, primarily literary and philological, which was rooted in the love of and desire for the rebirth of classical antiquity.[1] Humanism stressed the importance of classical languages, grammar and philology, cultivated epistelography, elevated rhetoric over dialectic, cherished poetry and music, emphasized moral over speculative philosophy, presented history as philosophy teaching by example, and held education at a premium. The key phrase came from Cicero's *De Oratore* : "For eloquence is nothing else than wisdom speaking copiously."

## II. RENAISSANCE HUMANISM AND AUGUSTINIANISM

The regular clergy contributed significantly to Renaissance culture and uniquely to the fusion of humanist and religious concerns. The role of the "religious," just as the revival of Christian antiquity during the Renaissance, has received far too little attention in scholarship.[2] From

---

[1] Hanna H. Gray, "Renaissance Humanism : The Pursuit of Eloquence," *Journal of the History of Ideas*, XXIV, 4 (October-December 1963), 497-514. P. 503 : True eloquence can be derived only from the "harmonious union between wisdom and style." Hanna H. Gray, "Valla's *Encomium of St. Thomas Aquinas* and the Humanist Conception of Christian Antiquity," Heinz Bluhm, ed., *Essays in History and Literature* (Chicago, 1965), pp. 37-51.

[2] Carlo Angeleri, *Il Problema Religiosa del Rinascimento : Storia della Critica e Bibliografia* (Florence, 1952) pays much attention to the historiography dealing with Franciscan naturalism and its supposed influence upon Renaissance realism in art and letters, but he offers no systematic treatment of the role of the religious or place of the orders in Renaissance culture. The concern of the humanists with the life of the religious, the *vita contemplativa* and *otium religiosum*, is examined by Charles Trinkaus, "Humanist Trea-

its very inception Renaissance humanism owed much to the regular clergy. In Florence the Augustinian monk Luigi Marsigli (c. 1330-1394), a friend of the cleric Petrarch, did a commentary on two Petrarchan poems. He gathered a group of intellectuals together at the church of Santo Spirito where they discoursed on the classics. The Camaldulensian Ambrogio Traversari (1386-1439) contributed in an important way to the revival of patristic studies.[1] The Carmelite prior general Baptista Mantuanus (1448-1516) wrote Christian poems with classical accouterments to counteract the pagan influence of Greek and Latin literature. Pico called him the most learned man of the period and contemporaries hailed him as a second Virgil. The young Luther and many other Northerners read his poems with deep appreciation.

Of special interest for the *initia reformationis* problem is the role played by Augustinianism and by the Augustinians in the development of the Renaissance culture. During the two centuries preceding the Reformation there was a lively resurgence of Augustinianism in European intellectual life of which the Reformation itself was in a sense at one point a manifestation. The influence of Augustine persisted, of course, in those medieval disciplines which carried through to the sixteenth century such as scholastic theology.[2] On the popular level, too, much religious and ascetic literature revealed the influence of Augustine. The Augustinian Canons and the Augustinian Hermits persisted in medieval piety, debated as to whether Augustine had been a monk, revived the cult of Monica, and copied their patron's works. But beyond the traditional concerns, Augustine had a critically important influence upon the two most characteristic intellectual currents in Renaissance intellectual life, humanism and Neo-Platonism. Petrarch, the father of humanism, and Ficino, the founder of the Florentine Platonic Academy, illustrate

---

tises on the Status of the Religious : Petrarch, Salutati, Valla," *Studies in the Renaissance*, ed. M.A. Shaaber, XI (1964), 7-45. See also the excellent comprehensive work, Charles Trinkaus, *"In Our Image and Likeness" : Humanity and Divinity in Italian Humanist Thought* (2 vols. Chicago, 1970).

[1] See Charles Stinger, "Humanism and Reform in the Early Quattrocento : The Patristic Scholarship of Ambrogio Traversari (1386-1439)," unpublished Ph. D. dissertation, Stanford University, 1971 ; Agnes Clare Way, "The Lost Translations Made by Ambrosius Traversarius of the Orations of Gregory Nazianzen," *Renaissance News*, XIV (1961), 91-96. Traversari's influence reached to the North where Lefèvre d'Étaples used his translation of Dionysius in his 1499 edition, though he might have used Ficino's had he known it.

[2] Karl Werner, *Die Scholastik des späteren Mittelalters*, III, *Der Augustinismus in der Scholastik des späteren Mittelalters* (Vienna, 1883).

the essential place of Augustine's Platonized and somewhat mystical theology in the central literary and philosophical movements of the Renaissance. Wherever Aristotle did not reign supreme, there was room for a burgeoning of Augustinian thought.[1]

Augustine played a key role in the humanists' cultural reorientation of the West. The humanists in turning away from medieval culture and theology developed a new intellectual norm, classical letters and pre-scholastic theology, specifically the church fathers and preeminently Augustine. Petrarch, Valla, and other humanists realized that Augustine lived while the Roman empire still existed and they cited him along with classical writers on matters of literary concern. Vives, Erasmus, and other humanists translated, edited, and commented on the fathers and especially on Augustine, with the same philological care as they devoted to the classics. The Platonism derived in part from the Augustinian current of the medieval period was reinforced by the discovery by Petrarch and other humanists that Augustine and Cicero both had preferred Plato to Aristotle. Ficino derived many substantive aspects of his Neo-Platonic philosophy from Augustine rather than from the school of Plotinus, Iamblichus, or Proclus.

The important role played by the Augustinians in conjunction with the Brethren of the Common Life in the revitalized spiritual life of the *Devotio Moderna* in the Netherlands and lower Rhinelands as well as their influence supportive of education must be recognized. Not only was this spiritual and educational force crucial for the northern Renaissance, providing an early introduction to the classics for Erasmus among others, but for the Reformation as well, not least of all through Luther's brief and mysterious encounter with the *Nollbrüder* in Magdeburg.[2] Augustine and Augustinianism had a pervasive influence also

---

[1] Paul Oskar Kristeller, "Augustine and the Early Renaissance," *The Review of Religion*, VIII, 4 (May 1944), 339-58. For Augustine's influence in general Kristeller, p. 340, n. 2, refers to the dated work by J.F. Nourrisson, *La Philosophie de Saint Augustine*, (Paris, 1865), II, 147-276, and to E. Portalie, "Augustinisme," *Dictionnaire de Théologie Catholique*, I, 2501-2561.

[2] P.O. Kristeller, "Augustine and the Early Renaissance," p. 345, n. 23, draws attention to the fact that Augustine exercized a powerful influence on Gerard Groote, the founder of the Brethren of the Common Life and that the decisive chapter 31 of their statutes, *De vita communi et paupertate*, begins with a quotation from Augustine. Despite R.R. Post's strictures against the thesis of Albert Hyma, Augustin Renaudet, and other scholars that the *Devotio Moderna* contributed to the growth and development of humanism and indirectly of the Reformation in the North, the significance of both the Brethren

on French humanism, Platonism, and Stoicism, but the direct line of impetus for the *initia Reformationis* involved rather Italy and Germany.[1]

A statistical survey of the regular clergy who contributed to humanism in Italy and Germany, most of them writing both neo-classical and religious treatises, reveals large numbers, important figures, and a fascinating ratio of Augustinians to other regulars. The data provided by a compilation from four sources yields a combined total of some 184 monks and brothers from the late Trecento through the Quattrocento to the mid-Cinquecento or approximately the time of Luther's death.[2] Of these, 41 were Dominicans, 36 Benedictines, 35 Augustinians, 30 Franciscans, 11 Camaldulensians, 11 Carmelites, and 21 others from other orders such as the Carthusians, Servitians, Humiliati, Vallumbrodians, or new groups like the Theatines. It is clear that the Augustinians played a larger role relative to their numbers than the other major orders.

---

and the Augustinians was basic. See the excellent review by Helmar Junghans of R.R. Post, *The Modern Devotion : Confrontation with Reformation and Humanism* (Leiden, 1968), in *Luther-Jahrbuch, 1970,* pp. 120-29. A far more positive assessment of the role played by the Brethren in education than that given by Post can be found in Julia S. Henkel, "An Historical Study of the Educational Contributions of the Brethren of the Common Life," unpublished Ph. D. dissertation, University of Pittsburgh, 1962; William M. Landeen, "The *Devotio Moderna* in Germany," Part III, *Research Studies of the State College of Washington,* XXI (1953); Kenneth A. Strand, "Luther's Schooling in Magdeburg : A Note on Recent Views," *Essays on Luther,* Kenneth A. Strand, ed. (Ann Arbor, Michigan, 1969), pp. 106-12. A picture of humanism in the Netherlands which is hardly complimentary is given by P.N.M. Bot, *Humanisme en Onderwijs in Nederland* (Utrecht and Antwerp, 1955), arguing that the humanists replaced complete classics with excerpts, produced lengthy pedantic books, and preferred moralizing Euripedes to the truly dramatic Aeschylus.

[1] See N. Abercrombie, *Saint Augustine and French Classical Thought* (Oxford, 1938), pp. 1-17, for a useful and reliable survey of Augustine's influence upon Renaissance thought. Jean Delumeau, *Naissance et Affirmation de la Réforme* (2nd ed. Paris, 1968), pp. 367-71, "Prédestination et Augustinisme" discusses the ongoing influence of Augustine on Catholic and Protestant thinkers alike and sees this historical fact as an ecumenical point of theological contact. On page 370, n. 2, he cites important articles on the Augustinianism of Luther by L. Saint-Blancat, L. Christiani, M. Bendiscioli, J. Cadier, P. Courcelle, as well as the books of A.V. Müller and P. Vignaux.

[2] Paul Oskar Kristeller, "The Contribution of Religious Orders to Renaissance Thought and Learning," *The American Benedictine Review,* XXI, 1 (March, 1970), 1-55; P.O. Kristeller, *Iter Italicum* (2 vols.; London and Leiden, 1963-1967). Rudolph Arbesmann, *Der Augustiner-Eremitenorden und der Beginn der humanistischen Bewegung* (Würzburg, 1965); L. Lauchert, *Die italienischen literarischen Gegner Luthers* (Freiburg, 1912).

A brief introduction to a few typical representatives of the *Ordo Eremeticorum Sancti Augustini* involved in the world of humanism may prove to be instructive. The three Augustinians cited in the preceding paper, Dionysius de Burgo S. Sepulchri, Bartholomaeus de Urbino, and Jean Coci did indeed contribute to the development of early Renaissance culture. One thinks immediately also of such major figures as Giles of Viterbo,[1] Girolamo Seripando,[2] Mariano da Genazzano, who was Savonarola's eloquent competitor in the Florentine duomo,[3] Paul of Venice, an Augustinian who transmitted Franciscan physics to the school of Padua,[4] and the renowned humanist Maffeo Vegio, who like Petrarch was personally involved in Augustine's thought and wrote a *Life of Saint Monica* which honored Augustine indirectly.[5] But six more average figures will better represent the group and a quick glance at their works will provide an overview of their intellectual interests and range.

Guilielmus Becchius, bishop of Fiesole (d. 1491 ?), wrote commentaries on Aristotelian *Economics*, *Ethics*, and *Politics*, a *Protesto*, dedicated a treatise *De Cometo* to Piero d'Medici, did a commentary on Porphyry's *Isagoge*, and wrote an apologetic *De falso dogmate Maumethi*, *De potestate spiritum*, and *De potestate papae et concilii*.

---

[1] John W. O'Malley, *Giles of Viterbo on Church and Reform : A Study in Renaissance Thought* (Leiden, 1968). The famous "Address to the Fifth Lateran Council" is translated in John C. Olin, ed., *The Catholic Reformation : Savonarola to Ignatius Loyola. Reform in the Church 1495-1540* (New York, 1969), pp. 44-53.

[2] Hubert Jedin, *Girolamo Seripando* (Würzburg, 1937).

[3] See Pasquale Villari, *La Storia di Girolamo Savonarola e de'suoi tempi* (Florence, 1930), I, 80 ff. on Genazzano as a popular preacher; II, 97, on Genazzano's conspiracy in Rome against Savonarola. Roberto Ridolfi, *Vita di Girolamo Savonarola*, secunda edizione, I (Rome, 1952), capitola V, "Predicatore dei disperati." La "giostra" col Genazzano, pp. 56-65. A thorough study of Italian "humanist homiletics" would be a very welcome addition to our knowledge of rhetorical culture.

[4] Bruno Nardi, *Saggi Sull'Aristolelismo Padovano da Secolo XIV al XVI* (Florence, 1958), pp. 75-93.

[5] Vittorio Rossi, *Il Quattrocento* (Milan, 1945), pp. 283-84, writes "Le Confessioni di Sant 'Agostino gli erano state alla riconquista della Verità e alla purificazione del costume e avevano acceso nel suo cuore quel fuoco d'amore e di pietà che tutto pervade il libro *De perseverantia religionis*, dedicato nel 1448 all sorella monaca." Anna Cox Brinton, *Maphaeus Vegius and his Thirteenth Book of the Aeneid* (Stanford, 1930), p. 12, discusses St. Augustine as the "unrivalled master of Vegio's heart" and lists eight of his works which bear witness to his special veneration of Monica and Augustine. Vegio's humanistic achievements were largely his Petrarchan poems and his treatise *De educatione liberorum*; Giuseppe Saitta, *Le Pensiero Italiano Nell'umanesimo e nel Rinascimento*, I (Bologna, 1949), 273-80.

Aurelius Lippus Brandolinus (1440-1497) did poems, orations, letters and sermons. He wrote *Paradoxa Christiana* (ed. 1531), *De humanae vitae conditione* (ed. 1543), *De ratione scribendi* (ed. 1549), *De comparatione rei publicae et regni* (ed. 1890 ?), *Epithoma in sacram Judeorum historiam, Rudimenta grammaticae*, in addition to commentaries on Virgil's *Georgics* and a translation of Pliny's *Panegyricus*.

Gabriel Buratellus attempted a *Praecipuarum Controversiarum Aristotelis et Platonis Conciliatio*, a harmonizing ambition shared with both Pico and Melanchthon.

Ambrosius Massarius de Cora (d. 1485) was more of an organization man or company hand. He published orations, a life of Augustine, a commentary on "his rule," a chronicle of the order, a *Defensarium ordinis Heremitorum S. Augustini* (against the Augustinian Canons), and a *Vita B. Christianae Spoletanae*, but also a commentary on Gilbertus Porretanus' *Liber sex principiorum*, and a treatise *De animae dignitatibus*.

Nicolaus Tridentinus Scutellius (d. 1542) was of a more philosophical bent of mind and could do Greek. He translated Iamblichus' *De mysteriis* and *De vita Pythagorae* (ed. 1556), a dialogue of Lucian and four hymns, Pletho's treatise on the difference between Plato and Aristotle, Orpheus' *De gemmis*, a treatise of Proclus, Porphyry, pseudo-Plato's *De iusto*, and other philosophical texts.

Sigfridus de Castello (c. 1500) corresponded with the German humanist Jacob Wimpfeling on the question of whether St. Augustine was a monk, which Wimpfeling had raised in chapter 31 of his *De Integritate*. Luther read it with approval at the time although in later life he referred to this controversy as the kind of quibble on which people under the papacy wasted their time.[1]

Humanism also penetrated the order of the Augustinian hermits in Germany. Relatively early the preacher from the Osnabrück Augustinian house, Gottschalk Hollen (d. 1481), disseminated humanist views which he had learned while studying in Italian convents. In his sermons he showed a preference for Ovid, Horace, Valerius Maximus, but also cited Petrarch and contemporary Italian humanists, as well as the Bible. Another humanist Augustinian in Germany was Casper Amman, who was provincial of the Rhenish-Swabian Province of the Order, a

---

[1] P.O. Kristeller, "The Contribution of Religious Orders," pp. 34, 36, 37, 46, 51. Paul Oskar Kristeller, *Le Thomisme et le Pensée Italienne de la Renaissance* (Montreal, 1967), pp. 51-56, discusses Dominican savants of theological and philosophical importance.

student of Hebrew. Johannes Lang of Erfurt was an excellent Graecist. Johann Altensteig was a pupil of the German humanist Heinrich Bebel. Hieronymus Streitel of Regensburg wrote history of a humanist type. The library of the Munich monastery contained works not only of antiquity but of Italian humanists as well.[1]

In the Catholic opposition to Luther during the decades prior to Trent, the Augustinians along with the friars provided leading polemicists. Ambrosius Flandinus (d. 1531), for example, a Platonist who published several volumes of humanist sermons, *Conciones quadragesimales* (Venice, 1523), *Conciones pre adventum*, and *De mundi genitura*, wrote against Pomponazzi in defense of the immortality of souls and against fatalism. Against Luther he wrote an *Examen vanitatis duodecim articulorum Martini Luther* (Parma ms.) and *Contra Lutheranos de vera et catholica fide conflictationes* (Genoa ms.). Augustina Steuco (1496-1549), celebrated for his biblical studies, coined the term *philosophia perennis* in 1540 for the combined Christian and Platonic tradition.[2]

A survey of the entire scene suggests the following conclusions and invites further study :

1. During the two centuries preceding the Reformation, there was a clear continuity of Augustine's influence in traditional theological and philosophical lines in areas less affected by Aristotelianism. There was also a general resurgence of Augustinianism which extended far beyond the new vitality within the order of hermits. This resurgence was manifested in the preoccupation with Augustine of Petrarch, Vegio, and many other Italian humanists, as well as Mutian, Pirckheimer, Erasmus, and other northern humanists, including adherents to the *Devotio Moderna* which had some impact on Luther himself.

---

[1] Helmar Junghans, "Der Einfluss des Humanismus auf Luthers Entwicklung bis 1518," *Luther-Jahrbuch*, XXXVII (1970), 54-55, cites the humanistic Augustinians in Germany named here, drawing on the older work of Hedwig Vonschott, *Geistiges Leben im Augustinerorden am Ende des Mittelalters und zu Beginn der Neuzeit* (Berlin, 1915), pp. 103-6, 134-36, 141-43, 157-59.

[2] L. Lauchert, pp. 239-40. Charles B. Schmitt, "Perennial Philosophy from Augustino Steuco to Leibniz," *Journal of the History of Ideas*, XXVII (1966), 505-32. Adolar Zumkeller, O.S.A., who has provided impressive source materials drawn from the Würzburg archives, *Urkunden und Regesten zur Geschichte der Augustinerklöster Würzburg und Münnerstadt von Anfängen bis zur Mitte des 17. Jahrhunderts* (Würzburg, 1966), p. 4, comments that a thorough history of these Augustinian monasteries satisfying all modern requirements has not as yet been written, a statement applicable to the entire history of the order in Germany.

2. The predominant thrust of Augustinian humanists South and North was naturally strongly in support of Platonism and Neo-Platonism in the later Quattrocento and early Cinquecento, a predilection which often led them to undertake an anti-Aristotelian polemic, against contemporary Aristotelians as well as against Aristotle himself. The Augustinians were therefore in phase with the most characteristic form of Renaissance philosophy of which the priest Marsiglio Ficino was the leading exponent. In April 1518, Luther expressed his strong preference for Plato and even Pythagoras over Aristotle, an order of priority that he retained in later years.

3. In view of the demonstrable steady intellectual commerce between Italy and Germany, the broader intellectual milieu within the order South and North merits further intensive study. Luther's *Romreise* is no more enlightening than the knowledge we have of his experience with the *Nollbrüder*, but it does illustrate the North-South contact. Such a study should encompass the traffic in books and manuscripts, as well as people, and the penetration of humanist ideas into septentrional Augustinianism.[1]

4. While there is a special point in beginning with Luther's immediate situation, his teachers and the Augustinian and nominalist and humanist books known to be available in the Erfurt library or prescribed for study, much can be gained by casting a wider net in the analysis of pre-Reformation Augustinianism. Such a study should be coupled with a comprehensive analysis of the conversion of regular clergy of all orders to the evangelical faith and their reeducation, in many cases for the Lutheran ministry, as well as an examination of their contribution to Protestant literature in subsequent decades. The humanist learning of the regulars, and specifically of the Augustinians, is important not only for the *initia Lutheri* but for the *initia Reformationis* as well. For it may well have been an important element favorable to the continuity of humanism in Protestant culture in the first critical decades of the Reformation, and during the centuries which followed. The resistance

---

[1] A comparison of the ideas representative of humanism and Augustinianism would be of interest, similar to Heiko Oberman's article "Some Notes on the Theology of Nominalism with Attention to its Relation to the Renaissance," *The Harvard Theological Review*, LIII, 1 (1960), 47-76, a study not entirely satisfying since it operates with only one side of the humanists' thought, stressing the *dignitas hominis* aspect without bringing out the *miseria hominis* underside of humanist anthropology. See Lewis W. Spitz, "Man on this Isthmus", *Luther for an Ecumenical Age*, Carl S. Meyer, ed. (St. Louis, 1967), pp. 43-49, 63-65, notes 50-64.

of highly spiritual and somewhat humanistic Augustinians to evangelical theology on the other hand reveals how wide the moat was over
which Luther leaped in his own appropriation of the Biblical message.

### III. Luther Senior and the Studia Humanitatis

One noted Augustinian reared in a nominalistic climate of thought
bitterly resented his scholastic upbringing and monastic entrapment. In
his *Address to the Municipalities* Luther exclaimed :

> How much I regret that we did not read more of the poets and the historians,
> and that nobody thought of teaching us these.  Instead of such study I was
> compelled to read the devil's rubbish—the scholastic philosophers and sophists
> with such cost, labor and detriment, from which I have had trouble enough to
> rid myself.

Luther's own relation to humanists and humanism, his personal interest in the *studia humanitatis*, his contribution to curricular reform at
Wittenberg, and yet that theological gulf that separated him from the
optimistic anthropology of humanism and from the synergistic moralism of Christian humanism have been examined closely by a number of
scholars.[1] On the other hand, much work does indeed remain to be done
on the *initia et exitus Lutheri senioris* with regard to humanism, a qualified and relative good which remained even after the young Luther had
consciously turned against monasticism and scholasticism. One may
well find in the voluminous writings of Luther's last three lustra clues to
his earlier thought or how he came to understand himself. If in the early
tension years he felt cultural deprivation, did he in later years compensate for the deficiency by study ? Can one make a choice between the
passages in the *Explanation of the 95 Theses* in which he came close to the
religious expressions of a Pico or Reuchlin, and his assertion against Eck
at the time of the Leipzig debate that *"Omnes homines aequales sunt in
humanitate, quae est omnium summa et admiranda aequalitas, ex qua om-
nis dignitas hominibus"* as the peak of Luther's affinity with humanism,
when in the *Disputatio de homine* of 1536 he can speak of divine reason
as a god and in his last great *Commentary on Genesis* can grow ecstatic
over the qualities of man and the glories of nature ? The attitude of the
mature Luther toward the *studia humanitatis*, moreover, was of critical

---

[1] The most recent examination of the problem is Helmar Junghans, "Der Einfluss des
Humanismus auf Luthers Entwicklung bis 1518," pp. 37-101. See also Peter Meinhold,
"Die Auseinandersetzung Luthers mit dem Humanismus und dem Spiritualismus,"
*Luther Heute* (Berlin und Hamburg, 1967), pp. 100-8.

importance for the beginnings and the development of the Reformation movement which accepted and transmitted the educational and cultural values of Christian humanism.

A reading of Luther's treatises from 1530 to 1546, of the *Tischreden* which begin in the summer of 1531, and of his voluminous correspondence may embolden one to venture a few judgments. There is little help to be found in secondary works, for Oswald G. Schmidt's old monograph *Luthers Bekanntschaft mit den alten Klassikern* (Leipzig, 1883) has not as yet been replaced by a more complete modern study. There are grave difficulties to be overcome in a reading of the sources as well. Not only is the authenticity of the *Table Talks* open to question, but, as Peter Meinhold has demonstrated in his impressive study of classical references in the Genesis commentary, it often remains difficult or impossible to establish whether a citation was Luther's or the transcriber's and editor's.[1] Despite these difficulties, at least a preliminary assessment may be made of the three most relevant points : 1. The older Luther's knowledge and utilization of the classics; 2. Luther's cultivation of the humanist discipline; and 3. Luther's relation to Italian and northern humanists from 1530 to his death.

1. Four months after Luther's demise Melanchthon wrote of him in the *Vita* :

> ... legit ipse pleraque veterum Latinorum scriptorum monumenta, Ciceronis, Virgilii, Livii et aliorum. Haec legebat non ut pueri verba tantum excerpentes, sed ut humanae vitae doctrinam, aut imagines, Quare et consilia horum scriptorum et sententias proprius aspiciebat, et ut erat memoria fideli et firma, pleraque ei lecta et audita in conspectu et ob oculos erant.[2]

Melanchthon seems to imply that Luther did his heavy reading in the Latin classics during his school days and as a student in the arts and with his marvellous memory retained and used what he had learned for life.

In 1531 Luther reminisced very touchingly about a certain young man who sold his *corpus iuris* and other books to a dealer but took his

---

[1] Peter Meinhold, *Die Genesisvorlesung Luthers und ihre Herausgeber* (Stuttgart, 1936), pp. 332-41 : "Luther war ein gründlicher Kenner der griechischen und römischen klassichen Literatur. Für seine genuinen Werke beweist das die Fühle der von ihm beigebrachten Zitate aus den alten Klassikern. Die Frage für die Genesisvorlesung ist, ob die sich hier findenden klassischen Zitate auf Luther oder auf die Bearbeiter zurückgehen." See also *LW*, I, x-xi.

[2] *CR*, VI, 157, no. 3478.

Virgil and Plautus along into the monastery.[1] With respect to Luther's frequency of citation, Melanchthon was quite right in pointing to Virgil and Cicero as Luther's favorite classics, for in the *Tischreden* alone there are 59 references to and from Cicero and about 50 from Virgil, although Livy fell aside, and there are 61 references to Aristotle. In his writings and correspondence (although his letters contain very few classical references), Aristotle, Cicero, and Virgil are most frequently cited and far more so than any other classical authors. The next in order of frequency of reference to and quotation from their works are Terence, Horace, Plato, Quintilian, Homer, and Ovid roughly in that order. Individual scattered references are to be found to Aesop, Plautus, Suetonius, Herodotus, Xenophon, Ammianus Marcellinus, Juvenal, Caesar, Aeschylus, Minucius Felix, Pliny, Tacitus, Demosthenes, Apuleius, Polycrates, Plutarch, Sulpetius, Severnus, Parmenides, Zeno, and a few others.[2]

Frequency of citation does not, of course, tell the whole story. Aristotle figures very prominently because of Luther's polemic against his intrusion into scholastic philosophy. Luther praised Aristotle's physics, metaphysics, and the *De anima* as his best books, but he regrets that Aristotle denies God tacitly.[3] Although he preferred Plato to Aristotle, he reproaches him for saying in the *De Ente* that "God is nothing and God is everything."[4] Philosophers in this tradition describe God as a circle in which He as midpoint is coterminous with the circumference, a kind of speculation which leads to pantheism. In Luther's clearly discernible hierarchy of classical authors Cicero is firmly established at the top. In his repeated comparisons of Cicero and Aristotle he pronounces Cicero more learned by far, a clear teacher, and, in books such as *De Officiis*, very wise. "If I were a youth," Luther exclaims, "I would devote myself to Cicero, but with my judgment nevertheless confirmed in the Sacred Scriptures." [5] Aristotle knows nothing about God and the immortality of the soul, but *Cicero longe superat Aristo-*

---

[1] *WA Tr*, I, 44, no. 116.

[2] For a list of the classical authors and Italian humanists whose works were published in Germany between 1465 and 1500 and the classical and humanist authors printed in German translations up to the year 1520, see Rudolph Hirsch, "Printing and the Spread of Humanism in Germany : The Example of Albrecht von Eyb," *Renaissance Men and Ideas*, Robert Schwoebel, ed. (New York, 1971), pp. 28, 31. Most of the classical and humanist authors whom Luther cited frequently had been published in Germany by 1520.

[3] *WA Tr*, I, 57, no. 135.

[4] *WA Tr*, I, 108, no. 257.

[5] *WA Tr*, III, 612, no. 5012.

104

*telem*, for in his *Tusculan Disputations* and *On the Nature of the Gods* he writes about the immortality of the soul, and his *De Officiis* is superior to the ethics of Aristotle.[1] He hopes that God will be merciful to Cicero and men like him, for he was the best, wisest and most diligent man.[2]

2. *Luther senior* retained a positive interest in the characteristic humanist disciplines. He had been the prime mover in the curricular reform at Wittenberg which introduced the humanist subjects at the expense of Aristotle and dialectic. In subsequent years he took an active interest in professional appointments to the chair of Greek, rhetoric, or similar subjects in the arts faculty.[3]

In the choice between rhetoric and dialectic Luther consistently held the former to be superior. Dialectic teaches and rhetoric moves the audience; dialectic belongs to reason, rhetoric to the will. He refers to Moses and St. Paul as great rhetoricians. St. Paul in Romans 12 distinguished between teaching and exhorting and except for one passage, all of Romans 4 is rhetorical.[4] On 22 February 1518, Luther wrote to Spalatin :

> I absolutely do not see how dialectic can be other than a poison to a true theologian. Grant that it may be useful as a game or an exercise for youthful minds, still in sacred letters, where pure faith and divine illumination are expected, the whole matter of the syllogism must be left without, just as

---

[1] *WA Tr*, III, 451, no. 3608d. Again in *WA Tr*, IV, 16, no. 3928, Luther relates that Cicero could comfort himself very nicely against death in the *Tusculan Disputations* so that Christians who have Christ as the conqueror of death should be able to do so much more. *WA Tr*, III, 4, no. 2808a, Luther observes that Cicero was the wisest and most prolific of all the philosophers and had read thoroughly the books of all the Greeks, but he could not rise above human wisdom.

[2] *WA Tr*, IV, 14, no. 3925.

[3] Thus he favored Veit Örtel in August 1541 for the Greek professorship since he had been taught in Deventer by Bartholomäus of Cologne, *WA Br*, IX, 482-84, no. 3649. Elector John Frederick wrote to Luther about appointing Mag. Holstein to teach rhetoric, *WA Br*, IX, 487-89, no. 3651.

[4] *WA Tr*, II, 360, no. 2199b. *WA Tr*, I, 120, no. 287 : Philippus Melanchthon : Duplex est orationis genus, dialecticum, id pertinet ad scholam, rhetoricum pertinet ad contiones publicas, ibi enim sunt tractandi loci pathetici in scholis tractandae disputationes, etc. *WA Tr*, I, 127, no. 309 : In omni oratione aut est exhortatio aut doctrina: doctrina dialectica, exhortatio rhetorica. *WA Tr*, II, 555-56, no. 2629a : "Dialectica ist, wen man ein ding unterschidlich und deutlich sagt mit kurtzen worten, rhetorica autem versatur in suadendo et dissuadendo; quae habet suos locos, bonum, honestum, utile, facile. Quae Paulus brevissime complexus est dicens : Qui docet in doctrina, qui exhortatur in exhortando...".

Abraham, when about to sacrifice, left the boys with the asses. This, Johannes
Reuchlin in the second book of his *Cabala* affirms sufficiently. For if any
dialectic is necessary, that natural inborn dialectic is sufficient, by which a man
is led to compare beliefs with other beliefs and so conclude the truth. I have
often discussed with friends what utility seemed to us to be gained from this
so sedulous study of philosophy and dialectic, and truly with one consent,
having marveled at, or rather bewailed, the calamity of our minds, we found
no utility, but rather a whole sea of hindrance.[1]

Luther held this position also in later years. Even when he allowed
the disputations to be reintroduced at Wittenberg, he did so only because they provided a useful exercise for youthful minds who would
soon be obliged to engage in apologetics, much as he himself made use
of syllogisms in controversy with scholastics to "beat them at their own
game". In his treatise *On Christian Doctrine* St. Augustine had written
that "the science of disputation is of great value for solving all sorts
of questions that appear in sacred literature." Luther was less impressed with this thought than were Abelard and the dialecticians. When in
later years Luther praised Ockham, his "dear master", as a great dialec-
tician, he had in mind the utility of dialectic as a mental tool but not as
an aid in theology.

Ockham alone understood dialectic [said Luther] that it has to do with defining and distinguishing words, but he was not able to speak out [eloquently].
But now, O God, I have truly lived to see such a noble time, so many reve-
lations, and truly as Christ says about the time of the last day : There will be a
flowering and then judgment day will come. All the arts flourish and when
that happens, as Christ says, summer is not far off.[2]

Luther repeats elsewhere the criticism that while Ockham was very wise
and learned he was deficient in rhetoric.[3] Cicero's rhetorical power and
Quintilian's instruction in rhetoric strongly attracted Luther to them.
Reading Quintilian is such a pleasure, he observed, and he draws the
reader along so that he is continuously impelled to proceed with

---

[1] *WA Br*, I, 149-50, no. 61. In the same letter Luther continues by saying that he
had written to Trutvetter, the prince of the dialecticians in our age (so it seems), that
dialectic "instead of being useful to theology is rather an obstacle to theological studies,
because theology uses the same vocabulary in a manner quite different from that of
dialectic. In what way therefore, I asked, can dialectic be of use, since once I begin to
study theology I am forced to reject the dialectic meaning of a word and have to accept
its [theological] meaning." This footnote translation is from *LW*, XLVIII, 57, no. 19.

[2] *WA Tr*, I, 85-86, no. 193.

[3] *WA Tr*, 137, no. 338.

reading, for he presses into one's heart.[1] Quintilian is opposed to ambiguity and offers other sound rhetorical advice.[2]

Luther's knowledge of classical poetry was limited in scope but he very much cherished what he knew, and cited certain lines quite freely and repeatedly. "Baptista Mantuanus was the first poet whom I read," he reminisced, "then the Heroiads of Ovid, and then Virgil, and afterwards I read nothing in the poets, for scholastic theology said it was an impediment." [3] Poets and playwrights portray the real world. Terence, Homer, and other poets were no lazy-dog monks but saw how things are with real people.[4] Terence is good for boys and girls, he thought, though Virgil is superior for adults. "I love Terence," he said, "for I see that it is good rhetoric to make a comedy out of a man sleeping with a maid; then he imagines what the father, what the servant, what the circle of friends say to that. *Sic ex qualibet causa potest fieri comoedia.*" [5] He advised a schoolmaster in Silesia who had been criticized for having his boys play a comedy of Terence to continue as he had done. For the boys should be encouraged to put on the plays, practice Latin, develop good artistry, see people well portrayed and all reminded of their duties. There is no reason because of obscenities not to do the comedies.[6] Luther was not about to see his Terence bowdlerized.

Luther's native genius for language carried over to a keen curiosity about philology, and an interest in historical and place names and etymologies reminiscent of Celtis, Aventine, and other German humanists. There is some doubt as to whether he himself was the author of a piece attributed to him, *Aliquot nomina propria Germanorum ad priscam etymologiam restituta*, 1544. However, he enjoyed playing with words, comparing Graecisms with Germanisms and toying with etymologies from Tacitus.[7]

---

[1] *WA Tr*, II, 411, no. 2299. *WA*, III, 73 fn., Quintilian's *Institutio oratoria* cited.

[2] *WA Tr*, I, 195, no. 446.

[3] *WA Tr*, I, 107, no. 256. A typical classical allusion is his *WA Br*, XI, 6-7, no. 4062, 4 January 1545, in counseling patience against one's enemies he cites Virgil's *Aeneid* : "Dabit Deus his quoque finem." *WA Tr*, III, 459, no. 3616a : Ovid excells all poets, even Virgil, in expressing feelings.

[4] *WA Tr*, I, 119, no. 285.

[5] *WA Tr*, 203-4, no. 467.

[6] *WA Tr*, I, 430-32, no. 867.

[7] *WA Tr*, III, p. 588, no. 3748; *WA Tr*, I, 110, no. 262; *WA Tr*, I, p. 123, no. 297. An excellent study of Luther's language skill in his Bible translation is that of the noted Germanist Heinz Bluhm, *Martin Luther Creative Translator* (St. Louis, 1965).

As a young *dozent* Luther had lectured on the ethics of Aristotle and he continued throughout his life to refer especially to the *Nichomachian Ethics*.[1] But, of course, he waged his theological battle against the Aristotelian premise that good works make a man good rather than that a good man does good works. And on a deeper level he fought the intrusion of Aristotelian anthropology and dialectic into scholastic theology. The fundamental difference between Aristotle and *Ecclesiastes*, he noted, is that Aristotle measures honesty by the best reason of life, but *Ecclesiastes* by the observance of the precepts of God.[2]

Luther's own very personal contribution to the cultivation of moral philosophy and prudential wisdom in the young was his edition of Aesop's *Fables*, *Etliche Fabeln aus Äsop 1530* done at the Coburg after meals, "to rest his weary head as great men need to do," said Mathesius in *Sermon VII* on Luther's life. The German humanist Heinrich Steinhöwel had published an edition with Johannes Zainer in Ulm between 1476 and 1480 based on the Phädrus-Romulus collection of the 4th and 5th centuries. In the front of that edition is a life of Aesop and in the appendix the fables of Avian and the facetiae of Petrus Alfonsus and Poggio with translations by Steinhöwel. Luther prepared his edition in 1530, although it was not printed until 1557, after his death. In a letter to Wenceslas Link in Nuremberg, 8 May 1530, he wrote, "I have also proposed to prepare the fables of Aesop for the youth and the common crowd so that they may be of some use to the Germans."[3] The fables which he chose taught moral lessons about folly, hatred, disloyalty, envy, greed, frivolousness, force. In the preface Luther quotes Quintilian's *Institutio oratoria* (V,11, 19) as saying the fables came from a wise Greek like Hesiod. Some of them, however, he believed to have been composed by two Christian bishops to teach schoolboys in a cryptic way at the time of the suppression of Christians by Julian the apostate.[4]

From the Aesop edition it is obvious that Luther's early emphatic advocacy of education for the youth continues throughout his life. His *Predigt, dasz man Kinder zur Schule halten solle* (1541) glows with the same fervor as his earlier sermon on keeping children in school and his *Address to the Councilmen of All Cities in Germany that They Establish*

---

[1] For example, *WA Br*, X, 575-76, no. 3992 (15 May 1544).

[2] *WA Tr*, I, 79, no. 168.

[3] *WA Br*, V, 309, no. 1563.

[4] *WA Tr*, VI, 16, no. 6523.

*and Maintain Christian Schools* (1524). The *Fakultäts-Zeugnissen* given to the university graduates and signed by Luther emphasized the young men's achievements in arts and letters, religion and piety, as well as their mastery of Latin, Greek, and Hebrew.

Similarly in his old age music provided Luther comfort as it had provided solace in his stormy youth. He wrote prefaces for musical works, περὶ τῆς Μουσικῆς, a *Vorrede auf alle guten Gesangbücher*, *Frau Musica, 1543,* and a *Praefatio zu Symphonicae iucundae.* He asked Elector John Frederick to appoint a musician to the university.[1] He sent his son John to study music with Marcus Crodel in Torgau.[2]

Luther's preoccupation with history actually increased during the last decade and a half of his life, as though his own advancing years developed in him a deeper interest in past ages. He wrote prefaces to a variety of "historical" works : *Vorrede zu Spalatin, magnifice consolatoria exempla et sententiae ex vitis et passionibus sanctorum... collectae; Vorrede zu Robert Barnes, Vitae Romanorum Pontificum; Vorrede zu Johannes Kymäus, Ein alt christlich Konzilium...zu Gangro; Vorrede zu Historia Galeatii Capellae,* 1539; *Vorrede zu Epistola S. Hieronymi ad Evagrium de potestate,* 1538; *Praefatio zu Georg Major Vitae patrum,* 1544; *Vorrede zu Papstreue Hadrian IV. und Alexandrus III. gegen Kaiser Friedrich Barbarossa,* 1545. From these various prefaces it is clear that Luther viewed history as a weapon in controversy. Twenty years after the Leipzig Debate of 1519 Luther reflected that at that time he had not been well versed in history and had attacked the Papacy *a priori* on the basis of Scriptures, but that now he appreciated the correspondence of the histories and Scripture and could attack the Papacy *a posteriori* from the histories.[3] The polemical and apologetic uses of history, whether the history of the patristic period, of the medieval papal period, or of lives of the saints are stressed most vigorously in the prefaces which Luther wrote. Moreover, in 1537 he wrote a blast of his own at the monstrous papal fraud of the Donation of Constantine, *Einer aus den hohen Artikeln des päpstlichen Glaubens, genannt Donatio*

---

[1] *WA Br*, IX, 340, no. 3583.

[2] *WA Br*, X, 132-35, no. 3783.

[3] *WA*, L, 5. John M. Headley, *Luther's View of Church History* (New Haven, 1963), p. 51. On the importance of history for Wittenberg theology in the first years of the Reformation, see D. Karl Bauer, *Die Wittenberger Universitätstheologie und die Anfänge der Deutschen Reformation* (Tübingen, 1928), pp. 80-98 : "Die Bereicherung der Wittenberger Theologie durch die Geschichte."

*Constantini.* He knew Hutten's edition done by Schöffer in 1520 of Valla's 1448 treatise. As a younger man Luther had been led by it to the conviction that the pope must be the anti-Christ.

Certain features of his view of history remain consistent with his more youthful period such as his idea that God calls out certain "wonder men" or "sound heroes" gifted with superior endowments to perform certain epochal deeds,[1] his conviction that the *verae historiae* show that the will of God is done also among the heathen nations,[2] and that history is philosophy teaching by example.[3] He still refers to the "histories" which provide an example of faith, but the "exemplarism" is considerably attenuated after the sobering experience of Müntzer and of the Münster radicals. He cautioned against mimesis or literally imitating in detail the lives of saints, heroes, or of Christ himself. Undoubtedly the discourse on history which most nearly approaches the humanist "pragmatic view" of history is his *Preface to Galeatius Capella's History* (1538) in which Luther tells us that historians are useful people and that rulers should support them, that the Germans should learn and write about their own early history, that God is everywhere at work in history so that at every point in time there are noteworthy deeds, that heroes are important in the scheme of things, and that historians are obligated to describe things as they actually happened without prejudice or flattery to men of power.[4]

---

[1] In his commentary on Psalm 101 of 1534-1535, for example, he adduces his theory of the role of the miracle men of history. *WA*, LI, 214-15 : "The healthy heroes are rare, and God provides them at a high price... In addition, we also follow the advice of the best people who live in our midst, until the time comes in which God again provides a healthy hero or a wondrous man in whose hand all things improve or at least fare better than is written in any book."

[2] *WA Tr*, I, 192, no. 441 : "Verae historiae apud gentes ostendunt voluntatem Dei tanquam mutae literae." *WA Tr*, I, 75, no. 158, one of the repeated references to the incident related in Theodoret's *Historia Ecclesiastica* which tells of the Persian king killed by flies in the siege of Nisibis by Sapor II.

[3] *WA Tr*, I, p. 374, no. 389 : Historiae sunt exemplar fidei.

[4] *WA*, L, 383-85; *LW*, XXXIV, 271-82. Perhaps Luther's focussing on the need for more knowledge of early German history was a reflection of Melanchthon's publication in 1538 of *Arminius dialogus Huttenicus, continens res Arminij in Germania gestas. P. Cornelii Taciti, de moribus et populis Germaniae libellus. Adiecta est breuis interpretatio appellationum partium Germaniae* (Wittenberg, 1538), *CR*, XVII, 611. A comparison of Luther's ideas of history with those of Melanchthon in his *Introduction to the Chronicon*, his preface to Hedio's *Chronicle* of 1539, or his slightly altered *Preface to Cuspinian's Caesares* of 1541, reveals many identical or similar views. On the Renaissance humanist attitude

As Luther's interest in history grew he appreciated the value of chronology as an aid to exegesis and for the light it shed on the history of the church. He prepared for his own use a *Reckoning of the Years of the World*, which was a chronological table so that he

> could always have before his eyes and see the time and years of historical events which are described in Holy Scriptures and remind himself how many years the patriarchs, judges, kings and princes lived and ruled or over how long a period of time one succeeded the other.

Inspired perhaps by Eusebius, whose chronicle he intensely admired, he worked out parallel traditions of Biblical history and secular events, with three columns, for the East, West, and German history. He projected the dates from creation forward to the year 1540, dividing the table up by millenia. He drew on contemporary histories to fix dates, but where there was a conflict between the Scriptural data and that of some other source, such as a chronology ascribed to Megasthenes he opted for the reliability of Scriptures.[1] He held that all the humanist disciplines together do not compare in value with the gospel and its promise for eternity.[2]

3. *Luther senior* distinguished among the humanists according to one basic criterion, whether or not they were favorably disposed toward the evangelical movement. As one might well expect, the older humanists, Italian and Northern, were on his blacklist and the younger who had turned evangelical for the most part received his commendation. Luther retained in later years his high regard for Lorenzo Valla. He praised him as the best Italian who disputed well in his *De libero arbitrio*, seeking simplicity both in piety and letters, while Erasmus seeks it only in letters and laughs at piety.[3] Sabellicus, the historian who had been so un-

---

toward history see Myron P. Gilmore, "The Renaissance Conception of the Lessons of History," *Humanists and Jurists* (Cambridge, Mass., 1963), pp. 1-37; Herbert Weisinger, "Ideas of History During the Renaissance," *Journal of the History of Ideas*, VI (1945), 415-35; Felix Gilbert, "The Renaissance Interest in History," *Art, Science, and History in the Renaissance*, Charles Singleton, ed. (Baltimore, 1967), pp. 373-87; and Nancy Struever, *The Language of History in the Renaissance; Rhetoric and Historical Consciousness in Florentine Humanism* (Princeton, 1970).

[1] "Supputatio annorum mundi", 1541, 1545, *WA*, LIII, 1-184. On chronology as the light of history, *WA*, XLIII, 138; on Scriptures and Megasthenes, *WA*, LIII, 24 and 27. J. Headley, pp. 51-52. Peter Meinhold, *Die Genesisvorlesung Luthers und ihre Herausgeber*, pp. 306-32, collates the *Supputatio* with the Genesis Commentary Chronology.

[2] *WA Tr*, I, 191, no. 439.

[3] *WA Tr*, I, 109, no. 259; *WA Tr*, II, 107, no. 1470. For the most part Luther considered Italians to be very superstitious and blind in their saint cults, *WA Tr*, III, 560, no. 3718.

complimentary to the Germans, wished to imitate Livy but nothing came of it.[1] With regard to Cardinal Bembo on Lutheranism, Luther merely commented that it is not fitting for a serious man to read such trifles.[2] The Erasmian Sadoleto he considered ingenious and learned, although "he wrote against us," but he showed in his commentary on the psalm *Misereri mei, Deus* that he does not understand the theological meaning of the *Deus absconditus*.[3]

Nor did Luther's opinion of the Northern humanists mellow with the years. Mutian remained for him an epicurean from whom Albert of Mainz learned the blasphemous joke that *Soli deo gloria* meant "Glory to God the Sun." [4] Crotus Rubeanus corrupted Justus Menius with his impious conversations. [5] Luther was saddened, on the other hand, by the death of Eobanus Hessus, the evangelical poet. He thought the Frenchman William Postel's effort in the *De orbis terrarum concordia libri IV* (1544) to convert the Turks, Jews, and other peoples by proving the articles of faith by nature and reason too ambitious, too much for one volume, and too "enthusiastic." [6] Luther was angered by the bawdy poems of a certain talented young poet named Simon Lemnius, who sold fifty copies of his poetry book before the church door at Pentecost in 1538. Luther thought the poems mocked university people and this suspicion was deepened by Lemnius' escape through the city gate when the town shepherd took his flock out in the morning.[7]

Erasmus remained for him a nutcracker, or mockingbird, who did not take Christ seriously. Luther considered Erasmus' *Copia* and *Adages* to be of value but thought all else would perish. Luther was ready to re-

---

[1] *WA Tr*, III, 459, no. 3616b.

[2] *WA Tr*, IV, 667, no. 5109.

[3] *WA Tr*, II, 8, no. 1248. Richard M. Douglas, *Jacopo Sadoleto, 1477-1547 Humanist and Reformer* (Cambridge, Mass., 1959), p. 47. The Commentary on Psalm 50 was Sadoleto's first exegetical work. Erasmus praised it but Luther found it to be untheological throughout, insensitive to the motive of grace, and neglectful of the role of Christ in the redemption of man. P. 118 : Commenting on Sadoleto's letter to Melanchthon Luther described the author as one "who was a papal secretary for fifteen years, certainly an able and cultivated man... but cunning and artful withal, in the Italian manner." See also Douglas, pp. 25, 27, 253 n. 64, 114, 116-17, 134, 149.

[4] *WA Br*, 11, pp. 168-69, no. 4146, Luther on Nikolaus von Amsdorf in Zeitz. Wittenberg, 19 August 1545. *WA Tr*, I, 186-87, no. 432.

[5] *WA Tr*, II, 627-28, no. 274la.

[6] *WA Tr*, V, 472, no. 6070.

[7] *WA*, L, 348-55 : *E. klärung gegen Simon Lemnius*, 16 June 1538.

lieve Erasmus of all embarrassment at being considered a Lutheran, for it is clear that "Erasmus believes implicitly whatever Pope Clement VII believes." Erasmus remained for him the great Epicurean.[1] With the single exception of Erasmus, however, one finds many more references in Luther's later writings to John Hus, Karlstadt, Müntzer, and comets than to all the Renaissance humanists together.

## IV. CONCLUSIONS

Approaching the headwaters of the Reformation from the angles both of the *initia Lutheri* and the *initia Reformationis* puts into clearer focus the point of confluence of the intra-personal and the broader societal intellectual forces at work. Following their combined course downstream deepens our understanding as to what that juncture meant to history.

1. Emphasis upon the Augustinian intellectual nexus within which Luther developed as a reformer, a nexus which combined and "domesticated" nominalist and humanist components, does make an understanding of Luther's development more intelligible. It seemed crystal clear to Luther that he owed nothing at all to humanism as such for the substance of his theology. "From Erasmus I have nothing," he asserted,

---

[1] *WA Tr*, III, 30, no. 2859a. The references to Erasmus are highly repetitive and too numerous to cite. Typical expressions are *WA Tr*, II, 346, no. 2170; *WA Tr*, IV, 574, no. 4902; *WA Tr*, III, 214, no. 3186a; *WA Tr*, III, 216, no. 3194; *WA Tr*, III, 107, no. 2939a; *WA Tr*, II, 363, no. 2205a; *WA Tr*, IV, 87, no. 4028 : Erasmi Roterodami epicurismi. One of his strongest blasts against Erasmus was *WA Tr*, IV, 37, no. 3963 : "Erasmi propositio et status fuit serviendum esse tempori. Tantum in se respexit. Vixit et mortuus est ut Epicurus, sine ministro et consolatione. Ist gefahren in bus correptam." Erasmus appears 182 times in the index to the *Tischreden*. In connection with a letter to Amsdorf Luther relieved himself of a vicious blast at Erasmus which was published separately in Antwerp, Basle, Cologne, Paris, Augsburg and elsewhere, *WA Br*, VII, 27-39, no. 2093, Luther to Nikolaus von Amsdorf, Wittenberg, c. 11 March 1534, in which he concludes, p. 38 : "Ego sane optarim totum Erasmum esse e nostris scholis explosum; nam si etiam non esset periciosus, tamen nihil est utilis, nullas res docet aut tractat." He expressed an opinion about Erasmus not a bit more flattering probably in 1543 in a letter to his son John, who had inquired of him what he thought of Erasmus, *WA Br*, VI, 565-66, no. 2076. The *Glossen zu Erasmus, Apophthegmatum opus*, 1543, a copy of Erasmus' work with Luther's marginal comments found in the Prince Stolberg Library shows that Luther consistently saw the shadowside of Erasmus' personality, *WA*, LIV, 101-6, 497-501 (Nachtrag), for Erasmus is an epicurean, a wordling, a mocker like Lucian, a man who despises God and religion without strong religious conviction, a despicable personality, one who has more words than content.

"for I have received everything from Dr. Staupitz, who gave me the favorable opportunity."[1] In his formal theology he was dependent upon the works of Augustinus Favorini, Jacobus Perez, Gregory of Rimini, and upon conversations with Staupitz. Erasmus provided philological instruments and a Greek text, Lefèvre contributed a highly spiritualized approach to exegesis, Reuchlin supplied a Hebrew grammar and vocabulary, but Luther's theology proper developed within the context of Augustinian thought as conditioned by nominalism and "in-house" humanism.

  2. In later years Luther was consistent in relating his evangelical breakthrough to a new understanding of the Word and a categorical rejection of his scholastic background. Consider this account of his conversation with Amsdorf on 2 February 1538 :

> That evening Luther in a happy mood conversed with Amsdorf discussing many things concerning the studies of the previous age when very ingenious men were occupied with vain readings, which sophisticated words are plainly unknown and barbarous to men of our century. For Scotus, Bonaventura, Gabriel, Thomas were men of great leisure when the papacy flourished and had to phantasize something. Gabriel writing a book on the Canon of the Mass, which book was in my judgment then the best; when I read it my heart bled. The authority of the Bible was nothing to Gabriel. I still have the books which martyred me so. Scotus wrote very well on the third book of the Sentences. The very ingenious Ockham was zealous in method; his desire was to expand and to amplify things to infinity. Thomas was most loquacious because he was seduced by metaphysics. Now God has wonderfully led us out and has led me unknowing through the affair for over twenty years.[2]

In view of Luther's explicit rejection of scholasticism and specifically of theological nominalism it would indeed be a mistaken notion to find the key to his reformatory development and evangelical solution in the theology he was reacting against. Similarly it is quite clear that Renaissance humanism even in the religious expression given it by the Erasmian *philosophia Christi* was only of marginal importance. Luther credited the power of the Word for his change, exercized upon him during the course of his intense Biblical studies and quite evident already in his first commentary on the Psalms. To be sure it would be a case of *petitio principii* to argue that Luther became a reformer as a *Schrifttheologe* without considering through what medium

---

[1] *WA Tr*, I, 80, no. 173 (*anno* 1532).

[2] *WA Tr*, III, 563-66, no. 3722. For an attack on the three sects of Thomists, Scotists, and Moderns see *WA Tr*, IV, 145, no. 4148.

and focus he read the Scriptures. Much insight is gained by paying close attention to the Augustinian mental setting from which he emerged. However, theological terms in the Scriptures, God, sin, righteousness, law, gospel, do not occur in a hygenically sealed package or as neutral objects whose interpretation is predominantly dependent upon the subjective outlook of the observer. Rather they appear in context and not infrequently, as Luther observed, are employed by master rhetoricians such as Moses and Paul. The Biblical passages are set in a Biblical world and have an impetus of their own which, when studied intensely, may well induce a changed or reformatory perception of theology. The fact that Luther's theological change was related so intimately to his personal religious seeking (he was a stormy petrel compared with serene Thomas) made his problem-solution more than an intellectual game.

Much can be gained by comparing the evangelical discovery of other reformers who attributed their conversion to the impact of the gospel, such as Vadian, who moved from a role as a humanist to reformer. On the other hand, a number of Luther's Augustinian opponents had backgrounds analogous to his own, but lacking his encounter with the Biblical world, they remained what he might have been without his long and arduous preoccupation with the Scriptures. To see his exegetical studies as the critical determinant in his evangelical theology is more than a mere begging of the question.

3. The examination of the *initia et exitus Lutheri senioris* reveals some interesting insights into his overall relation to humanism. Despite his avowed wish that he could earlier have devoted himself more fully to the liberal arts, there was no noticeable increase in his reading or mastery of the *studia humanitatis* in his later years. That Luther possessed a very considerable store of classical learning was evident even at the time of the controversy over the will with Erasmus. There are many more classical references in Luther's treatise *De servo arbitrio* (1525), though admittedly the longer one, than in that of Erasmus.[1] Luther continued in later years to call himself a *rusticus* as he did on that occasion !

4. With respect to the classics as a norm or form for theology and anthropology Luther remained the great *Aussenseiter*. One fact which marks the transition from Renaissance to Reformation is that now there

---

[1] E. Gordon Rupp, "Luther : Contemporary Image," *Kirche, Mystik, Heiligung und das Natürliche bei Luther*, Ivar Asheim, ed. (Göttingen, 1967), p. 13. Luther's allusions, Rupp observes, were frequent and often very subtle, so that it was not a case of Luther airing his classical knowledge, as Zwingli was wont to do.

were more leading intellectuals on the "outside" with him. This included not a few prominent Italians, who turned Protestant and came
to the North, although most of them veered toward Geneva.

A subtle test case for Luther's reaction to Renaissance humanism is
the question of the relationship of the power of the Word to induce
faith and the power of rhetoric to persuade. The temptation is always
present to see Luther's formula *verbum facit fidem* as an affective rhetorical religious manifestation of the power of the written and especially
of the spoken word. None of the scholastics brought *fides* and *verbum*
into direct correlation in the way that Luther did.[1] Luther encountered
a life-bringing Word (*vox divina*) in St. Bernard and other monastic prophetic types, and the power of words was explicitly and almost tediously
emphasized by the humanists. But it would be a fundamental error to
equate the *fidem facere* with the humanist *persuadere*. Faith is not for
him being persuaded and agreeing with human assertions. Faith is
unconditioned trust in the *promissa dei et beneficia Christi*.[2] Similar clear
distinctions and sharp contrasts between Luther's conception of God
and evaluation of man and those predominant in Renaissance humanism
and Platonism could easily be drawn.

5. The reasons for Luther's failure to follow through on his impulse
and desire to study the classics more thoroughly were largely practical
ones. Juvenal declared that men narrowly constrained by heavy duties
do not easily emerge from the shadows. Luther seemed to have no more
leisure in his later years than in his earlier period. From 1535 to 1545 he
served as dean. He wrote countless letters, many in behalf of students.
Some eighteen letters for students from the fourteen years between 1517
and 1531 are still extant; from the fourteen years between 1532 and
1546, some 57 letters are still extant. He was busy with the organization
of the evangelical churches. Moreover, he was intensely preoccupied

---

[1] Reinhard Schwarz, *Fides, Spes und Caritas beim jungen Luther* (Berlin, 1962), p. 422 :
"Bei keinem der Scholastiker ist also von der fides in der Korrelation zum verbum und
ohne ihre Unterordung unter die formierende caritas die Rede. Anders verhält es sich
bei Bernard." Schwarz stresses the critical importance of Scriptural studies in Luther's
ripening into a reformer, explicitly denying that his new theology was derived from an
Ockhamist, humanist, monastic (Bernard) or Augustinian theology or way of thinking,
*Vorgeschichte der reformatorischen Busstheologie* (Berlin, 1968), p. 297.

[2] Heinz Otto Burger, *Renaissance Humanismus Reformation. Deutsche Literatur im
Europäischen Kontext* (Berlin, 1969), pp. 418-24, especially p. 423, offers comments of
special value since Burger approaches Luther from a thorough study of the German
humanist background.

with teaching, preaching and defending the gospel, which had for him a higher priority than reading *belles lettres*.

6. However, his attitude toward the humanist disciplines remained positive, a fact of fundamental importance for the beginnings and the development of the magisterial Reformation and the form which the relation of evangelical religion to the learned tradition took. His attitude toward the young pro-evangelical humanists remained most cordial, toward Eobanus Hessus, the memory of Mosellanus, and Joachim Camerarius. "There are many living today," he said, "who are more erudite than Erasmus, such as our Philipp (Melanchthon), Joachim (Camerarius) and others." [1] Thus Luther's inner relation with Melanchthon remained harmonious despite their differences, such as in the interpretation of Augustine.

Finally, for the *exitus Reformationis* this positive stance of Dr. Luther toward the humanist disciplines helps to explain how many Renaissance cultural values were absorbed and transmitted by Protestantism to the modern world.[2]

On concluding these few remarks upon the subject of such magnitude with its vast implications, I feel very much as Luther did, not in his heroic moments making a great stand, but when he had come down from the pulpit feeling that he had not done so very well. "Ich habe mich offte angespeiet," he confessed, "wan ich vom predigstuel komen bin : Pfeu dich an, wie hastu gepredigt ? Du hast warlich wol ausgerichtet, nullum servasti conceptum." [3]

---

[1] *WA Tr*, IV, 567, no. 4908 (*anno* 1540).

[2] See the learned article of Professor Heinz Liebing, "Die Ausgänge des Europäischen Humanismus," *Geist und Geschichte der Reformation* (Berlin, 1966), pp. 357-76, and Lewis W. Spitz, "Humanism in the Reformation," *Renaissance Studies in Honor of Hans Baron*, Anthony Molho and John A. Tedeschi, eds., (Florence, Italy, 1971), pp. 643-62.

[3] *WA Tr*, IV, 446-47, no. 4719.

# VIII

# LUTHER AND HUMANISM

A most important aspect of the question of "Luther and Learning"
is that of his own relation to Renaissance humanism and of the
importance of humanism in turn for the Reformation movement.
This discussion of Luther and humanism will concentrate on three
major questions: 1. How much German and Italian humanism did
Luther know? Which humanists did he know, and how and when
did he make contact with them? 2. How extensive was Luther's
knowledge of the classics and how did his knowledge compare with
that of other contemporaries such as Erasmus? Did he know more
than representative medieval figures did? 3. In terms of substance,
what did humanism contribute to Luther's role as a reformer? The
answers to these questions about Luther and humanist learning
have tremendous implications for such larger issues as the relation
of the Reformation to the Renaissance and the place of the Renaissance and Reformation in the periodization of history.[1]

When Luther was on his way to the Diet of Worms he rode in a
wagon that was provided for him by the city council of Wittenberg.
He was accompanied by a modest entourage of his personal friends
and political folk associated with the Elector of Saxony. They were
met at the gate of Erfurt by Crotus Rubeanus, Luther's former
fellow student and friend at Erfurt who was rector at the university
there. Crotus hailed Luther "as a judge of evil, to see whose features is like a divine appearance." Crotus Rubeanus, along with
Ulrich von Hutten, had written *The Letters of Obscure Men*, and

he was a prominent member of Mutianus Rufus's humanist circle in Gotha. Eobanus Hessus, who became the most genial poet of the evangelical movement, cried: "Rejoice, exalted Erfurt, crown thyself . . . for behold, he comes who will free you from disgrace." That Luther was regarded as a fellow humanist, particularly by the younger humanists, is well-known. In 1517 Luther was thirty-four. Most of his followers were thirty years old or younger, and many of them were young humanists. Aesticampianus, Hutten's teacher, who was over seventy, was a rare exception. Most of Luther's opponents were fifty years old or older. Erasmus was just under fifty, and Dr. Johannes Eck, a major opponent, was a bit younger, but otherwise all of his opponents were much older men. The significant thing in our context is that these young humanists hailed Luther as a leader and saw him as a part of their enterprise. Luther responded to that kind of adulation in a very interesting way that I shall discuss shortly.[2]

Humanism is a protean concept. It has appeared in Western culture in varying modalities, and the type now under discussion must therefore be defined. Is it a matter of raising once again Tertullian's time-honored but terribly shopworn question about Jerusalem and Athens in his *Prescription Against Heretics:* What has Athens to do with Jerusalem, the church with the academy, Christians with heretics? Must we renew the modern debate between Wilhelm Dilthey, the father of modern intellectual history in the form of *Geistesgeschichte,* and Ernst Troeltsch, one of the great religious sociologists, as to how the Reformation related to Renaissance culture, medieval culture, and, by implication, to modernity?

There are massive numbers of books about the concept of the Renaissance and the meaning of humanism. The humanism that concerns us and our present topic is not the humanism that implies anthropocentrism, as in the Enlightenment. It is neither the new humanism of Wilhelm von Humboldt nor the secular humanism of Corliss Lamont. Still less is it the "progressive humanism" of the Marxists. Rather, I am talking about the Renaissance humanism of Luther's day. That humanism too has been given wildly contradictory definitions, but the seismographic needle has of late been settling down to one major indicator. Paul Oskar Kristeller related the humanists to the city secretaries in Italy, to the professors of rhetoric, successors to the practitioners and teachers of the *ars dictamis* in the medieval period. Hanna Holborn Gray, now president of the University of Chicago, broadened this definition to include a special emphasis on rhetoric and argued that many non-professionals practiced it, including bishops, doctors, lawyers, and pulpiteers. The German scholar Paul Joachimsen gave humanism a more ideological definition when he described it as a "desire for the rebirth of classical antiquity, both according to form and according to norm."[3] This definition will also serve as a useful one for the present discussion, because it suggests that humanism was a matter not only of style, good Latin, but of substantive questions that have to do with classical anthropology. It is at this point where the Reformation and the Renaissance style of humanism come into the most intimate contact and reaction. As we ponder their relation, a host of problems comes immediately to mind, such as the relation of Northern humanism to Italian humanism, of humanism to scholasticism, the role of humanism in the universities, and so on. On this particular occasion we are more interested in Luther's own relation to Renaissance humanism, his role in its survival and continuity into modern times.

Luther has been depicted by some scholars as a sickly product of a decadent or aberrant form of late scholasticism. Others have declared him to be the religious proponent and theological articulator of Renaissance humanism and his teaching to be the theological expression of the Renaissance. In actual fact, Luther's struggle was an elemental religious one. His question was How can I be sure that God is gracious to me, a sinner? We must also ask another question, namely, how did Luther reach his solution? Did he attain it with or without the help of Renaissance humanism? While his scholastic theological training posed and indeed created much of the question, humanist methodology facilitated his arrival at a solution. At the same time, only the Holy Spirit through the Word offered to him the basic solution, which he so gladly embraced in his tower experience.[4] The ways in which humanism facilitated his attaining that solution constitute the most important part of this discussion.

Let us turn now to the first of the questions posed at the beginning of this essay. From November 1517 until 1519 Luther adopted the humanist name "Eleutherius," the liberated one or the liberator—a name that Luther surely did not adopt out of respect for the thirteenth pope! The Greek word for "free," which appears in 1 Cor. 9:19, "For though I am free from all men, I have made myself a slave to all, that I might win the more" *(RSV)*, and John 8:32, "The truth will make you free" *(RSV)*, is the same word that Luther used as his "humanist" name. During those same years Luther called the gospel *eruditio divina,* a nice humanist affectation.[5] Not only was Luther a hero to the humanists, but he consciously associated himself with their methods and preferences. For example, in the Heidelberg Disputation, April 1518, in the philosophical theses 29–40, which Luther probably did not compose himself, he expressed an Augustinian preference for Pythagoras and Plato over Aristotle.[6] He spoke of man the midpoint in a manner worthy of Pico, although he may not have adopted this manner of speaking about man from Pico, but rather from Nemesius of Emessa, the Greek Church Father. There is a great parallel between Pico's *Oration on the Dignity of Man* and Nemesius, the Church Father's, description of man.

Another example of Luther's knowledge and recognition of humanism is provided in his *Operationes in Psalmos.* At the beginning of those lectures in 1518, Luther greeted the students and then spoke of the great flowering of the arts and sciences in their time.[7] He had after all himself been the major mover in the reform of the liberal arts curriculum at the University of Wittenberg, which culminated in the changes of 1518. Luther seldom talked about the Reformation movement, but he talked often about the curricular reformation at the University. He wished to alter the mental habits of the youth, he said, so that when they came from the arts level of study to the theological faculty, their minds would not have been molded by dialectic and syllogistic thinking. Finally, in his 1519 commentary on Paul's epistle to the Galatians, he included many Ciceronian and humanist expressions.

Luther had developed this humanist interest as his negative attitude toward scholasticism and its adverse effect on theology increased. In searching for its roots in his past, some scholars have pointed to Luther's supposed experience with the Brethren of the Common Life at Magdeburg, but we know too little about his contacts with the "Nollbrüder" there to draw any definite conclusions. On the one hand, there is a widespread myth that Luther was introduced to humanism while at Erfurt University through Crotus Rubeanus, who made contact for him with the circle of Mutianus Rufus, the canon at Gotha. But that theory is not only doubtful; it is wrong, since the Gotha circle was not formed until Luther had entered the monastery in 1505. On the other hand, the University of Erfurt was second perhaps only to Heidelberg in its openness to humanistic ideas and classical influences.

From its beginnings in 1502, the University of Wittenberg had experienced the presence of humanist scholars, such as Maternus Pistoris and Nikolaus Marschalk, who gave a commencement address in beautiful Latin.[8] Although as a new and undistinguished university, obviously Wittenberg was not a leader in the field, with the advent of Melanchthon in 1518 the strong advocate of humanism had arrived. Luther had wanted Peter Mosellanus for the position, but this was an instance when his judgment was in error.[9] It was Elector Frederick the Wise who had favored choosing Melanchthon, for somewhat political reasons, but Melanchthon proved to be far superior to Mosellanus in both brilliance and learning. Luther subsequently benefited from Melanchthon's tremendous knowledge of humanism and the classics. Luther's great impact on Melanchthon is well-known—how he bullied and used him, but always loved and respected him. That is only one part of the story, however, for Melanchthon also had a continuous influence on Luther through the years. One can almost see Luther's growing interest in humanist learning.

Melanchthon's appointment was indeed fortuitous, for there was very nearly a catastrophic appointment made at the university that might have led Luther to a negative attitude toward humanism. In January 1521 Georg Spalatin recommended Justus Jonas for a professorship in Wittenberg, but the Elector offered the vacant professorship to Mutianus Rufus, the cynical canon of Gotha. Although there is considerable controversy regarding how cynical Mutianus really was, Luther was quite convinced that he was very much an Epicurean, and it would have been painful for him to have had Mutianus on the faculty. Fortunately, Mutianus turned the position down, and Justus Jonas received the offer while he was with Luther at Worms in 1521. The appointment proved to be an important one in the long run.

Leif Grane has asserted that it is much easier to distinguish humanism and scholasticism in the abstract than to differentiate a humanist from a scholastic. There is presently a new trend in scholarship that emphasizes that in the older generation there were many men who were half humanist, half mystic, or half scholastic. Luther learned some humanist attitudes from the scholastics Jodocus Trutfetter and Arnold von Usingen, whom Luther later tried to convert to the evangelical cause. While a student at Erfurt, Luther also heard Jerome Emser lecture on Reuchlin's play *Sergius,* and he read Jakob Wimpheling's *De integritate.* He also learned to love the poems of the Christian poet Baptista Mantuanus, the general of the Carmelite order who wrote in the manner of Vergil. Thus it is a mistake to interpret Luther's relation to humanism so exclusively in the light of his controversy with Erasmus. Indeed, at first Luther did not even want to respond to Erasmus, but it was Kathie who badgered him until he did so. He finally dashed off his response, *De servo arbitrio,* in a matter of weeks in 1525, the same year as he married. In short, Luther's relation to humanism was much deeper and broader than scholars have realized, and his contact with Erasmus was but one important incident in a long lifetime of study.

Luther was not vindictive toward Erasmus, for he did a translation of one of Erasmus's writings and kept some of them on his own required reading list. Indeed, some of Erasmus's works were included in the readings that the visitors were to recommend for the evangelical schools. Luther opposed Erasmus not because of his humanist learning but for theological reasons. On certain occasions Luther even imitated Erasmus. For example, in 1517 Erasmus said, "We live at the dawn of a golden era." In 1524 Luther wrote to the city councils, "We live at the dawn of the new era." His optimism reflected his awareness of the new knowledge about the natural world that was coming to light. He kept this positive spirit and great interest in the natural world to the very end, as can be seen from his *Commentary on Genesis,* which he was writing during his final years.[10]

Luther's most dramatic encounter with German humanism was clearly the incident of the Reuchlin controversy, which also demonstrated the power of the printing press. The printing press played a key role in the success of the Reformation, but even before Luther there were three periods of much printing activity, one having to do with Savonarola, one having to do with Karlstadt's debates with the Thomist scholastics, and the third having to do with the Reuchlin controversy. Luther himself wrote a famous letter to Johannes Reuchlin when he was being persecuted for defending Hebrew letters. Indeed, eventually Reuchlin was threatened and summoned to Rome. In his letter Luther sided with Reuchlin against the scholastics and wrote: "Through your power the horns of this beast have been quite badly broken. Through you the Lord brought it about that the tyranny of the sophists has learned to attack the true friends of theology with greater caution, so that Germany could again breathe after having been not only oppressed but almost destroyed for some centuries thanks to scholastic theology. The beginning of a better knowledge could be made only through a man of great gifts. For just as God trod into dust the greatest of all mountains, our Lord Christ (if one may use this analogy), and thereafter from this dust allowed so many mountains to arise, so you also would have brought forth little fruit if you had not likewise been put to death and trod into the dust, from which so many defenders of the holy scriptures have arisen."[11] Luther did not hold up Christ as an example to be followed. He is the *exemplar, non exemplum,* for He shows how God deals with humankind. Christ is thus primarily an example of that divine action, not simply of how we are to relate to God through imitating Christ.

Luther also made use of Reuchlin's scholarship, employing both his Hebrew grammar and his dictionary. Reuchlin was not particularly appreciative, but when Luther became the center of attention, he said: "Thank God, now the monks have someone who will give them more to do than I have."

Francis Bacon, in *The Advancement of Learning,* Book I, underlined the linkage between Luther and the Renaissance. "Martin Luther," he wrote, "conducted (no doubt) by an higher providence, but in discourse of reason finding what a province he had undertaken against the Bishop of Rome and the degenerate traditions of the Church, and finding his own solitude, being no ways aided by the opinions of his own time, was enforced to awake all antiquity and to call former times to his succours to make a party against the present time. . . ." The cliché of Luther's going back to the sources, *ad fontes,* like the humanists, is in all the books, and there is indeed a positive analogy to be drawn. Does that similarity, however, make Luther a humanist? Could he have accomplished what he did without the assistance of the most progressive intellectuals of the time? The humanists, of course, insisted upon returning to the sources, and this idea was so implanted in people's minds that at least indirectly Luther was impressed by it. Nonetheless, one cannot take this conclusion too far. For example, the mere presence of many humanists at Erfurt does not of itself establish the linkage between Luther and humanism, any more than the presence of Italian Augustinian works in the Erfurt library proves that Luther studied them.

Let us now turn to our second question concerning Luther's knowledge of the classics. In short, what did Luther know about the classics and how much of a classicist was he? On the one hand, Luther often deprecated himself and his learning. He repeatedly called himself a *rusticus* and frequently affirmed that his Latin was barbarous.[12] On the other hand, there is counterevidence from other sources. For example, Gordon Rupp analyzed the *De servo arbitrio* and pointed out that there are many more, for its length, classical citations in Luther's treatise than in Erasmus's *De libero arbitrio*. Erasmus was very much a name-dropper and cited first one and then another author, but Luther put both quotations and ideas to genuine use. In fact, some of the editors of the Weimar edition were sleepily unaware of the extent of classical citations hidden in Luther's writings. To use his own analogy, they were sometimes like the nursemaid who dozes as she rocks the cradle. Certainly the notes on the classical citations in the *De servo arbitrio* are extremely inadequate.[13]

Luther did know the works of Lorenzo Valla, who is mostly appreciated for his work on the elegance of the Latin language and for his comments on free will. Indeed, Luther affirmed that Valla and John Wycliffe were his two most important authorities. He also kept in touch with Italian writings to a certain extent. Francesco Pico della Mirandola, Flacius Illyricus, and other Italians spent much time in Wittenberg. In *Culture and Anarchy*, published in 1869, the Victorian author Matthew Arnold wrote: "The Reformation has often been called a Hebraising revival, a return to the ardour and sincereness of primitive Christianity. No one, however, can study the development of Protantism and of Protestant

churches without feeling that into the Reformation, too—
Hebraising child of the Renascence and offspring of its fervour,
rather than its intelligence, as it undoubtedly was,—the subtle
Hellenic leaven of the Renascence found its way, and that the exact
respective parts, in the Reformation, of Hebraism and of Hellen-
ism, are not easy to separate."[14] That was Matthew Arnold's assumption, and though he grossly overstated the case, it is true that
the Renaissance penetrated not only Luther's mind but the Reformation movement as such to a much greater extent than scholars
have realized. Protestantism itself was clearly conscious of this
inheritance and exploited it.

We can now turn to the question of Luther's knowledge of the
classics. In 1524 he wrote to the councilmen of Germany: "Formerly no one knew why God had the languages revived, but now
for the first time we see that it was done for the sake of the gospel,
which he intended to bring to light and use in exposing and de-
stroying the kingdom of Antichrist. To this end he gave over
Greece to the Turks in order that the Greeks, driven out and
scattered, might disseminate their language and provide an incentive to the study of other languages as well."[15] That *translatio* myth
was transmitted into modern historiography largely through Theodore Beza and his history of Protestantism, but we know that
Greek learning came to the West long before the fall of Constantinople. When Luther entered the University of Erfurt in 1501, he
may have come into contact with good classicists, but we cannot
prove that to be the case. For example, in a letter of 1516 to
Mutianus Rufus he wrote "our friendship is of a relatively recent
date."[16] When he came to know Mutianus well, he began calling
him a skeptic and an Epicurean. He wrote to Staupitz that he
preferred to withdraw from the scene and to observe the pageant of
brilliant people in his times. From his earliest university days on,
Luther was aware of the great intellectual developments of his
times, including both humanism and the revival of the classics.

Indeed, Luther entered the monastery with Vergil and Plautus
under his arm—a sure sign of his appreciation of the classical authors. Clearly, Luther valued both the ideas and the eloquence to
be found in the classics. He once wrote: "Were I as eloquent and
rich in words as Erasmus, in Greek as learned as Camerarius, and
in Hebrew as skilled as Forstemius, and were I younger, ah, how I

would delve into the Word of God!"[17] In 1537 he wrote on the table with chalk in Latin: "Substance and words—Philip [Melanchthon]. Words without substance—Erasmus. Substance without words— Luther. Neither substance nor words—Karlstadt."[18] Eloquence was important to Luther as a worthy expression of substantive content.

In his 1524 letter *To the Councilmen of All Cities in Germany That They Establish and Maintain Christian Schools* Luther voiced his well-known lament: "How I regret now that I did not read more poets and historians, and that no one taught me them! Instead, I was obliged to read at great cost, toil, and detriment to myself, the devil's dung, the philosophers and sophists, from which I have all I can do to purge myself."[19] If he felt the deprivation of his early years, was he able in his later years to compensate for this deficiency? The evidence suggests that he was indeed able to do so. At the Leipzig Debate, for example, Dr. Eck expressed admiration for Luther's ability in Latin, and Peter Mosellanus, who presided at the occasion, commented upon the excellence and precision of his Greek.

Four months after Luther's death Melanchthon wrote in his *Vita* that Luther had read many ancient Latin authors, including Cicero, Vergil, Livy, and others. He read them, said Melanchthon, not as youths who make excerpts but for their images of human life and for purposes of teaching, and with his firm and true memory he retained them and kept them before his eyes. Melanchthon implies that Luther did his basic reading of the classics in school and as an arts student. The texts substantiate this view, for in the *Table Talks* there are 59 references to Cicero, 50 citations from Vergil, but the historian Livy falls to one side, and there are 61 references to Aristotle. In Luther's writings and correspondence, Aristotle, Cicero, and Vergil are most frequently cited, far more than any other classical authors, followed by Terence, Horace, Plato, Quintilian, Homer, and Ovid, roughly in that order. There are individual scattered references to Aesop, Plautus, Suetonius, Herodotus, Xenophon, Ammianus, Marcellinus, Juvenal, Caesar, Aeschylus, Minucius Felix, Pliny, Tacitus, Demosthenes, Apuleius, Polycrates, Plutarch, Sulpicius, Severnus, Parmenides, Zeno, and a few others. Most of the authors whom Luther cited frequently had been published in Germany by 1520. Frequency of reference or quotation does not, of course, tell us everything, for the references to Aristotle, for example, are frequently pejorative. The historians proved less quotable than the philosophers and rhetoricians, which does not mean that their total impact on his thought was of less importance. In addition, it is not always possible to tell which allusions came from reading and which from conversations with friends and colleagues.

Melanchthon was the person who had a formative influence on Luther's thought about history. Luther discussed history with him, he related, even on the journey to Torgau. In later years, between 1555 and 1560, Melanchthon gave lectures on world history. A comparison of Melanchthon's *Introduction to the Chronicon* and Luther's prefaces to various historical works such as Hedio's *Chronicle* of 1539 or Cuspinian's *Caesares* of 1541 reveals many similarities in their ideas about history. Twenty years after the Leipzig Debate Luther commented that at the time he had not been well versed in history and had attacked the papacy *a priori* on the basis of Scripture, but that now he appreciated the correspondence of the histories and Scripture and could attack the papacy *a posteriori* from the histories. In 1537, in fact, Luther wrote his own sharp attack on the monstrous fraud of the Donation of Constantine. As a younger man he had been led by Hutten's edition of Lorenzo Valla's *De donatione Constantini* to conclude that the papacy was the anti-Christ.[20]

Luther developed a deeper interest in history during the final three lustra of his life. He wrote prefaces to various "historical" works: *Vorrede zu Spalatin, magnifice consolatoria exempla et sententiae ex passionibus sanctorum . . . collectae; Vorrede zu Robert Barnes, Vitae Romanorum Pontificum; Vorrede Johannes Kymäus, Ein alt christlich Konzilium . . . zu Gangro; Vorrede zu Historia Galeatii Capellae, 1539; Vorrede zu Epistola S. Hieronymi ad Evangrium de potestate, 1538; Praefatio zu Georg Major Vitae patrum, 1544; Vorrede zu Papstreue Hadrian IV. und Alexandrus III. gegen Kaiser Friedrich Barbarossa, 1545*. These prefaces show that Luther shared with the humanists a passionate interest in history. He was interested in the entire sweep of history, not merely, like the annalists and chroniclers, in particular events. His writings are replete with historical reflections and judgments.

The rising tide of cultural nationalism, which antedated the Reformation by a century and a half, increased the humanists' interest in their own people's history. Histories should not be "cold and dead," but should serve useful moral purposes. Good history requires good historians, the "lion-hearted," men not afraid to write the truth.

Luther was also fascinated with the inner meaning and nature of history. He saw God as active everywhere in history, though He is often hidden, disguised as though concealed behind a mask (*larva*). Faith sees beyond fate and chance to the God whose Word reveals the true meaning and content of history. In his introduction to Galeatius Capella's history of the reign of Francesco II Sforza, Duke of Milan, who played a key role in the relations of Charles V and Francis I, Luther declared that "histories are . . . a very precious thing," for "histories are nothing else than a demonstration, recollection, and sign of divine action and judgment, how He upholds, rules, obstructs, prospers, punishes, and honors the world, and especially men, each according to his just desert, evil or good." He added: "The historians, therefore, are the most useful people and the best teachers, so that one can never honor, praise, and thank them enough."[21]

Arnold Berger has argued that Luther saw history as a completion of the Bible and as a kind of *Weltbibel*.[22] That may be something of an overstatement, but it is true that as Luther's interest in history grew he came to see the value of chronology as an aid to exegesis and as useful for the light it sheds on church history. In 1541 he constructed his *Supputatio annorum mundi* or *Reckoning of the Years of the World*, a chronological table, so that he "could always have before his eyes and see the time and years of historical events which are described in Holy Scriptures and remind himself how many years the patriarchs, judges, kings, and princes lived and ruled or over how long a period of time one succeeded the other."[23] Possibly inspired by Eusebius, whose work he admired, he wrote three columns of events and dates for East, West, and German history and worked out parallel traditions of biblical history and secular events. He projected the dates from creation to the year 1540, dividing the table by millennia. He listed the indulgence controversy as a major event of the sixteenth century! He drew on contemporary histories to fix dates, but where there was a conflict between the scriptural data and that of some secular source, such as the chronology ascribed to Megasthenes, he opted for the reliability of the Scriptures.

Although history was of great importance to the Wittenberg theology at the outset of the Reformation, and Luther promoted it at the university, there is no real evidence that he sought to have chairs of history established there. In his 1520 treatise *To the Christian Nobility of the German Nation Concerning the Reform of the Christian Estate*, he did, however, declare such a step to be desirable, but there is no evidence that he actively tried to implement it.

Not only did Luther have an impressive knowledge of the classics and a keen interest in history, but he also savored the use of words. Like a true linguist and rhetorician he enjoyed the mystery and beauty of language. Indeed, he even liked to play with words. Much of what he wrote consisted of a mixture of Latin and German, what is termed a macaronic text.[24]

Luther's 1524 letter *To the Councilmen of All Cities in Germany* is the best source for his views on the classical languages. His favorite classical author was Cicero, whom he valued much more highly than he did Aristotle. He held that whoever wants to learn true philosophy should read Cicero. He also approved of Cicero's moral philosophy and his speculation about proofs of the existence of God found in his work *De natura deorum*, which Calvin utilized in the first chapters of his *Institutes*. Luther admired Cicero's eloquence and once declared: "When I read Cicero's *Orations* I feel so ineloquent. I feel myself stammer as a child."[25] In many respects Cicero was Luther's model. When Luther talked about Eccles. 1:4, he said that Cicero had fully understood the meaning of vanity and vexation of the spirit. Even though he shared Erasmus's admiration for both Cicero and Seneca, he did not go so far as did Erasmus in the expression of it. For example, Erasmus said: "When I read pieces like that I can hardly refrain from crying out, 'O holy Cicero, pray for us' or another time, 'Holy Socrates, pray for us.' "[26] Luther did say that in the world to come Cicero will sit much higher than Duke George of Saxony or Margrave Joachim I of Brandenburg, who died between two whores. If they sat where Cicero does, they would be saved![27]

Of the historians, Luther particularly liked Livy for his style.

The German humanists, Ulrich von Hutten and Conrad Celtis, stressed the importance of the historian Tacitus. The belief that the Renaissance view of history was basically built on historical theories reflecting Livy is mistaken, for it was Tacitus who loomed large in their minds. He did so in part because he praised German virtue, but also because he described the decline of Rome. For the humanists it was very problematical to put those contradictory notions together, but it was not so for Luther. He used Tacitus to suggest the deterioration of the Germans since the pure and simple life in ancient times.[28]

Luther often included references to other classical authors in his works. He cited Pliny the Younger, for example, in his first sermon on the First Letter of Peter, of all places. Quintilian was his favorite rhetorician, as he was for most of the humanists. Luther also spoke of that distinguished man, Varro, from whom one could learn a whole array of information. He knew the geographer Pomponius Mela and used him in his commentary on Psalm 73. He termed Ovid an excellent poet, surpassing all others. According to Luther, he "masterfully expresses things in charming verse."[29] He quoted Ovid on man as the midpoint, who holds his hands upward toward the sky, hands up and eyes toward heaven, with feet planted on the ground—the only animal who can do so. In other words, Luther drew substantive things from some of the poets. He said, for example, that the enthusiasts or *Schwärmer* were like Icarus, fluttering around in the air too close to the sun. They would burn off their feathers and fall to the ground with their lofty, fluttery ideas. There are also at least twelve references in Luther's works to Horace's *De arte poetica.*

Luther also affirmed the importance of some classical authors whose works might appear to be more problematical. He advised a Silesian schoolmaster who had been criticized for having his students perform a comedy of Terence to keep on as he had done. The boys should be encouraged to put on the plays in order to practice their Latin, to develop good artistry, to see people well portrayed and reminded of their duties. Luther did not favor bowdlerizing Terence, for the obscenities show the pupils what life is really like.[30] Rather late in life Luther bought copies of Lucretius and Lucan. Of the skeptic Lucian he said that he liked such a person since he did not insinuate or beat around the bush. The skeptics were not like Erasmus, talking out of both sides of his mouth, but rather, they said clearly what they meant. Luther frequently used Lucian as a test of skeptical ideas.[31]

Limitations of space prevent a survey of Luther's knowledge of the Greek sources, but one must mention that Luther himself, as his personal contribution, put out an edition of Aesop's *Fables* that was used in the schools.[32]

We must now ask two questions about Luther's knowledge of the classical authors and texts. First, did he know more than any well-educated medieval figure who had completed secondary school? We must conclude that he did not know much more. He had an enormous and wonderful memory, and what he once learned he retained and continued to use. Second, did Luther, in his later years, learn even more of the classics and use them? Again, the answer must be in the negative. Certainly he did not learn a great deal more. One finds in the *Table Talks* of his later years the same style and the same references as in the early years. With more leisure he did not become a great humanistic scholar, as is sometimes said. He knew an impressive amount about the classics, much more than most educated moderns, and he was alert to Renaissance humanism and to the educational goals of the humanists. But the evangelical cause consumed his energies and prevented him from becoming an outstanding classical scholar or a giant among Renaissance humanists. Noble as were such pursuits, they were not his calling.

We may now turn to our third and final question. In terms of substance, what was the contribution of humanism to Luther's role as a theological and religious reformer? Bernd Moeller once stated with epigrammatic force: "Without humanism no Reformation." This assertion on the surface seems problematical, for Renaissance humanism did not lead to a radical Reformation in the Italy of Petrarch, Bruni, or Ficino, nor in the Spain of Cardinal Ximenes, nor in the France of Budé, Bodin, or Lefèvre d'Étaples. But in the German context humanism was clearly an essential precondition and a necessary catalyst for radical change. The Italian humanists considered scholastic theology, and some of them even Aristotelian natural science, to be a foreign import coming from the ultramontanes. The German humanists were increasingly repelled by scholasticism, admired Italian humanism, but were patriotically hostile to the Italian church and its exploitation of the German people.

The question posed here is whether Luther's reactions were the same or at least similar to those of the German humanists, and, if so, what impact humanism had upon his theology. It is clear that Luther was critical of scholastic theology, but not because the Latin was barbarous, nor merely because of the intrusion of dialectic, but preeminently because it represented a form of *theologia gloriae.* The adoption of the Aristotelian ethic reinforced the semi-Pelagian tendencies of medieval theology. Luther shared with the Christian humanists, most strongly represented in central and southern Germany, both a desire for religious enlightenment and some aspects of their cultural nationalism. His position is the same toward both mysticism with its "heavenly ladder" for ascending to the naked majesty of God and humanism with its optimistic anthropology, which did not fully grasp that sin or alienation from God is the root condition of man and that grace is a benignity whereby God by grace alone forgives man his sin and reconciles man to Himself. That difference was at the heart of the so-called free will controversy with Erasmus. The distinction has been made between humanist Christians and Christian humanism, a suggestion that is of some limited value, but that needs to be spelled out very carefully and specifically.[33] Luther has also been called a biblical humanist, a term not without its conceptual and substantive difficulties.[34] It is necessary to inquire more closely into Luther's theological and religious debt to humanism in order to place him with some precision on the spectrum of Renaissance humanism.

Such an inquiry should focus on Luther's exegesis, on his preference for rhetoric over dialectic, on the relation of moral philosophy to sanctification, on educational ideas, and finally, on the importance of the classical curriculum as a carrier of cultural and religious values.

Luther's professional calling was to teach as a *doctor in Biblia.* He was an exegete who lectured on the Scriptures as a professor for thirty-three years. In his exegesis he used the traditional sources and handbooks, such as Nicholas de Lyra's *Postillae,* extensively but not uncritically. Already in the *Dictata* or *First Lectures on the Psalms* of 1513–1515 and in his *Lectures on Romans* of 1515–1516, he made quite explicit his dependence on the French humanist Lefèvre d'Étaples, who had done annotations on the Psalms and the Pauline epistles. Lefèvre, in turn, learned much about biblical interpretation from Jean Gerson, a mystic and conciliarist whom Luther referred to as *Doctor Christianissimus*. The influence of the French evangelical humanist Lefèvre reinforced Luther's objection to the traditional fourfold interpretation of Scripture, for the allegorical, tropological, and anagogical interpretations allowed for too much subjectivity. Even in traditional university disputations they were not accepted as proofs of the truth of an argument. Along with Lefèvre, Luther insisted upon the historico-literal interpretation of the text, by which he, too, meant the spiritual message intended by the authors, holy men of God moved by the inspiration of the Holy Ghost. Whether this approach to exegesis, with its implied hermeneutics, was humanist in any generic or historical sense of the word may be debated, for what Luther owed to Lefèvre may have been a spiritual-evangelical approach rather than a humanist philological method. The fact that the line is hard to draw does not excuse us from making the attempt to draw it.

Another example may be of value in considering Luther as exegete, namely, his debt to Reuchlin, the great Hebraist. As is well-known, Luther, in contrast to supercilious Erasmus, was an ardent student and in due course a real master of Hebrew. Both his lectures and commentaries were mostly on books of the Old Testament, which he translated with the help of his "Sanhedrin." He used Reuchlin's Hebrew vocabulary and grammar, though he considered his cabalistic writings to be phantasmic and harmful. When Luther lectured on the Psalms, as the annotations in the *Dictata* make clear, he referred to Reuchlin's treatment of the seven penitential psalms. Since Luther's Hebrew was still weak in the mid-1510s, the precision of his knowledge of specific vocables and textual interpretations falls off in quality when he moves beyond Reuchlin's work.[35] Part way through his *Lectures on Romans* Luther switched to the newly published Greek New Testament text of Erasmus. Clearly Luther's dependence upon humanist philology and exegetical techniques helped him to transcend the inaccuracies, vagaries, and theological misconceptions of medieval exegesis. At the same time, for Luther the touchstone of interpretation remained the theological principle that an interpretation that exalts the *promissa dei et beneficia Christi* is the correct one. Any interpretation that diminishes those promises and benefits is false. It has been asserted that Luther was the first exegete since Irenaeus to enunciate so clearly a theological criterion for determining the biblical canon. He was also the first in a millennium to propose a simple religious criterion by which dark passages are to be understood in the light of a clear message. That is what Luther meant with the postulate that Scriptures are to be interpreted by the Scriptures *(Scriptura Scriptura interpretatur).* He did not mean, as a mere humanist might, that an obscure scriptural passage must be interpreted in the light of passages that are philologically or textually more comprehensible. Though Luther's biblical exegesis derived its formal method from the rules of rhetoric, the evangelical substance came from the Scriptures by listening with the help of the Holy Spirit to the Word.

Luther owed a great debt to humanism and to certain classics for his appreciation of rhetoric over dialectic. Like Ulrich von Hutten, who had declared that knowledge that merely convinces intellectually but does not lead to action is not truth, but philosophizing in the shadows, Luther held rhetoric to be a superior form of philosophy. The Scriptures are rhetorical and are not made up of labyrinths of syllogisms. That rhetoric was an important tool for Luther and for all evangelical preachers is virtually self-evident, and the newer studies of Luther's homiletics bear this fact out nicely.[36] Moreover, Luther's emphasis upon the spoken Word of the gospel *(Verbum evangelii vocale)* suggests an affinity between rhetorical expression and the Word as the carrier of the message of salvation.

Recently the attempt has been made to establish an interior connection between the rhetorical art of moving affections or emotions *(ars movendi affectus)* and the vivification *(vivificatio)* of the sinner by the Holy Spirit. In commenting on Psalm 119:25 in the *Dictata,* "Revive me according to thy word" *(RSV) (Vivifica me secundum verbum tuum),* Luther wrote: "This making alive takes place through the Spirit of God, namely, as a spiritual will. . . . No matter how learned and enlightened by faith a person may be, unless he wills and works by the same affect, he is not yet living."[37] On Psalm 119:37, "give me life in thy ways" *(RSV),* Luther commented: "It is the Spirit who makes alive and faith which justifies, as Paul says in Romans 1:17, for the just lives by faith. 'Revive me' *(vivifica me)* is to say 'justify me' *(iustifica me).*"[38] The conclusion follows that Luther linked *vivificatio affectu* with *iustificatio fide,* thus drawing upon a rhetorical locus at the very heart of his theology.[39] Again in the *Dictata,* commenting upon Psalm 119:17 (16), "Deal bountifully with thy servant, that I may live and observe thy word" *(RSV),* Luther wrote: "Christ's words not only have the power to teach *(vim docendi),* but also the power to move within *(vim excitandi seu movendi).* . . . A good speaker must know how to do three things, to teach, to delight, and to move. Therefore, I have never forgotten the words from the cross."[40] Christ seems to him to be the *bonus orator.*[41] Impressive though this argument identifying the *vivificatio ex affectu* and the *vivificatio ex fide* may be, in the final analysis it is not convincing. For Luther, in contrast to Petrarch and Agricola, only the Holy Spirit can turn the whole man around from unfaith to faith and eternal life, even though words constitute the external instrument and well-spoken words are able to move the emotions.

In addition to their emphasis on languages and philology and their preference for rhetoric over dialectic, the Renaissance humanists also stressed the fundamental importance of moral philosophy. Luther had lectured on Aristotle's *Nichomachean Ethics,* but had excoriated the Stagarite's intrusion into Christian theology. He was an admirer of Cicero and the Roman moralists, though he was not totally unaware of the potentially subversive nature of Stoic moral philosophy with its nontheistic presuppositions about natural law. Although Luther was, of course, opposed to the intrusion of moralism as a way to salvation, he appreciated the value of moral philosophy for natural man and for the regenerate Christian in conducting the affairs of this life. Revealed law, the Decalogue, the Sermon on the Mount, remain the spiritual standard for Christians. The law of love is the basis for all law and should also be such for all positive laws made by governments. Nonetheless, the experience of a statesman and moral philosopher such as Cicero can be of tremendous value to Christian and non-Christian alike in ordering the matters of this world. Once again, the humanist stress on moral philosophy finds a place in Luther's theology and has a certain utility, but it is not a source for nor a generic part of his theology.

Finally, Luther's educational goals and ideals were conditioned by Renaissance humanism. At no time in the history of the world, except perhaps our own, has so much attention been paid to educational theory and reform as in the age of the Renaissance and Reformation. The reformers were more egalitarian than the elitist Renaissance humanists and insisted upon universal compulsory elementary education for boys and girls. They also created the gymnasium and Lyceé for the gifted who could benefit from secondary education in order better to serve the bureaucracies of the state, the clerical positions of the church, and the very schools themselves. They revised the curriculum on the university level along humanist lines. Through the educational system, the Reformation, Protestant and Catholic, perpetuated humanist ideals, and classical letters and values. The reformers elevated the dignity of pedagogy by placing teaching as a divine vocation next to the ministry of the Word.

This understanding of the educability of men did not, however, constitute a contribution by humanism to Luther's theology as such. In his anthropology Luther was somewhat less optimistic than were humanist educators as to what could be accomplished through the teaching of the *humaniora,* or liberal arts, alone. Education has a lofty place in Luther's mind, but as such it has to do with earthly culture and human society and is not a prerequisite for entrance into the Kingdom of God. Learning does not of itself have salvific powers. It is the person who is enlightened by the Holy Spirit who is made wise unto salvation. Humanist educational theory did not contribute to the substance of Luther's theology nor change the nature of his Christian anthropology.

In conclusion, without the contribution of Renaissance humanism Luther could not have been the effective magisterial reformer he proved to be. He was alert to the newer intellectual currents of his time and appreciated the achievements of contemporary humanists. Just as he considered the Renaissance to be a John the Baptist pointing to the coming evangelical revival, so he himself used the new tools of humanist learning in behalf of the gospel. His student and first biographer, Johannes Mathesius, gave the following superscription to his collection of Luther's *Table Talk* from the winter of 1542–1543: *Evangelii occasi renascentis per doctorem.*[42]

Luther was himself a devotee of the classics, preeminently of Latin literature, but also of Greek and Hebrew. He contributed creatively through his own marvelous gift for languages to the development of new high German. He was appreciative of the fine arts and composed church music, hymns, and a revised liturgy. As an educator, in daily contact with the *Praeceptor Germaniae,* Philipp Melanchthon, he provided for the continuity of humanist learning into modern times—through the gymnasia, and both the new Protestant and reformed older universities. Humanism was important for Luther, and he, in turn, contributed to its ongoing presence and influence in the centuries that followed. Luther was deeply appreciative of the revival of the arts and liberal learning, the great achievements of Renaissance humanism. He wrote: "Now that God has today so graciously bestowed upon us an abundance of arts, scholars, and books, it is time to reap and gather in the best as well we can, and lay up treasure in order to preserve for the future something from these years of jubilee, and not lose this bountiful harvest."[43]

Leopold von Ranke, the great historian of the Reformation and the father of modern critical history, quite rightly paid this tribute to Luther, a man of learning as well as a great man of faith: "In no nation or age has a more . . . commanding and powerful writer appeared; and it would be difficult to find another who has so perfectly united popular and intelligent style and such downright homely good sense to so much originality, power and genius."[44]

## NOTES

1. The most excellent recent study of German humanism is that of Erich Meuthen, "Charakter und Tendenzen des deutschen Humanismus," in *Säkulare Aspekte der Reformationszeit,* ed. Heinz Angermeier and Reinhard Seyboth (Munich and Vienna, 1983), 217–76, with detailed bibliographic, analytical notes. The *XVIIIᵉ Colloque international de Tours: L'Humanisme allemand (1480–1540)* (Munich and Paris, 1979) contains a brief but significant article by Heinz Otto Burger, "Martin Luther und der Humanismus," 357–69. Otto Herding and Robert Stupperich, eds., *Die Humanisten in ihrer politischen und sozialen Umwelt: Kommission für Humanismusforschung 3* (Boppard, 1976), contains relevant essays. A handy book of sources in English translation is Reinhard P. Becker, ed., *German Humanism and Reformation* (New York, 1982). There is, of course, a vast German literature on the question of humanism and the Reformation, such as Martin Greschat and J. F. G. Goeters, eds., *Reformation und Humanismus: Robert Stupperich zum 65. Geburtstag* (Witten, 1969). I shall not, however, recapitulate the literature to which I have referred in earlier publications, for example, in the chapters, "Humanism in the Reformation," in *Renaissance*

*Studies in Honor of Hans Baron,* ed. Anthony Molho and John A. Tedeschi (Dekalb, Ill., 1971), 641–62, and "The Course of German Humanism," in *Itinerarium Italicum: The Profile of the Italian Renaissance in the Mirror of Its European Transformations,* ed. Heiko A. Oberman and Thomas A. Brady, Jr. (Leiden, 1975), 371–436. On the present state of research, see Dieter Wuttke, *Deutsche Germanistik und Renaissance-Forschung* (Bad Homburg, 1968).

2. On the humanists and Luther, reflecting the generation problem, see Herbert Schöffler, *Die Reformation: Einführung in eine Geistesgeschichte der deutschen Neuzeit* (Bochum, 1936), republished in his *Wirkungen der Reformation: Religionssoziologische Folgerungen für England und Deutschland* (Frankfurt a. M., 1960), 105–88; Bernd Moeller, "The German Humanists and the Beginnings of the Reformation," in *Imperial Cities and the Reformation: Three Essays,* ed. and trans. Erik Midelfort and Mark U. Edwards (Philadelphia, 1972), 19–38; and Lewis W. Spitz, "The Third Generation of German Renaissance Humanists," in *Aspects of the Renaissance: A Symposium,* ed. Archibald R. Lewis (Austin and London, 1967), 105–21, reprinted in *The Reformation: Basic Interpretations,* ed. Lewis W. Spitz, 2d ed. (Lexington, Mass., 1972), 44–59.

3. Paul Joachimsen, "Der Humanismus und die Entwicklung des deutschen Geistes," *Deutsche Vierteljahrsschrift für Literaturwissenschaft und Geistesgeschichte* 8 (1930): 419–20.

4. See Marilyn J. Harran, *Luther on Conversion: the Early Years* (Ithaca and London, 1983), "Luther's Tower Experience," 174–88.

5. On Luther's adoption of the name Eleutherius, see Bernd Moeller and Karl Stackmann, *Luder-Luther-Eleutherius: Erwägungen zu Luthers Namen, Nachrichten der Akademie der Wissenschaften in Göttingen I. Philologisch-Historische Klasse,* no. 7 (1981), 171–203.

6. WA 1:355, 16–19; *Luther's Works,* vol. 31: *Career of the Reformer: I,* ed. Harold J. Grimm (Philadelphia, 1957), 41–42. Theses 36 and 37 read: "Aristotle wrongly finds fault with and derides the ideas of Plato, which actually are better than his own. The mathematical order of material things is ingeniously maintained by Pythagoras, but more ingenious is the interaction of ideas maintained by Plato." 42. See also Karl-Heinz zur Mühlen, "Luthers Kritik am scholastischen Aristotelismus in der 25. These der 'Heidelberger Disputation' von 1518," *Lutherjahrbuch* 48 (1981): 54–79; and Helmar Junghans, "Die probationes zu den philosophischen Thesen der Heidelberger Disputation Luthers im Jahre 1518," *Lutherjahrbuch* 46 (1979): 10–59.

7. WA 5:19, 16–20; 20, 19–25; 26, 6–14. For Luther's role in university reform at Wittenberg, see Max Steinmetz, "Die Universität Wittenberg und der Humanismus (1502–1521)," 103–39, and Kurt Aland, "Die Theologische Fakultät Wittenberg und ihre Stellung im Gesamtzusammenhang der Leucorea während des 16. Jahrhunderts," 155–237, in *450 Jahre Martin-Luther-Universität Halle-Wittenberg,* vol. 1: *Wittenberg 1502–1817* (Halle, 1952). See also Martin Brecht, *Martin Luther: Sein Weg zur Reformation 1483–1521* (Stuttgart, 1981), "Universitäts-und Wissenschaftsreform im Bund mit dem Humanismus," 264–84.

8. *Nicolai Marscalci Thurii oratio habita albiori academia in alemania iam nuperrima ad promotionem primorum baccalauriorum numero quattuor et viginti anno domini mcccciii,* trans. with introduction and notes by Edgar C. Reinke and Gottfried G. Krodel (St. Louis, 1967), printed for Valparaiso University.

9. On Melanchthon's humanism, see Adolf Sperl, *Melanchthon zwischen*

*Humanismus und Reformation: Eine Untersuchung über den Wandel des Tradi-tionsverständnisses bei Melanchthon und die damit zusammenhängenden Grundfragen seiner Theologie* (Munich, 1959); Wilhelm Maurer, *Der junge Melanchthon zwischen Humanismus und Reformation*, vol. 1: *Der Humanist*, vol. 2: *Der Theologe* (Göttingen, 1967 and 1969), and Walter Elliger, ed., *Philipp Melanchthon: Forschungsberichte zur vierhundertsten Wiederkehr seines Todes-tages dargeboten in Wittenberg 1960* (Göttingen, 1961). On Mosellanus, see Os-wald Gottlob Schmidt, *Petrus Mosellanus: Ein Beitrag zur Geschichte des Humanismus in Sachsen* (Leipzig, 1867).

10. WA 42:4–56; *Luther's Works*, vol. 1: *Lectures on Genesis. Chapters 1–5*, ed. Jaroslav Pelikan (St. Louis, 1958), 3–73 on Genesis 1.

11. Johannes Reuchlin, *Johann Reuchlins Briefwechsel*, ed. Ludwig Geiger (Stuttgart, 1875), 311, no. 227, Luther to Reuchlin, 14 December 1518. Ludwig Geiger, *Johann Reuchlin: Sein Leben und seine Werke* (1871; reprint, Nieuwkoop, 1964), 353ff., discusses the relation of Luther and Reuchlin.

12. E. Gordon Rupp and Philip S. Watson, eds., *Luther and Erasmus: Free Will and Salvation*, vol. 17 in *The Library of Christian Classics* (Philadelphia, 1969). Luther, in the *De servo arbitrio*, wrote: "Yet not only do I not blame them, but of myself I yield you a palm such as I have never yielded to anyone before; for I confess not only that you are far superior to me in powers of eloquence and native genius (which we all must admit, all the more as I am an uncultivated fellow who has always moved in uncultivated circles), but that you have quite damped my spirit and eagerness, and left me exhausted before I could strike a blow." 101–2.

13. WA 18:600–787.

14. Matthew Arnold, *Culture and Anarchy*, ed. William S. Knickerbocker (1869; New York, 1929), 139.

15. WA 15:37, 11–26; *Luther's Works*, vol. 45: *The Christian in Society II*, ed. Walther I. Brandt (Philadelphia, 1962), *To the Councilmen of All Cities in Ger-many That They Establish and Maintain Christian Schools* (1524), 359.

16. WA Br 1:40, 7–8, no. 14 (29 May 1516). On 2 May 1515 Johann Lang had brought to Mutian a copy of Luther's sermon of 1 May along with Luther's greetings. On Luther's lack of contact with Mutian prior to that time, see Hans von Schubert, "Reformation und Humanismus," *Lutherjahrbuch* 8 (1926): 7.

17. WA TR 1:487, 21–23, no. 961.

18. WA TR 3:460, 38–40, no. 3619. *Luther's Works*, vol. 54: *Table Talk*, ed. and trans. Theodore G. Tappert (Philadelphia, 1967), 245.

19. WA 15:46, 18–21; LW 45:370.

20. Brecht, *Martin Luther*, 329–30. WA Br 2:48, 30–49, 29, no. 257 (24 Febru-ary 1520).

21. WA 50:383, 8; 384:2–5, 15–17. *Luther's Works*, vol. 34: *Career of the Reformer IV*, ed. Lewis W. Spitz (Philadelphia, 1960), 275–76.

22. Arnold Berger, *Martin Luther in kulturgeschichtlicher Darstellung* (1895; Berlin, 1919), 553.

23. WA 53:22–184; 22, 13–18. Ernst Schäfer wrote the pioneering work *Luther als Kirchenhistoriker: Ein Beitrag zur Geschichte der Wissenschaft* (Gütersloh, 1897). See also Karl Bauer, *Die Wittenberger Universitätstheologie und die An-fänge der Deutschen Reformation* (Tübingen, 1928), "Die Bereicherung der Wit-tenberger Theologie durch die Geschichte," 80–98. Werner Elert, *Morphologie des Luthertums hauptsächlich im 16. und 17. Jahrhundert*, vol. 1 (1931; Munich,

1958), 426, n. 2, discusses the question of whether Luther and then Melanchthon wished to establish chairs for historians, which would have been an advance over Italian universities. Three works on Luther's understanding of history especially worthy of mention are John M. Headley, *Luther's View of Church History* (New Haven, 1963); Heinz Zahrnt, *Luther Deutet Geschichte: Erfolg und Misserfolg im Licht des Evangeliums* (Munich, 1952); and Hans-Walter Krumwiede, *Glaube und Geschichte in der Theologie Luthers: Zur Entstehung des geschichtlichen Denkens in Deutschland* (Göttingen, 1952). On the importance of Luther and the Reformation for the history of universities, see the recent volume by Leif Grane, ed., *University and Reformation: Lectures from the University of Copenhagen Symposium* (Leiden, 1981).

24. Birgit Stolt, *Die Sprachmischung in Luthers Tischreden: Studien zum Problem der Zweisprachigkeit* (Stockholm, 1964), 8–15. See also the outstanding though still unpublished dissertation of Sandra Mosher Anderson, *Words and Word in Theological Perspective: Martin Luther's Views on Literature and Figurative Speech* (Ph.D. diss., Northwestern University, 1973). On Luther's genius for language, see also Heinz Bluhm, *Martin Luther: Creative Translator* (St. Louis, 1965).

25. Cited in Oswald Gottlob Schmidt, *Luther's Bekanntschaft mit den alten Classikern: Ein Beitrag zur Lutherforschung* (Leipzig, 1883), 14. The *Table Talk* is replete with comments on the excellence of Cicero on the subjects of proofs of the existence of God, the immortality of the soul, the rhetorical impact of the orator, the blessedness of life, and annihilation after death. One of the telling passages in which Luther draws a line between revelation and Cicero's natural wisdom occurs in *WA TR* 3:4, 19–24, no. 2808b; *LW* 54:171: "Experience demonstrates the efficacy of divine truth. The more it's read, the more it works. With all his wisdom and eloquence Cicero couldn't achieve this, although he was supreme in human wisdom. Such wisdom can't rise above its own level but must remain under it. Cicero was the wisest man. He wrote more than all the philosophers and also read all the books of the Greeks. I marvel at this man who, amid such great labors, read and wrote so much."

26. In Erasmus's colloquy *The Religious Banquet,* following a conversation about the wisdom of Cicero, Cato, and Plato, Erasmus has Nephalius declare: "Indeed, it was a wonderful elevation of the mind in a man who did not know Christ nor the Holy Scriptures and therefore I can scarce forbear, when I read such things of such men but cry out, *Sancte Socrates, ora pro nobis."* For a discussion of the problem, see Lewis W. Spitz, *The Religious Renaissance of the German Humanists* (Cambridge, Mass., 1963), 197–236; 212.

27. *WA TR* 5:311, 7–9, no. 5671; *LW* 54:475. Luther said that he hoped God would look with favor upon Cicero even though he was a pagan. *WA TR* 4:14, 1–4, no. 3925.

28. Frank L. Borchardt, *German Antiquity in Renaissance Myth* (Baltimore, 1971), 104–9. See also Hajo Holborn, *Ulrich von Hutten and the German Reformation,* trans. Roland H. Bainton (New Haven, 1937), 44–45; 55; 76–77; Lewis W. Spitz, *Conrad Celtis: The German Arch-Humanist* (Cambridge, Mass., 1957), 93–105.

29. Schmidt, *Luther's Bekanntschaft mit den alten Classikern,* 31.

30. *WA TR* 1:430–31, no. 867. See Schmidt, *Luther's Bekanntschaft mit den alten Classikern,* 23, 25. E. G. Sihler, "Luther and the Classics," in *Four Hundred*

*Years: Commemorative Essays on the Reformation of Dr. Martin Luther and Its Blessed Results* (St. Louis, 1916), 252.

31. Sihler, "Luther and the Classics," 253; Schmidt, *Luther's Bekanntschaft mit den alten Classikern*, 58.

32. *WA Br* 5:309, 13–15, no. 1563 (8 May 1530): "I have also proposed to prepare the fables of Aesop for the youth and the common crowd so that they may be of some use to the Germans." See Lewis W. Spitz, "Headwaters of the Reformation: *Studia Humanitatis, Luther Senior, et Initia Reformationis*," in *Luther and the Dawn of the Modern Era: Papers for the Fourth International Congress for Luther Research*, ed. Heiko A. Oberman (Leiden, 1974), 107.

33. Josef Ijsewijn, "The Coming of Humanism to the Low Countries," in *Itinerarium Italicum*, 282.

34. The term *biblical humanism* is, for example, used by E. G. Schwiebert, *Luther and His Times: The Reformation From a New Perspective* (St. Louis, 1950), "Triumph of Biblical Humanism in the University of Wittenberg," 275–302; and J. Lindeboom, *Het Bijbelsch Humanisme in Nederland* (Leiden, 1913).

35. Werner Schwarz, "Studies in Luther's Atittudes Toward Humanism," *Journal of Theological Studies* 6 (1953): 66–76. See also Hans Volz, "Luthers Arbeit am lateinischen Psalter," *Archiv für Reformationsgeschichte* 48 (1957): 44ff., 53; and Walter Koenig, "Luther as a Student of Hebrew," *Concordia Theological Monthly* 24 (1953): 845–53.

36. The latest excellent study of Luther's homiletics relates his sermonic method to rhetorical principles such as the *inventio, genus deliberativum, genus demonstrativum* and *iudicale*, and so forth, Ulrich Nembach, *Predigt des Evangeliums: Luther als Prediger, Pädagoge und Rhetor* (Neukirchen-Vluyn, 1972), 117–74. He relates Luther's sermons to Quintilian's teaching on counselling the people, 139–72, a point spelled out by Eric Wittenborn, *Luthers Predigt vom Jüngsten Tag (Theologische Darstellung, homiletische Form, grundsätzliche Bedeutung)* (Bonn, 1964), and Hermann Werdermann, *Luthers Wittenberger Gemeinde wiederhergestellt aus seinen Predigten: Zugleich ein Beitrag zu Luthers Homiletik und zur Gemeindepredigt der Gegenwart* (Gütersloh, 1929). Luther made immediate application to local problems when preaching in the City Church, where he had become a kind of assistant pastor shortly after his permanent return to Wittenberg, but much more formally and generally when preaching away from Wittenberg. He was always textual, with only about seventy of his some three thousand extant sermons not based specifically on a sermon text. See also Martin Doerne, "Luther und die Predigt," *Luther: Mitteilungen der Luthergesellschaft* 22 (1940): 36–77.

37. *WA* 4:320, 37–39.

38. *WA* 4:325, 8–9.

39. This argument is made by Heinz Otto Burger, "Martin Luther und der Humanismus," 364–67.

40. *WA* 4:284, 32–33, 36–285, 1.

41. Burger, "Martin Luther und der Humanismus," 366–67.

42. Ibid., 364.

43. *WA* 15:52, 25–29; *LW* 45:377. See Ernst Lichtenstein, "Luther und die Humanität," *Evangelische Theologie* 10 (1951): 393. Luther, nevertheless, gave precedence to the influence of the *Spiritus Sanctus* over human *ingenium*, to stammering religious truth over smooth human eloquence, and to Christian faith

94

over antique learning. See the excellent article by Helmar Junghans, "Der Einfluss des Humanismus auf Luthers Entwicklung bis 1518," *Lutherjahrbuch* 37 (1970): 37–101.

44. Leopold von Ranke, *Deutsche Geschichte im Zeitalter der Reformation*, vol. 2, 6th ed. (Leipzig, 1881), 56.

# HUMANISM AND THE PROTESTANT REFORMATION

T HE BRILLIANT, THOUGH ERRATIC, FRIEDRICH NIETZSCHE DE-scribed Luther as "a vengeful, unlucky priest who brought to shame the one cleverly refined beautiful brilliant possibility—Caesar Borgia as pope." (*Der Anti-Christ,* aph. 61). Of course, history was not Nietzsche's strong point, for Cesare Borgia, duke of Valentinois and Romagna and son of Pope Alexander VI, died in 1507 under trying circumstances, roughly a decade before the posting of the Ninety-five Theses by Martin Luther. Nevertheless, Nietzsche's thought does point up the fact that one school of writers in the historiographical tradition from Jacob Burckhardt's time to the present has seen Renaissance and Reformation, humanism and Protestantism, as antithetical. Another interpretive tradition has paired Renaissance and Reformation as twin sources of modernity, a view that has led to the periodization of history into ancient, medieval, and modern, with the modern beginning with the Renaissance. The debate over the relation between the two historic movements was given classical expression in the writings of Wilhelm Dilthey, who saw the Reformation as the religious expression of the Renaissance, and Ernst Troeltsch, for whom the Reformation represented the revival of other-worldly religiosity, antithetical both to the artistically ennobled naturalism of the Renaissance and to the secularized, scientized culture of modern times.[1] The role of humanism in the Reformation and the effects of Protestantism on humanism require a closer examination than they usually receive from cultural historians.

The term humanism is a protean concept, which has been used in varying modalities. The word has been associated in a general way with the rationalist and humanitarian concerns of the Enlightenment, with the "second humanism" of Wilhelm von Humboldt, who made reason and experience the sole touchstones of truth; with a variety of intellectual movements from the "new humanism" of the twentieth century, which is radically anthropocentric and antireligious; and even with the "progressive humanism" of the Communists. It has been claimed by the Neo-thomists at one extreme and the existentialists at the other. The term itself is of relatively recent origin, for a German philologist, F. J. Niethammer, coined the term in 1808 in order to describe a concept of secondary education that favored classical studies as the core of the curriculum. *Umanesimo* or *Humanismus* subsequently entered the scholarly and popular literature on the Italian and northern Renaissance, the form of humanism that Luther and the reformers encountered and that had such a formative influence on them. Renaissance humanism was itself not a simple and static cultural phenomenon, but gradually metamorphosed over the course of three hundred years, from the mid-fourteenth to the mid-seventeenth century. It was an intellectual movement initially and primarily literary and philological in nature, rooted in the love of and desire for the rebirth of classical antiquity in both form and norm.[2] Humanism associated ethical norms with aesthetic forms, the good with the beautiful, in a manner reminiscent of Plato. In looking backward toward classical antiquity, the humanists were not merely antiquarians, but they represented a certain way of assessing classical antiquity and relating it to the present. The term "humanism" was a derivative of the *studia humanitatis* or the liberal arts, those studies "worthy of a free man." This idea is said to have been largely inherited from Cicero, who believed that the orator or poet was best suited to teach the *humaniora* or humane studies. A humanist in the fifteenth century meant a student of the humanities in that classical context. Renaissance humanism contributed tremendously to the Reformation, and the Reformation, in turn, provided for the continuity of humanism into the seventeenth century or longer.

By the year 1517 humanism as a significant cultural movement at the forefront of thought was well established in the Germanies, in France, and in England, though perhaps to a lesser extent. The view that humanism was in the North derived largely from indigenous sources has lost ground in the scholarly opinion of the past two decades, so that the importance of Italian humanism for the North must be taken even more seriously.[3] Humanism was transmitted early and continuously to the Holy Roman Empire, at least as early as the conciliar period and throughout the fifteenth century to the time of Peter Luder, Samuel Karoch, and Rudolf Agricola, the father of German humanism, who died in 1485. Erasmus was indulging in a historical hyperbole when he made statements such as: "It was Rudolf Agricola who first brought with him from Italy some gleam of a better literature," or, "Agricola could have been the first in Italy had he not preferred Germany." Nevertheless, Agricola served not only as mentor, but also as a symbol to the so-called high generation of German humanists such as Conrad Celtis, Johann Reuchlin, Ulrich von Hutten, Conrad Mutian, Willibald Pirckheimer, and the rest.[4] Humanism penetrated courts and cities, and, though it met stronger resistance at the universities, it was well established in several

German universities such as Heidelberg, Erfurt, and Wittenberg before Luther became a student of the arts and law. Similarly the course of French humanism has been charted with greater precision by scholars of recent vintage. In the past century historians were apt to date the French Renaissance from the time of the invasion of Italy by Charles VIII (1494), but it is now established that French humanism was building up throughout the fifteenth century and by Calvin's time was already a well-represented cultural force, not only at the court of François I but in the universities, including one major approach to the study of the law, to which Calvin was introduced with powerful effect. Similarly, historians now appreciate the impact of Italian humanism even in England during the Quattrocento, so that the English scene in the study of classical culture was not so dismal then as has often been supposed. As English humanism entered the upper strata of English thought during that century it was not regarded as a new intellectual system that was incompatible with scholasticism. Most English humanists became ecclesiastical officials or civil servants, clerics being the mainstay of the governmental officialdom, the diplomatic corps, and the universities. As in the case of Germany and France, there was a continuous exchange of churchmen, diplomats, merchants, students, and artists between England and Italy throughout the century. It is not possible here to document the extent of these contacts, but appreciating the fact of their existence makes the emergence of John Colet and Thomas More and the reception of Erasmus seem less phenomenal than once supposed. Humanism was a well-established phenomenon and cultural force in each of the major countries that became Protestant.[5]

*       *       *

The magisterial reformers—Luther, Ulrich Zwingli, Calvin—benefited significantly from humanist learning, as did a small number of the radical reformers and a significant number of the Catholic reformers. Without the humanists and without humanism there would not have been a Reformation such as we know from history and from our own experience. Luther viewed the revival of learning in the Renaissance as a kind of John the Baptist that heralded the coming of the resurgence of the Gospel.[6] Zwingli not only was tutored by a learned uncle in the languages but also studied at Maximilian's University of Vienna, possibly with Conrad Celtis, the German archhumanist; read Erasmus assiduously and perhaps to his detriment; and mastered the art of rhetoric and much humanist or classical learning.[7] So did Joachim Vadian, reformer of St. Gallen.[8] Calvin has often been feted as a young humanist, and his early edition of Seneca's *De clementia* continues to be an object of wonder.[9] One should note also that a number of the Anabaptist reformers, especially among the Swiss Brethren, such as Conrad Grebel, were quite well-educated university men, who knew their patristic writings as well as many classical texts.[10] Among the evangelical humanists such as Michel Servet and Sébastien Castellio, the influence of humanist learning is also immediately apparent. Not always was such humanist input conducive to evangelical soundness, for it may be that although Erasmus lost the exchange with Luther on the freedom or bondage of the will with respect to man's ability to love God above all things and to believe in Christ as Redeemer on the basis of natural reason, he won the war with his rationalist and spiritualist approach to questions of biblical interpretation and understanding of the Sacrament, as reflected in Zwingli's and the reformed as well as the Anabaptist and spiritualist or evangelical-rationalist teachings. When humanism and Protestantism are considered, all too often attention is focused on the Luther–Erasmus exchange rather than on the broad exchange of influences and the counterpoint between humanism and Protestantism and, indeed, between humanism and Christianity whether Protestant or Catholic.

Protestantism was indebted to humanism on many grounds, but above all for the humanistic emphasis on the importance of the classical languages and scholarship. The importance of the languages for biblical studies, patristic learning, and classical erudition can scarcely be overestimated. Second, the humanists' emphasis on education was essential to the reformers' program for the opening of Scripture to the masses and for the elevation of the leaders of the evangelical movement to a position comparable to that of the most learned clergy of the traditional religion. Education was needed also for the lay leaders of the church and for the bureaucrats of the territorial states and the Protestant cities, Lutheran and Calvinist, and in due course for the Anglicans and Puritans. Third, the humanist emphasis on rhetoric, poetry, and history was of the essence for the Protestant movement. Clearly the stress on the spoken word of the Gospel and on preaching of the Word was central to the Protestants, who had much to learn from the humanists. Poetry was closely related to the rhetorical emphasis on *affectus,* and music became a major conveyor of the Gospel message and mover of emotion, which along with reason moved the will of man. History, so assiduously cultivated by the humanists, became for the reformers a mainline interest on two levels and for two reasons. The reformers were interested in history on two levels, of course, secular and sacred. They were also interested and, in fact, deeply concerned with history as a support for their essentially experiential rather than sapiential approach to religion or faith. For them biblical history told the story of God's people, not merely the history of old Israel and of the spiritual Israel—the church—but of individual be-lievers and heroes of the faith. Such history provided case studies of the way God deals with man, and secular history reveals in retrospect the *locutia* of God having spoken and acted in history.

In terms of theology proper there was a marked difference between evangelical theology and the religious assumptions both of the classical world and of Christian humanism, particularly in anthropology and so-teriology. The reformers' Christology contrasted strongly with the Chris-tocentrism of the Christian humanists. For the reformers Christ served as *exemplar,* demonstrating the way that God deals with man, grinding him down into the dust of death but raising him up again to eternal life. Christ was not merely an *exemplum,* a nice model to be followed in leading the Christian life. As long as they remained merely Christian humanists, without undergoing a conversion to the evangelical view, even the most religious of the humanists could scarcely grasp the depths of the sin-and-grace, law-and-gospel, life-and-death antinomies of biblical theology. Despite the theological shift effected by the Protestants, a change that Aristotle would characterize as a true *Metabasis eis allo genos* ("transformation from one dimension to another"), they were ap-preciative of humanist culture and viewed the life of the mind and higher culture as a sphere of faith's works just as were all other areas of life, and in so doing they legitimized religiously the humanists' achievements in the world of thought and learning. The reformers contributed to clas-sical learning through the work of their own savants, they broadened its influence on a larger segment of the population, they provided for the continuity of humanist disciplines through education, they perpetuated many humanist values and liberal arts education into modern times, and so they gave to humanism a new and longer life than it might otherwise have enjoyed.

\*       \* .     \*

Plutarch once observed that in criticizing lectures the auditor should im-prove upon them like Plato on Lysias and should not be as the Lacedae-monians said of Philip of Macedon: for on hearing that Philip had razed Olynthus to the ground, they said, "Yes, but to create a city as good is beyond the man's power." Luther, along with most Protestant reformers, was very critical of the schooling they had received from the elementary level right through their scholastic university studies. Luther in his *Ap-peal to the Municipalities of Germany* (1523), a writing that in the sphere of education was as important as his *Address to the Christian Nobility* (1520) in the area of general church reform, declared that his own schooling had been a disaster and that the schools needed radical change. He wrote that the schools "once were a hell and purgatory, in which we were tormented with the grinding cases and tenses and yet learned less than nothing despite all the flogging, trembling, anguish and misery we suffered at the hands of our brutal school masters. . . . How much I regret now that I did not read more poets and historians, and that nobody taught them to me. Instead, I was obliged to read at great cost, toil, and detriment to me the [scholastic] philosophers and sophists, from which I have had all I can do to purge myself."[11] Of that treatise Felix Rayther correctly observed that the whole little book is a eulogy of languages, for the state needs *rhetores* and *poetae*. "If it is necessary, dear sirs, to expend annually such great sums for firearms," Luther wrote to the councilmen, "for roads, bridges, dams, and countless similar things, in order that a city may enjoy temporal peace and prosperity, why should not at least as much be devoted to the poor needy youth?"[12] Luther's private correspondence is replete with admonitions to promote education and encouragement to pastors and teachers to devote themselves to improving the schools. In a letter to Jakob Strauss at Eisenach, April 1524, he wrote: "I beg you to do your utmost in the cause of the training of the youth. For I am convinced that the neglect of education will bring the greatest ruin to the Gospel. This matter is the most important of all."[13] In his *Sermon on the Estate of Marriage* (1519), he assured parents that they can please God, Christendom, the entire world, themselves, and their children in no better way than by educating their children. In his *Sermon on Keeping Children in School* (1530), he insisted that the civil authorities have a right to compel people to send their children to school. "It is true that it would be hard for me to ride in armor," he wrote. "But on the other hand, I should like to see the rider who could sit for a whole day and look in a book, even if he did not have to be concerned, write, or think. Ask a chancellor, preacher, or rhetorician what work writing and speaking are; ask a schoolteacher what labor teaching and educating youths are. The quill is light, that is true . . . but in this case the most noble parts of the human body are active here and do the most work, the best member (the head), the most noble member (the tongue), and the loftiest labor (speech), whereas in the case of the others either the fist, foot, back, or some similar member works along, and they can cheerfully sing joyously or joke freely, from which a writer must desist. Three fingers do it (they say of writing), but the entire body and soul are involved in the work."[14]

Luther was the first reformer to advocate universal compulsory education for boys and girls, for at least a number of grades, and if the boys had ability, and nature "had not denied them sense and wit," they should be encouraged and enabled to continue regardless of wealth and birth up to the university level. He was very likely the first person in the history of the world to do so. His motive was primarily religious but not exclusively so, for his thought was both humanistic and civic. "The prosperity of a country," he wrote in his *Address to the Municipalities,* "depends, not on the abundance of its revenue, nor on the strength of its fortifications, nor on the beauty of its public buildings, but it consists in the number of cultivated citizens, in its men of education, enlightenment and character."[15] That he favored education in order to provide bureaucrats for the government of the territorial states is an assertion that especially a social historian might assent to without heavy documentation. The magisterial reformers were fortunate to have as their successors men worthy of them. Calvin chose Theodore de Beze, a happy choice. Zwingli was followed by Heinrich Bullinger, a providential event, for Zwingli had not anticipated a change of authoritative venue when the Zurichers set out to battle against tremendous odds on his fateful day. Luther's successor was the least of all surprises, for it naturally proved to be Philipp Melanchthon, his associate through many years of reformatory effort. With respect to humanist education, Melanchthon, Johann Reuchlin's grandnephew, be it remembered, was even more zealous than Luther.

Luther himself never overcame a certain nonchalance and sense of irony about the achievements of worldly culture. In his transition period, when he was doing his *Lectures on Romans,* he wrote in his *Corollarium,* 7.6:

It is not the most learned, who read much and many books, who are the best Christians. For all of their books and all of their knowledge is "letter" and death for the soul. No, they are the best Christians who really with complete free will translate into action what the others read in books and teach to others. But they cannot act in that complete freedom if they do not through the Holy Spirit possess love. Therefore, one must fear for our times when, thanks to the multiplicity of books, men become very learned to be sure, but completely unlearned for Christ.

Subsequently Luther freed himself from some of his monkish inhibitions with respect to classical culture and reached a climax in his humanistic identification in 1519, when for a time he referred to himself as Eleutherios, the liberated one and the liberator. Even then he chose a moniker that could be either humanistic or biblical, for the pun on his own name was surely derived from John 8:31–36 and 1 Corinthians 9:19. Luther never confused the liberal arts, with all that they have to offer for this brief moment of time between the eternities of nontime, with the means of grace. He took an active part—in fact, played the role of initiator and leader—in the reform of his own university in favor of the humanistic liberal arts, for he found that students who came to the theological faculty with a background in dialectic and traditional disciplines were poorly equipped for theological studies. He instituted a curriculum that stressed languages and rhetoric instead.[16] The revised course of studies at Wittenberg, much like the humanistic curriculum introduced a short time thereafter at Louvain, served as a model for many new Protestant foundations as well as for those universities which were reformed along Protestant and humanist lines.[17]

If Luther was important for initiating the drive toward universal compulsory public education for all children and for his role in the reform of university education, his coworker Philipp Melanchthon merits credit for the important innovations in secondary education initiated under Protestantism. The *praeceptor germaniae* wrote an impressive number of tracts on behalf of humanistic studies and had a hand in the founding and development of the secondary schools that became preparatory academies for students destined for the universities or to serve church and state in some lesser capacity.[18] In Germany they were called *gymnasia* and in France developed into the *lycées*. In such orations as his *Oration in Praise of a New School* (1526), Melanchthon waxed eloquent with such passages as this: "For what else brings greater benefits to the whole human race than letters? No art, no work, not, by Hercules, the very fruits born of the earth, not, finally, this sun, which many have believed is the author of life, is as necessary as the knowledge of letters!" He was insistent that the ultimate end that education is to serve is not private virtue alone but the interest of the whole commonwealth. For religion itself to be rightly taught implies as a necessary precondition sound instruction in good letters.

No doubt the educator who most adequately fulfilled Melanchthon's vision of the ideal educator was Johann Sturm of Strasbourg, one of his students. Sturm not only wrote some prolix but nevertheless influential treatises, arguing the case for humanistic studies, he was also the director of one of the Protestant gymnasia, which became a model for many others, especially in the Calvinist areas of France, through the influence of Claude Baduel and of Calvin himself. Sturm influenced England directly through his close relation with Roger Ascham, the renowned English educator and tutor to Queen Elizabeth I, who even named one of his children John Sturm Ascham.[19]

In a second surge of Protestantism, the Genevans picked up the theme of compulsory universal attendance at free public schools. At

Guillaume Farel's insistence the General Council in Geneva met on 21 May 1536, and with uplifted hands the citizens pledged themselves to abandon idolatry, live by the Word of God—and to maintain a school to which all would be obliged to send their children and in which the children of the poor would receive a free education. "Thus," says Eugène Choisy, "was born the free and compulsory public school."[20] Could this claim be a slight Gallic exaggeration? The influence of Calvinist educational ideals in France and the story of the Calvinist academies has not as yet been told in detail and as a unified account, though we now have an excellent monograph on public schools in Renaissance France.[21]

A more obvious example of the impact of Protestantism on education is the case of Scotland, where Calvinism triumphed in Scottish Presbyterianism. John Knox, who pronounced Geneva "the most perfect school of Christ that ever existed on earth," was a prime mover. *The First Book of Discipline* (1560) laid out a plan for an educational system that set the goals, which were not fully realized until the 1890s. It envisioned a national education system in which, first, every church reader was to teach the rudiments of religion and education; second, every town church was to have a schoolmaster to teach Latin grammar; and third, every city, especially towns of the superintendent, was to establish a college of liberal arts with honest stipends for the masters. Then, it declared in words reminiscent of Melanchthon's, at the age of twenty-four the learner must be recovered to serve the church or commonwealth unless he is found to be needed as a reader in his college or university. Calvin had difficulty in setting up four colleges in Geneva, and the Scottish Presbyterians had to keep at the problem constantly. In 1616 they called again for a school in every parish, and eighty years later, 1696, an "Act for Settling Schools" once again attempted to set up a parochial system of education throughout Scotland. At the time of the Reformation in Scotland the revenues of the church, a mere eighty thousand pounds, were to go to the clergy, to education, and to the poor, but there was much resistance on the part of the landed aristocrats and wealthier clansmen. Lord Erskine, for example, refused to subscribe to the *Book of Discipline,* whereupon John Knox exclaimed: "Small wonder, for if the poor, the schools and the ministry of the kirk had its own, his kitchen would lack two-thirds and more of what he now unjustly possesses!"[22]

The nature of the impact of the English Reformation on education is still very much under discussion. Traditionally scholars have held to a positive assessment, and the assertion has been made that the dissolution of the monasteries made available wealth partially reinvested in education. For centuries Edward VI, and his counselors, were considered to be patrons of education; but revisionists assert that of the three hundred

Latin schools that were in existence in 1535, nearly all were swept away under Henry VIII and Edward VI, or plundered and damaged. The Puritans reasserted the necessity for universal compulsory education in England. Robert Cleaver, for example, in 1598 argued for the education of all children so that "they may read the word of God to their comfort and instruction to salvation." Finally, when Johann Amos Comenius in the seventeenth century demanded universal education, writing "let none therefore be excluded unless God denied him sense and intelligence," he was closing the historical circuit, for Comenius was the last senior bishop of the *Unitas fratrum* or Bohemian Brethren, forced into exile by the victory of the Counter-Reformation in Jan Hus's Bohemia.

Not only did the reformers throughout the movement advocate universal compulsory public education, which naturally was to include religious instruction, thus broadening the base of education beyond the Italian humanist ideal of education for the social and intellectual elite, but they reemphasized the need for the liberal arts for the truly educated person. They advocated at the university level the arts or classical curriculum, Plato's royal science. They stressed the need at the secondary level for preparation in the languages and sciences that would make that kind of classical education possible. Luther was enthusiastic: "Education is a divine gift to be seized upon by all." Luther was not reticent about expressing the practical value of the liberal arts. "The fine liberal arts," he wrote, "invented and brought to light by learned and outstanding people—even though those people were heathen—are serviceable and useful to people for this life."[23] When Margrave Georg of Brandenburg undertook the reformation of his territory, he asked Luther for advice on how to proceed. On 18 July 1529 Luther replied that he should establish one or two universities where not only the holy Scripture but also law and all sorts of arts would be taught. "From these schools," he explained, "learned men could be taken to serve as preachers, pastors, secretaries, councilors, and in other capacities for the whole principality. For this purpose the income of monasteries and foundations should be set aside for the purpose of maintaining good, learned men in the schools of honest salaries, viz., two theologians, two jurists, one professor of medicine, one mathematician, and four or five men for logic, rhetoric, etc."[24] Learning cannot be promoted as well in solitude as in a university, he argued, for association with other scholars provides incentive and example. Education, however, provides a source of personal and private pleasure and satisfaction.[25]

That Luther took his Vergil and Plautus into the monastery with him is well known. That he considered the rediscovery of the sciences and languages by the Renaissance humanists as providential, and that he saw the classical and biblical languages as the scabbard in which the word of God is sheathed, is all well known. He advocated the reading of Terence and Plautus in the schools in nonbowdlerized texts, so that the pupils would encounter life realistically. He urged that languages, history, singing, instrumental music, and all branches of mathematics be taught to children. But a somewhat less-known passage spells out Luther's advice on the proper assembling of a good library, including classical works:

> My advice is not to huddle together indiscriminately all sorts of books and to look only to their number and quantity. I would make a selection of books. There is no need of collecting the commentaries of all jurists, the sentences of all theologians, the questions of all philosophers, and the sermons of all monks. In fact, I would throw out such dung and furnish my library with the right sort of books, consulting with scholars as to my choice.
>
> First of all, the library should contain Holy Scripture in Latin, Greek, Hebrew, German, and in whatever other languages it may be available. Then there should be the best and oldest commentaries, if I could find them, in Greek, Hebrew and Latin. Then books that aid us in acquiring the languages, such as the poets and orators, no matter whether heathen or Christian, Greek or Latin, for these are the books from which one must learn grammar. Then should come books about the liberal arts and all the other arts; and finally also books of law and medicine, though here, too, a judicious choice of texts is necessary.
>
> Among the chief books, however, should be chronicles and histories in whatever language they may be had. For they are of wondrous value for understanding and guiding the course of the world, and especially for noting the wonderful works of God.[26]

If Luther took the lead in reforming university education at Wittenberg, his friend Melanchthon helped to develop the regulations that became normative and served as a model for all universities in Germany influenced by the Reformation, the *Leges academiae* of 1545. Melanchthon's orations from his inaugural lecture of 1518, *De corrigendis adolescentiae studiis*, on improving the studies of the young, through such orations as his *Encomium eloquentiae*, and through the addresses delivered at the founding of the new humanistic evangelical academies, consistently decried the spreading depreciation of classical culture, and urged the continued cultivation of the classics. His style of advocacy for the study of the classics was duplicated and in part imitated by other

Protestant reformed educators. Peter Schade (Petrus Mosellanus, 1493–1524) at the University of Leipzig, for example, delivered *An Oration Concerning the Knowledge of Various Languages Which Must Be Esteemed*. Ulrich Zwingli in his treatise *Of the Upbringing and Education of Youth in Good Manners* followed the promptings of his hero Erasmus, as well as some of the discourses of the church fathers on education. A friend of Melanchthon and Luther, Joachim Camerarius (1500–1574), who became a professor at Nuremberg, Tübingen, and Leipzig and a leader in the reform of university education at the latter two places, was a professor of classical Greek and the author of more than 150 treatises. He was an impassioned advocate of classical learning, as is reflected in such addresses as his *Oration on the Study of Good Letters and the Arts and of the Greek and Latin Languages* and his *Oration Concerning the Cultivation of Piety and Virtue by the Studies of Good Arts*. Camerarius himself translated Homer, Theocritus, Demosthenes, Sophocles, Lucian, and many other classical authors. One cannot help but be impressed with the fact that these reformers found the classics to be of value at all levels of education. In his *Instructions for the Visitors* sent to the local parishes to look into conditions, Luther together with his colleagues recommended that in the first division pupils be taught the Lord's Prayer, the creed, Donatus, and Cato; in the second, Aesop, Peter Mosellanus's *Paedagogica*, selections from the *Colloquies* of Erasmus, Terence, Plautus, doctrine, and the Bible; in the third, music, Vergil, Ovid, Cicero, composition, dialectic, rhetoric, and spoken Latin. Luther was innovative as an educator, urging a three-track system. "When the children have become well-versed in grammar," he wrote, "one should select the most gifted and form a third group."[27] He had an eye for the gifted children and their potential for society. "But the exceptional pupils who give promise of becoming skilled teachers, preachers, or holders of other spiritual offices," he insisted, "should be kept at school longer or altogether devoted to a life of study."[28] From the elementary level, then, through the university curriculum, the classics were recommended and used along the lines advocated by the humanist educators.

The Catholic apologist and historian Florimond de Raemond, who wrote at the end of the sixteenth century, argued that Strasbourg rather than Geneva had been the first and foremost gateway for heresy into France. The major reformer there was Martin Bucer, who was keenly interested in pedagogy and considered the school to be the *primarium membrum Ecclesiae*.[29] Not only did Calvin benefit from his two-year experience at Strasbourg, but others did likewise, such as the educator Claude Baduel, who went from there to Geneva and eventually on to become the reformer of education and refounder of the academy in Nîmes. The founding of the *Schola genevensis,* which developed into the University of Geneva, has been called the first external manifestation of the definitive triumph of the Calvinist idea, so that it was from that point that Geneva became the Protestant Rome and began to make universal history.[30] At the school's opening Calvin's fairly brief remarks and Theodore de Beze's *Address at the Solemn Opening of the Academy in Geneva* suggested the way in which the reformers would combine religion with humanistic classical culture. The distribution of the twenty-seven weekly lectures indicates the emphasis given: three on theology, eight on Hebrew, three on Greek ethics, five on Greek orators and poets, three on physics or mathematics, and five on dialectic or rhetoric. The influence of the Genevan academy, fused at times with that of the Haute École of Strasbourg—as in the case of the Académie de Lausanne—was determinative for the many reformed academies in France. By the beginning of the seventeenth century France and the smaller states around it that were later absorbed into the kingdom had eight Reformed academies, quite a sizable number considering the fact that the whole kingdom had only fifteen universities.[31] Moreover, the Genevan academy served as a model for many universities outside of France, for it contributed to the renewal of the Scottish universities of St. Andrews and Edinburgh, it was copied by Heidelberg University in the Palatinate when it turned Calvinist, and it influenced the founding of the University of Leiden in 1575 by William of Orange and of the Herborn Açademy founded in 1584.[32]

One final comment on Prostestantism and humanistic education is in order. Much has been said about the humanist teacher, tutors in a tradition represented in ancient times by such mentors to princes as Seneca and Quintilian, schoolmasters and educational theorists such as Vittorino da Feltre, Pier Paolo Vergerio the Elder, Guarino of Verona, Battista Guarino, or Leonardo Bruni. The reformers added a new dimension to the dignity and esteem of the teacher, for they emphasized the divine vocation of the teacher. Next to preaching the Gospel as a pastor of the whole congregation, the noblest calling was that of teacher to the young.

There was a discrepancy between the reformers" highest idealistic vision of what could be accomplished through church reform and education and their more realistic and at times disappointed expectations. Moreover, it is not surprising that actual achievements in education often fell far short even of their minimal expectations and wishes. Nevertheless, when due allowances are made for failures, education in the Protestant areas of Europe did make tremendous advances. Though it took until the nineteenth century, Scotland and three German territorial estates were the first to eliminate illiteracy, and classical studies flourished in the centuries that followed the Reformation, with Switzerland and Germany becoming the main centers for the study of Hebrew Scripture and language.[33]

*        *        *

The battle of the *viae* in the universities in late medieval times and the struggle between scholasticism and humanism during the Renaissance period have been wildly exaggerated. It is easier to define scholasticism and humanism in the abstract than it is to specify which person followed the one or the other discipline. There were half-scholastic humanists and half-humanist scholastics, and the conflicts at the universities were as often as not about who should be given which chairs than about the intellectual differences involved. It is true that the reformers across the board emphasized the utility of rhetoric and the value of poetry over that of dialectic or logic—a natural reaction to the scholastic preoccupation with syllogistic reasoning and the invasion of theology by the philosophy of Aristotle. To deemphasize the dialectical approach to theology Luther had suspended the university disputations, but then in the early 1530s restored them as having a certain value for training in apologetics and clear thinking. Similarly the young Melanchthon took a humanist line on dialectic. His first edition of the *Loci* or theological commonplaces is free of traditional dialectic, for he is devoted to humanistic rhetoric, follows the Topics of Aristotle rather than the Analytics, and takes his cue from Cicero and Quintilian. However, his later edition of the *Loci,* much larger and longer, is once again replete with technical terms drawn from traditional dialectic. Bearing these qualifications in mind, it is possible to assert that the reformers found rhetoric more in harmony with their scriptural concerns and biblical approach to religious truth.[34]

Luther once wrote to Georg Spalatin that he could see no utility in using dialectic in theology and did not believe that it could be anything else but a hindrance to the Gospel. Luther believed that the Scriptures themselves were fundamentally rhetorical, played on emotion, employed fine figures of speech, used stories to illustrate lessons, and nowhere were composed of labyrinthine syllogisms or dialectical proofs. His emphasis on the *verbum evangelii vocale* or spoken word of the Gospel underlines the affinity he felt between rhetorical expression and the spoken Word as the carrier of the good news of salvation. The church was there before the Gospels were committed to writing. When the good news is preached, confessed, or related, the Word of God is spoken. "The church," he declared, "is a mouth-house, not a pen-house."[35] As for the humanists, dialectic may convince intellectually on a certain plane, but rhetoric moves one to action. Hutten and Luther agreed that what one knows mentally which does not lead one to action, one does not really know.[36] The reformers' preference for rhetoric over dialectic reflects in a way a certain affinity to the humanists' anthropology, at least their definition of man borrowed from the Greeks as *Zoon logikon echon,* a living being having the power of speech.[37] The humanists saw man as less intellective, with the *ratio* in control of reflection and conclusion, than did the main-line scholastics, and the reformers, too, emphasized man as the *totus homo,* man as body, soul, and spirit, not compartmentalized. Man is wholly either rightly related to God or remains alienated from God. The Gospel does not merely change minds, but moves the heart, and for the reformers as for humanist rhetoricians, speaking with synecdoche, the heart stands for the whole man including his emotions. That rhetoric as a discipline became a valuable instrument for Protestant preachers and evangelizers is underlined by the recent studies of Reformation homiletics.[38]

The attempt has been made to relate the reformers' doctrine of *vivificatio* (vivification) of the sinner by the Holy Spirit to the rhetorical art of moving the affections (*ars movendi affectus*). In Luther one encounters many sentences such as "Revive me according to thy word" or "Christ's words not only have the power to teach, but also the power to move within." For Luther Christ is the model teacher and the ultimate orator, who instructs, delights, alarms, moves to action. The line of separation between humanist rhetorical theory and the Protestant use of the spoken Word of the gospel is a very thin one indeed, at least on the surface. The critical difference is, of course, that for the reformers the Word as gospel is the means of grace, whether preached or associated with the Sacrament, through which the Holy Spirit brings man from spiritual death to life. For all the power of the spoken word to move emotions, only the Holy Spirit can work faith and trust in the heart. Words are the external instrument through which internal change affecting the body, soul, and spirit of man is accomplished.

The emphasis on the value of rhetoric remained constant throughout the Reformation period. Melanchthon declared that much ruin happened to the church through the decline of grammar. He wrote a volume on rhetoric and in his oration *Encomium eloquentiae* or *Declamation on the Absolute Necessity of the Art of Speaking to Every Kind of Study* he praised rhetoric for its utility in service to church and state. His rhetoric text, *De rhetorica libri tres* (1519), followed along the lines of Rudolf Agricola's *De inventione,* linking German humanism and the Reformation. At Strasbourg the educator Johann Sturm wrote a variety of rhetorical works, including *De amissa dicendi ratione libri duo* (Lyons, 1542). The phenomenally productive Joachim Camerarius wrote a highly successful *Elementa rhetoricae* (Basel, 1541), published in many editions. Melanchthon had, after all, declared the two aims of classical study to be to stimulate *linguae cultum* and *ad vitae rationes formandas*. It is not possible in brief scope to trace the course of rhetoric through the subsequent course of Protestantism, but perhaps a single instance will suffice to illustrate the point. Laurence Chaderton, the Puritan head of Emmanuel College in Cambridge, made an eloquent statement on the importance of rhetoric and declared that "it teacheth truly to discern proper speeches from those that are tropical and figurative."[39] The tradition persisted well into modern times, including the most venerable of American university curricula and traditions.

A brief comment is called for on poetry as another instrument for moving the *affectus* or feelings of people. As is well known, Luther, the hymnodist, thought that song and music together had near-magical powers that approached those of the Word of God. Calvin's cherishing of Clement Marot (d. 1544), who resided at the court of François I and rewrote selected Psalms into hymn form, is well known. Perhaps he owed his sense of poetry as well as of literary style to Mathurin Cordier, the Rouen priest who had taught him so much about humanism. The savant Camerarius saw fit to write a biography not only of Melanchthon, but also of Eobanus Hessus (1488–1540) sometimes described as the first if not the foremost evangelical poet.

*        *        *

From Petrarch with his newly recovered sense of the past or of his distance from antiquity, through Valla and the Renaissance historians to the beginning of the sixteenth century, history loomed increasingly large in the consciousness of western man. T. S. Eliot referred to culture as "the incarnation of religion," or "lived religion."[40] The Christian religion, like the Jewish, is quintessentially historical. Protestant theology and religious belief alike reemphasized certain dimensions of the faith that had been forgotten or half-forgotten in the church, lost in the Neoplatonic clouds and in the varieties of labyrinthine dialectic. Protestant theology emphasized the concrete, the historical, the experiential rather than the sapiential. History moved into a new prominence in the mind of western man, history as the study of and reflection on past actuality. The Renaissance humanists had moved away from the mere annals and chronicles level of history characteristic of much medieval historical writing, that which was not at the other extreme of metahistory. The humanists stressed the pragmatic value of history, history as philosophy teaching by example. The reformers took up this view of the value of history but pressed on to stress history as evidence of the *locutia* of God, God having spoken, and the quality of *egisse*, God having acted in history. Moreover, on both sides of the theological divide, history became a weapon in controversy, which added to the urgency of its study.

Already at the time of the Leipzig debate in 1519 Luther had occasion to regret his historical deficiencies, for he spent weeks cramming on the history of the early church councils and the patristic writings. In his later years he tried to repair his deficiencies by reading history, with Melanchthon's encouragement. Luther related how even on the journey to Torgau, a time of high political tension between the princes and the emperor, he discussed history with Melanchthon at length. Between 1555 and 1560 Melanchthon gave lectures on world history, and he also edited Johann Carion's *Weltchronik* for publication. A comparison of Luther's various prefaces to historical works such as Caspar Hedio's *Chronicle* (1539) and Johann Cuspinian's *Caesares* (1541) with Melanchthon's *Introduction to the Chronicon* reveals the consanguinity of their views on history. Twenty years after the Leipzig debate Luther remarked that he had at that time not been well versed in history and had attacked the institution of the papacy a priori on the basis of the Scriptures, but that he now understood the correspondence of history with the Scriptures and could attack the papacy a posteriori.[41] The year after the Leipzig debate Luther had been led by his reading of Hutten's edition published by Schöffer of Lorenzo Valla's *De falso credita et ementita Constantini Donatione Declamatio* to conclude that the papacy was the Antichrist. In 1537 he wrote his own sharp attack on the "monstrous fraud" of the Donation of Constantine, using historical arguments.[42]

Luther's deepening interest in history is reflected in the various prefaces he wrote for historical works: Spalatin's edition of consolatory sentences from the lives of the saints, Robert Barnes's lives of the Roman pontiffs, Johann Kymaus's account of the council at Gangro, Galeazzo Capella's (1487–1537) history of the Sforzas, an edition of Jerome's letter to Evangrium, *De potestate,* Georg Major's Lives of the Fathers, a document of Popes Adrian IV and Alexander III against Emperor Frederick Barbarossa. These prefaces reveal that Luther shared the humanists' passion for the entire sweep of history as well as their interest in contemporary history, and that he shared their pragmatic predilection for drawing moral lessons from history. He stressed that histories should not be "cold and dead" but should serve moral ends.[43] In these prefaces, and most explicitly in the foreword to Galeazzo Capella's history of the reign of Francesco II Sforza, duke of Milan, Luther declares histories to be precious for they are nothing else "than a demonstration, recollection, and sign of divine action and judgment, how He upholds, rules, obstructs, prospers, punishes, and honors the world, and especially men, each according to his just desserts, evil or good." [44] In that same year, 1538, Melanchthon published a dialogue on Arminius and Tacitus on the Germans, which may have piqued Luther's interest in the Germans further.[45] In his later years Luther constructed a chronological outline of world history for his own use, the *Supputatio annorum mundi* (1541) or *Reckoning of the Years of the World*.[46] Inspired perhaps by Eusebius, whom he admired, he did three columns of events and dates for eastern, western, and German history and worked out the parallel traditions of biblical history and secular events down to his own day.

Among the ancient historians Luther's favorite was Livy, and he expressed regret that Livy had not written the Carthaginian side of the story as well as that of Rome. Like Celtis, Hutten, and other German humanists, Luther was much preoccupied with Tacitus, fascinated with his picture of the Germans as "noble savages" and of their vices as well. Suetonius and Sallust were also favorites for their accounts of Nero and imperial conspiracies. He was less interested in the Greek historians. In his *Address to the Christian Nobility of the German Nation* (1520), he urged that professorships of history be established in the universities; but there is no evidence that he took concrete steps as a university reformer to found them, for history continued to be subsumed under rhetoric and law.[47]

Various emphases in Luther's view of history are related to those of Renaissance humanism, and some introduce novelty. He was, of course, no philosopher of history, and his convictions developed out of his theological premises. Henri Strohl asserted that Luther's concept of an active and lively God, whose immanence and immediate presence are taken for granted in history, was new to the intellectual scene in the early sixteenth century.[48] "Sic enim ludit sapientia dei in orbe terrarum" ("Thus does the wisdom of God play in the world"), wrote Luther. Humanist historians had been attracted to the role of the individual in history. Luther pressed farther in this direction and developed a fascinating "hero in history" theory that reflected his own view of God. In his Genesis commentary Luther said of God, "Deus est heroicus sine regula!" ("God is a hero without compare!")[49].

In an absolute sense only God can be a true hero, but in a relative sense men, too, can achieve the status of the heroic makers of history. These men of action Luther calls heroes—*Helden, Wundermänner, Wunderleute*—and they serve God's purposes, however unwittingly. He created a "heroic hierarchy" in which he ranked people in accordance with the amount of Spirit in them. The biblical heroes began with Christ and ran the gamut downward from David and Abraham. The secular heroes included many classical figures such as Hercules, Achilles, Agamemnon, Hannibal, and Scipio, Cicero, Cyrus, Themistocles, Alexander, Augustus, Vespasian, and Naaman, with some figures such as Samson bridging religious and secular realms in his heroics. The number of heroes increases as he approaches his own time, but there are naturally also antiheroes. The most problematical are those unlikely people, such as the Virgin Mary, who seem to be chosen for special roles in history precisely because they are unlikely candidates. Here understanding "inner history" or salvation history proves to be the only resolution of the paradox. Luther's commentary on the *Magnificat* is the text that most directly struggles with the problem, explaining that the great *coram deo* are not necessarily the great *coram mundo!*[50] He brings out yet another dimension of the historical problem as seen theologically, the relation of the *deus absconditus* in nature and in history to the *deus revelatus* of Scripture. Luther's treatment of the *Magnificat* makes plain that for him God remains strangely abscondite, hidden in revelation. That he would choose this lowly maiden, of a despised people, from an obscure town in lowly Galilee defies all reason and must nevertheless (*Dennoch!*) be humbly accepted on trust. This dimension of inner history is an affront also to "religion," a rebuff to *theologia gloriae,* the birth of the *theologia crucis!* Luther's theological understanding of history conditioned the historical writing of Protestantism and introduced a dimension foreign to the approach of most humanist historiography.[51]

The German humanists had given a place of special honor to history. In his Heidelberg address Peter Luder praised rhetoric and poetry, but he gave the first place of importance to the study of history. From the fifteenth century to the seventeenth this emphasis on the importance of the study of history for human culture remained a constant in the Protestant tradition. From Felix Fabri, Sigismund Meisterlin, Lorenz Blumenau, Hartmann Schedel, Conrad Celtis, Jacob Wimpheling, Johannes Nauclerus, and other humanists through a long line of Protestant historians the humanist style of historiography prevailed, though the Protestants ever sought to espy the footsteps of God in history. Melanchthon based his *Chronicon* on Carion's simpler version of world history and did revealing prefaces to the histories of Caspar Hedio and Johann Cuspinian. Sebastian Franck's German chronicle of 1538 was intended "to point out the true kernel and main themes of our history." His was not a cultural nationalistic history, but rather an attempt to fill in the void left by the neglect of the Germans by the classical authors, and to respond to the defamation of Italian humanist historians. Notable among those detractors was Marcantonio Coccio (Sabellico), who also attracted Luther's attention. Johann Sleidan wrote on his *Commentarii de statu religionis et rei publicae Germanorum Carolo V. Caesare* until shortly before his death in 1556, a work depicting the German nation at its height under Charles V with a mission to the world, which proved to be an immensely popular theme.[52] Flacius Illyricus used history for apologetic purposes and gave it a distinctly polemical cast in his *Catalogue of the Witnesses of Truth* (1556) and the *Magdeburg Centuries* (1559ff.). These works precipitated a polemical response, of course, by such popular Catholic apologists as Florimond de Raemond and such learned scholars as Cesare Baronio (1538–1607), who spent thirty years gathering unpublished material in Vatican archives for his *Annales ecclesiastici a Christo nato ad annum 1198*, a reply to the *Magdeburg Centuries*. The Protestant historiographical line reaches down to the pragmatic church histories by Veit Ludwig von Seckendorff, a polemicist opposed by the Jesuit Louis Maimbourg, Johann Lorenz Mosheim, and the Helmstedt and Göttingen schools in the seventeenth and eighteenth centuries.

Calvin was too involved in churchmanship to write history himself, so that his treatise on relics is the closest approximation to critical history.[53] He was theologically involved in historical thinking along biblical lines, of course, seeing prefiguration in the Old Testament pointing forward and history moving on to the Eschaton. As he wrote to Charles V, the Reformation was a movement independent of human will so that he must go along with God's design and not oppose it. His successor as leader in Geneva, Theodore de Beze (1517–1605), professor of Greek in Lausanne and pastor and professor in Geneva, did some significant historical work, a *Vie de Calvin*, and an *Histoire ecclésiastique des églises réformées*, more a compilation of materials than an organic or analytical history. The tradition of polemical and pragmatic church histories persisted in the Calvinist tradition, carried along in a cacophonous dialogue with Jesuit and other polemical Catholic historians. In the French cultural milieu the study of legal history contributed to historical consciousness in a fundamental way.[54] It is not possible, nor is it necessary in order to make the point, to relate the ongoing concern with history in the Puritan and Anglican traditions where the debt to the humanist preoccupation with history continued to influence the Protestant intellectual ethos.

*          *          *

The historical interest in antiquity contributed to the continuous and growing interest in and knowledge of Christian antiquity and patristic writing. That Italian humanists were involved in the revival of Christian antiquity, as in the case of Ambrogio Traversari, for example, is coming to be increasingly appreciated. Erasmus, the prince of the northern humanists, of course, devoted his life's work to editions not only of the classics, but of the church fathers as well, such as Jerome (1516), Cyprian (1520), pseudo-Arnobius (1522), Hilary (1523), Ambrose (1527), Augustine (1528), Irenaeus (1526), Chrysostom (1530), Basil (1532), and a number of others. He recorded that his "mind was in such a glow" as he read Jerome! His editions were supplemented by Protestant scholars, and new Lives of the Fathers and patristic studies continued to expand during the subsequent century. One needs perhaps to be reminded that the church fathers in rethinking the universe in Christian terms incorporated much of the cultural good of the classical world in an overarching harmony. Their attitude was selectively but overwhelmingly positive toward the achievements of classical philosophy, history, and literature. Julian's effort to forbid Christians access to and the right to cite from classical authors failed. Gregory Nazianzus exulted: "By this measure Julian showed himself in advance to be conquered. He wished to overcome the Christians in a spiritual struggle, but robbed them in advance of their weapons. That is as though a champion were to challenge all men to a duel except the strong. He could, to be sure, forbid the Christians to speak Greek, but he could not keep them from speaking the truth."

Neither did the hostility of Tertullian to the classics prevail. Calling Plato a "grocery store of all heretics" and the philosophers the "patriarchs of heresy," Tertullian blamed them for the gnostic heresy and denied that they were inspired by an *anima naturaliter christiana*. In *De praescriptione*, 6, he decried the influence of Aristotle on Christian theology: "Unhappy Aristotle, who introduced dialectic for the benefit of heresy, the great master in building up and tearing down, ambiguous in its sentences, forced in its conjectures, ruthless in its arguments; a burden for itself, it discourses on everything so as not to have discoursed on anything." The more positive attitude toward the classics prevailed in Justin Martyr, Basil, Clement of Alexandria, Origen, Augustine, and a near patristic consensus. Justin Martyr argued in the *Apologia*, 1.46, "If Christ is the word of God himself, then he was that from eternity; then the Logos was eternal; then the Jewish conception of God was the absolute Reason from which also Greek wisdom came, then also Heraclitus and Socrates were Christians." His views were reminiscent of Philo's metaphor of the spoiling of the Egyptians for the appropriation of pagan cultural goods. Basil in his treatise "To the Youth, on How One Should Read the Classics" argued along the same lines as Plato, Plutarch, or

Seneca as to the utility of expounding the old poets. In the *Stromata,* 1.5, Clement of Alexandria wrote: "Philosophy educated the Greek people for Christ just as the law did the Hebrews. Thus philosophy was a forerunner insofar as it prepared the way for him who would be enlightened by Christ. It is a schoolmaster for Christ." Origen, whose standing as an orthodox churchman has been rehabilitated by the Roman Catholic church only in our own day, could write in the second *praefatio* of his *De principiis:* "That alone is to be accepted as truth which differs in no respect from ecclesiastical and apostolic tradition," and yet plead with his readers: "I beseech you then to draw from Greek philosophy such things as are capable of being encyclic or preparatory studies to Christianity, and from geometry and astronomy such things as will be useful for the exposition of holy Scriptures, or order that what the sons of the philosophers say about geometry, music, grammar, rhetoric, and astronomy, that they are handmaidens of philosophy, we may say of philosophy itself in relation to Christianity." Finally, Augustine himself in his *De doctrina christiana* declared most boldly: "If perchance those who are called philosophers have spoken things true and agreeable to our faith, especially the Platonists, not only are they not to be feared, but they should be appropriated from them as from unjust possessors for our own use."

It has perhaps been useful to rehearse some representative samples of patristic attitudes toward the classics, because the Fathers are considerably less known to today's readers than they were to the literate population of the Renaissance and Reformation period. That Petrarch recommended the Fathers as models and "princes" to be read and emulated in their way of life comes as no surprise to all who have come to realize that the Renaissance was not a revival of pagan antiquity, but had its deeply traditional Christian dimensions.[55] Typical of the magisterial reformers' appreciation of the church fathers was that of Philipp Melanchthon, whose understanding of the life of the one holy church through the centuries underlined the continuity in the line of great teachers from the prophets to the evangelists, apostles, church fathers, spokesmen of truth in the medieval period, and those in the latter days of humanism and reform. He articulated this idea with passion in his funeral oration over Luther: "After the apostles comes a long line, inferior, indeed, but distinguished by the divine attestations: Polycarp, Irenaeus, Gregory of Neocaesarea, Basil, Augustine, Prosper, Maximus, Hugo, Bernard, Tauler and others. And though these later times have been less fruitful, yet God has always preserved a remnant; and that a more splendid light of the gospel has been kindled by the voice of Luther cannot be denied."[56] John Calvin and other reformers achieved a knowledge of the church fathers that benefited from the emphases of Christian humanism but went well beyond the reach of the Italian humanists in that area of ancient thought.[57] The *testimonia patrum* continued to be valued all through the period, in the sacramental debates of Anglicans and Puritans, for example. Along with their utility as witnesses to the positions held in the early church, the Fathers provided reassurance to the reformers that the solution of the basic problem need not be religion or culture, religion without culture, or culture without religion, but religion and culture, each in its proper sphere and acceptably related to the other. As Paul Tillich once expressed his views: "Religion is the substance of culture and culture the form of religion."[58] Although the proposition is debatable for our times, unless one denatures religion with neologisms and idealist substitutes for historical content, as Tillich was wont to do, the statement applies to the early modern period of European history, when humanism and Protestantism flowed together to form the mainstream of higher culture.

\*    \*    \*

The problem of continuity or change is one of the perennial subjects on which historians exercise their ingenuity. When the discussion becomes tedious, as is often the case, readers are no doubt moved to agree with Lord Acton, when he wrote: "Better one great man than a dozen immaculate historians." Such problems are best discussed in a concrete historical setting such as the present one, the continuity of humanism through the Reformation period and the change that it underwent as it became allied with religious and sectarian interests. This discussion has necessarily been more suggestive than definitive, for a full discussion or a real history of the past actuality involved would require volumes. It has not been possible, for example, to include even in passing the radical Reformation, which is unfortunate for a number of reasons. Some of the Anabaptist leaders, particularly the Zurich group at the outset and some of those in the Netherlands as well, were educated men not only schooled in university learning, but "spiritualized" under the influence of Erasmianism. One thinks of Conrad Grebel, for example. Moreover, a good number of the spiritualists and evangelical humanists, a better term than "evangelical rationalists," were by way of humanist learning and overall educational achievement a match for the magisterial reformers. One thinks of Servet or Castellio by way of example. Nevertheless, when the dust had settled by the end of the sixteenth century over 90 percent of all Protestants—a conservative estimate, for perhaps 98 percent would be more accurate—were members of the four major confessions: Lutheran, Reformed, Calvinist, or Anglican. Anabaptism had nearly died out by the end of the century, to be reawakened in another manifestation in the century following. Though small in numbers, the radical reformers across the spectrum from the sectarian groups to the mystical and idealistic individual thinkers had an influence on the modern world of outsized proportions, and classical or humanist ideas made their contribution also there.

One extreme position on the matter of humanism and Protestantism is held by those who have seen the two as being in an essentially antithetical position, analogous to those who see largely a contrast between Renaissance and Reformation. A gross caricature of this position is the book of H. A. Enno van Gelder of the Royal Netherlands Academy of Sciences, *The Two Reformations in the 16th Century: A Study of the Religious Aspects and Consequences of Renaissance and Humanism* (The Hague, 1961). Van Gelder describes a second reformation, which he calls the major Reformation. The latter developed under the influence of the Renaissance and humanism, which caused a wider and deeper gap between the groups of those who were or who were not affected by it, since it was here a question of two completely different views of religion in general. These two views were the theological one and the philosophically ethical one, a Christian one compared with a classical one, an older compared with a more modern view. Van Gelder concludes that the origin of this major Reformation is to be found in Italy in the fifteenth century, that it extended in the sixteenth century over the whole of Europe and was destined, more than the other religious Reformation, to dominate cultural life in these regions. What is usually indicated as a middle path, preserving a happy mean between Catholicism and the Reformation, was in reality a thoroughly specific view of the Christian religion, a third path deviating more from the medieval point of view and leading more directly to the civilization of the modern period than Protestantism did. Van Gelder is not entirely mistaken, and yet his model does not fit the historical reality very conveniently.

The Reformation was a more immediately powerful historical force than was the Renaissance and its doctrines a more radical and powerful solvent of medieval orthodoxy than was Christian humanism. Humanism was partially subsumed under the religious drive of the Reformation and thereafter moved along with powerful sectarian streams.[59] But thanks to the magisterial reformers, who not only bestowed an *imprimatur* upon it, but understood the promotion of higher culture, too, as a *negotium cum Deo* (cooperative undertaking with God) humanism through approbation and amalgamation with religious reform received a broader, deeper, and longer-lasting impact upon modern European and western culture. As an intellectual movement humanism enjoyed an

impressive continuity and tremendous influence on modern cultural developments, only very rarely independently of religious forces. The idea
of discontinuity, a sharp break or disjunction between Renaissance humanism and Reformation religion is a historiographical convenience that
reinforces unfortunate secular and modernist prejudices at the expense
of historical veracity. The *Carmina Burana* in the twelfth century expressed nostalgia for the olden days when "florebat olim studium"
("study formerly flourished"). One can understand why men of the "late
Reformation" or those living through the seventeenth-century crises
would look back to the golden age of the Renaissance and the heroic age
of the Reformation and regret their fate at being born in their own times.
Actually the knowledge of the three philosophies expressed in three languages, Latin, Greek and Hebrew, was much more highly developed later
in the century than when northern humanism made its first amateurish
linguistic and literary efforts.

There was undoubtedly a certain loss of verve and spontaneity in
humanistic writings as they became increasingly humanistic studies of
the schools, but that loss was not nearly as total as some suppose. Cicero's definition of the best life—that for the learned and erudite man to
live is to think—gained the agreement of an ever-growing number of
people, as humanist ideals moved out from the courts and universities to
a broader spectrum of the middle-class population. It is difficult to con-
ceive of the Elizabethan age in England, of Shakespeare, without both
the advantage of classical inheritance mediated through the humanism
of a Protestant century and the intense earnestness about religious questions introduced and transmitted by Protestantism. If, as some have argued, the age of Elizabeth was the real English Renaissance, that French
humanism after the traumas of the religious wars culminated in the
French Enlightenment, and that the eighteenth-century Weimar culture
of the Germanies represented the culmination of the civilization of old
Europe, before the disintegrating forces of industrialization, democrati-
zation, and mass societies characteristic of the modern world set in, then
the amalgam of humanism and Protestantism may well be both appreciated and celebrated.

The Protestants through their educational programs, as was true
also of the Catholics, provided for the preservation of humanist culture
and for its continuity. Even the resurgence of Aristotelian dialectic in the
theological and philosophical faculties of the universities did not lead to
the suppression of the characteristic humanist intellectual interests and
disciplines: rhetoric, poetry, drama, moral philosophy, history, Platonism, and natural philosophy or science. Many external or social factors
can be adduced to explain the pattern of dispersion and the varying

fortunes of humanist culture during the three centuries that followed that first union of humanism and Protestantism. Commercial activity is said to have shifted away from central Europe, Italy, and the empire to the Atlantic seaboard, though there has been some revision regarding the extent of decline in the old centers of culture such as Venice. Political fortunes varied; as particularism grew more powerful in the empire, France became involved in civil wars, England underwent its revolutions, and the duels for hegemony between England and Spain or England and France, the rise of the Netherlands, all had an enormous impact on the cultural developments of the time. But despite all of the economic, political, and social pressures, the cultural alliance of humanism and Protestantism remained a powerful and constructive force in the life of western man.

It is not possible to elaborate here on the points of theological tension regarding anthropology and theology proper, between humanism and evangelical theology.[60] But it is interesting to note that the very year in which Luther made his stand—1521—saw the birth of "evangelical humanism" with the publication of Melanchthon's *Loci communes rerum theologicarum*. The *Loci* created for theology a new scholarly method that was quickly acknowledged and widely accepted, combining rhetoric and biblical content. He constantly reworked this volume, much as Calvin continuously revised the *Institutes,* creating a more elaborate statement but never departing from the humanist rhetorical premises. It became programmatic for theology and a statement approving the humanist approach to learning and culture, and its influence lasted for much more than a century.[61] The concern of the reformers, just as that of most humanists, was for church, commonwealth, and culture.

NOTES

1. W. Dilthey, "Auffassung und Analyse des Menschen im 15. und 16. Jahrhundert," in his *Gesammelte Schriften* (Stuttgart, 1940), 2:39–42, 53–63; E. Troeltsch, "Renaissance und Reformation," in his *Gesammelte Schriften* (Tübingen, 1925), 4:261–96.

2. P. Joachimsen, "Der Humanismus und die Entwicklung des deutschen Geistes," *Deutsche Vierteljahrsschrift für Literaturwissenschaft und Geistesgeschichte* 8 (1930): 419–80. The distinguished biographer of Vadian, the reformer of St. Gallen, declared Joachimsen's definition given here as the first clear formulation of the concept: W. Näf, "Aus der Forschung zur Geschichte des deutschen Humanismus," *Schweizer Beiträge zur Allgemeinen Geschichte* 2 (1944): 214.

3. R. Weiss, *The Spread of Italian Humanism* (London, 1964), addresses the problem of diffusion.

4. E. Bernstein, *German Humanism* (Boston, 1983), provides the very best

overview available in English. *German Humanism and the Reformation,* ed. R. P. Becker (New York, 1982), supplies most interesting texts in English. The best analysis in brief compass is that of E. Meuthen, "Charakter und Tendenzen der deutschen Humanisten," in *Säkulare Aspekte der Reformationszeit,* ed. H. Angermeier (Munich, 1983), 217–66.

5. On the matter of the spread of diffusion of Italian Renaissance humanism to the rest of Europe north and west of the Alps, see the *Festschrift* in honor of P. O. Kristeller, *Itinerarium Italicum: The Profile of the Italian Renaissance in the Mirror of Its European Transformations,* ed. H. A. Oberman and T. A. Brady, Jr. (Leiden, 1975). Also of special value are the essays by E. F. Jacob, "Christian Humanism," in *Europe in the Late Middle Ages,* ed. J. Hale et al. (London, 1965), 437–65; and C. Trinkaus, "Humanism, Religion, Society: Concepts and Motivations of Some Recent Studies," *Renaissance Quarterly* 29 (1976): 676–713. See also W. Kölmel, *Aspekte des Humanismus* (Westfallen, 1981), but not without reading the most acerbic review by R. N. Watkins, *Renaissance Quarterly* 35 (1982): 593–95. See also L. W. Spitz, "Humanismus/Humanismusforschung," in *Theologische Realencyklopädie,* ed. M. Greschat (Berlin, 1986), 15, *Lieferung* 5, 639–61.

6. *Weimar Ausgabe, Briefwechsel* (Weimar, 1933), no. 596, 3:50, lines 23–25. Luther's reference to the Renaissance revival of language and literature was originally published in a collection of letters addressed to the first Protestant poet—and some hold the greatest—of the first generation, Eoban Koch (Eobanus Hessus), *De non contemnendis studiis humanoribus futuro theologo maxime necessariis. . . .*

7. The most careful examination of Zwingli's move through Christian humanism to his discovery of St. Paul in Romans and his transformation beyond Erasmianism into a dedication to reform is that of W. H. Neuser, *Die reformatorische Wende bei Zwingli* (Neukirchen-Vluyn, 1977), 38–74.

8. See W. Näf's great volume: *Vadian und seine Stadt St. Gallen,* vol. 1, *Humanist in Wien* (St. Gallen, 1944), and vol. 2, *Bürgermeister und Reformator von St. Gallen* (St. Gallen, 1957). Vadian's statue to this day dominates the marketplace in St. Gallen.

9. There is naturally very little scholarly agreement regarding the significance of Calvin's *Commentary on Seneca's De clementia.* To reach one's own opinion one should see the translation with the introduction and notes by F. L. Battles and A. M. Hugo (Leiden, 1969), published for the Renaissance Society of America.

10. G. H. Williams, *The Radical Reformation* (Philadelphia, 1962), 93: "Grebel, a radical leader from a patrician family, was a humanist of refinement."

11. Luther, "To the Councilmen of all Cities in Germany that They Establish and Maintain Christian Schools," *Luther's Works,* 45, *The Christian in Society,* vol. 2, ed. W. I. Brandt (Philadelphia, 1962), 369–70, trans. A. T. W. Steinhaeuser, rev. W. I. Brandt.

12. Ibid., 350.

13. *D. Martin Luthers Werke. Kritische Gesamtausgabe. Briefwechsel* (Weimar,

1933), 3:276, lines 17–19. K. Holl, "Die Kulturbedeutung der Reformation," in *Gesammelte Aufsätze zur Kirchengeschichte,* vol. 1, *Luther* (Tübingen, 1932), 518: "Jedermann musste mindestens dahin gebracht werden, dass er die Bibel zu lesen und selbständig Belehrung aus ihr zu schöpfen vermochte." In his book, *The Doctrines of the Great Educators* (London, 1937), R. R. Rush argues that it was only on religious grounds that the Protestant faith in the universal education of the people could at that time be based. See also *A History of Religious Educators,* ed. E. L. Towns (Grand Rapids, MI, 1975).

14. The old classic work by F. V. N. Painter is still worth reading, *Luther on Education* (St. Louis, 1889). The most recent excellent work containing relevant essays is *Luther and Learning: The Wittenberg University Luther Symposium,* ed. M. J. Harran (Selinsgrove, PA, 1985). The citation from *A Sermon on Keeping Children in School* is to be found in *Luther's Works,* 46, *The Christian in Society,* vol. 3, ed. R. Schultz (Philadelphia, 1967), 249, in another translation.

15. *Luther's Works,* 45, 355–56.

16. H. Junghans, *Der junge Luther und die Humanisten* (Weimar, 1984), discusses the humanists in Luther's environment, his relation to humanists, the rhetorical observations in his *Dictata super Psalterium,* and his emphasis on the Word of God. The bibliography is very thorough. See also Junghans's two studies, "Der Einfluss des Humanismus auf Luthers Entwicklung bis 1518," *Luther Jahrbuch* 37 (1970): 37–101; and "Luther als Bibelhumanist," *Luther. Zeitschrift der Luther-Gesellschaft,* 1 (1982): 1–9. See also the excellent work of J. H. Overfield, *Humanism and Scholasticism in Late Medieval Germany* (Princeton, 1984), and *Die Humanisten in ihrer politischen und sozialen Umwelt,* ed. O. Herding and R. Stupperich (Bonn, 1976).

17. See *University and Reformation: Lectures from the University of Copenhagen Symposium,* ed. L. Grane (Leiden, 1981).

18. W. Maurer analyzes Melanchthon as a humanist, *Der junge Melanchthon,* 2 vols. (Göttingen, 1967–69). See also P. Fraenkel and M. Greschat, *Zwanzig Jahre Melanchthonstudium* (Geneva, 1967).

19. For Sturm and his school, see A. Schindling, *Humanistische Hochschule und Freie Reichsstadt. Gymnasium und Akademie in Strassburg* (Wiesbaden, 1977).

20. J. T. McNeill, *The History and Character of Calvinism* (New York, 1954), 135. See also Q. Breen, *John Calvin: A Study in French Humanism* (Grand Rapids, MI, 2d ed. 1968); and A. Biéler, *The Social Humanism of Calvin* (Richmond, VA, 1968).

21. G. Huppert, *Public Schools in Renaissance France* (Urbana, IL, 1984).

22. F. Farman, *Landmarks in the History of Education* (New York, 1952), 147.

23. *Weimar Ausgabe. Schriften,* 48:29; trans. in *What Luther Says: An Anthology,* ed. and trans. E. M. Plass (St. Louis, 1959), 1:450.

24. Ibid., *Briefwechsel* 5: 120.

25. Ibid., *Schriften,* 30^II: 565.

26. Ibid., 15: 51f. Scholars have in recent years given more attention to the role of libraries as a tool for recapturing the mindset of the literate classes in early modern times. See, for example, G. Strauss, "The Mental World of a Saxon Pastor," in *Reformation Principle and Practice: Essays in Honor of Arthur Geoffrey Dickens,* ed. P. N. Brooks (London, 1980), 157–70; B. Moeller, "Die öffentlichen Bibliotheken in Deutschland und die Reformation," summarized in *University and Reformation,* ed. Grane, 32–34, and in full in a publication of the Göttingen Akademie der Wissenschaften under the title "Die Entstehung der Ratsbibliotheken in Deutschland."

27. *Weimar Ausgabe. Schriften* 26: 239, lines 29ff.

28. Ibid. 15: 47, line 13.

29. See E.-W. Kohls, *Die Schule bei Martin Bucer in ihrem Verhältnis zu Kirche und Obrigkeit* (Heidelberg, 1963).

30. C. Borgeaud, *Histoire de l'Université de Genève,* vol. 1, *L'Académie de Calvin (1559–1798)* (Geneva, 1900), 81.

31. R. Stauffer, "Calvinism and the Universities," in *University and Reformation,* ed. Grane, 76–90, 87.

32. Ibid., 76–77.

33. See J. M. Kittelson, "Luther on Education for Ordination," *Lutheran Theological Seminary Bulletin,* 65 (1985): 27–44.

34. R. Lorenz, *Die unvollendete Befreiung vom Nominalismus. Martin Luther und die Grenzen hermeneutischer Theologie bei Gerhard Ebeling* (Gütersloh, 1973).

35. *Weimar Ausgabe. Schriften,* 10ᴵᴵ: 2, line 48.

36. Ibid., *Tischreden,* 2, no. 2199a. Luther argues the value of logic and rhetoric for fitting people for life.

37. See the article by L. W. Spitz, "Luther, Humanism and the Word," *Lutheran Theological Seminary Bulletin* 65 (1985): 3–26, and n. 15 for bibliography on rhetoric and the Word. See also Q. Breen, "John Calvin and the Rhetorical Tradition," in his *Christianity and Humanism: Studies in the History of Ideas,* ed. N. P. Ross (Grand Rapids, MI, 1968), 107–29; and B. Girardin, *Rhétorique et théologique:. Calvin et le commentairè de l'Epître aux Romains* (Paris, 1979).

38. U. Nembach, *Predigt des Evangeliums: Luther als Prediger, Pädagoge und Rhetor* (Neukirchen-Vluyn, 1972), 117–74, on Luther's homiletical method measured against rhetorical principles and the advice of Quintilian on counseling people. See also M. Doerne, "Luther und die Predigt," *Luther. Mitteilungen der Luthergesellschaft* 22 (1940): 36–77.

39. M. Curtis, *Oxford and Cambridge in Transition, 1558–1642* (Oxford, 1959), 206. Regrettably the whole Pierre de la Ramée (Peter Ramus) polemic and its place in French Protestantism must be passed over here.

40. T. S. Eliot, *Notes Towards the Definition of Culture* (London, 1948), 15, 33, 67–82.

41. *Weimar Ausgabe. Schriften,* 50: 5. See J. M. Headley, *Luther's View of Church History* (New Haven, 1963), 51. See the chapter in E. B. Fryde,

*Humanism and Renaissance Historiography* (London, 1983), "The Revival of a 'Scientific' and Erudite Historiography in the Earlier Renaissance," 3–31.

42. *Einer aus den hohen Artikeln des päpstlichen Glaubens, genannt Donatio Constantini.*

43. *Weimar Ausgabe. Schriften,* 43: 418.

44. Ibid. 50, 383–85; trans. in *Luther's Works,* 34 (Philadelphia, 1960), 275–78.

45. Philipp Melanchthon, *Arminius dialogus Huttenicus, continens res arminii in Germania gestas. P. Cornellii Taciti, de moribus et populis Germaniae libellus. Adiecta est brevis interpretatio appellatiorum partium Germaniae* (Wittenberg, 1938); *Corpus Reformatorum,* ed. C. G. Bretschneider and H. E. Bindseil (Halle, 1851), 17: 611–38 at 611.

46. *Supputatio annorum mundi. 1541, 1545, Weimar Ausgabe. Schriften* 52¹: 22–184, 679.

47. W. Elert, *Morphologie des Luthertums* (Munich, 1958), 1:426, n. 2, discusses the question as to whether or not Luther and then Melanchthon wished to establish chairs for historians, which would have been an advance over Italian universities. See D. K. Bauer, *Die Wittenberger Universitätstheologie und die Anfänge der deutschen Reformation* (Tübingen, 1928), 80–98: "Die Bereicherung der Wittenberger Theologie durch die Geschichte." The pioneering work still of value was E. Schäfer, *Luther als Kirchenhistoriker* (Gütersloh, 1897).

48. H. Strohl, *L'évolution religieuse de Luther* (Strasbourg, 1922), 161ff.

49. *Luther's Works,* 13, 172: God himself has "the fear-inspiring, stern, strict spirit of a hero." For Calvin's understanding of history, see H. Berger, *Calvins Geschichtsauffassung* (Zurich, 1955).

50. H. W. Beyer, "Gott und die Geschichte nach Luthers Auslegung des *Magnificat,*" *Luther Jahrbuch* 21 (1939): 110–34, writing on God and history in Luther's exegesis of the *Magnificat,* properly distinguished between "outer history," dealing with external goods or riches, wisdom, and power; and "inner history" or history within history, the real actuality that transpires inside a person such as Mary, a relation between God and the human being. But he does not bring out the dimension that did not escape Luther, namely, the importance to world history of the "inner history" also for the "external history" of mankind.

51. See the two excellent studies of faith and history in Luther: H.-W. Krumwiede, *Glaube und Geschichte in der Theologie Luthers. Zur Entstehung des geschichtlichen Denkens in Deutschland* (Göttingen, 1952); and H. Zahrnt, *Luther deutet Geschichte. Erfolg und Misserfolg im Licht des Evangeliums* (Munich, 1952).

52. In 1761 Heinrich Schütz wrote a critical commentary on the many works that were based on Sleidan's *opus* or even tangentially related to it. See W. Kögl, *Studien zur Reichsgeschichtsschreibung deutscher Humanisten* (Vienna, 1972), dissertation, 16–18, n. 37.

53. John Calvin, *Three French Treatises,* ed. F. M. Higman (London, 1970), 46, refers to a work on the beginnings of critical history in the Middle Ages: A. Lefranc, "Le traité des reliques de Guibert de Nogent, et les commencements de la critique historique au Moyen Âge," in *Études d'histoire du Moyen Âge, dédiées à Gabriel Monod* (Paris, 1896), 285–306. I owe this reference to Bruce Tolley.

54. See D. R. Kelley, *Foundations of Modern Historical Scholarship: Language, Law, and History in the French Renaissance* (New York, 1970).

55. See, for example, Petrarch's *De otio religioso,* in which he points to the Fathers as models, and the excellent analysis by C. Trinkaus, "Humanist Treatises on the Status of the Religious: Petrarch, Salutati, Valla," *Studies in the Renaissance* 11 (1964): 7–45, at 16, reprinted in his *The Scope of Renaissance Humanism* (Ann Arbor, MI, 1983), 195–236; and in his *In Our Image and Likeness: Humanity and Divinity in Italian Humanist Thought* (Chicago, 1970), 2:651–62, at 655–60. On the other hand, some humanists such as Ermolao Barbaro the Younger resisted the idea of directing their energies toward the Fathers: *Epistolae, orationes, carmina,* ed. V. Branca (Florence, 1943), ep. 72, 1:92. Luther once commented in the *Table Talks* that there is far more wisdom in Aesop than in Jerome!

56. Philipp Melanchthon, "Funeral Oration Over Luther," in *The Protestant Reformation,* ed. L. W. Spitz (Englewood Cliffs, NJ, 1966), 70. On Melanchthon's impressive knowledge of patristic authors, see P. Fraenkel, *Testimonia Patrum: The Function of Patristic Argument in the Theology of Philipp Melanchthon* (Geneva, 1961).

57. A major work on Calvin and the church fathers awaits its author, but an exemplary monograph is B. Warfield, *Calvin and Augustine* (Philadelphia, 1956). See also L. Nixon, *John Calvin's Teachings on Human Reason* (New York, 1963). H. R. Van Til, *The Calvinistic Concept of Culture* (Grand Rapids, MI, 1959), includes such challenging essays as "Augustine, the Philosopher of Spiritual Antithesis and Cultural Transformation." The scholarly world awaits with keen anticipation the publication of W. Bouwsma's Calvin studies, for his mastery of Renaissance culture, keen perception of the Stoic and Augustinian elements in humanist thought, and deep appreciation of Calvin's theological wisdom will lend great authority to his analysis.

58. P. Tillich, *The Protestant Era* (Chicago, 1938), 57.

59. On the continuity of humanism in confessional alliance with Lutheranism, see M. P. Fleischer, *Späthumanismus in Schlesien. Ausgewählte Aufsätze* (Munich, 1984). Also of interest is H. Schöffler, *Deutsches Geistesleben zwischen Reformation und Aufklärung: Von Martin Opitz zu Christian Wolff* (Frankfurt am Main, 3d ed. 1974).

60. The theological differences and varying emphases between Christian humanism and evangelical theology with respect to anthropology and theology proper are spelled out by E. Wolf, "Reformatorische Botschaft und Humanismus," in *Studien zur Geschichte und Theologie der Reformation. Festschrift für Ernst Bizer,* ed. L. Abramowski and J. F. G. Goeters (Neukirchen, 1969), 97–119.

61. W. Maurer, "Melanchthons *Loci communes* von 1521 als wissenschaftliche Programmschrift," *Luther Jahrbuch* 27 (1960): 1–50. Joachimsen, "Humanismus und die Entwicklung," 475, said of the *Loci communes:* "Das Ergebnis ist eine Theorie der inneren Erfahrung, die ganz auf die reformatorische abgestellt ist und sich anheischig macht, diese Erfahrung in eine logische Deduktion von allgemein gültigem Charakter zu verwandeln."

# X

## *Luther's Importance for Anthropological Realism*

Such an elaborate and kindly introduction as that which Professor John Headley has just given me is designed less for the benefit of the audience than of the speaker. It is intended to prevent a last-minute failure of nerve on his part in the presence of such a distinguished group of scholars. When I consider us *Wandervögel* of the academic world on the Chatauqua circuit the lines of Hilaire Belloc come to mind: "We circulate throughout the Land / The second rate, and second hand!" The English humorist Potter defined the art of lecturemanship as the art of getting people to take notes even when you don't know what you are talking about. There is many a man, says the pundit, who does not need an introduction but who could certainly stand some good conclusions, so I may turn to Professor Headley later in the hour for further assistance.

Jacob Burckhardt had a point when he refused to "hawk" his lectures beyond the gates of Basel, for if a lecture is what it should be, it takes a man's energy. Dour Burckhardt disapproved of academic conferences where scholars "come to sniff each other out" like dogs in a pack. Hopefully he would at least approve of today's enterprise, for we shall play with ideas through the centuries in a style for which he set a brilliant precedent.

Though anthropological realism may suggest *African Genesis* or *The Naked Ape*, the fact is that Luther will perform more like a highbrow Alley Oop who lived in the sixteenth century, but had an important impact upon the nineteenth-

## Luther's Importance

and twentieth-century anthropological realists. This undertaking is difficult, for the *Einflusz* problem is one of the most difficult in intellectual history. Renaissance scholars are well aware of the pitfalls, for they recall the way in which Petrarch and Dante were exploited as symbols of cultural nationalism and natural superiority in the *risorgimento* and Fascist periods of Italian history. The outsized men of history may live again (*vir redivivens*) as their ideas, understood as they intended, stir up the minds of a later generation. Their ideas may be misunderstood with regrettable results, or by a *felix culpa* may be misinterpreted with fortunate results. Their thought may be vulgarized, understood on a lower level or transferred to a different context in such a way as to do violence to their inner essence. These are the hazards involved in the study of influence.

A single example will serve as a caveat. Socrates, a figure relatively neglected or sublimated during the Renaissance, or perhaps merely overshadowed by his great pupil Plato, received singular attention during the nineteenth century. But how different were the responses to his thought and reaction to his person! Hegel found Socrates to be subversive, for he not only cultivated subjectivity at the expense of the objective nature of truth, but he undermined the authority of the state by challenging the presuppositions upon which its concept of law depends. Jacob Burckhardt thought Socrates pitiful in that, as an exercise in futility, he actually tried to improve men. Nietzsche criticized Socrates for introducing a questioning criticality, a compunction for self-analysis which sapped the natural instincts and spontaneity of man. Sören Kierkegaard came closest to a positive evaluation of Socrates, appreciative above all of his contribution to the "concept of irony." Like Socrates, Luther, too, nearly became all things to all men. He was less remote, spoke to issues directly and with great urgency, but his influence emerged nevertheless in varying modalities. As in the case of Socrates the "reception" depended in no small part on the receivers. What games people play!

### 1. *Luther and Idealism*

Luther's impact upon modern thought was strangely bifurcated. On the one hand, he figured as a major influence upon and as a cultural symbol for the *Aufklärung* and German idealism. On the other hand, his religious thought and specifically his anthropology was of enormous importance as source and resource of anthropological realism. This dual thrust resulted less from opposing elements in his thought than from the fact that different aspects of his theology came into play as the modern intellectual configuration shifted and contributed to the change.

Luther belonged to the top-level tradition of Christian rationalism in the sense that he considered man's reason to be the most wondrous and majestic of God's creations. Even after the fall of man, reason remains a kind of god, a beautiful light, a sun, and a divine thing to rule over everything in this world. Some of Luther's expressions in praise of natural reason impress a man of our times as extravagant, unreal, and even naive. For in a day in which men understand all too well the obstacles to rational behavior and the dark forces of the subconscious, they are less apt to laud the powers of reason. In a post-Freudian, highly empirical, almost anti-intellectual society, men are less likely to rely with any great sense of security upon reason even in temporal things. With Pareto's reminders in *Mind and Society* how many decisions are made and actions taken simply in response to "derivations and residues," in accordance with learned or inherited responses, fully cushioned by rationalizations, men are a bit cautious about extolling the powers of *ratio* as Luther did. For Luther natural reason, as God created it, was king of creation.

Nevertheless, for Luther reason was not absolute; in matters having to do with God and man's relation to Him reason is blind and a false guide. It cannot show the way or find the path that leads from sin and death to righteousness and life. It remains in darkness. In religion the fond conceit of reason sets itself up as judge over what can and cannot be God's will. This "rationalism" of arrogant reason is inevitably inclined toward moralism. As the devil's harlot it tempts man to rely upon his own good works as though he were in a position to make demands upon God rather than acknowledging that he is in every respect a debtor to God. Compared with the light of God's Word in religion man's reason is but a candle in the sun. In commenting upon Psalm 119:105 ("Thy word is a lamp unto my feet, and a light unto my path"), Luther wrote:

> Reason, too, is a light, and a beautiful light. Yet it cannot point to or find the way or the foot that will lead from sin and death to righteousness and life, but remains in darkness. Just as our tallow and wax candles do not illuminate heaven or earth but the narrow nooks in houses. The sun, however, sheds light on heaven, earth, and everything. In just that way God's Word is the true sun which gives us an eternal day in which to live and to be happy. Such a Word is given richly and sweetly in the Psalms. Blessed is the man who delights in it and gladly sees this light, for it shines gladly. But moles and bats, that is, the world, do not like it.[1]

Luther uses the word "reason" in yet a third way as "regenerate reason." The man whose trust (*fiducia*) in God has been awakened by the Holy Spirit has a new, alive, hopeful outlook on life. His perspective on life is radically altered because of his new relationship to God. Reason for such a man is the "best instrument" for ordering a life of love for his fellow man in accordance with the Word and will of God. In the *Table Talks* Luther explained in clear and simple words how regenerate reason serves the man of faith.

> Before faith and the knowledge of God reason is darkness in divine matters, but through faith it is turned into a light in the believer and serves piety as an excellent instrument. For just as all natural endowments serve to further impiety in the godless, so they serve to further salvation in the godly. An eloquent tongue promotes faith; reason makes speech clear, and everything helps faith forward. Reason receives life from faith; it is killed by it and brought back to life.[2]

Enlightened reason does not have the capacity to discover new truths in natural theology independently of revelation.

Rather, it orders life willingly in accordance with the requirements of the Word, in the footsteps of the Master. The *ratio theologica* is the reason of the *homo theologicus*. Here, too, the formula *simul justus et peccator* applies; for the regenerate reason, too, is at one and the same time justified, considered holy in God's eyes, while remaining imperfect, deficient in sanctification as a present reality.

Luther's use of the term "reason" was complex and his expressions must always be read in context. Nor can it be asserted that he was always careful to define and distinguish, but was perfectly capable in rhetorical outbursts of mixing various uses of the term together in the same passage. Reason can be used in an instrumental sense as the ability to draw logical conclusions. It can be considered a cultural factor in the secular realm. It can serve as a principle or criterion of a total world view in a philosophical or natural-religion sense.[3] Luther's main concern, however, was theological, that "the thing itself be distinguished from its abuse." A distinguished Reformation scholar, Brian Gerrish, has in a recent book spelled out the three-fold distinction which Luther made between natural reason ruling within its own proper domain of worldly matters, natural reason illegitimately carrying over into the domain of spiritual matters certain propositions derived from the secular realm (e.g., the virtues are rewarded), and regenerate reason working legitimately within the domain of spiritual matters by humbly adopting presuppositions derived solely from the "Word."

The natural reason which deals with mundane affairs is, as Luther's language often seems to suggest, a 'practical reason,' approaching at times our own notion of "common sense"; and to this extent natural reason, even within its proper boundaries, may appear to be a material as well as a formal conception, since it implies the adoption of certain concrete attitudes of mind. When the natural reason trespasses on the domain of spiritual matters, it is unambiguously a concrete, material attitude of the unregenerate man; here we have seen, *ratio* is a certain definite *opinio*. The regenerate reason, finally, is in the main a formal conception; reason here is a tool, an instrument, an organ. But since regenerate reason tends to coalesce with the notion of faith, in this context also *ratio* may sometimes take into itself a certain material content.4

It is quite obvious that Luther normally employs synecdoche, using reason for the whole man. Thus natural reason is really the reason of natural man and regenerate reason is actually the reason of regenerate man. Beyond this he frequently does hypostatize reason in a substantial and material sense, while at other times it retains a purely formal aspect.

In terms of the impact of Luther's distinctively Christian rationalism upon enlightenment and idealist thought, it was fortuitous that Luther associated an appeal to reason with the demands of conscience in his dramatic address at the Diet of Worms:

Since then your serene majesty and your lordships seek a simple answer, I will give it in this manner, neither horned nor toothed: Unless I am convinced by the testimony of the Scriptures or by clear reason (for I do not trust either in the pope or in councils alone, since it is well known that they have often erred and contradicted themselves), I am bound by the Scriptures I have quoted and my conscience is captive to the Word of God. I cannot and I will not retract anything, since it is neither safe nor right to go against conscience.5

The *ratio evidens* to which Luther appeals seen in context as well as in the light of other references is the reason of regenerate man informed, as is his conscience, by the Word of God.6 In earlier centuries, however, the *ratio* in this famous reply was understood to mean magisterial reason, just as conscience was understood to be the subjective sensitivity of an autonomous individual asserting his freedom from heteronomous controls. Luther as the protagonist of reason, conscience, and freedom—this was the Luther who appealed to the men of the Enlightenment and the transcendental idealist philosophers.

There is a discernible difference in the way in which the English and French Enlightenment intellectuals and the German *Aufklärung* thinkers related to Luther's Reformation. Hume and Gibbon were contemptuous of the theological concern of the reformers. It is a curious development to find that in England many of the Victorians in the next century were critical of "Luther's rationalism and Erastianism."[7] Voltaire despised the Reformation as a "quarrel of monks" and sneered that "one cannot read without a mixture of contempt and pity the manner in which Luther treats all his opponents and particularly the Pope." The men of the *Aufklärung* were critical of Luther, but by no means contemptuous. They were critical of the medieval remains in his thought, but they were appreciative of his battle for the freedom of conscience, which for them was the essence of the Reformation. In Luther the gold of religious and ethical autonomy was still mixed with slag. They considered further purification and the completion of what Luther had begun to be their task. It was no mere theatrical gesture, therefore, or act of hypocrisy, when the men of the *Aufklärung* constantly called upon the name of Luther, for they considered him to be the leader of the first attack wave, while they constituted the phalanx of hoplites which would win the final victory of reason over superstition and the forces of darkness. "Reformation" became one of their favorite words, "reformation" as freedom and "reformation" as cultural reform and resurgence. They staged "reformations" of dogmatics, jurisprudence, orthography, the book trade, hymnbooks, and of Lutheranism itself. The majestic Goethe in the *Frankfurter gelehrten Anzeigen* in 1772 mocked the "iconoclastic Zeal" of the "enlightened reformers" of his day. Hamann commented ironically on the "epidemic reformation swindle" and the fact that "reformation" was such a favorite word in the *Aufklärung*.[8]

German transcendental idealism inherited certain basic ways of interpreting Luther's importance for humanity and higher culture. The idealists in general valued his contribution to the full development of individual personality and the "deepest inwardness," the critical role of private conscience and conscientiousness, and the advancement of liberty. The great Luther scholar Karl Holl, in an essay on the cultural

X

significance of the Reformation, commended the positive influence which Luther had upon Kant and Fichte, who, in the
spirit of Luther, deepened the Leibnizian idea of personality.⁹
Along with the concept of an unconditioned law, he argued,
they received the concept of sin.

In advancing from the narrowness of naturalism to the
breadth of an ethical understanding of man, Fichte believed
that he had arrived at the essence of man's reality. The nub
of his anthropology is presented in his *Die Bestimmung des
Menschen* which he published in 1800. Dealing with doubt,
knowledge, and faith, Fichte struggled with the question of
the doubt which the human self feels about its own reality
when confronted by the external world, a doubt with which
the naturalistic or "scientific" point of view threatens to over-
whelm man. He wished to assert the validity of the knowledge
of self and faith as the action by which the self affirms itself as
the sole reality. What is real is the knowing mind of man,
which gives to the external world such reality as it has. Through
the exercise of freedom the self determines what it is. The determination of the self does not lie in knowledge alone, but in
action in accordance with that knowledge. In the third book,
entitled "Faith," Fichte exhorted: "'Your determination does
not lie in mere knowledge but in action in accordance with
your knowledge: this message rings aloud in my inmost soul as
soon as for a moment I collect myself and look into myself.
You exist not merely for the purpose of idle self-contemplation
or brooding over pious feelings. No, you are there to act; your
action and your action alone decides your worth."¹⁰ Man becomes sure of the world surrounding him because it is the
sphere and the object of his dutiful action, his ethical conduct.
Man does not act because he knows, but he knows because he
is called to act—as a member of two orders of life, the spiritual
in which man prevails by the effect of a pure will and the sensual in which he participates through individual actions.

The heart of Fichte's anthropology is that man through an
act of will transcends the limitation of natural determination
to the sphere of his true freedom. Fichte's philosophy has been

glorified as the "'philosophy of freedom," for central to his thought is man in his moral aspect and therefore in the light of human freedom. Fichte's absolute subjectivism and argument for the autarchy of man are subject to a variety of serious criticisms from both naturalistic and theological positions, but a critique is not the purpose here. The point to be made is that when Fichte said, "One decision and I rise above nature," he was generally understood to be expressing the same confidence as Luther in personal liberty and the right to make ethical decisions in the world of action. Man has the ability to tear himself free from what he is by nature and to raise himself into the freedom of the spirit. The intellectual world of idealism took Fichte's message in the same sense as the literary world understood the popular poet and dramatist Schiller. When Schiller emboldened Western man with his slogan "Du kannst, denn du sollst" (You can, for you should), he, too, was believed to be reflecting Luther's view of man's moral essence. The individual freed from heteronomous controls of an ecclesiastical or regimental kind must make and is able to make free moral decisions. In June, 1790, Fichte wrote to his bride: "I shall always be called a heretic for that is certain . . . I know very well how I think; I am neither a Lutheran nor Reformed, but a Christian. And if I must choose, since a Christian congregation really exists nowhere, that congregation is dearest to me where one can think the most freely and live most tolerantly."[11] In spite of this protest of his independence, Fichte was indebted to the reformers as a theologian and in no small part because of the influence of Kant, his great master. On July 4, 1791, Fichte as a thirty-year-old theologian met Kant face to face in Königsberg. Under Kant's protection and influence he wrote his first book, *Critique of All Revelation*, which Kant later publicly spoke of as a "bad book."

Kant, as the most brilliant exponent of high idealism, was known as "the Protestant philosopher." On first examination, his transcendental criticism of the traditional metaphysical arguments concerning the soul, the universe, and God seemed diametrically opposed to Luther's theology, arriving at an agnostic position so far as human understanding as a basis for a priori synthetic judgments is concerned. But what Kant took away in his *Critique of Pure Reason* he sought to restore in his *Critique of Practical Reason*. The moral law is supreme and the individual is more certain of the moral imperative "I ought" than of any other fact of experience. Consideration of pleasure or of interest must give way to the demands of conscience, for nothing can gainsay the voice of conscience, although the individual is free to obey or to disobey the universal and necessary moral law. The moral law implies the existence of a Law Giver. Christ was the exemplification of the highest moral perfection. Historical faith is the vehicle of rational faith.

Energetic efforts have been devoted to analyzing the dogmatic sources of Kant's religious thought.[12] He seems to have known among Luther's writings only the small catechism. Nevertheless, a generic relationship between Kant and Luther's thought is discernible. Both were opposed to speculative religious metaphysics, for they agreed that precise scientific statements about God and transcendent reality were not possible for speculative reason. For Kant the postulates of practical reason, for Luther the faith experience were firmer grounds for establishing religious reality. Although Kant did not know the depth of sin and radical evil as the primal experience of man (*Urerlebnis*) as did Luther, he acknowledged the feeling of guilt. An ethic of intention was common to both; but for Kant the law, the duty to love the neighbor as oneself, informed and quickened conscience; for Luther the God of justice stood back of that law. The God of mercy and forgiveness meant nothing to Kant and everything to Luther.

In view of the fundamental differences between Luther and Kant it is fascinating to observe how the younger idealists loved to link Kant with the Luther of *On the Liberty of the Christian Man*. They were seen as partners in the promotion of freedom, education, liberalism, the sovereignty of conscience, and idealism. Whoever wanted to be a Christian had to be an idealist. Even in later scholarship, Kant was frequently described as having successfully put Luther's ethical religious feeling upon the foundation of reason.[13] The way in which later scholars, including such great minds as Karl Holl and Wilhelm Dilthey, analyzed Luther's thought using Kantian concepts provides a further demonstration of how in the idealist tradition Kant and Luther were linked together as intellectually of the some genre.

For nearly four decades the transcendental idealists were concerned about the relationship of Kant's phenomenal and the noumenal world. They shared a common metaphysical vision of the ultimate unity of thought and being. In the mystery of feeling, in an encounter with the divine, or in speculative thought, man transcends himself to understand, experience, or feel the ultimate unity of reality. This vision served for a time as an epistemological ground for the knowledge of God and served as a support for religion.[14]

Hegel in particular emerged as a patron and protector of religion. He went beyond Kant's critique not by a strict epistemological analysis but on the basis of his own metaphysical vision of the identity of thought and being, idea and reality. Hegel's early theological writings were heavily influenced by Luther. In his maturity he still considered himself to be a Christian thinker and a Lutheran. He was throughout many of his major works preoccupied with Christian themes. The process of reconciliation for Hegel was essentially the process in which the implicit unity of the divine and human natures becomes explicit. This process must take place in rational consciousness; thought and knowledge and the reconciling work of Christ must be understood in those terms. The unity of the divine and human natures is known insofar as it is embodied in the real immediate event of the incarnation. This unity is known ". . . in no other way than for this unity to manifest itself in a completely temporal, perfectly common appearance in the world in one of these men—in this man, who at the same time becomes known as the divine Idea, not as a teacher, not only as a higher being in general, but as the highest, as God's Son."[15]

## Luther's Importance

Hegel stressed repeatedly that the historical incarnation was essential for man to gain an immediate certainty of the truth. If truth is "to become certain to men, God must appear in the flesh in the world." In writing on the incarnation Hegel reiterated that it is man's destiny to know the identity of his own nature with God. This Hegelian reading of Christianity set the stage for a first-rate tragicomic production, the left-wing Hegelian inversion which precipitated a major crisis in religious thought. Proceeding from Hegel's system, with its many affinities to Luther's theology, Bruno Bauer, David Friedrich Strauss, Ludwig Feuerbach, and Karl Marx turned against it and confronted Christianity with a modern challenge more fundamental than had the philosophers of the Enlightenment. The nineteenth-century "realists" identified Christianity closely with idealism. Belief in God was associated with the realm of the spirit, the supersensory, supernatural realm. This is the meaning of Nietzsche's devastating thrust: "Christentum ist Platonismus fürs Volk."

*Lutherus redivivus!* Intellectual history at this point unveiled one of Clio's little surprises, for at this very critical juncture in Western thought Luther's theology became a central focus of discussion. Luther scholasticized, moralized, catechetically domesticated, tamed, could be employed by the idealists for their purposes. But there was another side to Luther available for exploitation. Aldous Huxley once referred to the reformers as "sweaty realists" in their view of man. Realism in the nineteenth-century context meant thinking anthropologically. Man is the central reality, and through the understanding of man, man is enabled to interpret the realities of nature and religion around him, for they are not beyond him. Man does not begin with the world outside or a system of thought provided objectively by reason. Through an understanding of man, as his experience has shaped him, man as the prime reality comes to understand what it is necessary for him to understand about reality. The battle between idealism and realism has long since been decided in favor of realism, anthropological realism and not that of mere empiricism. Luther participated in the operation.[16] Erasmus once said of Luther: "God has given us a radical physician!"

## II. *Luther's Anthropological Realism*

As the key witness in the case of the anthropological realists against the idealists' spiritualization of Christianity, Luther's understanding of man is of critical importance. Luther, much more so than Calvin or Zwingli, linked together the *cognitio dei et hominis*. Man is a central concern for Luther precisely because man is a central concern for God. God is the highest concern for Luther just as he should be for everyman. The God who loves man and whom man can in turn love is known in the God-man, Christ, alone. The incarnation is the focus of both theology and anthropology.

It will be useful to rehearse the basic elements of Luther's view of man before exploring in greater detail two points of crucial importance for the nineteenth-century realists' reading of Luther, namely, his giving priority to experience and being over thought and action and his intense concentration upon God in the human Jesus. While Luther's anthropology is in the main-line Western Christian tradition, formally acknowledging, for example, the body/soul dichotomy, immortality of the soul, man's rationality, and the like, he deviates in both emphasis and substance on important matters. There is no mistaking the ways in which he differs from the Renaissance Platonic idealization of man. The humanists, rationalists, and idealists agreed in their own times that Luther had a "too dark and pessimistic view of man."

Luther did not feel comfortable operating with the dichotomy of a body/soul division or the trichotomy of body/soul/spirit. He was too thoroughly Hebraic, thanks to his intense study of the Old Testament, to read Saint Paul through Hellenistic eyes. He objected strenuously to Erasmus' exegesis of Saint Paul's epistles interpreting "spirit" as that ethereal side of man which draws him upward toward God while "flesh" is the bodily side of man that keeps him earthbound. "In my temerity," Luther declared, "I do not distinguish body, soul, and spirit, but present the whole man unto God." Just as he controverted the humanist Erasmus, so he directed a major apologetic against the scholastic Latomus on the very question of sin and righteousness in man.[17] Against this "sophist," who had defended the University of Louvain's condemnation of Luther's theology, Luther explained his position that man in the flesh is entirely sinner and that man in the spirit is the man of faith who is entirely forgiven by God. The man of faith is at the same time justified and righteous in God's eyes, while in reality he remains spotted with sin, as he and his neighbor know *(simul justus et peccator)*. In the course of his argument Luther comments as follows upon Romans 7:21 ("I find then a law, that, when I would do good, evil is present with me"): "For it is no one else," Luther explains, "who wishes to do the good than he to whom the evil clings. The spiritual man wishes to do the good as a whole man *(totus homo)* but the fleshly man hangs on to him as not entirely a whole man *(minus totus)*."[18]

This emphasis upon the *totus homo* is in line with Luther's exegesis in his *Lectures on Romans,* where in commenting on Romans 7:25 ("Therefore I with the mind serve the law of God, but with the flesh, the law of sin"): "This is the most telling passage of all," Luther writes. "Notice that one and the same man serves both the law of God and the law of sin, that he is righteous and at the same time he sins. He does not say: 'My mind serves the law of God,' nor 'My flesh serves the law of sin,' but he says, 'I, this whole man *(totus homo)*, this person here, stand in this double servitude.' He therefore gives thanks that he serves the law of God and he asks for mercy that he serves the law of sin."[19] This concept of man as a single unity, a *totus homo,* was an important development away from the Platonic conception of the soul as prisoner in the body, so common to the medieval ascetic and Renaissance metaphysical doctrine of man.

Secondly, Luther's realism is evident in his stress upon sin as man's primal experience *(Urerlebnis)*. He deepened the conception of sin by describing it as the root condition of man, a state of unspirituality in which man is estranged from God. Sin is not a simple single transgression of the law, but a state of indifference and hostility to God which makes even "good" works, which in structure conform to the law, sinful.[20] It is not merely a matter of deficiencies or individual flaws, as Horace described man in the *Satires* (I, iii, 68): "No one is born free from vices." It is a total, all-comprehending state of the total man. Man's natural condition is to be self-loving, self-seeking, self-serving, for man is by nature turned in upon himself (*incurvatus in se*).[21] Man in this condition is not a mere automaton, one who against his will or with no will at all lives out his life condemned to an inherited state of spiritual death. Luther distinguishes *necessitas* and *coactio*, for while man is necessarily as natural man engulfed in this condition of unspirituality, he is not coerced. His is a religious necessity, not a metaphysical determinism. His predicament is more desperate precisely because he willingly lives out his life in an abyss of self-centeredness in which he does not wish to love God above all things or his neighbor as much as himself. The enslaved will (*servum arbitrium*) remains *arbitrium, voluntas*, will. Man in this condition remains man with a potentiality for spiritual liberation. He is not, says Luther to Erasmus, a goose or a stone. He is a person fitted (*aptus*) with a disposition (*dispositiva qualitas*) and passive aptitude (*passiva aptitudo*) for a spiritual awakening or rebirth. The man in whom the Holy Spirit works faith in God is thereby given a freed will (*arbitrium liberatum*), a will which can desire and perform acts of love pleasing to Him, for they are done in a state of spiritual life. Royal liberty (*libertas regia*) is the happy possession of men who have come to trust in God.

Thirdly, Luther's realism is evident in his assessment of man's anxiety in living toward death. Man, spiritually dead, lives in a constant state of anxiety (*angst*), for away from God life is meaningless and empty. Man thrown into the world lives out his life toward death in dread. "Indeed," Luther commented in 1519, "death is on all sides, whatever they [men] see and feel. They are stretched out between life and death:

## Luther's Importance

They dread death; they do not have life."[22] That is the message of his *Sermon on the Preparation for Death*, 1519,[23] and of the somber *Invocavit* sermons preached during Lent in 1522.[24] His theme in the discourse on Psalm 90, delivered in 1534, was "In the midst of life we are in death" (*Media vita in morte sumus*). Man is afflicted with calamities, miseries, brevity of life, torments of afflicted conscience, desperation, temporal and eternal death. The author of the psalm is a "most Moses Moses, that is, a severe minister of death, of the wrath of God and of sin."[25] Life taken as a whole is like a besieged city surrounded on all sides by death. Man lives constantly in a "border situation" (*Grenzsituation—a sein zum Tode*) and on the razor's edge between life and death. Life's very transiency is its most disconcerting feature.

Luther saw the reality of death with clear eyes. A close brush with death had triggered his decision to enter the monastery, and he never forgot that death is man's nextdoor neighbor. The world is on a daily and continuous march toward death. The death of an animal, the death of a heathen, the death of a Christian are three kinds of death. The death of a Christian is the most poignant, for beyond the physical end of life, the question of the man's relation to God comes into play. There is no greater power on earth than death, for the world itself will one day come to an end.[26]

Luther's anthropological realism was stark realism. Also Christian existence is subjected to constant shattering. The theologian is made by living, dying, being damned, not by understanding, reading, or speculating.[27] The believer is sustained by a theology of hope. Everyone must do his own believing, Luther constantly asserts, just as everyone must do his own dying.

Fourthly, Luther's anthropological realism is evident in the interior theological context in that he insists upon the reality of faith as experienced and the priority of suffering to being, of being to thought and action. Luther abhorred speculation in theology and stressed the immediate, concrete, and personal dimension of religion. The most important words in religion, he once observed, are the personal pronouns, the "I," "Thou," and "he," my brother. His theology was marked by a strange dynamic concreteness. Faith is *fiducia* or trust in God, not *credulitas* or credulous acceptance of particular propositions about God. His writings are studded with statements that to trust is instantaneously to possess the object of faith. "As you believe, so you have!" he exclaimed.[28] "You have as much as you believe (on account of the promise of Christ)," he repeated time and again.[29] At times he seems almost to hypostatize faith. Faith is the *vita cordis*, the very life of the heart, and a *vita experimentalis*, the experimental or experiential life of the spiritual man.

The relationship of faith and experience is a subtle question related directly to the problem of being preceding action. On the one hand, Luther divorces faith from subjective human feelings and assumptions. Faith is invisible and hidden, even insensible.[30] Faith lives in darkness and may even be described as "blind."[31] Luther exerts every effort to direct faith to an objective ground in the Word outside the self's own feelings, which so readily deceive and are subject to sudden change. On the other hand, Luther does not really wish to divorce faith from experience, but wants merely to underline the fact that the experience of faith is an experience of another kind. It is the work of the Holy Spirit and should not be confused with emotions or mystical experiences of any other kind. Where a man has experienced something of God's goodness and love, where holy joy fills the heart, there the Holy Spirit has been the teacher.[32] The experience of faith in this sense is truly an experience which contrasts markedly from the experience of natural man who lives without the awakening of faith.[33] The content of faith, the Word, may be objectively understood, but must be subjectively apprehended. The story of Redemption remains speculation, theory, mere idle historical knowledge, unless a man believes that his cause was involved and that all was done for him.

Not only is the experience of struggle and the release of faith essential for the believer, but is indispensable to the the-

ologian, if he is to understand his subject. "Experience alone
makes the theologian," Luther reiterated.³⁴ The true theologian
is not the one who knows great things and teaches many things,
but the one who lives in a holy and "theological" way.³⁵ Luther's scholastic master Gabriel Biel had asserted that "reading [Scriptures], meditation and prayer" make the theologian.³⁶
Already in 1513 Luther substituted *experientia* as the third
component in the right formula. In the preface to the first part
of his German writing of 1539 Luther coined his oft-cited
definition: "Prayer, meditation, and the experience of struggle
[*tentatio*] make a theologian." The way in which a theologian
understands the Word depends upon his prior disposition.³⁷

The power and persuasive thrust of Luther's theology was
a result of a subtle fusion of his own personal religious experience and the product of his scientific labors as an exegete.
Interestingly enough he at times associates personal experience
with conscience, while the Scriptures serve as both source and
norm of truth. In 1530 he wrote in a *Rhapsodia* about justification:

> The miracles of my teaching are experiences, which I prefer to
> the resurrection of the dead. . . . Since this experience is more cer-
> tain than life itself, it is not a deceiving sign for me, but serves
> instead of many thousands of miracles, since it agrees with the
> Scriptures in all things. You have two most faithful and invincible
> witnesses, namely Scripture and conscience, which is experience.
> For conscience is a thousand witnesses, Scripture an infinite num-
> ber of witnesses.³⁸

Theology is real and concrete, involving the whole man.
It is therefore not to be confused with the abstractions of metaphysics or scholastic distinctions. This drive away from an in-
tellectualized scholastic theology toward a theology of experience emerged powerfully in his crucial *Lectures on Romans*
of the years 1515-1516. In a striking passage Luther hits at the
religiously irrelevant word games of the scholastic theologians
and presses for an understanding of man's deeper needs. His
reflections on Romans 8:19 ("For the expectation of the crea-

ture waits for the revelation of the sons of God") are to this point:

The apostle philosophizes and thinks about the things of the world in another way than the philosophers and metaphysicians do, and he understands them differently from the way they do. For the philosophers are so deeply engaged in studying the present state of things that they explore only what and of what kind they are, but the apostle turns our attention away from the consideration of things as they are now, and from what they are as to essence and accidents, and directs us to regard them in terms of what they will be. He does not speak of the "essence" of the creature, and of the way it "operates," or of its "action" or "inaction," and "motion," but, using a new and strange theological word, he speaks of "the expectation of the creature." By virtue of the fact that his soul has the power of hearing the creature waiting, he no longer directs his inquiry toward the creature as such but to what it waits for. But alas, how deeply and painfully we are caught up in categories and quiddities, and how many foolish opinions befog us in metaphysics! When shall we learn to see that we waste so much precious time with such useless studies and neglect better ones?[39]

In commenting on Romans 8 he carries on his argument according to the *analogia fidei* rather than the *analogia entis*:

Would it, then, not be sheer madness on our part to sing the praises of philosophy? For is it not so that while we think highly of the science of the essences and actions and inactions of things, the things themselves loath their essences and their actions and inactions and groan under them? . . . The apostle is therefore right when, in Colossians 2:8, he speaks up against philosophy and says: "Beware lest any man cheat you by philosophy and vain deceit according to the tradition of man." If the·apostle had wanted to understand any philosophy as something good and useful, he certainly would not have condemned it so unequivocally! We conclude, therefore, that anyone who searches into the essences and functionings of the creatures rather than into their sighings and earnest expectations is certainly foolish and blind. He does not know that also the creatures are created for an end. This passage shows this clearly enough.[40]

## Luther's Importance

Luther's powerful emphasis upon experience, the soul-struggle and the effect of God's grace upon man through the gift of faith was central to his whole theology. His basic ground of objection to scholastic theology was the failure of the doctors to deal adequately with sin and grace. They do not weigh the seriousness of sin as heavily as they should, acting as though sin could be removed by the flick of an eyelash, as darkness is by light. Unlike the fathers such as Augustine and Ambrose, the scholastics follow Aristotle instead of Scriptures. In his *Nicomachean Ethics* Aristotle bases sinfulness and righteousness and the extent of their actualization on what a person does.[41] Luther declares that it is God's grace that makes a man righteous, grace understood as a benignity, when God forgives a man his sin at a particular time and place. The man thus justified in God's eyes does good works. Luther explained this point with epigrammatic brevity and force:

Indeed, neither the works which precede nor those which follow make a man righteous—how much less the works of the law. Not those which precede, for they only prepare a man for justification; nor those which follow, for they require that justification be already accomplished. For we are not made righteous by doing righteous deeds. But we do righteous deeds because we are righteous. Therefore grace alone *(sola gratia)* justifies.[42]

Such was the religious ground upon which he objected to Erasmus' way of interpreting *Romans*, as though Saint Paul with *law* meant merely the ceremonial laws. In a letter to Spalatin, October 19, 1516, dating from the time of his preoccupation with *Romans*, Luther explained that Erasmus was wrong in his interpretation, for it is not as Aristotle thought that we are made righteous by doing righteous deeds, but by having become and being righteous we do righteous deeds. It is "first necessary that the person be changed, then the works." "I do this," Luther concluded, "for the sake of theology and the salvation of the brethren."[43] In fact, Luther emphasized this very crucial idea that man's condition determines the spiritual quality of his thought and action in his exegesis of

Romans 1:17, which he frequently described as the "great breakthrough" for his Pauline theology.[44] In asserting that "the good tree brings forth good fruit," in that sequence, Luther could, of course, appeal to authority higher than his own. In his commentary on Ecclesiastes Luther carried this argument over to the case of the skeptic. His despair, Luther stressed, is not the result of the vanity of all things in themselves or merely the transiency of life. Rather, it is the result of the anterior condition of the inner man which determines his negative perception of the world outside.

Luther spelled out the sequence of events in the marginal gloss to Romans 12:1 following, it is curious to note, the Aristotelian *progressio a non esse ad esse*, the progression from nonbeing to being, which is familiar also from scholastic theology. Luther explains:

So far the apostle has spoken about what it means to become a new man, and he has described the new birth which bestows the new being (John 3:3ff). But now he speaks about the works of the new birth; one who has not yet become a new man presumes that he is doing them—but in vain. For being comes before doing, but being-acted-upon comes even before being. Hence, becoming, being, acting, follow one another.[45]

In the corollary Luther gave this sequence of five stages in natural growth according to Aristotle (privation, matter, form, operation, and passion) a theological application. In the case of the Spirit, he explained, not-being is something without a name, and man in sin; becoming is justification; being is righteousness; acting is to act and live righteously; to be acted upon is to be made perfect and complete. These five are somehow always in motion in man.[46] "I do not have vision," Luther argued, "because I see, but because I have vision therefore I see."[47] Neither the external piety of a priest nor the human imitations by a monkey make them essentially righteous human beings.[48]

The initiative in man's justification lies with God. The

Holy Spirit changes the will or "inner spirit" of man. One cannot answer the question why it is I who is *re*born anymore than one can answer the question why it is I who was born. Luther cites Augustine's *De Spiritu et Litera* to establish that it is God himself who gives what he commands of man.49 "Now, this sublime power that is in us is not, so the apostle asserts," writes Luther, "a product of our own, but it must be sought for from God. This is why it is *shed abroad* and in no way brought forth from us or originated by us. And thus *by the Holy Spirit*; it is not acquired by moral effort and habit as the moral virtues are. *In our hearts*, i.e., deep down in the innermost parts of the heart and not on the surface of the heart in the way foam lies on water."50 Such is the divine initiative!

A fifth and final aspect of Luther's anthropological realism is his stress upon the hypostatic union of the divine and human natures in Christ. His stress upon Christ's humanity and the communication of divine attributes to Christ's human nature sets him apart not only from humanism and scholasticism but, in emphasis, even somewhat from the other magisterial reformers. His exalted view of the human nature of Christ brought into focus God's unbounded love for man. Luther's sacramental teaching of the ubiquity of Christ and real presence is dependent upon his high Athanasian Christology. Moreover, Christ was proof of what man as man could have been, were it not for the fall of man. He followed Saint Paul in seeing Adam as the archetype of fallen man and Christ as the archetype of perfect man. All this is known and very well understood by those who know and understand Luther at all. But it is necessary to raise a special question at this point, for it became a vital issue at a later time. Luther was impressed, as was Calvin after him, with man's ingenious ability to create religions. Man's resourcefulness is unlimited in making gods of all sorts and of seeing in those idols the very qualities which man would most like to see there. With respect to the High God, man projects upon God the terror or love which in reality is in his own heart. Luther was no religionist and an old German monograph is entitled *Luther's Criticism of All Religion*![51] How does one determine whether when a natural man to whom the gospel story is mere history sees God in Christ beckoning him, he is not merely projecting his own exalted view of man upon a divine Christ?

As a man believes, he has! Luther plunges ahead without dreaming or caring what use would be made of his words. In his exposition of the first commandment in the *Large Catechism*: "How often I have said that the trust and faith of the heart alone make both God and idol. If the faith and the trust is right, then your God is right, and, contrariwise, where the trust is false and wrong, there the right God is also not present." "So it is," says Luther, "with our faith and unbelief: whoever portrays Him in his heart as merciful or angry, sweet or sour, he has Him just that way."[52] One of Luther's least guarded expressions reads: "Just as I think about God, so he is to me!"[53] Such statements occur in his scholarly as well as in his popular writing. In his key exegetical work, the *Commentary on Romans*, for example, he offers his corollary to Romans 3:5 ("But if our unrighteousness commend the righteousness of God, what shall we say? Is God unrighteous who taketh vengeance? [I speak as a man]"):

God is mutable to the highest degree. This is obvious, because one can justify and judge him, according to Psalm 18, 26: "With the elect thou wilt be elect, and with the perverse thou wilt be perverted." For as everyone is in himself, so God is to him objectively. If he is righteous, God is righteous; if he is pure, God is pure; if he is unjust, God is unjust, etc. So he will appear as unjust to those who are eternally damned, but to the righteous, as righteous, and so he is in himself. This change, however, is extrinsic. This is plainly implied in the word "Thou wilt be judged." For as God is judged only from the outside, on man's part, so he is also justified only from the outside. Hence, one can necessarily say only extrinsically of God: "That thou mayest be justified."[54]

Luther's intention is perfectly clear, but his vulnerability to exploitation is all too obvious from our vantage point.

## Luther's Importance

### III. *Anthropological Realism and Luther*

The great Protestant philosopher of the *Aufklärung*, Immanuel Kant, in his work *Religion Within the Limits of Reason Alone* (1793) introduced a thought "concerning the universal subjective ground of the religious illusion" which seemed to subvert the independent authenticity of revelation and thereby to anticipate the realists' criticism of religion. He wrote:

> Anthropomorphism scarcely to be avoided by men in the theoretical representation of God and His being, but yet harmless enough (so long as it does not influence concepts of duty), is highly dangerous in connection with our practical relation to His will, and even for our morality; for here *we create a God for ourselves*, and we create Him in the form in which we believe we shall be able most easily to win Him over to our advantage and ourselves escape from the wearisome uninterrupted effort of working upon the innermost part of our moral disposition.[55]

Kant went on to argue that it is in no way reprehensible to say that every man *creates a God* for himself, for he must always compare any revealed God with his own ideal in order to judge whether he is entitled to regard and honor it as God. All the artificial self-deceptions in religious matters have a common base, Kant concluded.[56] Among the three divine moral attributes, holiness, mercy, and justice, man habitually turns directly to the second in order to avoid the forbidding condition of conforming to the requirements of the first! Kant was getting uncomfortably close to depth-psychologizing *sola gratia*.

But even if Kant in his old age had not moved in this direction, another child of the *Aufklärung*, illegitimate and romantic, Johann Gottfried Herder, would have turned Western thought down such a road. In his *Ideas* (1784) on history Herder put the whole ponderous thought into a single capsule: "Religion is man's humanity in its highest form."[57] Even when looked upon solely as an exercise of the understanding, this ordained Lutheran minister went on, it is the most sublime flowering of the human soul. He gives the following account of the origin of this precious blossom:

As soon as man learned to use his understanding when stimulated ever so slightly, as soon, that is, as his vision of the world became different from that of the animals, he was bound to surmise the existence of invisible, mighty beings which helped or harmed him. These he sought to make his friends, or to keep as his friends, and thus religion, whether true or false, right or wrong, became the teacher of mankind, the comfort and counsel of a life so full of darkness, danger and perplexity.[58]

He went on to describe religion as a "childlike service of God, an imitation of the highest and most beautiful qualities in the human image, and hence that which affords the deepest satisfaction, and most effective goodness and human love."[59]

Neither Kant nor Herder, of course, thought that their psychological, phenomenological, or evolutionary historical explication of religion and its origins really brought into question the objective reality of a transcendent Deity. The noumenal world could not be touched by phenomenological explanations. When, however, the moment came that a radical materialist entered the ring armed with such argumentation, a "fatal mutation" suddenly occurred. That moment was the publication in 1841 of Ludwig Feuerbach's *The Essence of Christianity*. How fascinating that Feuerbach should come from left-wing Hegelianism, for Hegel had in his great synthesis sought to combine rationalist and romantic elements, Kant and Herder, into one harmonious system. In writing on the incarnation Hegel had pontificated that it is man's destiny to know the identity of his own nature with God. An inversion of this hypothesis was easy enough and not long in coming. It was God's destiny in the year of our Lord 1841 to learn of the identity of His own nature with man. Compared with Hegel's grand system, Feuerbach's thought seems simple, unilinear, trifling. But Feuerbach needed only one spade, an ace, with which to undermine and topple Hegel's proud tower.

In his *The Essence of Christianity* Ludwig Feuerbach

shocked the intellectual world with the radical assertion that all religion is anthropology. Years later in his *Lectures on the Essence of Religion* he provided a summary of his own doctrine:

> I now come to those of my writings which embody my doctrine, religion, philosophy, or whatever you may choose to call it, and provide the subject matter of these lectures. This doctrine of mine is briefly as follows. *Theology is anthropology*: in other words, the object of religion, which in Greek we call *theos* and in our language God, expresses nothing other than the essence of man; man's God is nothing other than the deified essence of man, so that the history of religion or, what amounts to the same thing, of God—for the gods are as varied as the religions, and the religions are as varied as mankind—is nothing other than the history of man.[60]

Christianity differs from the religions of uncivilized peoples only in transforming the phenomena that arouse man's fear not into special gods, but into attributes of one God. God is the epitome of all realities or perfections, a compendious summary devised for the benefit of the limited individual, an "epitome of the generic human qualities distributed among men, in the self-realization of the species in the course of world history."[61] His most radical phrase was: "Man and man, the unity of I and Thou, is God." *Homo homini deus est*! Now in arguing that not the attribute of divinity but the divinity of the attribute is the first truly divine being, Feuerbach did not consider himself to be an atheist, but rather the discoverer of the true wealth of religion, for the only true atheist is the man to whom these attributes mean nothing. Feuerbach's notorious "Der Mensch ist was er isst" (man is what he eats) was intended to express not a materialistic theory of human nature, but simply a plea in favor of the human right of healthy survival.[62] If theology is anthropology, it remains that a high regard for man's being is reflected in theology. In God as subject man can only perceive that which is a predicate or quality of himself. Humanism is raised to the level of religion. "The beginning, middle, and end of religion is man."[63] In the divinity of Christ the believer sees projected the best qualities of collective man.

"Thus Christ," Feuerbach stated enthusiastically, "as the consciousness of love, is the consciousness of the species. He therefore who loves man for the sake of man, who rises to the love of the species, to universal love, adequate to the nature of the species, he is a Christian, is Christ himself."[64]

Feuerbach thus offered an analysis not only of the metaphysical idea of God as the absolute, but also of the personal God as revealed in the Scriptures. The idea of a personal God is the ultimate religious idea, for in the personal God man has arrived at the most perfect possible projection of himself. Luther as the great preacher of the "Word made flesh" naturally intrigued Feuerbach, who recognized Luther and Augustine to be "the two great matadors" of Christendom.[65] He thought of Luther as "der erste Mensch" of Christendom and often used to say humorously of himself, "Ich bin Luther II." In later years Feuerbach repeatedly said that his work *The Essence of Christianity* really presupposed his study of *The Essence of Faith According to Luther*, even though the *Luther* came several years later (1844).[66] Although he assured his publisher that it was the "deepest thing that has ever been written on the essence of Luther,"[67] he was far from satisfied with it. In a letter of May 13, 1844, to his friend Christian Kapp, he described it as too casually written, brief where ideas still needed explication and repetitious where ideas had already been expressed.[68] In a newly discovered fragment of a draft of a letter to Arnold Ruge in Paris, April, 1844, Feuerbach referred to Luther as the "Essence of Christianity on German soil," the well-grounded German resolution of the "deepest and most powerful essence of mankind." His book, he confided, is studded with citations to gain the respect of the learned crowd.[69]

Feuerbach considered his book to be as much pro as anti-Luther, a contradiction which lies in the nature of the situation.[70] As an idealism the Christianity which Luther espoused was a source of alienation, in turning man's attention away from the individual men. Yet in emphasizing the triumph of God's merciful forgiveness coming from His heart over the wrath against sin which comes from His moral essence, Luther offered the loftiest concept of eternal, changeless, fatherly love. Christ as the daily mirror and true picture or image of God reflects the best that is in mankind. Feuerbach knows his Luther well and exploits effectively those unguarded statements about having the God one believes in. Luther is proof for his thesis that faith in the goodness of God is the form in which man affirms himself, the way in which each man makes Luther his contemporary. Feuerbach exploited (1) Luther's conception of faith; (2) his Christology, especially the communication of attributes (*communicatio idiomatum*) of the divine to the human nature of Christ; and (3) his conception of the real presence in the Sacrament.

While Luther did come exceedingly close to Feuerbach in some of his expressions, he would have been horrified at the idea that Christ as true God was merely the objectivized essence of the human species. Rather, he believed faith itself to be the work of God who has created both man and his consciousness of God. Man in nature cannot know or of his own reason and strength come to trust in the God of love. God must create the new man of faith. Luther even seems to have anticipated Feuerbach's approach in his commentary on the *Magnificat* and other passages presenting his *theologia crucis* when he confesses that the form which God's self-disclosure took is precisely not the form which man would have anticipated or desired. In the introduction to a sermon on Luke 24:13-25, which Luther preached in the city church in Wittenburg in 1534 he emphasized, as he consistently did, that the Scriptures are not a depository for human notions about God, but the vehicle which God uses to address man.

It is a fascinating spectacle to observe the way in which the greatest theologian of our day, Karl Barth, reacted to the Luther-Feuerbach concatenation on theology proper. Karl Barth in his early years was alarmed, not to say terrified, at Luther's earthy way of portraying God's consanguinity with man through the incarnation. Luther did not provide safeguards against the reversibility of his propositions as they were turned about by Feuerbach. Lutheran theology, he warned solemnly, has "guarded itself perhaps all too rigidly against the Calvinist corrective."[71] After all, Hegel had emphatically declared that he was a good Lutheran, and so did Feuerbach, in his own way and upon his own level. Barth himself thought it necessary with respect to his thought about God's own being to go to school with Anselm.[72]

Barth thought that the experience-theology of the early nineteenth century was immediately vulnerable to Feuerbach's manipulation. Feuerbach, he explained, sought to take Hegel and Schleiermacher seriously, completely seriously, at the point where they concurred in asserting the nonobjective quality of God. He wanted "to turn theology, which itself seemed half-inclined towards the same goal, completely and finally into anthropology; to turn the lovers of God into lovers of men, the worshippers into workers, the candidates for the life to come into students of the present life, the Christians into complete men; he wanted to turn away from heaven towards the earth, from faith towards love, from Christ towards ourselves, from all, but really all, supernaturalism towards real life."[73] Barth conceded that what appears to be a weakness in Feuerbach's position, namely the sensory and natural quality of his thought might also be its particular strength.

Beyond the usual criticism of Feuerbach, especially that he did not consider nature as *extra nos* (outside of us) and stubbornly resistant to an anthropomorphic explanation, Barth advanced two lines of objection to his thought. First, he believed that Feuerbach's conception of "Man's essential being" or the "consciousness of the species" which he made the measure of all things and in which he thought he saw man's true divinity might very well be a fiction just like Hegel's "Reason" or any other abstraction. The true man, conceived in real existential terms, is the individual man. Secondly, he believed that Feuerbach did not take cognizance either of man's wickedness or of his mortality. Thus his abstraction of the divinity of man in general is much less impressive when considered concretely in the individual case.[74] Barth makes the same criticism as Marx, that Feuerbach in following the left-wing Hegelian line of Max

Stirner is too abstract, too ideal, too far from concrete reality, for the unique individual is important. Before God we are liars. We can lay claim to His truth, certainty, salvation only by grace.[75] Barth considered Feuerbach as basically a man of one idea, trivial and superficial, but one who, because of his impact on modern thought, had to be reckoned with seriously.[76]

Barth is a big man, capable of executing reversals with grace and charm. Among the surprising turns in his thought is his new appreciation of Luther's Christology, taming down his own stress upon God as being "wholly other." He is very ingenious in explaining that on Renaissance grounds of "man the measure" theology had been unable to give an effective answer to Feuerbach, when, invoking Luther's sanction, he theorized that statements of the Christian faith are in reality statements of more or less profound human needs and desires projected into the infinite. For that reason early in his career Barth stressed the disjunction of the divine and human. Now (1956), *mutatis mutandis*, Barth announces a great turning point in his own thought, a *Wendung*! The prevailing theological interest in the existence of the believing man would not necessarily have been erroneous had it been a matter of shift in tone and emphasis for serious and pertinent reasons. The Scriptures, after all, speak emphatically enough of the commerce of the believing Israelites and the believing Christians with God. How else, Barth asks, could they testify on behalf of Him who was very God and very man? Then he with great temerity asserts: "The theologians should not have hesitated so long to appeal to Luther, especially the early Luther, and to the early Melanchthon! And how much assistance and guidance could they have received had they paid any attention to Kierkegaard! There is no reason why the attempt of Christian anthropocentrism should not be made, indeed ought not to be made."[77]

No sooner had Feuerbach published his book on *The Essence of Christianity*, than that brilliant "maker of modern history" Karl Marx perceived that Feuerbach could very well use Luther in support of his thesis. In January, 1842, Marx wrote his brief comment on *Luther as Umpire between Strauss and Feuerbach*, which he sent off to the *Deutschen Jahrbücher* in November for publication. David Friedrich Strauss had on a platform of radical historical skepticism and religious illusionism argued against the reality and utility of miracles. Feuerbach had written on miracles and had used Luther's picture of the world as a drunken peasant who when pushed into the saddle of a horse from one side falls off the other. Thus the intellectual world having been helped up from a one-sided rationalism has toppled over into historicism and empiricism. Miracles, as Luther appreciated, tell us something profound about man. Luther knew that all the works of nature are miraculous, just as is the real presence of God under the bread in the sacrament.[78] At this juncture in the debate Marx intervened with his decisive judgment in favor of Feuerbach. He quoted a long passage from Luther's commentary on Luke 7 in which he treats the miracle of resurrection from the dead and concluded:

> In these few words you have an apology for the whole Feuerbach writing—an apology for the definitions of providence, omnipotence, creation, miracle, faith as they are presented in this writing. Oh, shame yourselves, you Christians, shame yourselves that an *antiChrist* had to show you the essence of Christianity in its true unconcealed form! And you speculative theologians and philosophers, I advise you: free yourselves from the concepts and prejudices of speculative philosophy, if you wish to come in another way to things as they are, that is, to the *truth*. And there is no other way for you to *truth* and *freedom* except through the *Feuer bach* [stream of fire]. Feuerbach is the .purgatory of these times.[79]

Marx and Engels moved rapidly beyond Feuerbach, however. In *The Holy Family*, 1845, a wicked attack on Bruno Bauer "and company," Marx criticized Feuerbach's cult of the abstract man and urged that it be replaced by the science of real men and their historical development. In *The German Ideology*, completed in 1846, Marx and Engels devoted Part One to Feuerbach, but their reference to him was oblique and they used him more as an occasion for presenting their materialistic philosophy rather than for offering a thorough critique of his thought. Later Engels criticized Feuerbach severely in his *Ludwig Feuerbach and the Outcome of Classical German Philosophy* for ignoring the new knowledge about man and nature provided by modern science and for not pursuing consistently the implications of materialism. The new immense advances in science, Engels believed, were making possible in an approximately systematic form a comprehensive view of the interconnection of the different spheres in nature, of which Feuerbach seemed to be unaware.[80] Engels even speaks of Feuerbach's "astonishing poverty" when compared with Hegel in the doctrine of moral conduct and philosophy of law.[81]

But perhaps the most damning charge which Marx and Engels leveled against Feuerbach was that he was like the idealist philosophers, who were speculative rather than relevant and active in effecting change. Marx had been born a Jew, but when Karl was six years old his father Heinrich embraced Christianity and, with his wife and children, was baptized and became a member of the Evangelical State Church (Lutheran combined with Reformed). Marx rebelled against that church as a devotee of the *status quo*, although he was grateful that his father's conversion had freed him of the burden of Judaic legalism. Marx articulated his impatience with Feuerbach's "half-way" ideology in his famous *Theses on Feuerbach*. Thesis XI reads: "The philosophers have *interpreted* the world in various ways; the point, however, is to *change* it."[82]

Another development in nineteenth-century anthropological realism related to an important aspect of Luther's thought may be tagged "voluntarist." The great pessimist Arthur Schopenhauer and the irrepressible Friedrich Nietzsche with their stress on the priority of will and the will to power as the mainsprings of human action acknowledge Luther, rightly or wrongly, as a predecessor on the road to this great insight. Luther's overall assessment of human nature, of course, was a more likely antecedent than the optimism of some of Luther's contemporaries or of the official philosophy of the Enlightenment. But it was rather the facet of Luther's anthropology having to do with the priority of suffering or becoming to being, and being to thought and action to which they attached themselves. This assumption was clear in Feuerbach's thought—in fact, was necessary to his conclusions. Man necessarily thinks and acts as he is. On the loftiest plane, when he thinks about God, he unconsciously thinks about him as he himself is. He creates him in the image of man. Schopenhauer called on Luther to support the psychology on which he based his voluntarism.

In his major work *The World as Will and Idea* Schopenhauer repeatedly cited Luther as an authority who favored determinism over freedom and will prior to reason, because being precedes thought and action. That the will is not free, he argued, is an original evangelical doctrine powerfully developed by Augustine against the platitudes of the Pelagians. Luther made it the main point of his book *De servo arbitrio*. Grace effects faith; faith receives righteousness as a gift; it comes upon us from outside and is not a product of our free will.[83] Good works, Luther declares in his book *De libertate Christiana*, follow freely from faith and do not produce rewards.[84] That Saint Paul, Augustine, and Luther taught that works cannot justify a man, Schopenhauer argues, is a result in the final analysis of the fact that *operari sequitur esse*, doing follows upon being. Hence men who are in essence all sinners cannot do good works.[85] In acting we merely experience what we are, a depressing thought in Schopenhauer's context. This association of his own key dogma with Luther's thought was no mere sport or device on the melancholy German's part. For in his early prize-winning essay on *The Freedom of the Will*, crowned by the royal Norwegian Society of the Sciences in 1839, Schopenhauer had already declared: "Especially do I call upon Luther who in his book written for that express purpose, the *De servo arbitrio*, fought against freedom of the will with all his might."[86]

Nietzsche moved on to the will to power. As a "realist" Nietzsche mocked Christianity as the "Platonism of the masses." In his early years Nietzsche knew and admired Luther as a great German, a religious and cultural giant to be revered like Schiller and Goethe. In his later years Nietzsche became a bitter

## Luther's Importance

assailant of Luther, who had revitalized Christianity with its slave morality and inhibited man in his quest to break through beyond himself.[87] Despite this rejection, Nietzsche could not rid himself of certain attitudes and hypotheses absorbed in his youth and associated with Luther. "We Germans are still very young," he wrote, "and our last achievement is still Luther and our sole book is still the Bible. The Germans have never moralized."[88] He continued to value Luther's German modesty, a virtue Wagner did not possess.[89] Luther is an artist, pure and selfless.[90] Schopenhauer is simple and honorable, but crude, like Luther.[91] He observed Luther's identification with the lower classes and thought that Luther would shake up the propertied classes in the modern world.[92]

Moreover, many aspects of Nietzsche's thought are reminiscent of Luther's, such as his view of history as the arena in which the powers of this world struggled for mastery. But more relevant to the question of anthropological realism is the fact that on several occasions when Nietzsche discussed ethics, he reverted to Luther's analysis of being and action, and did so consciously. In answer to such basic questions as How deep is the ethical? Does it merely belong to that which is acquired by learning? Is it a means of expression? all deeper men are unanimous in their opinion. Luther, Augustine, Paul come to mind, for they agree that our morality and its accomplishments are not to be explained in terms of our conscious will, in brief, that the explanation as the basis of utilitarian purposes is not adequate.[93] Citing Luther with approval in this point was not necessarily very flattering, coming from Nietzsche. Luther, Augustine, Paul teach the absolute depravity of man, lack of freedom to do good, eventually grace, for sick men look for a cure.[94] Luther "belonged," for the world is an *Irrenanstalt*, a madhouse.

For Nietzsche, as for Luther, thought and action are secondary manifestations of man's inner self. Nietzsche believed man to be driven by the will to power, not to be confused with the individual's empirical will, which only indirectly and partially gives expression and an outlet to the basic driving will inherent in every action, the will to power. Man cannot transcend what he is. Like Feuerbach, and in a special way, Marx, and Schopenhauer, Nietzsche accepted the premise that *operari sequitur esse.*

What a marvelous spectacle! Luther's influence in evidence not only upon transcendental idealism, but also upon anthropological realism! In his commentary on Psalm 14:4-6 Luther declared that he was no prophet, but was sure of his message. The more people despise him, he warned, and honor themselves, the more they must fear that he is a prophet.[95] He was a prophet in that he "proclaimed" that in the final analysis man can understand what he really is in a primary or ultimate context only if word comes to him from outside himself. Anthropology in the most fundamental sense is dependent upon theology. He was a prophet in that he unknowingly "foretold" developments in intellectual history which have unfolded gradually in modern times.

That Luther's world of thought should have shaped the thought-world of the German idealists and realists was in a way inevitable, for they were conditioned by a culture based upon the Reformation experience and the Christian tradition. Luther's theology, with its paradoxes, could when taken in part rather than as a whole, which is impossible for philosophy, provide an intellectual thrust in the direction of either idealism or realism. In a good many passages our moderns seem to be blissfully unaware of how new insights have been suggested by or conditioned by the religious base and component of their thought. Like Cyrus of old men are used in a way unknown to them. In his autobiography *To Have Lived These Days* Harry Emerson Fosdick offers a portion of the book under the caption "Ideas that Have Used Me."

In some cases it is clear that a happy misunderstanding (*felix culpa*) of Luther's thought helped to propel a modern ideology forward. By taking his stand and thereby introducing religious pluralism, Luther certainly made decisive a historical contribution to the liberal option in subsequent human history. But the way in which the Enlightenment understood his

## Luther's Importance

idea of conscience and Christian liberty as a mandate for the autonomous individual to oppose tradition, authority, and community was clearly a misapprehension and misapplication of his ideas. Similarly, the way in which the realists applied his theological premise of an unfree will as though he were a metaphysical determinist was clearly a case of misunderstanding. The transposition of the priority of being to thought and action, which Luther in the first instance derived from the *sola gratia* polemic against salvation by good works, from the theological realm to a general ontological context could more easily be justified, for Luther leaves the possibility for such a transfer open and even suggests it himself.

Feuerbach and Schopenhauer in certain passages seem to be exploiting the authority of Luther to support unorthodox positions in a conscious way. This is a case of the tyranny, as Lord Chesterfield once put it, which the living exercise over the dead. It is like Kaiser Wilhelm quoting John Knox to the effect that "one man with God is always a majority." Luther contributed to, but was also used by, idealists and realists alike. Both groups failed to appreciate his deepest concerns, the primal anxiety and dread (*Urgrauen*) which oppresses mortal man, the concern to find gracious the God who is the final ground of being, the conviction that the divine initiative changes man's being, makes of him a new creature, the theology of hope and joy. Other moderns, the existentialists and post-liberal theologians have been able to wrestle more seriously with Luther's thought in its third and fourth dimensions.

Ever since Copernicus, Nietzsche observed, man has been falling from the center of the universe toward an X. Lacking a precisely defined cosmology, religious thinkers, idealists such as Kant and realists such as Feuerbach, have been forced to retreat to the domain of man's inwardness.[96] Biblical imagery has been internalized, the principle of analogy between heaven and earth has given way to a dialectic of identity or alienation between Creator and creation, and a language characterized by the free associative interplay of imagery.[97] Evidence of Luther's precocity and one clue to his impact on post-Reformation thought is the fact that while the Copernican cosmology was still intact, he replaced a synthetic with an antithetical dialectic, the *theologia crucis*. Luther's biblical realism in anthropology has remained disconcertingly relevant down to present times.

# Notes

1. *Weimar Ausgabe (W.A.)*, 48, 76, No. 100, ll. 1-12, Cf. *W.A.* 6, 291, 8-14: "The effort to establish or defend the divine order with human reason, unless it has already itself been grounded and enlightened by faith, is as pointless as throwing light on the bright sun with a dark lantern or resting a rock on a reed. For Isaiah in chapter 7 makes reason subject to faith and says: Unless you believe, you will not be understanding and reasonable. He does not say: Unless you are reasonable, you will not be believing."

I am grateful to the National Endowment for the Humanities for providing with a senior fellowship the sustained time for preparing this lecture for publication, which at the time of delivery was neither written out nor thought out.

2. *W.A.Ti.* 3, 104, No. 2938a, 24-29: "optimum instrumentum." *W.A.* 40ᴵ, 412, 20: "Alia ratio generatur quae est fidei."

3. Half a century ago Hans Preusz distinguished these three uses of *ratio* by Luther, "Was bedeutet die Formel 'convictus testimonüs scripturarum aut ratione evidente' in Luthers ungehörnter Antwort zu Worms?" *Theologische Studien und Kritiken*, 81 (1908), 62 ff.

4. Brian Gerrish, *Grace and Reason* (Oxford, 1962), p. 168. Gerrish's analysis is substantially in agreement with a work done independently by Bernhard Lohse, *Ratio und Fides: Eine Untersuchung über die ratio in der Theologie Luthers* (Göttingen, 1958).

5. *Career of the Reformer*, II, 113, in *Luther's Works*, George Forell, ed., Vol. XXXII (Philadelphia, 1958).

6. See Berhard Lohse, "Luthers Antwort in Worms," *Luther: Mitteilungen der Luthergesellschaft* (1958), No. 3, pp. 124-134.

7. I owe this observation to Professor William Baker, a close student of English historiography in the Victorian age.

8. Fritz Blanke, "Hamann und Luther," *Lutherjahrbuch*, X (1928), 28-29. See Horst Stephan, *Luther in den Wandlungen seiner Kirche* (2nd ed.; Berlin, 1951), pp. 35-67.

9. Karl Holl, "Die Kulturbedeutung der Reformation, 1911," *Gesammelte Aufsätze zur Kirchengeschichte*, I: *Luther* (6th ed.; Tübingen, 1932), 468-543, 531; translated as *The Cultural Significance of the Reformation* (New York, 1959), p. 134.

10. Fichte, *Die Bestimmung des Menschen*, Book 3: *Glaube, Sämmtliche Werke*, II (Berlin, 1845), 249; translated in Karl Barth, *Church Dogmatics*, III, part 2 (Edinburgh, 1960), 99.

11. Cited in August Messer, *Fichtes religiöse Weltanschauung* (Stuttgart, 1923), p. 21. It is interesting to note that a recent not very ecumenical Catholic study of Luther's theology criticizes Luther's concern with self and individual salvation for its subjectivism and personalism, almost as though Luther had been a Fichtean, or at least a Methodist, distorting spirituality; see Paul Hacker, *Das Ich in Glauben bei Martin Luther* (Graz, 1966).

12. See, for example, Joseph Bohatec, *Die Religionsphilosophie Kants in der "Religion innerhalb der Grenzen der bloszen Vernunft"* (Hildesheim, 1966).

13. See Bruno Bauch, *Luther und Kant* (Berlin, 1904), p. 169; Ernst Katzer, *Luther und Kant* (Gieszen, 1910).

14. Joseph C. Weber, "Feuerbach, Barth and Theological Methodology," *Journal of Religion*, 46, No. 1 (January, 1966), 24.

15. Hegel, *Philosophie der Geschichte*, IIIᴵ, 131, Johannes Hoffmeister, ed., *Vorlesungen über die Philosophie der Weltgeschichte* (Hamburg, 1955), cited in Stephan Crites, "The Gospel According to Hegel," *Journal of Religion*, XLVI,

No. 2 (April, 1966), 254. The entire article, pp. 246-263, is excellent and offers a useful corrective to Walter Kaufman, *Hegel* (New York, 1965), sec. 65.

16. Georg Wünsch, *Luther und die Gegenwart* (Stuttgart, 1961), p. 99.

17. *Rationis Latomianae pro incendiariis Lovaniensis scholae sophistis redditae, Lutheriana confutatio*, 1521, *W.A.* 8, 43-128.

18. *W.A.* 8, 122, 22-25.

19. *W.A.* 56, 347, 1-7; trans. Wilhelm Pauck, *Luther: Lectures on Romans* (London, 1961), p. 208. A monograph on the subject which would benefit from supplemental scholarship is Erdmann Schott, *Fleisch und Geist nach Luthers Lehre unter besonderer Berücksichtigung des Begriffes "totus homo"* (Leipzig, 1928).

20. *W.A.* 10¹, 1st half, 508, 20.

21. *W.A.* 56, 356, 4-7: "Et hoc consonat Scripturæ Quæ hominem describit incuruatum in se adeo, ut non tantum corporalia, Sed et spiritualia bona sibi inflectat et se in omnibus querat. Quæ Curuitas est nunc naturalis, naturale vitium et naturale malum."

22. *Operationes in Psalmos, W.A.* 5, 207, 32-34.

23. *W.A.* 2, 685-697: *Eyn Sermon von der bereytung zum sterben.*

24. *W.A.* 10ᴵᴵᴵ, 1-64: *Acht Sermone D.M. Luthers von ihm gepredigt zu Wittenberg in der Fasten.*

25. *W.A.* 40ᴵᴵᴵ, 484-594: *Enarratio psalmi XC per D.M. Lutherum in schola Witenbergensi anno 1534 publice absoluta.*

26. See Carl Stange, *Luthers Gedanken über die Todesfurcht* (Berlin, 1932) p. 8: Luther: "Denn Auf Erden kann nichts Höheres begegnen weder der Tod, da die Welt und alles miteinander musz aufhören." *Erlangen Ausgabe* 14², 133; *W.A.* 37, 535, 23-24.

27. *W.A.* 5, 163, 28-29: "Vivendo, immo moriendo et damnando fit theologus, non intelligendo, legendo aut speculando."

28. *W.A.* 40ᴵ, 444, 14: "Quia sicut credit, sic habet," *W.A.* 18, 769, 17-18; "Atque ut credunt, ita habent," *W.A.* 18, 778, 13-14.

29. *W.A.* i, 543, 8-9: "tantum habes, quantum credis"; 595, 5: "tantum habes quantum credis."

30. Cf. *W.A.* 18, 633, 7: "Altera est, quod fides est rerum non apparentium Ut ergo fidei locus sit, opus est, ut omnia quae creduntur abscondantur"; *W.A.* 5, 86, 33-35: "Atque ita oculus fidei in tenebras interiores et caliginem mentis suspicit nihilque videt, nisi quod attenuatur suspiciens in excelso expectansque, unde veniat auxilium ei." *W.A.* 5, 623, 40-624, 2: "Agat ergo secundum fidem, idest insensibilitatem, et fiat truncus immobilis ad has blasphemias, quas in corde suo suscitat satanas."

31. *W.A.* 7, 551, 19-21: "Sein geist ist *sanctum sanctorum*, gottis wonung ym finsternn glauben on liecht, denn er glawbt, das er nit sihet, noch fulet, noch begreiffet." See Walther von Loewenich, *Luther als Ausleger der Synoptiker* (Munich, 1954), pp. 83-88, on this problem of faith and existential experience.

32. *W.A.* 7, 548, 10-11: "Unnd da ist denn der heilig geyst, der hat solch uberschwenklich kunst und lust ynn einem augenblick ynn der erfarung geleret." So also *W.A.* 9, 98, 21, in which Luther commends Tauler's theology as being "sapientia experimentalis et non doctrinalis. Quia nemo novit nisi qui accipit hoc negotium absconditum."

33. *W.A.* 18, 605, 32-34 (the famous lines of the *De servo arbitrio*): "Spiritus sanctus non est Scepticus, nec dubia aut opiniones in cordibus nostris scripsit, sed assertiones ipsa vita et omni experientia certiores et firmiores."

34. *W.A.Ti.* 1, 16, No. 46, l. 12.

35. *W.A.* 5, 26, 18-20.

36. Heiko Oberman, " 'Justitia Christi' and 'iustitia dei.' Luther and the

## Luther's Importance

scholastic doctrines of justification," *Harvard Theological Review*, 59 (January, 1966), 1-26.

37. *W.A.* 4, 511, 13: ". . . Qualis tu es in dispositione, tale est [verbum] tibi."

38. *W.A.* 30^{II}, 672, 37-673, 13-17.

39. *W.A.* 56, 371, 2-14; trans. Wilhelm Pauck, *Luther: Lectures on Romans*, pp. 235-236.

40. *W.A.* 56, 372, 5-25; trans. Wilhelm Pauck, *Luther: Lectures on Romans*, p. 237.

41. *W.A.* 56, 273, 8-9.

42. *W.A.* 56, 255, 15-19.

43. Wilhelm de Wette, *Briefwechsel*, I (Berlin, 1825), ep. 22, p. 40: "prius necesse est personam esse mutatam, deinde opera."

44. *W.A.* 56, 172, 9-11: "Sicut Aristoteles 3. Ethicorum manifeste determinat, secundum quem Iustitia sequitur et fit ex actibus. Sed secundum Deum precedit opera et opera fiunt ex ipsa." This is a major theme in Luther's works, repeated in his *Sermon on Good Works, The Liberty of the Christian Man*, and elsewhere.

45. *W.A.* 56, 117, 25-29; trans. Wilhelm Pauck, *Luther: Lectures on Romans*, p. 321, n. 1.

46. *W.A.* 56, 441, 23-442, 1-5; trans. Wilhelm Pauck, *Luther: Lectures on Romans*, p. 322. *W.A.* 56, 441, n. 23, explains that the terms are derived from Aristotle via such medieval handbooks on physics as Ockham, *Summule in lib. physicorum*, c. IX, c. XXV f. Cf. *W.A.* 4, 113, 14-15: "Ratio omnium est haec regula, quod nos justi non sumus ex operibus, sed opera justa ex nobis primo justis."

47. *W.A.* 4, 19, 21-24, incorrectly cited in Erich Seeberg, *Luthers Theologie: Motive und Ideen*, I (Göttingen, 1929), 107, n. 3, as *W.A.* 7, 19.

48. *W.A.* 56, 248, 27-33; *W.A.* 56, 249, 1-11.

49. *W.A.* 56, 264, 5-8.

50. *W.A.* 56, 307, 16-21; trans. Wilhelm Pauck, *Luther: Lectures on Romans*, p. 162.

51. Herbert Vossberg, *Luthers Kritik aller Religion* (Leipzig, 1922).

52. *W.A.* 37, 589, 35-57.

53. Cited in Georg Wünsch, *Luther und die Gegenwart*, p. 117.

54. *W.A.* 56, 234, 1-9; trans. Wilhelm Pauck, *Luther: Lectures on Romans*, pp. 84-85. Cf. G. Wünsch, *Luther und die Gegenwart*, p. 117.

55. Immanuel Kant, *Religion Within the Limits of Reason Alone* (Chicago, 1934), pp. 156-157.

56. *Ibid.*, p. 188.

57. Herder, *Ideen zur Philosophie der Geschichte der Menschheit* (2nd ed.; Leipzig, 1921), p. 153.

58. *Ibid.*, p. 154.

59. *Ibid.*, p. 155. These three Herder citations are taken from Karl Barth, *Protestant Thought: From Rousseau to Ritschl* (New York, 1959), pp. 213-214, who cites another edition of the *Ideen*.

60. Ludwig Feuerbach, *Lectures on the Essence of Religion* (New York, 1967), p. 17.

61. Ludwig Feuerbach, *The Essence of Christianity* (New York, 1957), p. xvi.

62. Melvin Cherno, "Ludwig Feuerbach and the Intellectual Basis of Nineteenth Century Radicalism" (dissertation, Stanford, 1955), p. 52.

63. *Essence of Christianity*, p. 184.

64. *Ibid.*, p. 269.

65. *Sämmtliche Werke*, XII (2nd ed.; Stuttgart-Canstatt, 1960–), p. 83.

66. *Das Wesen des Glaubens im Sinne Luthers* (1844), trans. Melvin Cherno, *The Essence of Faith According to Luther* (New York, 1967).

67. *Sämmtliche Werke*, XII, 108.

68. *Ibid.*, XIII, 136. He repeated the complaint in a letter of October 15, 1844, also to Kapp.

69. Werner Schuffenhauer, *Feuerbach und der junge Marx* (Berlin, 1965), p. 83.

70. *Sämmtliche Werke*, II, 405, cited in S. Rawidowicz, *Ludwig Feuerbachs Philosophie. Ursprung und Schicksal* (2nd ed.; Berlin, 1964), p. 16, n. 4.

71. Karl Barth, *Protestant Thought*, p. 359.

72. See Barth's very brilliant book *Anselm: Fides Quaerens Intellectum* (Richmond, Va., 1960), in which he argues that since Anselm was arguing within the "theological circle," assurance of God resting upon anterior faith, he was not vulnerable to the criticism of Aquinas and Kant, as they supposed.

73. Karl Barth, *Protestant Thought*, p. 355.

74. *Ibid.*, p. 359. See the excellent article by Joseph C. Weber, "Feuerbach, Barth, and Theological Methodology," *Journal of Religion*, 46, No. 1 (January, 1966), 24-36.

75. See the very perceptive introductory essay to Feuerbach's *The Essence of Christianity* (New York, 1957), pp. x-xxxii, criticisms, pp. xxvii-xxviii. Karl Löwith, ed., *Die Hegelsche Linke* (Stuttgart-Canstatt, 1962), p. 11, observes that Feuerbach and the young Hegelians worked up to a superficial level and provided further proof of Jacob Burckhardt's dour observation that after 1830 the world grew more "common."

76. Barth's criticism that Feuerbach did not take death seriously is both unfair and yet justifiable. In his thesis at Erlangen, *De Ratione una universali infinita* (1828), pp. 11-68, Feuerbach included thoughts on death and immortality, a theme to which he frequently returned. Nature brings death, immortality is a projection. Any ethic based on immortality is a miserable construction. See Feuerbach, *Sämmtliche Werke*, I: "Gedanken über Tod und Unsterblichkeit"; "Todesgedanken, 1830"; "Die Unsterblichkeit vom Standpunkt der Anthropologie, 1846-1866"; *Sämmtliche Werke*, XI, 69-324. At the same time Barth's criticism is justified from the point of view of Barth (and Luther), since Feuerbach did not take seriously sin as the "sting of death," viewing death merely in a naturalistic, not a theological context. For Barth's own anthropology the reader can profitably study his *Church Dogmatics*, III, part 2 (Edinburgh, 1960), chap. x: "The Creature," and IV, part 1 (Edinburgh, 1961), chap. xiv: "Jesus Christ, the Lord as Servant."

77. Karl Barth, *The Humanity of God* (Richmond, Va., 1960), pp. 24, 26. Of relevance is his small study *Christ and Adam: Man and Humanity in Romans 5* (New York, 1957). Walther von Loewenich, *Luther und der Neuprotestantismus* (Witten, 1963), p. 261, criticizes Barth for giving a distorted picture of the experience-theology of the nineteenth century, for it did not consider religious experience to be the only source of faith, but only a way of making certainty greater. Since the Holy Spirit must work through experience there is no point in ridiculing experience as subjectivism.

78. Feuerbach, "Ueber das Wunder" (1839), *Sämmtliche Werke*, VII, 1-41; *Lectures on the Essence of Religion*, p. 146.

79. Marx-Engels, *Werke*, I (Berlin, 1961), pp. 26-27. See Werner Schuffenhauer, *Feuerbach und der junge Marx*, 24-25. The embattled Strauss published his *Streitschriften zur Vertheidigung meiner Schrift über das Leben Jesu und zur Charakteristik der gegenwärtigen Theologie*, 3 vols., in 1837.

80. Frederick Engels, *Ludwig Feuerbach and the Outcome of Classical German Philosophy* (New York, 1941), pp. 18 ff, 28, 46.

81. *Ibid.*, p. 36.

82. Text translated in Engels, *Ludwig Feuerbach*, Appendix A, pp. 73-75. If this present discussion of Luther, Feuerbach, and Marx seems to be improbable, confer the relatively brilliant comparison of Pascal and Marx in Lucien Goldmann, *The Hidden God: A Study of Tragic Vision in the Pensées of Pascal and the Tragedies of Racine* (New York, 1964), pp. 278-282. There is, of course, a vast literature on Christianity and Marxism in general, of which at least one ambitious title merits special mention, Nicholas Lobkowicz, ed., *Marx and the Western World* (Notre Dame, 1967), in which the editor discusses Marx's attitude toward religion sympathetically and James L. Adams offers a distinctively Protestant point of view.

83. Schopenhauer, *Die Welt als Wille und Vorstellung*, I (Wiesbaden, 1965), 480.

84. *Ibid.*, p. 482. On p. 621 Schopenhauer refers to Luther's ethic of selfless love.

85. Schopenhauer, *Die Welt als Wille und Vorstellung*, II (Wiesbaden, 1961), 693, from chap. 48: "Zur Lehre von der Verneinung des Willens zum Leben."

86. Schopenhauer, *Parerga, Sämmtliche Werke*, III (Frankfurt am Main, 1962), 583-584. In chap. iv of the *Über die Freiheit des Willens* he discusses Luther as his forerunner.

87. Cf. the closely documented articles by Heinz Bluhm on Nietzsche and Luther: "Das Lutherbild des jungen Nietzsche," *PMLA*, 58 (1943), 246-288; "Nietzsche's Idea of Luther in *Menschliches Allzumenschliches*," *PMLA*, 65 (1950), 1053-1068; "Nietzsche's View of Luther and the Reformation in *Morgenröthe* and *Die Fröhliche Wissenschaft*," *PMLA*, 68 (1953), 111-127. See also Emanuel Hirsch, "Nietzsche und Luther," *Lutherjahrbuch*, II-III (1920/1921), 61-106.

88. Nietzsche, *Werke*, XIII (Leipzig, 1903), 333.

89. *Ibid.*, X, 441.

90. *Ibid.*, p. 433.

91. *Ibid.*, p. 301.

92. *Ibid.*, pp. 290, 307.

93. *Ibid.*, XIII, 215, No. 506.

94. *Ibid.*, pp. 301-303.

95. *W.A.* 7, 373, 17-29. Luther compares himself with Balaam's ass which God chose to use even though there were enough other asses around.

96. Jacob Taubes, "Dialectic and Analogy," *Journal of Religion*, 34 (1954), 111-119, 115. See also Paul Wernle, *Allegorie und Erlebnis bei Luther* (Bern, 1960).

97. See the intriguing study by Friedrich Karl Schumann, "Gedanken Luthers zur Frage der Entmythologisierung," *Wort und Bestalt* (Witten, 1956), pp. 165-178.

# XI

## MAN ON THIS ISTHMUS

THE INCOMPARABLE Hegel said of Leopold von Ranke, the father of modern critical history, "Er ist nur ein gewöhnlicher Historiker!" Literati of all schools have been quick to agree with Aristotle's pronouncement in the *Poetics* that history is less philosophical than poetry. Moreover, historians are acutely aware of the inherent difficulties of their task, as Thomas Carlyle expressed it in one of his purple passages: "Listening from a distance of centuries across the death-chasms and howling kingdoms of decay, it is not easy to catch everything." A present-day Carlyle, Britain's late statesman-historian Sir Winston Churchill, in one of his less optimistic moments declared: "History with its flickering lamp stumbles along the trail of the past, trying to reconstruct its scenes, to revive its echoes, and kindle with pale gleams the passion of former days." [1] Contemporary philosophers such as Martin Heidegger in the *Holzwege* not only emphasize the mysterious nature of history but seem to revel in it. And even the keen and sober historian of early modern times, Jacob Burckhardt, who wrote the essay on the Italian Renaissance characterized by Lord Acton as "the most penetrating and subtle treatise on the history of civilization that exists in literature," was not at all confident of the historian's ability to reach the inner core of historical happenings. "Mighty events like the Reformation," he confessed, "elude, as respects their details, their outbreak, and their development, the deductions of the philosophers, however clearly the necessity of them as a whole may be demonstrated. The movements of the human spirit, its sudden flashes, its expansions and its pauses, must forever remain a mystery to our eyes, since we can but know this or that of the forces at work in it, never all of them together." [2] In the presence of philosophers and historians all these difficulties, confessions of limitations, and fear of futility might well inhibit a hard-working, dirt-farming, garden-variety common historian. And yet the Reformation historian has the words of that bumptious young German humanist Ulrich von Hutten ringing in his ears, "Even if we do not succeed, there is merit in having tried!"

An occasion such as the 450th anniversary of Luther's epoch-making act on 31 October 1517, moreover, calls for a theme sufficiently grand to merit the attention of all whom Goethe has characterized as the "higher thinkers," which necessarily draws the historian away from the comforts of his own detailed and carefully circumscribed research to the larger arena of religious and cultural history. When confronted with the question of a suitable *terminus a quo* in his *Reflections on History,* Jacob Burckhardt settled on the problem of anthropology as the most suitable *Anknüpfungspunkt,* and a lesser historian may well emulate his example. "We, however," wrote Burckhardt, "shall start out from the one point accessible to us, the one eternal center of all things — man, suffering, striving, doing, as he is and was and ever shall be. Hence our study will, in a certain sense, be pathological in kind." [3] The problem of man is central for every historian who has a humanistic rather than a hominal view of history, that is, who views man as the subject of history as well as merely an object in history. The place of man in the total scheme of things is of singular importance for the historian of the Renaissance and Reformation period when Western man, for better or for worse, grew increasingly self-conscious about his position in the world and universe.

One badly dated way of viewing the phenomena of Renaissance and Reformation is in terms of a sharp contrast in their conceptions of man. One view of Western cultural history, widespread in popular literature and even in some purportedly scholarly writing to the present day, sees the Renaissance conception of man as one of lofty appreciation and the Reformation view as one of abject denigration.[4] The picture of the Renaissance man as a lusty, amoral, ebullient type in contrast to the timid, inhibited, repressed Reformation man owes a great deal to Friedrich Nietzsche, for whom Burckhardt developed a distinct dislike when they were together at Basel. Upon hearing one of Burckhardt's lectures on his *Weltgeschichtliche Betrachtungen* (reflections on world history), Nietzsche paid him the compliment of saying that for the first time in his life he had enjoyed listening to a lecture. Considering Nietzsche's depiction of Renaissance man, it is doubtful whether he understood Burckhardt. Conrad Burdach, a serious historian of the Renaissance and an advocate of a theory of the northern origin of the phenomenon, has composed a montage of Nietzschean terminology that may well serve to mark one polar extreme of interpretation:

> Renaissance Man is the free, genial personality, fresh and wanton in bold sinfulness, the type of an aesthetic immoralism, the domineering, fame-seeking, power-hungry, insatiable voluptuary, the frivolous despiser of religion, who nevertheless keeps peace with the church and its servants, because he views it as an indispensable device for managing the masses by deception.[5]

This portrait, coupled with Nietzsche's expressed regrets that the Reformation had unfortunately intervened to prevent the Renaissance popes from secularizing Western culture painlessly from on top, represents the extreme caricature of a contrast between the Renaissance and Reformation views of man that has been maintained in varying shadings of chiaroscuro. It is one that needs radical rethinking and adjustment. In reality, the synthesis achieved during the patristic period of the double aspects of man's dignity and misery, both having classical and Biblical sources, was maintained and reemphasized during the Renaissance and Reformation era. And if the balance has been disturbed in modern or postmodern times, it needs to be restored for the mental health and spiritual welfare of man.

The Biblical root of the conception of the dignity of man lay in the account of man's creation. In reason, moral judgment, free will, and immortality of the soul man was made in the image of God. The creation motif lies behind the psalmist's expression: "I have said, Ye are gods; and all of you are children of the Most High" (Ps. 82:6). The second Biblical basis for acclaiming the supreme worth of man was the incarnation, the appearance of the *Deus humanatus*. This guarantee of the genuine value of human flesh pointed to man as the chief object of God's concern. The New England poet Robert Frost

25

suggested a dimension of the incarnation that was important to the humanists in the lines:

> God's descent into flesh was meant
> As a supreme demonstration
> Of the merit of risking spirit
> In substantiation.

These are the double grounds for human worth capsulated in the *Formula missae* and intoned in parishes throughout Christendom through the long centuries, when during the preparation of the cup for Mass the priest murmured the words: "Deus qui humanae substantiae dignitatem mirabiliter condidisti et mirabilius reformasti," or: "God who has marvelously created the dignity of human substance and has more wondrously reformed it." Such a theme repeated before peasants and wool carders as well as before kings and prelates was sure to impress itself deeply upon the mind of the Latin West.

Classical antiquity served as a second major source of the cultural emphasis on man's supreme worth. Glorification of man was common in high Hellenic culture. A most striking statement of the awesomeness of man and his magnificent achievements comes from the second chorus of Sophocles' *Antigone:*

> Much is there passing strange;
> Nothing surpassing mankind.
> He it is loves to range
> Over the ocean hoar,
> Thorough its surges' roar,
> South winds raging behind. . . .
> Now bends he to the good, now to the ill,
> With craft of art, subtle past reach of sight.[6]

The radical anthropocentrism of Protagoras' *homo mensura* and the extreme views of the Sophists fed into a rhetorical stream of commonplaces lauding man. For Plato man was the midpoint of the universe, and in middle Platonism and Neoplatonism the philosophical notion of man as the microcosm was further developed. From Hellenic sources the rhetorical and philosophical traditions of the Latin West drew an exalted image of man. The Stoics saw in the universe a community of gods and men. The figure of Cicero loomed even larger in the later tradition than in his own times. For Cicero man is remarkable in his terrestrial achievements, building colorful and beautiful structures and cities and with the strength of his own hands establishing his own empire on earth. Man's reason desires to explore the secrets of a higher world. In one of his most famous passages in the

*De natura deorum* Cicero exclaimed: "Great and special endowments have been bestowed upon men by the gods. In the first place they made them tall and upright, raised aloft from the ground, that they might be able, through their gaze being turned upon the sky, to obtain a knowledge of the divine existence. For men are formed from the earth, not as mere inhabitants and occupants, but as spectators of the things above them in the sky, the spectacle of which is afforded to no other race of animate beings."[7] The poet Ovid in his *Metamorphoses* presented a picture of the formation of man reminiscent of the Genesis account. Prometheus constructs man out of earth and water after the image of the gods and teaches him to lift his face to the heavens. His upright position characterizes him as the ruler of the earth and its living essence. In his hymn of creation Ovid wrote:

> But something else was needed, a finer being,
> More capable of mind, a sage, a ruler,
> So Man was born, it may be, in God's image,
> Or Earth, perhaps, so newly separated
> From the old fire of Heaven, still retained
> Some seed of the celestial force which fashioned
> Gods out of living clay and running water.
> All other animals look downward; Man,
> Alone, erect, can raise his face toward Heaven.[8]

Ovid wrote of the "god within us," a phrase parroted faithfully by the Renaissance humanists and a thought given renewed emphasis by the microcosm-macrocosm dogma of the Neoplatonists of the Florentine school.[9]

The first great synthesis of Biblical and classical theological and anthropological motifs was made by the patristic writers, the Greek fathers in the first instance and the Latin fathers in the second. This fact needs reemphasis in this connection, not because it is unknown but because its great importance in the Renaissance and Reformation periods with the revival of Christian antiquity has not been sufficiently appreciated. If St. Paul's sermon on Mars' Hill became the *locus classicus* — and no pun is intended — for Christian humanism, then the expressions of the apologists spelled out precisely the positive attitude of the main-line patristic appreciation of classical culture that became programmatic for the fathers through the second to the fifth centuries. Justin Martyr's declaration that "whatever has been well said belongs to us Christians," or his reference to Christian theology as "the only philosophy which I find useful and adequate," are well known. In his first *Apology* he was very explicit: "We have been taught that Christ was First-begotten of God (the Father) and we have indicated above that He is the Word of whom all mankind partakes. Those who lived by reason are Christians, even though they have been considered atheists: such as, among the Greeks, Socrates, Heraclitus, and others like them." [10]

The instrumental value of the classics for the Church Fathers in their monumental effort to rethink the universe in Christian terms was recognized by many. Gregory of Nazianzus, for example, declared that Julian the Apostate with his measure forbidding Christians to teach and study the classics openly declared himself conquered in advance. He wished to overcome the Christians in a spiritual struggle by robbing them beforehand of their weapons. That is as though a champion were to challenge all men to a duel except the strong, Gregory asserted. He could, to be sure, forbid the Christians to speak correct Greek, but he could not keep them from speaking the truth.[11] That great, comprehensive mind of Clement of Alexandria, himself a product of a milieu which had absorbed and integrated Greek thought with a culture of greater antiquity, laid out the program of cultural and religious synthesis most systematically. Philosophy educated the Greek people for Christ just as the Law did the Hebrews. Thus philosophy was a forerunner insofar as it prepared the way for him who would be enlightened by Christ. It is a "schoolmaster for Christ." [12] There were warnings in great number, of course, from all of the fathers against the lasciviousness of some classical writings and against the demonic nature of the antique gods. Tertullian, that dour rigorist, referred to the philosophers as the "patriarchs of heresy" and blamed Greek philosophy for the Gnostic deviation. He called Plato a "grocery store for all the heretics," and in the De praescriptione haereticorum he attacked Plato's greatest student: "Unhappy Aristotle who introduced dialectic for the benefit of heresy, the great master in building up and in tearing down, ambiguous in its sentences, forced in its conjectures, ruthless in its arguments; a work of contentions, a burden even for itself, it discourses on everything so as not to have discoursed on anything." [13] But even Tertullian spoke of an anima naturaliter christiana, which suggested that the divine logos had not left natural man without some light of truth.

One positive result of this synthetic approach to the Christian and classical traditions was the emergence in many of the Fathers of a euphoric assessment of the dignity of man. To personalize this general proposition, the example of Origen and Nemesius will prove to be illuminating. The Alexandrian Father Origen had discoursed eloquently on the utility of Greek philosophy as a preparation for theology. He wrote:

> I beseech you to draw from Greek philosophy such things as are capable of being encyclic or preparatory studies to Christianity, and from geometry and astronomy such things as will be useful for the exposition of Holy Scriptures, in order that what the sons of the philosophers say about geometry and music and grammar and rhetoric and astronomy, that they are the handmaidens of philosophy, we may say of philosophy itself in relation to Christianity.[14]

Man, as Origen saw him, is a free creature of reason gifted above all with the power of speech, ἑκούσιον καὶ λογικόν ζῷον. It was Origen's *Commentary on Genesis*, in turn, which inspired Nemesius, bishop of Emesa, to one of the grandest encomiums on the dignity and excellence of man in all patristic literature:

> When we consider these facts about man, how can we exaggerate the dignity of his place in creation? In his own person, man joins mortal creatures with the immortals, and brings the rational beings into contact with the irrational. He bears about in his proper nature a reflex of the whole creation, and is therefore rightly called "the world in little." He is the creature whom God thought worthy of such special providence that, for his sake, all creatures have their being, both those that now are, and those that are yet to be. He is the creature for whose sake God became man, so that this creature might attain incorruption and escape corruption, might reign on high, being made after the image and likeness of God, dwelling with Christ as a child of God, and might be throned above all rule and all authority. Who, then, can fully express the pre-eminence of so singular a creature? Man crosses the mighty deep, contemplates the range of the heavens, notes the motion, position, and size of the stars, and reaps a harvest both from land and sea, scorning the rage of wild beasts and the might of whales. He learns all kinds of knowledge, gains skill in arts, and pursues scientific enquiry. By writing, he addresses himself to whom he will, however far away, unhindered by bodily location. He foretells the future, rules everything, subdues everything, enjoys everything. He converses with angels and with God himself. He gives orders to creation. Devils are subject to him. He explores the nature of every kind of being. He busies himself with the knowing of God, and is God's house and temple. And all these privileges he is able to purchase at the cost of virtue and godliness. But we must not let ourselves appear to any to be making out of place, a panegyric on man, instead of a straightforward description of his nature as we proposed to do.[15]

During the Renaissance period, as in medieval times, this work of

Nemesius was regularly ascribed to Gregory of Nyssa, the most prominent Christian philosopher of the fourth century. This was due in part to textual imprecision, but in large part also to the tone reminiscent of many of Gregory of Nyssa's flights of rhapsody about the human spirit. In his *Great Catechetical Discourse* and in his treatise *On the Creation of Man* Gregory depicted man as he was created in God's likeness, enjoying the gifts of intelligence, free will, charity, purity, and happiness. In the fifth chapter of his treatise *De hominis opificio,* he describes God in His own atelier, so to speak, busy painting His own portrait, omitting none of His perfections in His own likeness, human nature itself. Above all, the Divinity is intellect and reason.[16] In the Latin West the figure who cast his shadow over all the medieval centuries was St. Augustine. If, as Santayana once observed, no sermon is complete without a quotation from St. Augustine, then certainly no general chapter on Western intellectual history can pass him by. Augustine served as a primary channel for a certain expression of optimism and recognition of human worth during the Middle Ages, paradoxical though it might seem. His conviction that God had made man for man's own sake out of His own immense goodness, for the perfect God had no need of man for the Divinity's sake, reemphasized the creation basis for the primordial worth of man. He could speak of man as "opus eius tam magnum et admirabile."

In Book XIX of the *City of God* Augustine undertook to demonstrate Christianity's superiority over the pagan philosophies by helping man to transcend earthly sorrows and to attain to the eternal joys of heavenly life. Basically Augustine contrasts the miseries of this present life with the glories of the life to come, but in Chapter 24 he spells out the positive aspects of terrestrial life with such enthusiasm that taken alone without reference to the general argument the chapter constitutes a brief for the value of life in the here and now. In Chapter 24 of Book XXII Augustine came to speak again of the blessings with which the Creator has filled this life, obnoxious though it is because of the curse. The rich and countless blessings with which the goodness of God, who cares for all He has created, reflect His retributive justice, according to Augustine. The two major blessings are propagation and conformation, the first providing an ongoing genesis and the second assuring the continued sustenance of creation. Man's soul is thus gifted with a mind in which reason and understanding become capable of receiving knowledge and of understanding what is true and of loving what is good. By this capacity the soul drinks in wisdom and becomes endowed with those virtues by which in prudence, fortitude, temperance, and righteousness it makes war upon error and the other inborn vices and conquers them by fixing its desires on no other object than the supreme and unchangeable Good. Even in the body the goodness of God is apparent in the marvelous organs of sense and the rest of the members. And all the rest of creation with all its beauty and utility, the manifold and various loveliness of sky and earth and sea would fill a volume.[17] Augustine, to be sure, inserts these passages in the middle of a stream of thought with quite a different tendency. They have a grudging tone and are introduced with the concession that, if God had withdrawn His blessing completely and if man had lost his original image entirely, nothing would remain. This cannot be acclaimed as a bold humanistic assertion. Nevertheless, in the following centuries these statements were there for all to see.

One declamation of Lactantius, a Latin Father dubbed the "Christian Cicero," is reminiscent of the mood of the Greek Fathers. Lactantius had been a professor of rhetoric before his conversion to Christianity and became tutor to Crispus, the son of Constantine. His work on man as God's creation, then, stands in the rhetorical tradition and has roots in Latin as well as Greek antiquity. In his *De opificio Dei* Lactantius appealed to the creation motif as the ground for human dignity. "For that creator and father-God has given to man sense and reason, so that it might be apparent from this that we have been created by him, since he is himself intelligence, sense, and reason," he wrote.[18] He continued with a commentary on the superiority reason gives to man over the animal kingdom.

The tradition of Christian rationalism, with its culmination in St. Thomas Aquinas, kept reason central as man's basic claim to humaneness, for the final end is that knowledge of God which includes the faculty of intellect. Although with the ascendancy of the ascetic emphasis in medieval monasticism and with its Near Eastern source of origin and its Neoplatonic and partly Scriptural rationale, the assessment of the dignity of man in his natural estate under God's general providence was minimized. Even within the theology of the monks it remained an articulated theme. Bernard of Clairvaux might well serve as a striking example. He could refer to man as "celsa creatura in capacitate majestatis" and base such a lofty claim on man's dignity in creation, his rule over nature, and the power of his dominion.[19] In his *Meditationes piissimae* Bernard developed his ideas in a treatise entitled *De cognitione humanae conditionis,* with the first chapter *De dignitate hominis* making the argument for man's dignity on the basis of the persistence of the image of God in man and the advice for man to look within himself to discover God there. Many people know many things, he argues, but they do not know themselves. They seek God through exterior things and desert their own interior realm, for God is within. Man should therefore return from the exterior to the interior things and ascend from lower to higher things and hence come to a knowledge of God. In making progress in a knowledge of himself, man gains a knowledge of God. Man is made in God's image and similitude, which God wished to give to no other creature, and man's creation in this image involves his possession of memory, intelligence, and will or love. His full manhood is realized in his knowledge and understanding of the Son, in whom God is revealed.[20]

While the dignity-of-man theme persisted in the medieval period to a much greater extent than is commonly realized, the basis of that dignity was almost universally held to be the religious ground of his being. The various medieval renaissances from the Iro-Celtic to the 12th-century Renaissance merely suggested the anthropocentric classical context for allegations of human worth, for they were predominantly classical in form rather than in norm. With the coming of the Italian Renaissance a perceptible shift in emphasis became evident. Due in large part to the new verve of bourgeois society, for taken as a whole the humanists in a city such as Florence represented the upper levels of the population in wealth and political power, a new appreciation of man's innate and acquired worth and a new confidence in man's ability to control his environment emerged.[21]

Petrarch, the father of Renaissance humanism, was a self-conscious and in some respects self-assured and highly individualistic person, though it is no longer in vogue to tag him as the "first modern man." In his *De sui ipsius et multorum ignorantia* (on his own ignorance and that of many others) Petrarch declared all knowledge of nature useless unless one knows man and his place in the universe; for that reason men should not neglect to know themselves. In his *Ascent of Mount Ventoux* he quoted Seneca to the effect that "nothing is admirable besides the mind; compared to its greatness nothing is great," a thought then nearing the end of its second millenium in longevity.[22]

In Boccaccio, Petrarch's contemporary and admirer, a programmatic note was struck for the Renaissance humanists. He was born in Paris, it must be conceded to the historiographical revisionists, and his *Decameron* did depend on the medieval *fabliaux*.[23] But his *De genealogia deorum gentilium*, which he began about A. D. 1350, is an Italianesque handbook of mythology without a medieval equal. In it Boccaccio introduced the second Prometheus theme into humanis-

XI

tic literature. If God as the first Prometheus created man as a natural being, the second Prometheus, the learned man, creates anew. He makes of natural man civil man, known for his morals, knowledge, and virtue. If nature produces man, learning forms him anew and reforms him.[24]

The engagement of such civic humanists in the *vita activa* as Coluccio Salutati, whose *De laboribus Herculis* as a handbook of mythological allegories was intended to supplement Boccaccio's work, was in itself testimony of the feeling of confidence in the individual's position and capacity to achieve in public life. In striving to maintain and extend republican ideals of statehood these *viri docti* reformed not only man but men in the collective. Salutati was the undisputed leader of the humanistic movement for some 32 years from the death of Petrarch in 1374, and it was Petrarch who initially inspired him to his passionate interest in the classics until his own passing in 1406. He handed the torch of civic humanism with its explicit recognition of the importance of the *vita civile* to his two most important disciples, Leonardo Bruni and Poggio Bracciolini, both of whom succeeded him in turn as chancellors of the city of Florence.

Leon Battista Alberti (1404–1472), himself a religious but of a well-established Florentine family, in the Preface to that famous handbook of bourgeois virtues, the *Della famiglia,* urged the importance of the activist response to life's challenges, declaring that "fortune places under a yoke only him who submits to her." Even though the stream of life may seem to be directed by fate or fortune, he asserted in the *Intercoenales* of 1443, much can be accomplished in human affairs through prudence and industry.[25]

Three archetypal discourses on the dignity-of-man theme in Italian Renaissance humanism illustrate the varying emphases within conventional statements on the same motif. The first, written about the middle of the Quattrocento, was Bartolommeo Fazio's (1400?–1457) *De excellentia et praestantia hominis,* written for "the first Renaissance pope," Nicholas V. Stating in the Preface that this work was intended to be a companion piece to Innocent III's *De contemptu mundi,* Fazio stressed the importance of the power of reason in man working in harmony with the senses to achieve the conquest of nature. God created man and endowed him with reason so that he could know, love, and possess the supreme good, which is God himself. The supreme end of man is to serve God for his own sake, but since man can add nothing to God's divinity, this service of God takes the form of service to man.[26] In words reminiscent of Cicero he rehearsed man's

33

achievements, for "men have known secrets, constructed cities, invented shelter and clothing, founded laws, apprehended the turnings of the heavens and the motions and course of the stars, discovered medicine, besides so many arts, so many sciences such as among the first, philosophy, that master and leader of good living which first incites and establishes in us the worship of God and thence all works of virtue." All the powers of man's mind should lead him to contemplate divine things.[27] In Fazio the human achievements are only of transient value, and the ground for optimism in the final analysis is metaphysical or religious.

The second even more renowned expression of the dignity-of-man theme was that of Giannozzo Manetti, born in Florence in 1396 and died as an exile in Naples in 1459. Had Manetti known in 1451 and 1452, when he composed the treatise, of his total ruin and disastrous flight from Florence, he might have written differently. Manetti was in the activist tradition of civic humanism, however, and once responded to a question of King Alphonso of Naples as to what comprises the whole duty of man with the answer: *Intellegere et agere* (to understand and to act). The *De dignitate et excellentia hominis* was dedicated to King Alphonso and stressed man's achievements as evidence of human worth. He rehearsed the achievements of man from the building of the pyramids in antiquity to the construction of the dome of Brunelleschi in his native Florence. The artists, rhetoricians, poets, historians, jurists, philologists, doctors, and astrologers through the long centuries have served as witnesses of man's great excellence. The climax of the treatise was reached in the grand encomium on human powers in these lines:

> The genius of man is such that all these things, after that first new and rude creation of the world, seem to have been discovered and completed and perfected by us with a certain unique and extraordinary acumen of the human mind. For things which are perceived are ours, that is, are human things, since they have been made by men, all houses, all towns, all cities, in short, all edifices on earth, which certainly are so great and such that they ought rightly to be considered the works of angels rather than of men, on account of this great excellence of theirs. Ours are the pictures, ours the sculptures, ours are the arts, ours the sciences.[28]

Once again the creation and the new creation by the *vir doctus* is stressed. In Book IV of the treatise Manetti went beyond Fazio, whose work he cited in the Preface, to undertake a detailed refutation of Innocent III's *De contemptu mundi,* urging the physical as well as the mental and spiritual capacities of man as grounds for his value and the worthiness of life in the present world.

The third treatise, which may very well be the best-known document of Italian humanism, was Giovanni Pico della Mirandola's *Oratio de dignitate hominis*. He wrote it probably in 1486 as an introduction to the debate on his 900 propositions projected for January 1487, a disputation never held, thanks to ecclesiastical intervention. Pico, it is interesting to note, entitled his piece simply *Oratio*, and the subtitle *De dignitate hominis* was added by his editors, although it applies specifically only to the first part of the oration. The subject of the second half is that all conflicting schools of philosophy can be reconciled in a grand unity. As an admirer and understudy of Marsilio Ficino, Pico was familiar with his Neoplatonic approach to anthropology. Ficino had manipulated the traditional schemes in his *Theologia Platonica*. He had placed the rational soul at the center of the universe and had emphasized the importance of man's central position as the *copula mundi*, or midpoint in the totality of things, as well as man's universality. Man should dominate as lord and ruler, as the very rival of nature. Man can through astronomy even understand the heavenly sphere and his own place in the center of total reality. Pico stressed rather man's mobility and freedom, his potentiality for rising to great heights or for sinking to bottomless depths, sharing in the properties of all other things and finding his place where he wills it to be. It was this idea of man's freedom that drove Pico to put man outside the chain of being. Man must make the choices that will assure his upward movement to communion with angelic beings, an ascent aided by true philosophy, which recognizes the deep inner harmony of all sincere and genuine assertions of the mind.[29] The *Oratio* was composed, after all, in a burst of enthusiasm at a time when Pico was immersed in the study of Hebrew Gnostic literature and cabbalistic mysticism and was writing a treatise on love and beauty. The Hermetic literature was ecstatic about man, the great miracle who enjoys mental freedom.

The Italian Aristotelian Pietro Pomponazzi of Mantua (1462 to 1524) emphasized the humanistic conception of the dignity and worth of the individual soul. In his treatise *On the Immortality of the Soul* he argued that the excellence of man consists in his moral virtue and not in contemplation. In this emphasis he was not merely departing from the medieval ideal of the *vita contemplativa* but was differing with Aristotle, who in one passage in the *Nicomachean Ethics* had stressed the great value of contemplation. Pomponazzi knew little

Greek, and his humanist anthropology reflected the moralistic emphasis of the Latin classics and Italian humanism. It was, however, Pico's rhetorical statement that remained the Renaissance apotheosis of *homo sapiens* at its apogee, and that less than a decade before the disastrous invasion of Italy by Charles VIII and the beginning of a new time of troubles.

The *dignitas hominis* theme was reflected with varying brilliance also in septentrional, or transmontane, humanism. In following their Italian predecessors as well as the classical texts the German humanists lauded the *dignitas essendi,* the grandeur of the human spirit, and the "incredible power of the human mind." Among the French humanists Carolus Bovillus provides an excellent example of the lofty appreciation of man and above all of the learned man. In his *Liber de sapiente,* written in 1509 and published two years later, he developed the Prometheus theme once again. Following Pico's line, he held that man, being outside the order of all things, was free to become all things. Imitating Prometheus, man scales the heights of angelic intellection and governs the earth like a second god. Man resembles the divine Prometheus in his creative power and re-creates himself with learned wisdom. He is a man by nature because of his rational soul, and a true man by virtue because he is wise.[30]

A single example from Spanish humanism must suffice, the most obvious choice being Juan Luis Vives' *Fabula de homine,* an allegory portraying man as the son of Jupiter, born to play on the world-stage as he wills. The dependence on Pico's conception of the dignity of man is apparent throughout, stressing Pico's analysis of body and soul as equal parts of the human being, who is free to ascend or descend as he wills. Jupiter determines the creation of the world as a stage, prescribing no particular form to man, but gives to man an unlimited power of self-transformation. Man finally transforms himself into the person of Jupiter, thus becoming immortal. Once again the classical influence, specifically Cicero's *De legibus* and his *De natura deorum,* is evident, and the Biblical notions of the Creation and the Incarnation are suggested.[31] Vives (1492–1540) wrote the *Fabula* shortly after he first met Erasmus in Louvain in 1518, and it is intriguing to suppose that the prince of the northern humanists may have inspired him to do this Promethean allegory, for Erasmus was given to playing with mythology, such as the story of Cain deceiving the angel guarding the gates of Paradise and obtaining seed from which to grow outsized fruit, which Erasmus told at Colet's dinner table in November 1499. The statements on man's free will in the

*De libero arbitrio* were ambivalently mild compared with the ecstatic rhapsodies on the infinite resources of the human genius in the *Hyperaspistes* that followed the *Arbitrio*. In the *Enchiridion* he asserted that "the human spirit has never demanded anything of itself with vigor that it did not accomplish. A large part of Christianity is to wish to be a Christian with the whole heart." His whole confidence in the educability of man was in the tradition of the *vir doctus* as a second Prometheus.

The magisterial reformers had a loftier view of natural man in his natural estate than is often realized. Luther praised man's reason as the highest creation of the Almighty and marveled at the great achievements of man and the excellence of society and government also among the heathen. In his comments on Genesis 2:7 he referred to the creation as the primary basis of human dignity and worth:

> Here Moses returns to the work of the sixth day and points out whence the cultivator of the earth came, namely, that God formed him from a clod, as a potter forms a pot out of clay with his hands. For this reason he did not say above, as in the case of other creatures: "Let the earth bring forth man," but: "Let Us make a man," in order to point out the superiority of the human race and to disclose the unique counsel of God, of which He availed Himself when He created man, although after this man increased and multiplied in the same manner as the other beasts. For the semen congeals in the womb and is given form in an identical manner. Here there is no difference between a pregnant cow and a woman with child. But Moses shows that in their first state there was a very great difference, inasmuch as man was created by a unique counsel and wisdom and shaped by the finger of God.
>
> The difference between the origin of man and that of cattle also points to the immortality of the soul, of which we have previously spoken. Although all the remaining works of God are perfect objects of wonder and are very sublime, this nevertheless proves conclusively that man is the most outstanding creature: when God creates him, He takes counsel and employs a new procedure. He does not leave it to the earth to produce him, like the animals and the trees. But He Himself shapes him according to His image as if he were God's partner and one who would enjoy God's rest. And so Adam is a dead and inactive clod before he is formed by the Lord. God takes that clod and forms from it a most beautiful creature which has a share in immortality.[32]

Luther even adopted the humanists' imagery of man as the microcosm in a surprising passage on man as the *imago Dei*:

Here Moses does not employ the word "similitude," but only "image." Perhaps he wanted to avoid an ambiguity of speech and for this reason repeated the norm "image." I see no other reason for the repetition unless we should understand it for the sake of emphasis as an indication of the Creator's rejoicing and exulting over the most beautiful work He had made, so that Moses intends to indicate that God was not so delighted at the other creatures as at man, whom He had created according to His own similitude. The rest of the animals are designated as footprints of God; but man alone is God's image, as appears in the *Sentences* (Peter Lombard's). In the remaining creatures God is recognized as by His footprints; but in the human being, especially in Adam, He is truly recognized, because in him there is such wisdom, justice, and knowledge of all things that he may rightly be called a world in miniature. He has an understanding of heaven, earth, and the entire creation. And so it gives God pleasure that He made so beautiful a creature.[33]

In a fairly typical passage, Luther in fact lauded the new and pending conquests of nature with a verve characteristic of the humanists. Luther, like Aeneas Silvius and Erasmus, hailed the dawn of a golden age, a *güldene Zeit*.[34] In an unstudied and spontaneous expression of confidence in man's triumphs he exclaimed:

We are at the dawn of a new era, for we are beginning to recover the knowledge of the external world that we had lost through the fall of Adam. We now observe creatures properly, and not as formerly under the Papacy. Erasmus is indifferent and does not care to know how the fetus is developed in the uterus of the mother and is ignorant of the dignity of marriage. But by the grace of God we are beginning to recognize in the most delicate flower the wonders of divine goodness and omnipotence. Therefore we praise, bless, and give thanks to Him and we see in His creatures the power of His Word. He spoke and things stood fast. See that force display itself in the stone of a peach. It is very hard, and the germ it encloses is very tender; nevertheless, when the moment has come, the stone must open to let out the young plant that God calls into life. Erasmus passes by all that and takes no account of it and looks upon external objects as cows look at a new gate.[35]

Not only did Luther deliver a good many encomiums on the glories of human reason in the natural world, but he personally took the initiative in introducing the humanist curriculum into the University of Wittenberg as a replacement for the scholastic routine.[36] It is at the point of human-divine encounter that Luther most emphatically distinguishes between human and divine wisdom. There is no redemptive power in human knowledge and the arts:

> True it is that human wisdom and the liberal arts are noble gifts of God, good and useful for all sorts of things so that one cannot get along without them in this life. But we can never learn from them in detail what sin and righteousness are in the sight of God, how we can get rid of our sins, become pious and just before God, and come to life from death.[37]

Theology provides the infinite wisdom that cannot be learned.[38]

The case of Calvin and a humanistic view of man in the natural sphere of life has been made so well that it hardly needs retelling. Calvin as a young French humanist had edited a work of Seneca and had imbibed a large component of particularly Latin classical thought. It has been argued that this mental set remained with him after his religious conversion and affected his ethical and social thought. Recent scholarship has gone so far as to trace an increasing influence of Platonic thought in Calvin. Expressions of high regard for man's status as creature in the natural world are to be found not only in the young Calvin but also in the final editions of the *Institutes* and throughout his works.[39] Zwingli's *anderer Geist* was suffused with Erasmian anthropology to the point of extending instrumental reason to a magisterial role also in the realm of religion.[40] The optimism of 18th and 19th century Europe and 19th and 20th century America is so familiar as to make a full-dress rehearsal unnecessary.

If this euphoric view of life were the only or even the predominant one, the historian would find it a simple task to correlate a psychic and an intellectual ascending curve with the rise of the West in economic and political power. But at the high risk of easing the reader into a slough of despondency, it is mandatory to turn now to that other more somber view of man which has been a constant in Western culture from Biblical and classical times to the present. The very psalm of Asaph which called men "gods" and the children of the Most High continued with the somber reminder: "But ye shall die like men and fall like one of the princes. Arise, O God, judge the earth; for Thou shalt inherit all nations" (Ps. 82:7-8). This recognition of human frailty and mortality is a constant in the Biblical view of man, a view reflected upon more deeply and with greater agony in the struggles of Job and in the doubts of the Preacher. For St. Paul the body is the "body of this death." The ultimate hope of deliverance comes from the Beyond and points to the great Beyond.

In Hellenic and Roman classical culture the pessimistic view of man is not exclusively a characteristic of the decline or disintegration of classical culture. What is rather astonishing is the appearance of this corrosive mood at the very apogee of the golden ages. Among the Greeks rhetoricians, philosophers, and dramatists joined in a chorus of low notes. The Sophist antiphon argued that life should not be exalted as great and elevated since everything is small, mean, short, and mixed with misery. Not some ecstatic cultist of mystery and darkness but the measured and moderate Aristotle queried: "What is man? A true mark of weakness, the prey of the moment, a toy of fortune, a picture of sudden change, now subject more to envy, now more to misfortunes; the rest is slime and gall." [41] Aristophanes in *The Birds* echoed this sad refrain:

> Ye children of man! Whose life is a span
> Protracted with sorrow from day to day
> Naked and featherless, feeble and querulous
> Sickly, calamitous creatures of clay!

The Roman writers recognized that man's infirmities are both physical and psychological. In the Augustan age Vergil described the mood of the times not only in his paean of praise to Aeneas and the emperor but also in lines suggesting the coming of an early frost, killing flowers still in bloom. Pliny in his *Natural History* contrasted the physical weakness of man with the strength of animals, which are armed with natural weapons against their enemies and enjoy natural protection against the weather. Man alone sheds tears and begins life by crying. Nature asks a cruel price for her generous gifts, making it hardly possible to judge whether she had been more a kind parent to man or more a harsh stepmother.[42] Seneca, the author of so many humane treatises on kindness, gratitude, and graciousness, could yet advocate a necessary suicide. In many places, as in his *De consolatione ad Helviam matrem,* he lamented the great feebleness of the human body.[43] Plutarch in the *Moralia* has a witty dialog between Odysseus and Gryllus, his companion metamorphosed into a pig, entitled "Beasts Are Rational." In it he compares man unfavorably with the animals, arguing that animals are in full possession of all the virtues and even possess reason, but are free of all the desires that drive men through the world and lead them to make war on each other. He concludes that men are less fortunate than the animals.[44] And in the *Tusculan Disputations* Cicero added to the list of physical ills the psychic sufferings of man: "For nature has given to us infirm bodies and added to them intolerable sorrows and incurable diseases, and also gave minds suitable to the sorrows of the bodies and separately entangled in their own troubles and anxieties." [45]

The laments about the human predicament which can be heard even in the great age of Roman society increased to a mighty chorus during the centuries of imperial decline, dissolving at last in the tears of Jerome in Bethlehem for the fallen city. A necessary component for the health of Rome's body psychic as well as body politic was missing. Perhaps the lines of Matthew Arnold, who coined the beautiful phrase "sad lucidity of soul," are not too severe in depicting the Roman debacle:

> On that hard Pagan world disgust
> And secret loathing fell.
> Deep weariness and sated lust
> Made human life a hell.
> Stout was its arm, each thew and bone
> Seem'd puissant and alive —
> But, ah! its heart, its heart was stone
> And so it could not thrive! [46]

Dante in the *Convivio* relates that when he was in despair over the death of Beatrice, he turned to Boethius' *Consolation* and was like a man who looks for silver and finds gold. Boethius was not only a major formative influence upon the Middle Ages but also continued to be one of the most widely read and appreciated philosophers through the Renaissance period, particularly in northern Europe. Boethius in prison has Philosophy sitting down on the foot of his bed, beholding his dejected eye and his face disfigured with grief, and bewailing his wretched condition in the moving strains:

> Ah! hapless state of human race!
> How quick do all their pleasures pass!
> And too, too weak their minds to bear
> Life's varied scenes of woe and care.
> When grief's sharp thorn the heart assails,
> Of wisdom's sons the purpose fails;
> Their boasted vigour soon gives way,
> Dark melancholy clouds their day;
> The helm no longer reason steers,
> But lawless passion domineers.

The message seems to be that very few people die laughing. The medieval mood can hardly be characterized as hilarious, and the medieval image of man has been depicted in sufficiently grey tones often enough to do more than justice to this aspect of that phase of

Western culture. The great archetypal figure St. Bernard followed his chapter on the dignity of man with one entitled *De miseria hominis,* which reflected the major motifs in the melancholy dirge on man's transiency and frailty.

The most celebrated document of despondency over the human condition and the one against which Manetti was reacting specifically was Innocent III's *De contemptu mundi seu de miseria humanae conditionis,* in which he made the utmost of the dust-to-dust and ashes-to-ashes realities and rehearsed the most disgusting side of human life: the lice, spittel, urine, feces, the brevity of time, old age, the various labors and sorrows of mortals, the precariousness of life, the constant nearness of death, the many kinds of torments and sufferings of the human body, and his proclivities for sin and propensities for evil. It is true that Innocent planned to write the corresponding essay on the dignity of man, but he was caught up in administration and never rounded out the picture. Thus the total effect of this writing from such a lofty source was to underline in black the sorry side of human life.[47]

The closing epoch of the Middle Ages following the Black Death in the 14th century was the most gloomy in the history of all Europe. This age was more acutely aware than any before it of the brevity of life and the certainty of death. The suffering of the sick, the horrors of disease, the sudden, unpredictable coming of death were vividly described by popular pulpiteers such as Jacopo Passavanti and depicted in the paintings in murals and altarpieces.[48] At the very end of the era more was written about the *miseria* of human life than ever before. A characteristic expression of the depressed feeling of the time was Giovanni Conversino da Ravenna's (d. 1408) *De miseria humanae vitae.* Curiously the very advocates of Petrarchan humanism were major contributors to this body of gloom-filled literature.[49]

Eugenio Garin, the great Renaissance scholar at the University of Florence, once remarked that the Renaissance was a splendid but not a happy age. No longer is Petrarch, the father of Renaissance humanism, hailed as the first to embrace life in the world wholeheartedly. Petrarch is seen more as a man torn between conflicting world views, between a desire for the *vita activa* and the *vita studiosa* and even the *contemplativa.* He was a man full of self-doubt and agonized misgivings, given to serious reflection on central problems of existence in such treatises as his *De vera sapientia* or his *De vita solitaria.* His *Ascent of Mount Ventoux* is no longer understood as a new discovery and appreciation of nature but as a skillful literary artifice depicting

the meandering path of life and culminating in the introspective reflections on the summit as Petrarch reads and reflects on St. Augustine's
*Confessions,* where his eyes first fell upon the lines: "And men go to
admire the high mountains, the vast floods of the sea, the huge streams
of the rivers, the circumference of the ocean, and the revolutions of
the stars — and desert themselves." [50] He now, Petrarch relates, turned
his inner eye toward himself. Probably in June 1354 the prior of the
Milanese Certosa brought a letter to Petrarch from the Grand Prior
urging him to complete the unfinished treatise of Innocent III on *The
Dignity of Man.* Petrarch replied that he was preoccupied with a work
of his own on the remedies against the effects of fortune, *De remediis
utriusque fortunae.* In the *De remediis* he incorporated a dialog, *De
tristitia et miseria,* that brought to a head the opposition of Reason to
Sorrow and Fear, which are the children of Adversity, with Reason
contriving sufficient cause for considering life in spite of everything
as happy and pleasant. For Petrarch such a conclusion did not come
easily or with firm and lasting conviction.[51]

With Petrarch there entered into the body of Renaissance thought
the concept of the melancholy of the exquisitely cultivated isolated
individual, the special psychic anguish of the man of genius. In his
*Secretum,* or *De contemptu mundi,* which originally carried the subtitle of *De secreto conflictu mearum curarum* (the secret conflict of
my desires), Petrarch in three dialogs explored the agony of his soul
with St. Augustine, probing his difficulties and suggesting remedies,
some of which were not genuinely Augustinian. Particularly the second dialog analyzes the feelings of sin and guilt, and then he finally
comes to the heart of the matter, which is the problem of melancholy
and a despair that opens the way to destruction. He describes the state
of melancholy of the soul with the analogy to a besieged castle. This
melancholy is not the conventional *tristitia* (sorrow or sadness), but
rather *accidia* (deep melancholy). No longer is *accidia* the old *Kloster-
krankheit,* the monks' sin of sloth or malaise induced by routine living,
nor the vice defined by scholastic theology and berated by popular
preachers. In Petrarch it is related uniquely, if not exclusively, to the
pursuit of learning and wisdom.[52]

The concept of melancholy emerged in the Renaissance in at least
four basic modalities. The most easily defined was the medical notion
that identified *melancholia* and *mania* as a disease involving a disturbed balance of the humors, which should be medically treated and
is subject to physical correction. This Renaissance theory had Galenic
antecedents.[53] The second was the more traditional identification of

melancholy with the sin of sloth, and the way these two were combined to keep the catalog of cardinal sins within the prescribed limitation of seven is fascinating. Dante ingeniously suggested biting insects as the proper eternal retribution for sloth, and Thomas a Kempis suggested branding with red-hot pokers as a fitting reward. A third was associated with the struggle against the tyranny of *Fortuna,* a melancholy induced by the hopelessness of the struggle against the impersonal forces of *Fatum* or *Tyche Fortuna,* which was a nearly constant preoccupation of major Renaissance thinkers. Finally, melancholy was considered an all but inevitable concomitant of *ingenium,* or genius, which produced or was accompanied by an "enthusiasm" that was mystical and poetical in nature and either drove the intellectual into a state of restlessness, Augustine's *cor irrequietum,* or went so far as to reduce him to inertness and total immobility of mind and body. Although Aristotle formally associated genius and melancholy in classical times, the germ of this conception lay in Plato, especially in the *Phaedrus,* and this conception was reactivated through the agency of Marsilio Ficino.[54]

In Petrarch the third and fourth varieties of melancholy, the brooding over fortune and the pangs of genius, are clearly in evidence and subtly fused. A variety of reasons might be suggested for the misgivings and suffering of Petrarch. Quite obviously he was paying the price for the wider intellectual horizons his superior knowledge of the classical world revealed to him. Secondly, his psychic insecurity may well have resulted from an increasing individualism, for self-consciousness precipitated his self-doubts and a need for reassurance. Third, since the revival of Roman antiquity was not merely the revival of major classics but to a large extent a resurgence of late classical antiquity with the pessimistic cultural motifs far advanced, Petrarch may have absorbed attitudes characteristic of this declining epoch. Melancholy of the Aristotelian, Neoplatonic, or Hermetic-Magian kind shadowed the humanists through the Renaissance. The melancholy of Albrecht Dürer's famous·woodcut of 1514, *Melancholia I,* was of the Saturnine type, influenced by the natural and spiritual magic of Agrippa of Nettesheim, whose popular book on the occult sciences Dürer knew well. The woodcut with the figure of Melancholy brooding, surrounded by all the instruments of learning but reduced to absolute inertness by *accidia,* may well serve to illustrate this dark stream running through Renaissance humanism. The difficulty of these cultural giants is pointed up in André Gide's clever lines: "When one has ability, one does what one wishes. When one has genius, one does what one can." [55]

The Italian civic and literary humanists took up the theme of human misery and the comforts of otherworldliness, all the more surprising in view of their general affluence and established position in the urban society of the Renaissance.[56] Coluccio Salutati (d. 1406), the celebrated Florentine chancellor, about 1381 wrote a treatise on the world and religion, *De seculo et religione,* designed to strengthen a Camaldolese monk in his determination to remain in his monastery. The first book deals with the evils of secular life and the second with the joys of the monastic life.[57] Salutati's two leading protégés, Leonardo Bruni and Poggio Braccolini, each produced works discussing the limitations to human happiness. Leonardo Bruni (d. 1444) wrote an introduction to moral discipline which stressed the difficulty of achieving happiness while allowing for its possibility.[58] Poggio Braccolini (d. 1459), who as an old man of 72 had already lived a successful life by worldly standards, composed a work on the misery of the human condition which complained about everything the world might offer man.[59] Poggio had been haunted by the ironic spectacle of grandeur and decay presented by the Roman ruins and describes them in his *De varietate fortunae.* It has even been plausibly argued that Manetti's optimistic work on man's dignity and excellence was just a shade removed from a fundamental pessimism and that the arguments were adduced more in a search for reassurance than from a natural conviction. He wrote it, apparently, at the height of his career and not long before he was ruined by confiscatory taxation and forced into exile, a development, as noted above, that might understandably have changed the emphasis of his work. The end of the *Quattrocento* with the triumph of factionalism within and the domination by barbarian invaders from without saw the depths of depression, strikingly expressed by Machiavelli or by Guicciardini (d. 1540), the historian of Italy in those last decades. Guicciardini wrote: "When I consider how many accidents and perils of infirmity, of chance, of violence, and in infinite ways, the life of man is subjected to . . . I marvel all the more to see an old man or a fruitful year." [60] He was the chronicler of the denouement of the Italian Renaissance.

To the Florentine Platonists goes the credit, however, of wrestling most seriously in metaphysical terms with the place of man in the total scheme of things. Marsilio Ficino himself suffered from acute melancholy for three years prior to entering the priesthood. He was the author of the *De vita triplici,* that "diatetic of the Saturnine man" which became a classical document of Platonic anthropology. But precisely because of his celebrated treatise on the dignity of man, it is Pico who startles the Renaissance student the most with his compensatory emphasis on man's dependency on God, to whom he is immediately related without being bound to the restricting limitations of nature as such. That Pico had strong ties with traditional scholastic theology has long been known, for it is evident in the structure of his *Conclusiones,* and in his famous letter to Ermolao Barbaro he made his enthusiasm for the scholastics explicit:

> I was so troubled by your remarks that I blushed and grew ashamed of my studies. What, six years wasted in trying to understand, with so much labor, a thing which you consider so foolish! On St. Thomas, Duns Scotus, Albert, Averroes, I have, then, squandered my best years! . . . Nevertheless, I tell myself as a kind of consolation, that if one of these philosophers returned, he would know very well how to defend himself, for they were men well equipped with arguments. Well and good; our scholastic is loquacious; he will offer you his apology with as little rudeness as possible. "We were famous in our time, Ermolao, and we shall remain so, not in the schools of the grammarians or with pedagogues, but in the circles of the philosophers and among the wise: there it is not a question of who was the mother of Andromache or the children of Niobe, and similar nonsense, but of the reasons of things human and divine. It was to study and unravel these things that we were so subtle, so sharp, so penetrating that we may seem to have been, here and there, too meticulous and pedantic, if indeed one can be too scrupulous in the search for truth. Let him who accuses us of dullness and heaviness come and fight with us. He will see that these barbarians had Mercury in their hearts, if not on their lips, and that in lieu of eloquence they had wisdom, that wisdom which, far from uniting itself to eloquence, ought to dispense with it." [61]

Years later Melanchthon still thought it useful in the interests of the humanist rhetorical tradition to compose a reply to Pico's letter. Familiarity with this aspect of Pico's thought helps one understand the turn toward high theology which Pico took and the deeply personal religious interest he developed. It comes as a great surprise to the casual student of the Renaissance to encounter in the brilliant Pico, archetype of Renaissance humanist individualism and lofty view of man, such moving expressions of man's complete dependence on God as the following statements. The first is taken from Pico's *Commentary on Psalm Sixteen,* the most complete of his exegetical writings on the Psalms:

*Conserva me Domine.* That is to say, keep me good Lord: which word "keep me," if it be well considered, taketh away all occasion of pride. For he that is able of himself anything to get is able of himself that same thing to keep. He that asketh then of God to be kept in the state of virtue signifyeth in that asking that from the beginning he got not that virtue by himself. He then which remembreth that he attained his virtue not by his own power but by the power of God, may not be proud thereof but rather humbled before God after those words of the apostle: *Quid habes quod non accepisti* — What hast thou that thou hast not received. And if thou hast received it, why art thou proud thereof as though thou had not received it? Two words then there be which we should ever have in our mouth: the one — *Miserere mei Deus,* keep me, good Lord, when we remember our virtue.

The second is the summary of Pico's *Exposition of the Lord's Prayer:*

All consideration of this Prayer is reduced to a consideration of Christ's cross and our own death. Our own death shows us truly that we are pilgrims on earth, and the death of Christ made us sons of God; so that, thinking neither of an earthly father nor of an earthly fatherland, we may rightly say: "Our Father, who art in heaven." Our death keeps us from seeking our own glory, for we shall soon be dust and ashes; and Christ's death makes us desire God's glory, for on our behalf He did not shrink from the disgrace of the Cross. Therefore we shall say: "Hallowed be Thy Name," as if we were saying: "Not to us, Lord, not to us, but to Thy name give glory." Moreover, if we remember that all men swiftly perish through death, we shall want Christ to rule among them.[62]

In the light of such expressions and making allowances for the influence of Savonarola upon him in the last years, Pico's famous *Oratio,* it might be argued, described man before the Fall and was not intended to eliminate the need for grace nor meant to assay how much supernatural help man needs in the fallen estate. Though Pico's *Oratio* was the apotheosis of man in the Renaissance, it cannot fairly be argued that his religious expressions constitute the nadir of the Renaissance regard for man.

In a twofold sense Pietro Pomponazzi represented a more modest evaluation of man's place within total reality, as is evident from the well known position taken in the *De immortalitate animae* that contrary to the assertions of the Platonists, the immortality of the soul must be accepted on the authority of the church and not upon rational or empirical proofs, and in the position that the excellence of man consists in his moral virtue, not in contemplation. Man cannot think outside the sensible world and can understand his life only from within the world. In this emphasis on the corporal confines of real man Pomponazzi was dependent on Alexander of Aphrodisias, who allowed even less room for the nonmaterial element in man than Aristotle, to say nothing of Plato. What man thinks has, therefore, only a relative and not an absolute value. Theoretical speculations must always remain unsatisfying. Only by limiting himself to the things he is capable of achieving, Pomponazzi continued, can man build a harmonious existence. To be satisfied with what comes to him and with what he can have must be the mark of the measured man. Because it is vain to fear the inevitable, man should "thank God and nature and always be ready to die and not to fear death." In Pomponazzi Italian humanism has clearly moved far from the ecstatic reaches of Fazio, Manetti, or Pico's treatises on the dignity of man.

In humanism beyond Italy two examples of the shadow side must suffice, the one surprising and the other well known. Juan Luis Vives was a fine Erasmian Spanish humanist and the author of the *Fable of Man* discussed above. Yet this secure Christian humanist had his dark side, for he believed that man's intellect was weak, that he can comprehend but little in this life, and that what he does understand is uncertain and obscure. Man's mind, imprisoned in the flesh, lies in darkness and ignorance, and his heart is filled with deep and somber secrets.[63] The example easy to anticipate is, of course, Montaigne, with intriguing turns of phrase such as "Who knows when I am playing with my cat but that my cat is killing time with me." Luther's own *Anfechtungen* and bouts with melancholy are so well known and the picture of man's shortcomings drawn by those sweaty realists, to use Huxley's phrase, the reformers, that an elaborate discussion is not really called for.[64] In the historical literature of recent decades the dark undertow of the age of the Enlightenment has been discovered, but for a cultural manifestation analogous to the humanists' *accidia* the intellectual historian must turn to Chateaubriand and the Romantics.

"Western civilization has begun to doubt its own credentials," wrote Andre Malraux in his *Psychologie de l'art*.[65] This mood of disenchantment and loss of confidence began to develop seriously in the course of the 19th century with such voices as the somber Sören Kierkegaard and with the wars and pending destruction accelerated enormously during the first half of the 20th century. In 1843 Kierkegaard wrote in this vein:

Our age reminds one vividly of the dissolution of the Greek city-state: everything goes on as usual, and yet there is no longer anyone who believes in it. The invisible spiritual bond which gives it validity no longer exists, and so the whole age is at once comic and tragic — tragic because it is perishing, comic because it goes on. For it is always the imperishable which sustains the perishable, the spiritual which sustains the corporal.

It is as though man today were apprehensively echoing timid Erasmus' famous words: "Videmus fatalem quondam rerum humanarum mutationem!"

The secure and limited world of antiquity and the medieval periods has been badly shattered by four major successive blows: the Copernican revolution, the theory of Darwinian evolution, the Freudian discovery of the world of the subconscious, which Freud himself compared with the Copernican revolution, and post-Newtonian physics, which has unsettled the legal mechanics of the world machine. In writing his *Paradise Lost* John Milton presented a description of the Ptolemaic and Copernican systems, though he used a cosmological framework older than that employed by Dante. The question in early modern times weighed on sentient man's mind in a worrisome way. In 1611 John Donne, the English parson-poet, conceded to the Copernicans that "those opinions of yours may very well be true . . . (in any case they are now) creeping into every man's mind." In his poem on *The Anatomy of the World,* which represented "the frailty and decay of this whole world," Donne reflected the unsettling effect of Copernicanism:

> [The] new Philosophy calls all in doubt,
> The element of fire is quite put out;
> The Sun is lost, and the earth, and no man's wit
> Can well direct him where to look for it.
> And freely men confess that this world's spent,
> When in the Planets, and the Firmament
> They seek so many new; then see that this
> Is crumbled out again to his Atomies.
> 'Tis all in pieces, all coherence gone;
> All just supply, and all Relation:
> Prince, Subject, Father, Son are things forgot,
> For every man alone thinks he hath got
> To be a Phoenix, and that then can be
> None of that Kind, of which he is, but he.[66]

The impact of the new cosmology on man's view of his own position in the universe was given somber expression by Blaise Pascal when he wrote:

When I consider the short duration of my life, swallowed up in the eternity before and after, the little space which I fill, and even can see, engulfed in the infinite immensity of spaces of which I am ignorant, and which know me not, I am frightened, and am astonished at being here rather than there, why now rather than then?[67]

Modern man has learned to roll with the punches with greater skill than Donne or Pascal, but something analogous to the effect of Copernicanism on them is mirrored in the impact of the new physics on our own contemporaries. A precocious young poet, Barbara Baier Solomon, compressed the ideas, though overstating the case, into a few lines:

Newton's world no longer exists
In quantum paths chance persists
Subtle device an extension
Of random chance to man's intention.[68]

Very possibly, however, the new anthropologies of developmentalism and depth psychology have contributed equally to man's downward assessment of man, whether rightly or wrongly so. The worry about man himself was well phrased by New England's poet laureate Robert Frost when he said: "You cannot frighten me with your enormous spaces, It is the void in man that gives me pause."

The nestor of Renaissance historians, Jacob Burckhardt, was both prophetic and historical, it seems, when he raised the question in his *Reflections on History*, "Will optimism continue to survive and how long? Or, as pessimist philosophy of today might seem to suggest, will there be a general change in thought such as took place in the third and fourth centuries?"[69] The answer to his second question that wells up from the demimonde of intellectual life in our day is a shrill yes. Jacques Kerouac, spokesman for the ragged edge of the younger set, advertises his contempt for history as being neither true nor valuable. Norman Mailer defines a hipster as "a man who has divorced himself from history, who does not give a damn about the past." On a considerably higher level existentialist Sartre cites the reasons why man is not bound by history. For a large segment of the population, cut off from a serious bond with the past, whatever value and meaning there is in life is created by the self, while all outside belongs to the mysterious and impenetrable unpattern of an unreal reality. It could be plausibly argued that a Christian like Cardinal Newman and a pagan like Seneca had infinitely more in common than a large part of the postmodern generation (if the reader will forgive the use of this faddish term) has with either Christianity or paganism. It is no longer possible to ignore this loud chorus of "existential screaming," for it is both symptom and sickness.

What is, however, more decisive is the plaintive song of responsible intellectuals, particularly of the younger men. Without embarking on a discussion of the anatomy of revolution and the desertion of the intellectuals, we can at least suggest that the intellectuals have frequently proved themselves to be sensitive to great human problems and were their articulate heralds long before society had followed fateful tendencies toward final consequences. Only a few examples from the voluminous "viewing with alarm" literature will have to suffice. The key word is alienation.

A brilliant young Harvard-trained psychologist now at Yale, Kenneth Keniston, spoke out in the Phi Beta Kappa journal on the problem of Western man:

> This is an age that inspires little enthusiasm. In the industrial West, and increasingly now in the uncommitted nations of the East, ardor is lacking; instead men talk of their growing distance from one another, from their social order, from their work and play, and even from the values that in a perhaps romanticized past seem to have given their lives cohesiveness and direction. Horatio Alger is replaced by Timon, Napoleon by Ishmael, and even Lincoln now seems pallid before the defiant images of "hoods" and "beats." The vocabulary of social commentary is dominated by terms that characterize this distance: alienation, estrangement, separation, withdrawal, indifference, disaffection, apathy, noninvolvement, neutralism — all these words describe the increasing distance between men and their former objects of love, commitment, loyalty, devotion and reverence. Alienation, once seen as the consequence of a cruel (but changeable) economic order, has become for many the central fact of human existence, characterizing man's "thrown-ness" into a world in which he has no inherent place. Formerly imposed *upon* men by the world around them, estrangement increasingly is chosen *by* them as their dominant reaction to the world.[70]

The shift in literature from a preoccupation with the alienation of the outsider, the member of a minority group, to a concern for the alienation of the common man as a metaphysical malady is highly indicative. The American historian and presidential advisor Eric Goldman once commented sardonically that when the American Negroes have achieved all their realizable goals, they will discover what the emancipated Jews learned: that life itself is fundamentally empty. *Der Mann ohne Eigenschaften* was the title of Robert Musil's important Austrian novel which earlier in the century suggested the line literature of despair would take. Contemporary man fears loss of self in the economic, social, and even cultural processes of mass society.

One very common diagnosis of the problem relates man as victim to the robotization and mechanization of man in an industrial society. The prolific journalist and articulate humanist Joseph Wood Krutch has emphasized this aspect of the problem. A montage of thoughts derived from his book *Human Nature and the Human Condition* will serve to bring out the concern of an honest contemporary social critic.

We lost what had been from about 475 B. C. until about seventy-five years ago the supreme conviction that what was best in man was that which was least like the machine.

Even though modern man may labor at the machine to provide the good things of life for others, he believes that these good things are the wealth and the power produced by the machine. During the two centuries just past more and more human beings have become accustomed to doubt that they are the sons of God and that they have immortal souls. Modern man regards himself as just another animal, another machine. He is only what circumstances and reflexes make him at any given moment. Reason is mere rationalization. Choice is an illusion. Standards are prejudices. Man is not Homo Sapiens, man the thinker, but merely Homo Faber, man the machine-tender.

He has become the master of know-how, but he is less and less capable of reason, wisdom and love. Even in the eighteenth century when men became more inclined to appeal to right reason than to revealed religion, they had ideals; they distinguished between right and wrong, purity and impurity, the courtly and the vulgar. But today's key words are wealth, power, progress, prosperity, welfare, adjustment, security and peace of mind. Love, whether considered as caritas or merely as eros, eludes us. Psychiatrists speak of the "incapacity to love." Millions are "alienated" from their world, unhappy strangers in their only home.[71]

Man is more than a metabolic engine merely reacting to his environment. On the other hand, he is never governed entirely by reason and by conscious aims. His whole being is intertwined with that of his family and associations, his religion and total culture. When the individual man is cut off from his own tradition and isolated from his own kind, the whole of human society is weakened. Where natural forms of association and sound influences from the higher life no longer provide the basic assumptions on which the reality of life is based, the way is opened wide for alien influences and corrosive forces to debilitate the individual and enfeeble all of society. If religion is in some sense the vibrant heart of a culture, then the question how well Christianity is maintaining its hold on Western society is a central concern.

A century ago the French historian and religious biographer Ernst Renan expressed his misgivings as to the future of Christianity in these words: "We are living off of the shadow of faith. We will be living on the shadow of the shadow, on the scent left in an empty bottle. Will it last?" [72] This challenge from an honest critic of the last century has become the militant theme of many bumptious crusaders in the 20th century. One German journalist, publisher, and public orator, Gerhard Szczesny, has attracted astonishingly large crowds of university students with his lectures announcing the end of the Christian era. He is taken seriously by the present generation of university youth. He declares:

> Today the real Christian creed, viewed in the broad, scarcely survives as a vitally creative force. The peoples of the West, as they live out their lives — and this takes into account the majority of those who call themselves Christians — in their thinking and behavior have ceased to pay the least attention to Christianity's idea of God and the hereafter, or the Christian notion of sin and grace. Christianity was once a faith that really pervaded human existence. But it has been supplanted by a kind of indifferent tolerance of that theological phraseology which, every Sunday, resounds from pulpit and loudspeaker.[73]

A fascinating development within the communist world has been the debate in recent years about alienation within a communist society. Marx had described alienation or the isolation of man from his environment and within it as a social phenomenon that was a product of capitalism, and until a short time ago good communists declared that alienation was impossible in societies of their creation. Now revisionists concede that communism has created forms of alienation peculiar to itself; and Eastern European writers, when liberated from the narrow dictates of the party, consistently turn to themes of solitude and despair.

In the democratic West the cultural and religious dislocations of our times are recorded with seismic sensitivity in both contemporary literature and the arts, in which traditional ideas and familiar forms are turned and distorted nearly beyond recognition. Empty sounds and meaningless lines symbolize the loss of content and meaningfulness in much of the life of contemporary man. It is plain irresponsible nonsense to characterize alienation and estrangement as universally

53

present in our society. There is much that is sound and solid in the cultural and religious body of Western man. It is, nevertheless, urgent to note that many intellectuals believe that our culture stands at one of those critical turning points marked by the breakdown of the old and the emergence of a new. The possibility that their analysis is accurate exists, and the probability of their warnings becoming self-fulfilling prophecies is high. An unwholesome paranoia of the leaders in thought can easily infect the multitude. In intellectual history the tendency or direction of movement is more significant than the quantified proportions of opinion at any given point. An ideology of despair in the midst of plenty and of melancholy profundity that repudiates the present and foresees illness in the future is to be taken seriously by all concerned men. The deepest theme in history, Goethe observed, has been posed by the conflict of faith and unfaith.

If the history of mankind teaches nothing else, it demonstrates that man is a durable and resilient creature. Western culture has twice gone through cultural crises that seemed to presage to men of those days the end of their culture and to promise only dark days for man. Friedrich Nietzsche, with insight becoming his brilliance, pronounced: "Before one seeks man, one must have found the lantern — must it be the lantern of the Cynic?" [74] During the first major crisis of Western culture, when the classical world was in noticeable decline, the golden age giving way to the silver and the silver age to lead and iron, and crepuscular shadows were enveloping the earth, the Church Fathers held aloft a lantern to send out light in the gathering gloom. Clement of Alexandria in his *Stromata*, that patchwork quilt of old and new thought, spoke for them all when he wrote:

> With the lamps of the wise virgins lighted at night in the great darkness of ignorance, which the Scripture signified by "night," wise souls, pure as virgins, understanding themselves to be situated amidst the ignorance of the world, kindle the light, and rouse the mind, and illumine the darkness, and dispel ignorance, and seek truth, and await the appearance of the Teacher. [75]

During the second major crisis precipitated by the deaththrows of medieval civilization, the Reformers with their rediscovery of the historical core of Christianity and a new declaration of its evangelical affirmations gave to the faith a new lease on life. Albrecht Dürer, whose *Melancholia I* symbolized the shadow side of the Renaissance, in the year 1516 did a drawing *Der Verzweifelnde* (the despairing man) which captured the anguish of his own and his fellowmen's uncertainty. When Dürer encountered Luther's proclamation of the

Kerygma (the glad tidings), he was swept along with the excitement of a new discovery. His response to the news after Worms that Luther had been killed was a disconsolate cry: "Who now will give us certainty?" A few characteristic expressions from Luther himself will bring out the tone as well as accentuate the theme of his message that "the Christian need not be melancholy."

Luther's assessment of the human situation was positive and rooted in the basic Christian optimism with its theological premise:

> We have more occasions for joy than for sadness; we believe in the living God, and Christ lives, and we, too, shall live. (John 14:19) Sadness is born in us. . . . But God is the Spirit of gladness. He saves us. . . . We must hold on to the fact that God does not desert his own. He did not create man with a head to hang down like the beasts but to be held erect so that man can look toward the heavens.[76]

In this final sentence Luther reverts to the thought of Ovid and Cicero on man, whose feet are planted on the earth but whose hands and head can be raised to the heavens.

In his commentary on Ecclesiastes Luther undertook to wrestle with the problems posed by skepticism and the theme of the vanity of all things. He was concerned to combat the view that the world is a *fatum* and that life is perpetually consumed by time, and stressed instead the need for personal faith and an activist engagement. Vanity does not lie in man's world, that is to say, in things *sub sole* (under the sun), but rather in the void, that is, within man himself — *vanitas in humano corde!* Luther's response to the total questioning of natural man is the universal answer of Christian faith. He recognized that epistemological skepticism is only one small twig on the large tree of doubt about life's meaning and purposes. In his famous reply to Erasmus, "Spiritus sanctus non est Scepticus," Luther was indulging in an unfair innuendo against Erasmus, but beyond that was offering his religious response to the doubt of an age.[77]

The man of faith must ideally take the good and the bad, the pleasant and the unpleasant things alike as from God's hands.[78] But to live in the midst of the world and to preserve a quiet and peaceful heart — that is an art! [79] The great danger for the individual is to become isolated and turned in upon himself *(incurvatus in se)*. The man of faith has been recommissioned to care for all creation and to become a co-worker with God. This challenge to an activist program in the realms of social, political, economic, and cultural life is a most wholesome corrective and antidote to sloth, melancholy, and other sickness of the soul. Once faith has been implanted, Christians should

**55**

be very busy toward the neighbor, zealous of good works, burning with love toward the neighbor. Thus life *coram Deo* leads to a constructive and meaningful life *coram mundo*.[80]

Luther spent a lifetime combatting melancholy and communicating a sense of confidence to his fellowmen. There is even a bit of bravado in his protestations of courage and Christian nonchalance, to borrow Reinhold Niebuhr's phrase. It came to the surface particularly in crisis situations, as in 1522 when desertions from his cause were numerous and he wrote to Elector Frederick of Saxony:

> Have a little confidence in me, fool though I am, for I know these and other like tricks of Satan. I do not fear him because I know that this hurts him. Yet all of this is only a beginning. Let the world cry out and pass its judgments. Let those fall away who will — even a Saint Peter or persons like the apostles. They will come back on the third day, when Christ rises from the dead. This word in II Cor. ch. 6, must be fulfilled in us: "Let us approve ourselves in tumults," etc.[81]

Or again, during the trying days of the Augsburg Diet in 1530, Luther allegedly wrote on the wall in the Koburg the words of the psalm for his own encouragement: "Non moriar sed vivam et narrabo opera Dei." He found it necessary to encourage Melanchthon and the less stalwart evangelicals at the Diet:

> I am displeased with your miserable worries, with which you write you are consumed and which rule so in your heart. This shows the magnitude of our unbelief, not the magnitude of our cause. For the same cause was greater in the time of John Hus and many others than it is with us. But just as the cause is great, so is its author and initiator, for the cause is not ours. Therefore, why do you continually and without intermission weaken? If the cause is false, let us renounce it. If it is true, why do we make him a liar in such great promises with which he commands us to be of a calm and quiet mind?[82]

Luther's correspondence is studded with letters of a *Seelsorger* combatting depression and melancholy in men who have turned to him for help. Luther sent Matthias Weller a characteristic bit of advice on the problem of his psychological depression.

Grace and peace in Christ.
Honorable, kind, good Friend:

> Your dear brother has informed me that you are deeply distressed and afflicted with melancholy. He will undoubtedly tell you what I have said to him.
> Dear Matthias, do not dwell on your own thoughts, but listen to

what other people have to say to you. For God has commanded men to comfort their brethren, and it is his will that the afflicted should receive such consolation as God's very own. Thus our Lord speaks through Saint Paul, "Comfort the fainthearted," and through Isaiah: "Comfort ye, comfort ye my people. Speak ye comfortably." And elsewhere our Lord indicated that it is not his will that man should be downcast, but that he should rather serve the Lord with gladness and not offer him the sacrifice of sorrow. All this Moses and the prophets declared often and in many places. Our Lord also commanded us not to be anxious, but to cast our cares upon him, for he careth for us, as Saint Peter taught from Ps. 55. . . .[83]

In the Table Talk Luther reverted to this theme frequently, as though he perceived an infectious malady spreading through society. Especially throughout the last 15 years of his life he warned that solitude produces melancholy and urged comradeship and social contacts as a cure, together with playing the lute, prayer, and a host of common-sense devices.[84] Luther was candid enough to admit that for all the sound advice he freely dispensed, he found that applying the same to himself was another matter. To Conrad Cordatus he wrote: "This is in accord with the saying, 'Good cheer is half the battle,' and, 'A merry heart doeth good like a medicine: but a broken spirit drieth the bones.' I give you this advice although I confess that I do not take it myself." [85]

That was Luther in another day and another age, at the end of the Middle Ages, which the medievalist Norman Cantor has described with the rubric "the life and death of a civilization." [86] The problem confronting contemporary man may very well be that of Albrecht Dürer's "Who now will give us certainty?" With Erasmus we too see a certain fatal mutation in human affairs, but need it be fatal?

The audacious survey now happily completed of man's view of man and his prospects through the long millenia of Western history at least suggests, if it does not confirm, certain tentative conclusions. A time-line perspective of the problem of man's ambiguous position in the total scheme of things and of man's ambivalent assessment of that position suggests that the range of human possibilities is fortunately limited at the extremes of both pessimism and optimism. The human habitation is provided with both a floor and a ceiling. As Hegel once reminded his lady friend and future wife, Marie Tucher, "In all not superficial minds a sense of sadness is linked with all sense of happiness," and the reverse is fortunately also usually true.[87] In the grand sweep of Western history there have been periods of decline in which the general mood was depressed and periods of ascent in which the mood was exuberant. But in each period the counterpoint of expectation or despondency found expression through some articulate spokesmen and was recorded for our contemplation. This chiaroscuro treatment of the human landscape displays broad areas of light and shadow. But close study of the detail reveals also that many of the leading figures in pronouncing upon either the grandeur of man's dignity or the abjectness of his misery have in their own persons given expression also to the antithetical aspect. The picture in terms of broad cultural analysis is complicated in two ways, then: first by the fact that both motifs were present in varying degrees in at least the major figures referred to and, second, by the fact that both motifs were found in varying degrees in all the cultural epochs traversed. The line runs not merely among men but through each man, marking off sectors in history of varying areas.

From within his own historical perspective man remains a mystery to man. It is ironic, in fact, that the world of nature should seem to be more accessible to human understanding than the world of history, which man makes and in which he is intimately involved. Alexander Pope's lines have a kind of permanent validity, so far as the really important questions of human life are concerned:

> Placed on this isthmus of a middle state,
> A being darkly wise yet rudely great:
> With too much weakness for the stoic's pride,
> He hangs between; in doubt to act, or rest,
> In doubt to deem himself a God, or Beast;
> In doubt his Mind or Body to prefer,
> Born but to die, and reas'ning but to err;
> Alike in ignorance, his reason such,
> Whether he thinks too little, or too much:
> Chaos or thought and passion, all confus'd;
> Still by himself abus'd, or disabus'd;
> Created half to rise, and half to fall;
> Great lord of all things, yet a prey to all.
> Sole judge of Truth, in endless error hurl'd:
> The glory, jest, and riddle of the world! [88]

If the temper of our times is one of gathering darkness with all the attendant apprehension and anguish of soul, then some comfort can be derived from the fact that our civilization has responded twice before in a positive way to similar disintegrating maladies. Ideas have exercised a powerful force upon men who collectively make history. The quality of the ideas and the evocative and creative efforts of men acting upon those ideas will determine what man's past will come to be in the future.

ἄνωθεν τὸ φῶς (From above the light) is the motto of Concordia Seminary. The words of a forceful contemporary poet who has himself wrestled with the dark melancholy, meaninglessness, and alienation of our times, W. H. Auden, express this thought with beauty and power:

> Defenseless under the night
> Our world in stupor lies;
> Yet, dotted everywhere,
> Ironic points of light
> Flash out wherever the Just
> Exchange their messages;
> May we (I), composed like them
> Of Eros and of dust,
> Beleaguered by the same
> Negation and despair
> Show an affirming flame.

## NOTES

1. Samuel Eliot Morrison, *Vistas of History* (New York: Alfred A. Knopf, 1964), p. 21.
2. *The Civilization of the Renaissance in Italy* (New York: Harper & Brothers, 1954), p. 342.
3. *Force and Freedom. Reflections on History* (Boston: Beacon Press, 1964), pp. 80—81. The section "Fortune and Misfortune in History," pp. 347—70, is a notable attempt to guard against wishful thinking in history.
4. Typical of this view is H. A. Enno van Gelder's *The Two Reformations in the 16th Century* (The Hague: Martinus Nijhoff, 1961), a book that reflects an interpretation more current thirty or more years ago than today.
5. *Reformation, Renaissance, Humanismus* (Berlin, Leipzig: Gebrüder Paetel, 1926), p. 90. The sober Dutch cultural historian Jan Huizinga described the humanists in similar terms: "If ever an elite, fully conscious of its own merits, sought to segregate itself from the vulgar herd and live life as a game of artistic perfection, that was the circle of choice Renaissance spirits," *Homo ludens* (London: Routledge & K. Paul, 1949), p. 180.
6. Sir George Young, *The Dramas of Sophocles Rendered in English Verse Dramatic and Lyric* (London and Toronto: J. M. Dent & Sons, 1931), pp. 11—12.
7. Marcus Tullius Cicero, *De natura deorum,* trans. Francis Brooks (London: Methuen & Co., 1896), Ch. lvi, p. 146. The preceding chapter describes the marvel of the human physical organism.
8. *Metamorphoses* I, 72—84, trans. Rolfe Humphries (Bloomington, Ind.: Indiana University Press, 1955), p. 5.
9. This dogma is found also in northern humanists, for example, *Der Briefwechsel des Konrad Celtis,* ed. Hans Rupprich (Munich: C. H. Beck'sche Verlagsbuchhandlung, 1934), Br. 275, pp. 499 ff., lines 121 ff.; Johannes Tolhopf to Celtis, Br. 101, p. 166, line 22.

10. Justin Martyr, J. P. Migne, ed. *Patrologiae Graecae,* (Paris: Apud Garnier Fratres, editores et J. P. Migne successores, 1884), VI, col. 397. Hereafter cited as either Migne, P. G., or Migne, P. L., *Patrologia Latina,* as the case may be. *Apologia* I, 46.

11. "Contra Julianum I," Migne, P. G., XXXV, cols. 535—38. See Herbert W. Rüssel, *Gestalt eines christlichen Humanismus* (Amsterdam: Akademische Verlagsanstalt Pantheon, 1940), p. 75. Marcel Guignet, *Saint Grégoire de Nazianze et lá Rhétorique* (Paris: Alphonse Picard et fils, 1911), pp. 43—70, depicts Gregory's attitude to the classics as ambivalent, even contradictory. St. Basil's "Exhortation to Young Men on How They Might Derive Profit from Pagan Literature," *St. Basil: The Letters,* trans. Roy J. Deferrari (Cambridge: Harvard University Press, 1950), IV, 378—435, argued for the utility of the classics on grounds similar to those of Gregory, even adducing the examples of Plato, Plutarch, and Seneca, who themselves expounded the old poets.

12. *Stromata* I, 5, *The Ante-Nicene Fathers,* eds. Alexander Roberts and James Donaldson (Grand Rapids, Mich.: Wm. B. Eerdmans Publishing Co., 1962), II, 305.

13. Tertullian, *De Praescriptione Haereticorum,* VII, 6, *Corpus Christianorum. Series Latina* (Turnholti: Typographi Prepols Editores Pontifici, 1954), p. 192. See his *Apologia adversus Marcionem* I, 1, for a Prometheus reference; also p. 442.

14. Origen really desired to be orthodox, moreover, as is evident from his statement in the *De principiis, praefatio* 2: "That alone is to be accepted as truth which differs in no respect from ecclesiastical and apostolic tradition." The way in which Origen's orthodoxy has been refurbished by recent scholarship is evident in Jean Daniélou, *Origen* (London and New York: Sheed and Ward, 1955), p. 310: "He is of that rare class of men whose genius is equalled only by their sanctity."

15. *De natura hominis,* Migne, P. G., XL, cols. 532C—533B. Translated in William Telfer, ed. *Cyril of Jerusalem and Nemesius of Emesa* (London: SCM Press Ltd., 1955); LCC IV, 254—56. This panegyric reflects the Posidonian doctrine that man is the apex of the natural order. A rhetorical commonplace, it is related or indebted to Cicero's *De natura deorum,* II, 153.

16. Alcuin A. Weiswurm, "The Rational Nature of Man," *The Nature of Human Knowledge According to Saint Gregory of Nyssa* (Washington, D. C.: The Catholic University of America Press, 1952), p. 62. See Gregory of Nyssa, "Restoring God's Image," *From Glory to Glory* (New York: Charles Scribner's Sons, 1961), pp. 112—17; Roger Leys, S. J., *"Anthropologie," L'Image de Dieu chez Saint Grégoire de Nysse* (Brussels: L' Édition Universellé, 1951), pp. 59—119.

17. Saint Augustine, *The City of God* (New York: Random House, 1950), pp. 850 to 855. In the *De doctrina christiana* Augustine asserts the utility of classical thinkers in a way reminiscent of the Greek Fathers: "If those who are called philosophers, especially the Platonists, have said things by chance that are truthful and conformable to our faith, we must not only have no fear of them, but even appropriate them for our own use from those who are in a sense their illegal possessors," *Christian Instruction,* Ch. 40, John J. Gavigan, O. S. A., trans. *Writings of Saint Augustine,* (New York: CIMA Publishing Co., Inc., 1947), IV, 112.

18. *De opificio Dei, vel formatione hominis,* Migne, P. L., VII, col. 14. In Book II, Ch. 10, of his *The Divine Institutes,.* Lactantius opposes the Genesis creation account to the Prometheus legend. *The Fathers of the Church,* (Washington, D. C.: The Catholic University of America Press, 1964), XLIX, 138—43. Lac-

tantius, *Div. Instit.* II, 2: "Deus unicus qui universa condidit, qui hominem de humo struxit, hic est verus Prometheus."

19. Saint Bernard, *Opera omnia*, (Paris, 1839), I, cols. 284D, 2594A, 1332A. Of all the creatures under heaven man is nearest to God. Ibid., col. 2331C.

20. Ibid., Tomus V, volumen secundum, pars prior, cols. 661—64. William of St. Thierry (d. 1148), Bernard's precise contemporary, referred to the image-of-God idea in addressing man: "O image of God, recall your dignity; let the image of the author shine brightly in you," *Expositio altera super cantica canticorum*, Migne, P. L., CLXXX, col. 494C. On William see Etienne Gilson, *La Philosophie au Moyen Age* (Paris: Payot & Cie, 1952) pp. 300—01. In the East an 11th-century Byzantine poet John Mauropus could pray for Plato and Plutarch, for they were both closely related to Christ's laws in their teaching and ethic. The dignity-of-man theme persisted also there.

21. The growth of secularism and its effect on the spiritual and intellectual life of Europe is emphasized by the noted Renaissance scholar Wallace K. Ferguson in his article "The Church in a Changing World, a Contribution to the Interpretation of the Renaissance," *American Historical Review*, LIX (Jan. 1953), 1—18, as well as in his major text *Europe in Transition* (New York: Houghton Mifflin Co., 1962).

22. The Seneca passage is his *Epistles*, 8, 5, cited in Ernst Cassirer and others, *The Renaissance Philosophy of Man* (Chicago: University of Chicago Press, 1948), p. 44.

23. Johan Nordström, *Moyen Age et Renaissance* (Paris: Librairie Stock, 1933), adduces these facts to promote his northern and specifically French origin of the Renaissance thesis.

24. *De genealogiis deorum gentilium*, Book IV, Ch. 44, a cura di V. Romano (Bari: Gius. Laterza & Figli, 1951), I, 198—202: "Circa quos secundus Prometheus insurgit, id est, doctus homo, et eos tanquam lapideos suscipiens quasi de novo curret, docet et instruit, et demonstrationibus suis ex virtutibus insignes, adeo ut liquido pateat alios produxisse naturam, et alios reformasse doctrinam. . . ." See Georg Habich, "Ueber 2. Prometheus — Bilder angeblich von Piero di Cosimo," *Sitzungsberichte der Bayerischen Akademie der Wissenschaften, Philos. Phil. Klasse, 2. Abhandlung* (Munich, 1920), pp. 1—18.

25. See Berthold L. Ullman, *The Humanism of Coluccio Salutati* (Padua: Editrice Antenore, 1963), pp. 39—70. Leon Battista Alberti, *Intercoenales*, in ed. *Prosatori Latini del Quattrocento*, ed. Eugenio Garin (Milan: Riccardo Ricciardi Editore, 1952), p. 656: "Contra vero Fortunam esse duram sensi nobis qui eo tempore in fluvium corruissemus quo perpetuo in nisu undas nando superare opus sit: plurimum tamen in rebus humanis prudentiam et industriam valere non ignorabimus."

26. Charles Trinkaus, *Adversity's Noblemen: The Italian Humanists or Happiness* (New York: Columbia University Press, 1940), pp. 64—65.

27. Ibid., p. 96.

28. Giannozzo Manetti, *De dignitate et excellentia hominis*, in Eugenio Garin, *Filosofi italiani del Quattrocento*, Pagine scelte, tradotte e illustrate (Florence: Felice Le Mounier, 1942), p. 238. See the excellent article by August Buck, "Die Rangstellung des Menschen in der Renaissance: dignitas et miseria hominis," *Archiv für Kulturgeschichte*, XLII (1960), 61—75. See A. G. Auer, "Manetti und Pico della Mirandola, de hominis dignitate," *Vitae et veritate* (Duesseldorf: Patmos Verlag, 1956), pp. 83—102.

29. The contrast between Pico and Ficino is not fundamentally one of an immanent as opposed to a transcendant basis for the dignity of man as suggested by

Giovanni Semprini, *La Filosofia di Pico della Mirandola* (Milan: Libreria Lombarda, 1936), pp. 63—65. A superior treatment of the question is in Eugenio Garin, *Giovanni Pico della Mirandola: Vita e dottrina* (Florence: Felice Le Monnier, 1937). See also Paul Oskar Kristeller, *Eight Philosophers of the Italian Renaissance* (Stanford: Stanford University Press, 1964), pp. 54—71. Eugenio Garin gives a summary of his views in *Der italienische Humanismus* (Bern: Verlag A. Francke, 1947), pp. 123—25.

30. *De sapiente*, xix, 341, xxi, 369, cited in Eugene F. Rice, Jr., *The Renaissance Idea of Wisdom* (Cambridge, Mass.: Harvard University Press, 1958), pp. 119, 121. Rice's excellent chapter on "The Wisdom of Prometheus," pp. 92—123, is germane to the theme of the *vir doctus* as the second Prometheus.

31. Ernst Cassirer and others, *The Renaissance Philosophy of Man*, pp. 385—97. See Otis H. Green, "The Concept of Man in the Spanish Renaissance," *The Rice Institute Pamphlet*, XLVI (Jan. 1960), 49—50: Cervantes has Don Quixote express a Pico-like thought when he says, "I know who I am and who I may be if I choose." Book I, Ch. 5.

32. LW I, 83—84.

33. Ibid., I, 68.

34. WA XXXIX 1, 41: ". . . und ist ja itzund eine güldene Zeit, darin man wohl und reichlich auch leichtlich gelehrte und feine Leute erziehen kann."

35. Luther, WA, Tr I, No. 1160, pp. 573—74.

36. On this point see Kurt Aland, "Die theologische Fakultät Wittenberg und ihre Stellung im Gesamtzusammenhang der Leucorea während des 16. Jahrhunderts," *450 Jahre Martin Luther Universität Halle-Wittenberg*, (Wittenberg: Selbstverlag der Martin Luther Universität Halle-Wittenberg, 1952), I, 155—237. On Luther's appreciation of natural reason in its proper sphere, as distinguished from regenerate reason of the man of faith and the arrogant reason of the man of unfaith speaking to questions of faith, see two admirable monographs, Bernhard Lohse, *Ratio und fides. Eine Untersuchung "über die ratio in der Theologie Luthers* (Göttingen: Vandenhoeck & Ruprecht, 1958) and Brian Gerrish, *Grace and Reason: A Study in the Theology of Luther* (Oxford: Clarendon Press, 1962). Luther's disputation on man proposed theses on reason as operative on the natural plane and as blind with reference to God's inner nature and the true essence of ultimate reality, WA XXXIX/1, 175—80.

37. WA XXXXVIII, 78.

38. WA XXXX/3, 63, 17: "Ideo Theologia est infinita sapientia, quia nunquam potest edisci."

39. The pioneer study on this subject was Quirinus Breen's University of Chicago dissertation, *John Calvin: A Study in French Humanism* (Grand Rapids, Mich.: Wm. B. Eerdmans Publishing Company, 1931). Josef Bohatec, the Czech scholar who taught in his final years at the University of Vienna, argued in his *Budé und Calvin. Studien zur Gedankenwelt des französischen Frühhumanismus* (Graz: Verlag Hermann Böhlaus Nachf., 1950) that the humanistic orientation of Calvin's thought did not make a telling impact on his high theological concerns about God, freedom, and immortality. The two strongest assertions of a Platonic influence on Calvin's anthropology and on his theology in general are an article that has been the center of considerable debate, Roy Battenhouse, "The Doctrine of Man in Calvin and in Renaissance Platonism," *Journal of the History of Ideas*, IX (Oct.—Dec. 1948), 447—71, and a recent analysis of Calvin's "humanism," Jean Boisset, *Sagesse et sainteté dans la pensée de Jean Calvin. Essai sur l'humanisme du reformateur français* (Paris:

Presses universitaires de France, 1959), pp. 4, 222 f., 296, etc. The tendency to develop the humanist influence in Calvin is evident from the summary work of François Wendel, *Calvin. Sources et évolution de sa pensée religieuse* (Paris: Presses universitaires de France, 1950).

40. The tie between Zwingli and Italian humanism was made over a century ago by Christoph Sigwart, *Ulrich Zwingli. Der Charakter seiner Theologie mit besonderer Rücksicht auf Picus von Mirandola dargestellt* (Stuttgart: Besser Verlag, 1855). Early humanist influences on his anthropology are delineated in Arthur Rich, *Die Anfänge der Theologie Huldrych Zwinglis* (Zurich: Zwingli Verlag, 1949). See also the references in Bard Thompson, "Zwingli Study Since 1918," *Church History,* XIX (June 1950), 116—28.

41. See Jacob Burckhardt, "Der griechische Pessimismus," *Gesammelte Werke,* (Basle: B. Schwabe, 1956), V, 349—67, especially pp. 365, 370. In the *Nicomachean Ethics* VII, 15, 1154b, 7, Aristotle wrote: "To see and to hear are laborious, as natural discourses testify."

42. Pliny, *Natural History* (Cambridge, Mass.: Harvard University Press, 1942), p. 507—13.

43. L. Annaeus Seneca, *Opera* III, *Dialogi* IX, ed. Carolus Fickert (Lipsiae: Sumptibus Librariae Weidmannianae, 1845), 355—57. So also his *Ad Paullinum de brevitate vitae,* ibid., 267—312.

44. Plutarch, *Moralia,* (Cambridge, Mass.: Harvard University Press, 1957), pp. 487—533.

45. M. Tullius Cicero, *Tusculanarum Disputationum ad M. Brutum. Liber Quintus,* Ch. 1, lines 20—24; *M. Tullii Ciceronis Opera* (Turici: Sumptibus ac Typis Orellii Füsslini et Sociorum, 1861), IV, 331.

46. Matthew Arnold, *Poems* (London: Macmillan and Co., 1903), I, 306; from *Obermann Once More, Elegiac Poems.*

47. Innocent's treatise is in Migne, P. L., CCXVII, cols. 701—46. A new English publication provides a translation of both Innocent III's and Manetti's treatises in *Two Views of Man;* Pope Innocent III, *On the Misery of Man,* and Giannozzo Manetti, *On the Dignity of Man,* ed. Bernard Murchland (New York: Frederick Ungar Publishing Co., 1966).

48. See Millard Meiss, *Painting in Florence and Siena after the Black Death* (New York: Harper Torchbook, 1964), p. 74.

49. Hans Baron, "Franciscan Poverty and Civic Wealth as Factors in the Rise of Humanistic Thought," *Speculum,* XIII, 1 (Jan. 1938), 12. In n. 3 Baron locates Conversino's *De miseria* as Codex IX, 11, fol. 55ᵛ-57ᵛ, of the Querini-Stampaglia Library in Venice.

50. *Confessions* X, 8, 15, cited from Petrarch, *Ascent of Mount Ventoux,* Ernst Cassirer and others, *Renaissance Philosophy of Man,* p. 44.

51. See the account in Ernest Hatch Wilkins, *Petrarch's Eight Years in Milan* (Cambridge, Mass.: Mediaeval Academy of America, 1958), p. 66, and in his *Life of Petrarch* (Chicago: University of Chicago Press, 1961), pp. 138—40.

52. Siegfried Wenzel, "Petrarch's *Accidia,*" *Studies in the Renaissance,* VIII (1961), 36—48, an excellent study, draws the lines too sharply, however, in concluding that Petrarch's *accidia* belongs no longer to the system of Christian moral theology but to the pursuit of secular wisdom.

53. See Richard Walzer, *Greek into Arabic. Essays on Islamic Philosophy* (Oxford: B. Cassirer, 1962), pp. 142—57.

54. See the unpublished dissertation (Stanford Univ., 1965) by Noel Brann, "The Renaissance Passion of Melancholy."

55. Of the extensive contemporary literature on melancholy in the Renaissance a few titles of special interest are: Lawrence Babb, *The Elizabethan Malady* (Lansing: Michigan State University Press, 1951); Rudolf and Margot Wittkower, *Born Under Saturn* (New York: Random House, 1963); Raimond Klibansky, *Saturn and Melancholy* (London: Thomas Nelson, 1964); Erwin Panofsky and F. Saxl, *Albrecht Dürer*, 2 vols. (Princeton: Princeton University Press, 1945), I, 156—69. In the brilliant recent study of Frances A. Yates, *Giordano Bruno and the Hermetic Tradition* (Chicago: University of Chicago Press, 1964), pp. 102—3, 110—11, 144—45, the author stresses the Hermetic sources for the dignity-of-man theme in Pico. The Hermetic root of the melancholy theme might also be sought there.

56. Lauro Martines, *The Social World of the Florentine Humanists* (Princeton: Princeton University Press, 1963), documents the solid footing of the Florentine humanists in their society, using 11 full studies and 45 special cases to demonstrate that the humanists were men of means connected by family ties and position in the state to the upper classes of society. The work of Martines has in effect reduced to shambles Alfred von Martin's *Sociology of the Renaissance* (New York: Oxford University Press, 1944). The book of Trinkaus, *Adversity's Noblemen: The Italian Humanists on Happiness* (New York: Columbia University Press, 1940), while mistakenly still basing its explanation of the insecurity of the humanists on the older notions of their uncertain status in society, is still of great value in presenting systematically the humanists' treatises in a thorough survey of their writings on this theme.

57. Berthold L. Ullman, *Coluccio Salutati de seculo et religione* (Florence: In aedibus L. S. Olschki, 1957). For an analysis of this work see B. L. Ullman, *The Humanism of Coluccio Salutati* (Padua: Editrice Antenore, 1963), pp. 26—30, 90—92. Charles Trinkaus, "Humanist Treatises on the Status of the Religious: Petrarch, Salutati, Valla," *Studies in the Renaissance* XI (1962), 20—34, suggests that Salutati used new arguments classical in origin, such as the poverty and vigor of early Rome, to support the promonastic arguments and saw no contradiction between his humanist values and the received traditional views of medieval asceticism, as a layman willingly granting spiritual superiority to the regular life of the religious.

58. Hans Baron, ed. "Isagogicon moralis disciplinae," *Leonardo Bruni Aretinos humanistische-philosophische Schriften* (Leipzig, 1928), 20—41, cited in Trinkaus, *Adversity's Noblemen*, p. 43.

59. *De miseria humanae conditionis, Libri II, Opera omnia* (Basel, 1538), pp. 86 to 131, cited in Trinkaus, *Adversity's Noblemen*, p. 44.

60. Francesco Guicciardini, *Ricordi*, 161, cited in Buck, *Rangstellung*, p. 69.

61. Victor Michael Hamm, trans. *Pico della Mirandola. Of Being and Unity (De ente et uno)*, (Milwaukee: Marquette University Press, 1943), pp. 4 ff.

62. Both Pico selections are cited from the excellent article of John Warwick Montgomery, "Eros and Agape in the Thought of Giovanni Pico della Mirandola," *Concordia Theological Monthly*, XXXII, 12 (Dec. 1961), 743—45. For a systematic presentation of Pico's theology, including such concepts as his understanding of original sin, proceeding from Pico's view of man, analyzing his dependence on Platonic and patristic sources, and treating the more formally theological aspect of his thought, see the work of Engelbert Monnerjahn, *Giovanni Pico della Mirandola. Ein Beitrag zur philosophischen Theologie des italienischen Humanismus* (Wiesbaden: Franz Steiner Verlag GMBH, 1960).

63. Otis H. Green, "The Concept of Man in the Spanish Renaissance," *The Rice Institute Pamphlet, Renaissance Studies*, XLVI, 4 (Jan. 1960), 46. Jan Huizinga, *The Waning of the Middle Ages* (London: Edward Arnold & Co.,

1937), and Rudolf Stadelmann, *Vom Geist des Ausgehenden Mittelalters* (Halle/Salle: Max Niemeyer Verlag, 1929), have characterized the culture of northern Europe, France, the Court of Burgundy, and the empire in dour terms as one of disintegration, pessimism, skepticism, resignation, as well as partially of emancipation.

64. Paul Bühler, *Die Anfechtung bei Martin Luther* (Zürich: Zwingli Verlag, 1942) is a good example of the extensive literature on the question. An uncomplicated treatment is Roland H. Bainton, "Luther's Struggle for Faith," *Church History*, XVII (Sept. 1948), 193—206. Heinz Bluhm, "Luther's View of Man in His First Published Work," *Harvard Theological Review*, XL (April 1948), 103—22, describes the emergence of the Augustinian-Pauline view of man in Luther's *Die Sieben Busspsalmen*, spring 1517.

65. Cited in Eric R. Dodds, *The Greeks and the Irrational* (Berkeley: University of California Press, 1951), p. 254.

66. *Complete Poetry and Selected Prose of John Donne*, ed. John Hayward (Bloomsbury, Nonesuch Press, 1929), p. 202. See the chapter on "The Assimilation of Copernican Astronomy," Thomas S. Kuhn, *The Copernican Revolution* (Cambridge, Mass.: Harvard University Press, 1957), pp. 185—228.

67. *Pensées*, ed. Léon Brunschvicq (Paris: Librairie Hachette et cie, 1904), II, 126, fragment 205.

68. "Within the Indeterminate Universe," *Sequoia*, VII, 3 (1962), 29.

69. Burckhardt, *Force and Freedom*, p. 300.

70. "Alienation and the Decline of Utopia," *The American Scholar*, XXIX, 2 (Spring 1960), 1.

71. (New York: Random House, 1961), pp. 98, 101, et passim.

72. Adolf Harnack, *Martin Luther in seiner Bedeutung für die Geschichte der Wissenschaft und der Bildung* (Giessen, 1911), p. 28.

73. Gerhard Szczesny, "The Future of Unbelief," in *The Fate of Man*, ed. Crane Brinton (New York: George Braziller, 1961), p. 23.

74. *Menschliches, Allzumenschliches*, II, *Nietzsches Werke* (Leipzig: C. C. Naumann, 1900), III, 205; Zweite Abteilung: "Der Wanderer und sein Schatten," No. 18: *Der Moderne Diogenes*.

75. Bk. V, Chs. iii, iv, *The Ante-Nicene Fathers*, II, 448.

76. WA, Tr II, 2342a, cited in *What Luther Says*, ed. Ewald M. Plass (St. Louis: Concordia Publishing House, 1959), III, 1244, Nos. 3966—67.

77. WA XVIII, 605, 32.

78. "Summa summarum: res non sunt in manu nostra, sed Dei." WA XX, 47, 16.

79. WA XX, 190, 3 and 18 ff.: "Qui vult versari in medio mundo et servare *cor pacatum et quietum*, das ist ein Kunst."

80. WA XX, 152, 6: ". . . cum plantata est fides, hoc agendum est, ut Christiani sint negociocissimi erga proximum et prorsus nullum hic agant Sabbatum sed sint Zelotae bonorum operum, ardeant in charitate erga proximum et Sabbatum tantum agant coram Deo." On Luther's commentary on Ecclesiastes see the excellent study of Eberhard Wölfel, *Luther und die Skepsis. Eine Studie zur Kohelet-Exegese Luthers* (Munich: Christian Kaiser Verlag, 1958), pp. 39, 52, 120, 173—74, 197, 232—33. See also Horst Beintker "Die Überwindung der Anfechtung durch den Glauben," *Die Überwindung der Anfechtung bei Luther* (Berlin: Evangelische Verlagsanstalt, 1954), 115—79.

81. Luther to Elector Frederick of Saxony, Feb. 24, 1522, *Luther: Letters of Spiritual Counsel*, ed. Theodore G. Tappert (Philadelphia: The Westminster Press, 1955), p. 140.

82. WA, Br V, 399—400. On this exchange of correspondence see H. Fausel, "Luther und Melanchthon während des Augsburger Reichstags," *Theologische Aufsätze. Karl Barth zum 50. Geburtstag* (Munich: Chr. Kaiser Verlag, 1936), 405—16.

83. WA, Br VII, 104—6, trans. in Tappert, *Letters of Spiritual Counsel*, p. 96. See also Luther's letter to Jonas von Stockhausen on fighting melancholy, Tappert, *Letters*, pp. 88—90.

84. WA, Tr IV, No. 4857, versus the *Vita solitaria;* WA, Tr II, No. 1270, on how God hates our afflictions when they drive us to despair.

85. WA, Br VIII, 79, 80, trans. in Tappert, *Letters*, pp. 99—100.

86. *Medieval History. The Life and Death of a Civilization* (New York: The Macmillan Co., 1963).

87. *The Philosophy of Hegel*, ed. Carl J. Friedrich (New York: Random House, 1954), p. xxxix.

88. *An Essay on Man* (London: Methuen & Co. Ltd., 1950), pp. 53—56.

# INDEX